Design and Deploy Microsoft Azure Sentinel for IoMT

Enhance IoMT Cybersecurity Operations with Intelligent Analytics

Puthiyavan Udayakumar
Dr. R Anandan

Apress®

Design and Deploy Microsoft Azure Sentinel for IoMT: Enhance IoMT Cybersecurity Operations with Intelligent Analytics

Puthiyavan Udayakumar
CSE-Technology, VISTAS,
Chennai, India

Dr. R Anandan
CSE-Technology, VISTAS,
Chennai, India

ISBN-13 (pbk): 979-8-8688-2039-7
https://doi.org/10.1007/979-8-8688-2040-3

ISBN-13 (electronic): 979-8-8688-2040-3

Copyright © 2025 by Puthiyavan Udayakumar, Dr. R Anandan

This work is subject to copyright. All rights are reserved by the Publisher, whether the whole or part of the material is concerned, specifically the rights of translation, reprinting, reuse of illustrations, recitation, broadcasting, reproduction on microfilms or in any other physical way, and transmission or information storage and retrieval, electronic adaptation, computer software, or by similar or dissimilar methodology now known or hereafter developed.

Trademarked names, logos, and images may appear in this book. Rather than use a trademark symbol with every occurrence of a trademarked name, logo, or image we use the names, logos, and images only in an editorial fashion and to the benefit of the trademark owner, with no intention of infringement of the trademark.

The use in this publication of trade names, trademarks, service marks, and similar terms, even if they are not identified as such, is not to be taken as an expression of opinion as to whether or not they are subject to proprietary rights.

While the advice and information in this book are believed to be true and accurate at the date of publication, neither the authors nor the editors nor the publisher can accept any legal responsibility for any errors or omissions that may be made. The publisher makes no warranty, express or implied, with respect to the material contained herein.

Managing Director, Apress Media LLC: Welmoed Spahr
Acquisitions Editor: Smriti Srivastava
Development Editor: Laura Berendson
Editorial Assistant: Jessica Vakili

Cover designed by eStudioCalamar

Cover image designed by Pixabay

Distributed to the book trade worldwide by Springer Science+Business Media New York, 1 New York Plaza, New York, NY 10004. Phone 1-800-SPRINGER, fax (201) 348-4505, e-mail orders-ny@springer-sbm.com, or visit www.springeronline.com. Apress Media, LLC is a Delaware LLC and the sole member (owner) is Springer Science + Business Media Finance Inc (SSBM Finance Inc). SSBM Finance Inc is a **Delaware** corporation.

For information on translations, please e-mail booktranslations@springernature.com; for reprint, paperback, or audio rights, please e-mail bookpermissions@springernature.com.

Apress titles may be purchased in bulk for academic, corporate, or promotional use. eBook versions and licenses are also available for most titles. For more information, reference our Print and eBook Bulk Sales web page at http://www.apress.com/bulk-sales.

Any source code or other supplementary material referenced by the author in this book is available to readers on GitHub. For more detailed information, please visit https://www.apress.com/gp/services/source-code.

If disposing of this product, please recycle the paper

Table of Contents

About the Authors xvii

About the Technical Reviewer xix

Acknowledgments xxi

Introduction xxiii

Chapter 1: Get Started with Microsoft Sentinel and IoMT 1

Introduction to IoMT 2

    The Evolution of IoMT 3

    Components and Architecture 4

    Real-World Applications and Use Cases 7

    Advantages and Outcomes 8

    Regulatory Landscape and Standards 9

    The Road Ahead: The Future of IoMT 10

    The Expanding Threat Surface of IoMT 11

    Common Cybersecurity Threats in IoMT 11

    Global Regulatory and Legal Pressures 15

    Challenges in Implementing IoMT Cybersecurity 16

    Opportunities for Innovation and Resilience 16

    Best Practices for Securing IoMT 17

Get Started with Microsoft Sentinel and the World of IoMT 18

    Microsoft Sentinel Viewpoints of IoMT 20

Microsoft Sentinel for IoT 22

    Activate OoB (Out of Box) Security Contents 23

    Microsoft Sentinel Collects Data at Scale 25

    Microsoft Sentinel (Detect, Investigate, Respond) 27

    Detect Threats with Microsoft Sentinel 28

TABLE OF CONTENTS

    Incidents 30

    Hunts 30

    Notebooks 30

    Automation Rules 31

    Playbooks 31

Unifying Security Operations 31

    The Growing Risk Surface of IoT and IoMT 32

    Unified Security Begins with Microsoft Defender Portal 32

    Microsoft Sentinel: Cloud-Native SIEM for Total Visibility 33

    Microsoft Defender XDR: Correlated Threat Detection and Response 33

    Security Exposure Management: Proactive Risk Mitigation 33

    Generative AI: Moving from Data to Actionable Intelligence 34

    Unified, Scalable Strategy for IoT and IoMT Security 34

    Framework of a Unified Approach to Security Operations 34

    Protecting Critical Assets Across the Enterprise 35

    Simplifying Security Management 36

    Working with the Microsoft Defender Portal 39

    The Unified Security Hub 39

    Key Services in the Portal 39

    Defender XDR 40

    Sentinel 40

    Threat Intelligence 41

    Exposure Management 41

    Defender for Cloud 41

    Getting Access 41

    Navigating the Portal 41

    Managing Security Exposure 42

    Investigating and Responding to Threats 42

    Deepening Threat Intelligence 43

    Managing Assets 43

    Improving Your Security Operations Center (SOC) 43

Understanding Microsoft Defender XDR in the Microsoft Defender Portal	44
Unified Visibility Across the Organization	46
Real-Time Collaboration and Workflow Collaboration	46
Unified Security with Microsoft Defender and Sentinel	47
Bringing Microsoft Sentinel into the Defender Portal	48
Integrate Microsoft Defender XDR with Microsoft Sentinel	51
Incident Correlation and Alerts	52
Defender for Cloud Integration	53
Incident Generation	53
Microsoft Copilot in Microsoft Defender	53
Microsoft Defender for Cloud	60
Enhanced Investigation Experience in Microsoft Defender XDR	61
Planning Best Practices for Unified Security Operations	**66**
Planning Your Deployment	69
Identify Data Security and Privacy Practices	71
Planning Your Log Analytics Workspace Architecture for Microsoft Sentinel	73
Identifying Your Data Sources	74
Summary	**75**

Chapter 2: Architecting and Deploying Microsoft Sentinel 77

Implementing Zero Trust with Sentinel	78
Making Zero Trust Work in Healthcare	81
Common Challenges in Healthcare Environments	81
Real-World Steps for Implementing Zero Trust in Healthcare	82
Enhancing Cybersecurity Resilience with Microsoft Defender XDR and Sentinel	85
Understanding Microsoft Defender XDR and Sentinel	86
Integrating XDR and Sentinel: A Unified Defense Strategy	86
Reinforcing Zero Trust with Defender XDR and Sentinel	87
Verify Explicitly	87
Use Least Privileged Access Controls	88
Assume Breach	88
Planning and Prerequisites	89

TABLE OF CONTENTS

- Implementing Components of Microsoft Defender XDR 90
- Expanding Security with Defender for Cloud and Security Copilot 90
- Configuring Microsoft Sentinel for Detection and Analytics 91
- Optimizing Analytics and Threat Detections 91
- Role Management and Secure Access 92
- Changing Security Operations with Unified Tools 92

Designing and Architecting Workspaces and Tenants 95
- Single Workspace 95
- Multiple Workspaces 96
- Evaluating the Need for Multiple Workspaces 98
- Managing Workspaces Across Multiple Azure Tenants: Strategy Overview ... 104

Migrating to Microsoft Sentinel 106
- Phases of Migration 108
- Phase 1: Discovery 109
- Phase 2: Design 110
- Phase 3: Implement 110
- Phase 4: Operationalize 111
- Achieving the Sentinel Advantage 112

Optimized Data Collection 112
- Best Practices for Data Collection in Microsoft Sentinel 114
- Prioritizing and Filtering Log Data 114
- Handling Special Data Collection Scenarios 115
- Working with Custom and Operational Logs 116
- Collecting from Cloud and Endpoint Sources 116
- Understanding Data Connectors in Microsoft Sentinel 117
- What Is a Data Connector? 117
- Types of Data Connectors 118
- Common Use Cases 118
- How Data Connectors Work 119
- Benefits of Using Sentinel Connectors 120

TABLE OF CONTENTS

Integrating Threat Intelligence 120
    Threat Intelligence Integration: Overview 120
    Operational Use Cases 121
    Sources of Threat Intelligence 122
    Understanding Cyber Threat Intelligence (CTI) 122

Effective Log Management 127
    Optimize and Increase Efficiency 130
    Implement a Tiered Log Retention Strategy 130
    Export Logs Efficiently Using Native Integrations 131
    Automate Schema Mapping and Table Management 131
    Integrate ADX Tables for Seamless Querying 131
    Customize Retention and Lifecycle Policies 132

Data Normalization and ASIM 134
    How ASIM Normalization Works 135
    The Value of Normalized Data in ASIM 135
    Everyday Use Cases for ASIM (Advanced Security Information Model) 136
    ASIM Components 137

User and Entity Behavior Analytics (UEBA) 144
    Security-Driven Use of Behavior Analytics 144
    Understanding Behavior with Entity Context 145
    UEBA's Role in Threat Detection 146
    The Way UEBA Models Behavior 146
    Detecting Insider Threats and Compromised Accounts 147
    UEBA Is More Than Just Users 147
    Integration with Microsoft Sentinel's Security Operations 147
    Reduced Alert Fatigue Using Intelligent Analytics 148
    Continuous Improvement 148

Utilizing Copilot for Security Architects 150
    Integrating Security Copilot with Microsoft Sentinel 153
    The Core Capabilities of the Integration 153

Summary 156

TABLE OF CONTENTS

Chapter 3: Engineering Microsoft Sentinel for Security Operations 159

Microsoft Sentinel for Security Engineers 160
Understanding the Role of Microsoft Sentinel 163
Connecting Data Sources—The First Step 164
Detecting Threats Through Analytics Rules 164
KQL Capabilities for Security Engineers 165
Automating Your Response with Playbooks (SOAR) 165
Workbooks, Watchlists, and Threat Intelligence 166
Building a Smarter SOC 166
Reinventing Security Operations with Microsoft Sentinel 167
A New Class of SIEM for a New Class of Threats 167
Key Features That Distinguish Sentinel from the Competition 167
Building Blocks of Sentinel's Modern Security Model 170
The Numbers Tell the Story 172
Future-Proofing the Security Operations Center 172

Leveraging Threat Intelligence 173
What Does Microsoft Sentinel Do to Manage Threat Intelligence? 173
Value of Threat Intelligence for Security Engineers 174
Combining and Handling Cyber Threat Intelligence 177
Using Threat Intelligence to Detect and Respond 177
Connecting Microsoft Defender Threat Intelligence to Microsoft Sentinel 178
Connecting the TAXII Threat Intelligence Connector in Microsoft Sentinel 180
Connecting Microsoft Sentinel with the Threat Intelligence Upload API 181
Step-by-Step: Setting Up the Threat Intelligence Upload API 182
Validating Ingestion and Watching STIX Objects 183
Turning Threat Data into Real-Time Alerts 184
What You Need Before You Start 184
Creating a Rule That Uses Threat Intelligence 185
Understanding the Rule Logic 185
Defining Incident Settings and Automation 186
To Finalize the Rule 186

TABLE OF CONTENTS

Integrating Threat Intelligence 120
    Threat Intelligence Integration: Overview 120
    Operational Use Cases 121
    Sources of Threat Intelligence 122
    Understanding Cyber Threat Intelligence (CTI) 122

Effective Log Management 127
    Optimize and Increase Efficiency 130
    Implement a Tiered Log Retention Strategy 130
    Export Logs Efficiently Using Native Integrations 131
    Automate Schema Mapping and Table Management 131
    Integrate ADX Tables for Seamless Querying 131
    Customize Retention and Lifecycle Policies 132

Data Normalization and ASIM 134
    How ASIM Normalization Works 135
    The Value of Normalized Data in ASIM 135
    Everyday Use Cases for ASIM (Advanced Security Information Model) 136
    ASIM Components 137

User and Entity Behavior Analytics (UEBA) 144
    Security-Driven Use of Behavior Analytics 144
    Understanding Behavior with Entity Context 145
    UEBA's Role in Threat Detection 146
    The Way UEBA Models Behavior 146
    Detecting Insider Threats and Compromised Accounts 147
    UEBA Is More Than Just Users 147
    Integration with Microsoft Sentinel's Security Operations 147
    Reduced Alert Fatigue Using Intelligent Analytics 148
    Continuous Improvement 148

Utilizing Copilot for Security Architects 150
    Integrating Security Copilot with Microsoft Sentinel 153
    The Core Capabilities of the Integration 153

Summary 156

TABLE OF CONTENTS

Chapter 3: Engineering Microsoft Sentinel for Security Operations 159

Microsoft Sentinel for Security Engineers 160

    Understanding the Role of Microsoft Sentinel 163

    Connecting Data Sources—The First Step 164

    Detecting Threats Through Analytics Rules 164

    KQL Capabilities for Security Engineers 165

    Automating Your Response with Playbooks (SOAR) 165

    Workbooks, Watchlists, and Threat Intelligence 166

    Building a Smarter SOC 166

    Reinventing Security Operations with Microsoft Sentinel 167

    A New Class of SIEM for a New Class of Threats 167

    Key Features That Distinguish Sentinel from the Competition 167

    Building Blocks of Sentinel's Modern Security Model 170

    The Numbers Tell the Story 172

    Future-Proofing the Security Operations Center 172

Leveraging Threat Intelligence 173

    What Does Microsoft Sentinel Do to Manage Threat Intelligence? 173

    Value of Threat Intelligence for Security Engineers 174

    Combining and Handling Cyber Threat Intelligence 177

    Using Threat Intelligence to Detect and Respond 177

    Connecting Microsoft Defender Threat Intelligence to Microsoft Sentinel 178

    Connecting the TAXII Threat Intelligence Connector in Microsoft Sentinel 180

    Connecting Microsoft Sentinel with the Threat Intelligence Upload API 181

    Step-by-Step: Setting Up the Threat Intelligence Upload API 182

    Validating Ingestion and Watching STIX Objects 183

    Turning Threat Data into Real-Time Alerts 184

    What You Need Before You Start 184

    Creating a Rule That Uses Threat Intelligence 185

    Understanding the Rule Logic 185

    Defining Incident Settings and Automation 186

    To Finalize the Rule 186

Monitoring Alerts and Incidents	186
What Is the MITRE ATT&CK® Framework?	187
Leveraging MITRE ATT&CK® for IoMT Security	189

Creating Watchlists in Sentinel 191

Practical Scenarios for Watchlist Use	192
Important Considerations and Limitations	193
Creating Watchlists	194
Deploying Watchlists in Microsoft Sentinel	194
Uploading a Watchlist from a Local Folder	195
Uploading a Watchlist from a File You Created (Without a Template)	195
Uploading a Watchlist Created from a Template (Preview)	196
Creating a Large Watchlist from a File in Azure Storage (Preview)	197

Developing Content with Kusto Query Language 200

What Is a Kusto Query?	201
What Is a Query Statement?	201
What Can You Do with KQL?	202
Core Operators: Filter, Sort, Take, and More	204
Summarizing and Aggregating	205
Column Control: project, project-away, and extend	206
Working with Multiple Tables: union and join	207
Parsing and Transforming with evaluate	208
Using Variables with `let` Statements	208

Building Effective Analytics 209

Analytics Rules: The Workhorse of Threat Detection	209
Types of Analytics Rules in Microsoft Sentinel	209
Rule Access and Permissions	211
Indication from Detection to Action: Incidents	212
Role of Threat Hunting in Modern Security Operations	212
Launchpad for Discovery: Built-In Queries	213
Managing and Modifying Hunting Queries	214
Creating Custom Queries Using KQL	214

TABLE OF CONTENTS

Community Contributions and Continual Improvement 215
Practical Considerations for Threat Hunting Success 215
Turning Data into Threat Intelligence 216
Security Orchestration, Automation, and Response (SOAR) 220
    Components to Understand in Automation Rules 223
    Incident Automation Versus Alert Automation 223
    Triggers in Automation Rules 224
    Conditions for Rule Execution 224
    Establishing Automation Actions 224
    Playbook and Advanced Automation 225
    Managing Order of Execution 225
    Common Use Cases and Scenarios 226
    Managing Automation Rules 226
    Exporting and Importing Automation Rules 227
    Multitenant Considerations 227
    Automating Incident Response Through Playbooks in Microsoft Sentinel 228
Workbooks, Reporting, and Data Visualization 230
    Commonly Used Workbooks in Microsoft Sentinel 232
SOC Optimization Using Microsoft Sentinel for IoMT 234
    Centralized Visibility and Unified Data Ingestion 234
    Threat Detection and Behavioral Analytics 234
    Automation Using Playbooks 235
    Improved Threat Intelligence Integration 235
    Incident Investigation and Root Cause Analysis 235
    Compliance and Risk Management 236
    Ongoing Improvement and SOC Maturity 236
    Managing Device Diversity and Complexity in IoMT 236
    Intended Use Cases for Healthcare Models 237
    Integration with Existing Security and IT Ecosystems 238
    Scaling Operations 238
    Measure and Mature the Effectiveness of the SOC 239
Summary 240

TABLE OF CONTENTS

Chapter 4: Threat Detection, Investigation, and Response 243

Microsoft Sentinel for Security Analysts 244
- Understanding the Microsoft Sentinel Role 247
- Connecting Data Sources—The First Step 247
- Detecting Threats with Analytics Rules 248
- Power of KQL for Engineers 248
- Automating Response with Playbooks (SOAR) 249
- Workbooks, Watchlists, and Threat Intelligence 249
- Building a Smarter SOC 249
- Reinventing Security Operations with Microsoft Sentinel 250
- A New Breed of SIEM for a New Breed of Threats 251
- Key Innovations That Make Sentinel the Best 251
- Building Blocks of Sentinel's Modern Security Model 254
- Sentinel's Quantifiable Value 255
- Future-Proofing the Security Operations Center 256

Crafting Threat Detection and Analytics Rules in Microsoft Sentinel 256
- Understanding Analytics Rules in Sentinel 257
- Establishing High-Quality Detections 258
- Enriching Detections with Threat Intelligence 259
- Watchlists and Custom Lists 259
- Alert Fatigue 259
- Automation and Integrating with Your Incident Response Processes ... 260
- Detection Rule Lifecycle 260
- Continuous Improvement and Inter-Team Collaboration 261

Understanding Incidents and Alerts in the Microsoft Defender Portal 261
- Alerts: The Frontline Signals 261
- Incidents: The Complete Attack Narrative 262
- Correlation and Intelligence in Action 263
- Alerts and Source of Detection Events 263
- Investigation and Response Tools 263
- Incident Management 264

xi

TABLE OF CONTENTS

Automated Investigation and Remediation 264
Attacks Disruption 264
Sentinel Automation Rules 264
Advanced Hunting 264
AI-Assisted Security Operations 265
A Unified Framework for Detection and Response 265
Managing Incidents in Microsoft Defender 265
The Role of Incidents in the Security Workflow 266
Triage: Prioritizing Incidents to Determine When to Take Action 266
Assign Ownership 267
Setting Severity 267
Applying Tags 267
Investigation and Resolution 267
Changing Incident Status 268
Classification of Incidents 268
Adding Investigation Notes 268
Audit and Reporting 269
Renaming Incidents 269
Reviewing the Activity Log 269
Exporting Incident Reports 269
Improving Efficiency Through Automation 270
Investigating Security Incidents 270
Alert Correlation and Incident Merging in the Microsoft Defender Portal 273
Planning an Incident Response Workflow in Microsoft Defender 275
Investigating Security Incidents Involving IoT Devices Using Microsoft Sentinel 277
Automating Incident Response in IoMT Ecosystems with Microsoft Sentinel 279
The Role of IoMT in Modern Healthcare Security 280
Know the Specific Threats in IoMT Environments 280
Building an Automated Incident Response Process for the IoMT 281
Phase 1: Normalize Your IoMT Telemetry Using ASIM 281
Phase 2: Analytics Rules to Detect IoMT Threats 281

- Phase 3: Automation Rules to Trigger Playbooks 282
- Phase 4: Create Logic App Playbooks for Response 282
- Continuous Monitoring and Optimization 283
- Example: Ransomware Attack Targeting Imaging Devices 284
- Streamlining Automation via Sentinel Capabilities 284
- Further Considerations with Playbooks and Automation Rules 285
- Strategic Use of Automation Tools and Playbooks 285
- Conclusion 286

Disrupting Attacks Effectively 286
- Motivations of Attacks in IoMT 286
- Examples of Attack Disruption Techniques Found in IoMT 288
- Challenges to Disruption of an IoMT Attack 289
- The Way Ahead: In-Use Disruption Attacks to IoMT Security Posture 289
- MS Sentinel, Making Disruption Attacks Effective 290
- Key Capabilities in Microsoft Sentinel to Disrupt Attacks 290
- How Sentinel Disrupts Attacks on IoMT 291
- Building Disruption Workflows in Sentinel 292

Using KQL for Analysts 292
- The Importance of KQL Within Microsoft Sentinel 293
- A Brief Understanding of the KQL Query Structure 294
- Best Practices for Writing KQL Queries in Sentinel 295
- Using KQL in Incident Management with Microsoft Sentinel 296
- How KQL Is Used in Incident Investigation 297
- Steps to Use KQL in Incident Management 298

Hunting for Threats 300
- Why Hunt for Threats in the IoMT Environment? 300
- The Problems Associated with Reactive Security 301
- Adversaries Are After IoMT 301
- Why Threat Hunting Matters for the Analyst 302
- Key Domains for Threat Hunting 302
- Role of Baseline Establishment 304

TABLE OF CONTENTS

How the Intelligence in Threat Intelligence Can Supercharge Threat Hunting 304
Visibility of Devices Can Be Challenging; Potential Workarounds Are Available 305
Collaborating with Clinical Teams on Hunting 305
Automating and Scaling Threat Hunts 306
Creating a Threat Hunting Program in Healthcare 306
Ongoing Education and Engaging in the Community 306
Embracing a Proactive Security Philosophy 307
Why Alert-Only Security Doesn't Cut It 307
The Foundation: Sentinel Hunting Queries 308
Building a Valuable Hypothesis 308
Refining the Results: Identifying the Noise 309
Hunting for Threat Campaigns 309
Mitigating Detection Gaps with MITRE ATT&CK 309
Hunting in Microsoft Sentinel: Prebuilt or Custom Paths 310
Managing the Hunt Workspace 310
From Hunt to Detection: Creating Analytics Rules 310
Real-Time Monitoring via Live Hunting 311
Bookmarking Findings 311
Incident Beacon 311
Visualize Your Connections 312
Hunting Across Multiple Workspaces and Tenants 312
Controlling Access and Permissions 312
Understanding and Quantifying Hunting Effectiveness 313

Hunting with KQL 314
The Basics: A Read-Only, Data-Flow Language 314
The Structure of a Query: Building Your First Hunt 315
Important Operators: Your Threat Hunting Toolbelt 316
Understanding the Schema: The Blueprint of Your Data 318
Threat Hunting with the MITRE ATT&CK Framework 319
The Structure of ATT&CK: Tactics and Techniques 320
From Framework to Hunt: A Hypothesis-Driven Approach 320

- Using ATT&CK with Microsoft Sentinel 322
- A Practical Example: Hunting for Scheduled Task Abuse 322

Integrating Threat Intelligence into Response Strategies 324
- Building Threat-Intelligent Security Architectures using Microsoft Sentinel 325
- To Engineer Sentinel to Activate Threat Intelligence 326
- Using Detect and Response Capabilities with Threat Intelligence 326
- Enabling Analysts to Leverage Intelligence in Investigations 327
- Automating Response Actions with Intelligence at the Core 328
- Integrating Continual Threat Hunting and Strategic Defense 328
- Working with Threat Intelligence in Microsoft Sentinel 329
- A Transition to the Defender Portal 329
- Access the Threat Intelligence Interface 330
- Creating Threat Intelligence Objects with STIX 330
- Evolving and Managing Threat Intelligence 330
- Ingestion Rules Switch: To Suppress Source Data Ingestion 331
- Making Relationships Between Threat Intelligence Objects 331
- Viewing Threat Intelligence 331
- Tagging Threat Intelligence 332
- Querying Threat Intelligence Data 332
- Visualizing Threat Intelligence Using Workbooks 332

Using Copilot for Security Analysts in the Embedded Experience 333
- Internet of Medical Things (IoMT) View 336
- The IoMT Security Challenge: A Complex, Critical Space 336
- From Design to Deployment: Designing and Deploying Secure IoMT Solutions ... 338
- The Security Analyst's Resource: Changing Operational Practices 338

Summary 340

Index 343

About the Authors

Puthiyavan Udayakumar is a seasoned infrastructure architect and senior infrastructure consultant with more than 16 years of experience in the IT industry. He is a Master Certified Architect by OpenGroup and holds numerous IT certifications. Throughout his career, he has excelled as an infrastructure solution architect and senior engineer, specializing in designing, deploying, and rolling out advanced on-premises, cloud, IoT, and cybersecurity solutions. He possesses robust expertise in on-premises, cloud, IoT, and cybersecurity, including project management and Agile delivery services. He has also authored more than ten books on various topics related to information technology.

Dr. R. Anandan completed his undergraduate degree, doctorate in Computer Science and Engineering, and postdoctoral degree in Computer Science and Engineering in Mexico. He is an IBMS/390 mainframe professional and a chartered engineer from the Institution of Engineers in India and received a fellowship from Bose Science Society, India. He has completed seven certification courses (mainly from CISCO). He has published more than 140 research papers in various international journals such as Scopus and SCI. He has presented 90 papers at various international conferences. He has received 18 awards from national and international agencies. He has authored and edited 27 books. He is also an editor for publishers such as Springer, Wiley, World Scientific Press, and Nova Publishers.

About the Technical Reviewer

Kasam Shaikh is a prominent figure in India's artificial intelligence landscape, holding the distinction of being one of the country's first four Microsoft Most Valuable Professionals (MVPs) in AI. Currently serving as a senior architect, Kasam boasts an impressive track record as an author, having authored five best-selling books dedicated to Azure and AI technologies. Beyond his writing endeavors, Kasam is recognized as a Microsoft Certified Trainer (MCT) and influential tech YouTuber (@mekasamshaikh). He also leads the largest online Azure AI community, known as DearAzure | Azure INDIA, and is a globally renowned AI speaker. His commitment to knowledge sharing extends to contributions to Microsoft Learn, where he plays a pivotal role.

Within the realm of AI, Kasam is a respected Subject Matter Expert (SME) in Generative AI for the Cloud, complementing his role as a Senior Cloud Architect. He actively promotes the adoption of No Code and Azure OpenAI solutions and possesses a strong foundation in hybrid and cross-cloud practices. Kasam Shaikh's versatility and expertise make him an invaluable asset in the rapidly evolving landscape of technology, contributing significantly to the advancement of Azure and AI.

In summary, Kasam Shaikh is a multifaceted professional who excels in both technical expertise and knowledge dissemination. His contributions span writing, training, community leadership, public speaking, and architecture, establishing him as a true luminary in Azure and AI. Kasam was recently recognized as a top voice in AI by LinkedIn, making him the sole exclusive Indian professional acknowledged by both Microsoft and LinkedIn for his contributions to artificial intelligence!

Acknowledgments

I extend my heartfelt gratitude to the Acquisitions Editor, Smriti Srivastava, whose insightful guidance, thoughtful feedback, and steadfast support were instrumental in shaping and refining this manuscript. Her dedication and vision continue to elevate Apress to new heights.

Special thanks to Deepa Shirley Tryphosa Chellappa for her tireless efforts in making the book materialize. Thanks to all Apress production team members.

Introduction

Microsoft Sentinel for Internet of Medical Things (IoMT) provides advanced threat detection, investigation, and automated response for connected medical devices, guaranteeing real-time protection in healthcare environments. By integrating medical device logs, applying AI-driven analytics, and leveraging Security Orchestration, Automation, and Response (SOAR), Sentinel helps mitigate cyber risks such as ransomware, unauthorized access, and device exploitation. This cloud-native SIEM and SOAR solution enables healthcare organizations to strengthen security, maintain compliance, and safeguard patient data in an increasingly connected medical landscape.

The book helps Azure administrators, network and security administrators, architects, and developers to understand and get in-depth knowledge in Microsoft Sentinel for IoT/IoMT.

In Chapter 1, "Get Started with Microsoft Sentinel and IoMT," readers are introduced to Microsoft Sentinel, a powerful cloud-native Security Information and Event Management (SIEM) and Security Orchestration, Automation, and Response (SOAR) solution. This section explains the core concepts of Sentinel, its role in securing IoMT (Internet of Medical Things) ecosystems, and the fundamental features that make it an essential tool for modern security operations. We cover key elements like data collection, threat intelligence, and log management, providing a foundational understanding for security professionals new to Sentinel. The chapter also includes an introduction to how Sentinel can unify and enhance security across diverse environments, making sure that healthcare systems remain protected against increasingly sophisticated cyber threats.

Chapter 2, "Architecting and Deploying Microsoft Sentinel," dives into the design and deployment of Microsoft Sentinel for IoMT environments, focusing on architecting a scalable, secure workspace. It covers essential practices such as Zero Trust architecture, tenant configuration, and data integration to guarantee seamless ingestion from connected medical devices. Readers will learn of ASIM (Azure Security Information Model) for data normalization, log transformation, and User and Entity Behavior Analytics (UEBA), which help detect irregularities across IoMT devices. Additionally, we explore the migration to Microsoft Sentinel from legacy systems, making sure that

INTRODUCTION

organizations can smoothly transition to the cloud-based platform while maintaining operational efficiency and securing sensitive medical data.

In Chapter 3, "Engineering Microsoft Sentinel for Security Operations," we focus on the operationalization of Microsoft Sentinel within healthcare environments. Security engineers will learn how to configure and customize analytics for IoMT-specific threats, integrate threat intelligence into their workflows, and create tailored KQL (Kusto Query Language) queries. This chapter also explores the creation of workbooks for real-time reporting and visualization of IoMT device data. We will dive deep into Security Orchestration, Automation, and Response (SOAR) to help engineers automate threat response and optimize Security Operations Center (SOC) workflows for faster and more efficient incident resolution.

Chapter 4, "Threat Detection, Investigation, and Response," focuses on the critical tasks of threat detection, incident investigation, and response within IoMT environments. Security analysts will learn to create analytics rules specific to medical devices and healthcare networks, enabling them to identify suspicious activity and vulnerabilities early. The chapter details how to investigate incidents effectively using the KQL query language while automating response workflows to mitigate threats quickly. We also cover advanced topics like attack disruption techniques and how threat intelligence can be integrated into the incident response process. By the end of this section, readers will be equipped with practical tools for threat hunting and will understand how to leverage Sentinel's embedded features, including Copilot for Analysts, to streamline their security operations.

CHAPTER 1

Get Started with Microsoft Sentinel and IoMT

IoMT, or the Internet of Medical Things, is changing patient care and medical device management as digital healthcare grows. Connected medical devices are becoming more common, which raises security concerns. Microsoft Sentinel plays a role in protecting the Internet of Things by offering security information and event management (SIEM) capabilities. It provides organizations with a strong and scalable solution that helps them respond effectively to cybersecurity threats in the IoMT ecosystem.

This chapter looks at Microsoft Sentinel's role in securing Internet of Medical Things environments as the Internet of Things expands. The Internet of Medical Things includes a specialized industry focused on medical devices and healthcare technology. Sentinel's cloud-native design allows healthcare providers to quickly collect, detect, analyze, and respond to security incidents across IoT devices at the point of care. By using AI and machine learning, Sentinel improves its ability to spot issues within connected healthcare devices, protecting patient data and ensuring compliance with regulations.

Connecting, managing, and securing Internet of Medical Things devices is crucial for maintaining a secure IoMT environment using the Azure IoT Reference Architecture. Along with real-time monitoring and detailed threat intelligence, Microsoft Sentinel provides automated incident response, creating a resilient and secure IoMT ecosystem. Sentinel also integrates smoothly with Azure's IoT cloud platform.

The last section of this chapter explores the merging of Extended Detection and Response (XDR) and Security Information and Event Management (SIEM) systems. It highlights how these two important elements can work together within a single security operations platform. The combination of XDR and SIEM will enable us to create a more thorough and effective approach to cybersecurity. By the end of this chapter, you should understand the following:

- Introduction to IoMT
- Get started with Microsoft Sentinel and World of IoMT
- Microsoft Sentinel for IoT
- Unified Security Operations Platform
- Planning best practices for Unified Security Operations

Introduction to IoMT

The digital revolution is creating a major fundamental shift in healthcare. The digital revolution in healthcare encompasses more than simply digitizing medical records and implementing telehealth. It is more than merely a change in what or how to create delivered care; it is occurring in the way we organize the delivery of care. The Internet of Medical Things (IoMT) will facilitate a network for defining, delivering, and managing clinical outcomes, including the integration of medical devices, clinical applications, and health IT into a single device or application. Clinicians and caregivers will be able to communicate and collect real-time data on patient health from the IoMT devices.

The IoMT is highly convenient; it is a collection of patient-wearable sensors and implantable health monitors connected to mobile health applications and devices that continuously collect and transfer data regarding a patient's clinical care pathways. All patients are vulnerable to acute health events that can cause life-threatening or systemic health changes. The application of these IoMT devices helps minimize significant health risks by preventing health problems from developing, reducing emergency department visits, and optimizing each visit to healthcare delivery. Many of the IoMT devices have features that allow for real-time analysis of a patient's assessment history, which will maximize clinical decision-making and address a patient's health problem earlier. For example, if an IoMT monitoring device is worn and detects an abnormal change in the patient's vital signs that, for example, impacts the patient's heart (e.g., sudden heart rate change) or systemic health (e.g., huge blood sugar spike), the device could immediately report to a healthcare provider.

Due to this connectivity, patients are provided with a more personalized treatment plan and more patient-centered care. The IoMT gives providers continuous access to reliable, real-time, and relevant patient information, enabling them to tailor treatment protocols to the individualized needs of patients. By moving from reactive treatment to proactive patient care, patient participation in monitoring health and well-being improves. It also enables shared decision-making, where patients and doctors can collaborate using real data, rather than relying on check-ins every few months.

Health systems also gain efficiencies through the Internet of Medical Things (IoMT). IoMT data enables hospitals and providers to enhance workflow efficiency, optimize inventory management of medical resources by utilizing medical assets more effectively, and reduce the burden on providers. IoMT analytics help hospitals achieve cost savings and improve efficiencies in their resource offerings by predicting patient needs, tracking patient bed occupancy, and streamlining patient diagnostic procedures. In addition, another practical advantage of remote monitoring is that it allows hospitals to remotely monitor in-person patients for their health, which is even more complicated in rural areas or areas with limited healthcare resources.

In summary, IoMT is not merely a modernization of healthcare delivery; it represents a substantial shift towards faster, more intelligent, and more connected healthcare. With the integration of artificial intelligence (AI), machine learning (ML), and edge computing, the IoMT ecosystem will continue to evolve and enhance the delivery of next-generation healthcare and public health outcomes. Overall, IoMT will help transform healthcare from a data-siloed entity to a data-driven, patient-centric, and efficient manner of delivering care.

The Evolution of IoMT

While it is possible to understand the impact of IoMT, tracing some of the historical developments that culminated in its emergence is also beneficial. All of this connects back to the broad category of IoT. IoT is the concept that everyday objects are part of a larger system, connected through the internet, which enables data collection and sharing. The evolution of IoT into a sub-field called IoMT came from the increased ability to remotely monitor patient health while at the same time using the data to make more informed decisions and ultimately providing improved patient care.

Telemedicine, a type of remote care that emerged in the last decades of the 20th century, is now more feasible with the shift towards mobile, cloud, and wireless technologies, allowing holistic IoMT models to emerge. Monitoring devices that assess vital signs (blood glucose, heart rate) began including sensors and wireless communication modules. Further developments in cloud computing technologies and the continued digitization of health records acted as a jump to innovations in IoMT.

Some of the developments during this short period include

- The emergence of wearable fitness and health devices in the early 2010s
- increasing FDA approvals of connected medical devices like Bluetooth glucose monitors
- Integration with EHRs and the advent of the HL7 and FHIR standards
- Artificial intelligence (AI) and machine learning (ML) could be applied to the continuously collected health data

Components and Architecture

The architecture of the Internet of Medical Things (IoMT) is a multi-layered and complex architecture intended to provide the capability to collect, communicate, process, and use data in real-time in a variety of healthcare settings. Architecture is an essential aspect of being able to deliver a seamless, effective, and personalized experience in the provision of healthcare. Each layer is equally significant, and together they become an integrated ecosystem that connects the patient, the medical device, the healthcare provider, and the data ecosystem. Learning this architecture is fundamental to understanding how IoMT operates and the disruption to modern healthcare.

IoMT consists of multiple layers that enable components to work in tandem to provide an integrated healthcare experience. Figure 1-1 shows elements that comprise the IoMT ecosystem at a high level.

Figure 1-1. IoMT Ecosystem

A key component of the IoMT architecture is medical devices, which generate data in real time. Devices of this type include wearable monitors, like ECG patches and fitness trackers; implantable devices like pacemakers; and diagnostic machines in clinics, such as MRIs and CT scanners. Medical equipment used by patients at home, such as blood glucose meters, digital thermometers, and blood pressure cuffs, also plays a vital role in patient monitoring. Patient engagement is ensured by these devices being intelligent, non-invasive, and user-friendly, ensuring they are reliable and easily accessible.

A medical device has actuators and sensors that can monitor the heart rate, temperature of the body, oxygen level in blood, blood sugar, and even device position in the body. They are needed for event-based notification and ongoing monitoring. Actuators, while less common, can perform some action in response to data, for example, insulin delivery through a smart pump. Sensors and actuators together form the sensing interface between the human organism and the digital health platform.

Once data is gathered, the communication modules operate. In general terms, these are the mechanisms that transmit the information from the device to the central data repository or analysis system. Different transmission technologies exist, and the average age of the wearables we will be using has employed several different technologies based on existing infrastructure. Wi-Fi, Bluetooth, Zigbee, LTE, and, as of late, 5G, which will allow for rapid communication with the lowest latency possible. It should be noted that with low power consumption and extensive coverage (vast coverage areas), Narrowband IoT (NB-IoT) does provide reliable service. These communication modules connect devices, regardless of their location, to the cloud (e.g., tracking a patient within the hallways of a hospital, while at home, or when mobile).

In many instances, before the data arrives at centralized servers, the data is operationalized using data aggregators and gateways, usually built into edge computing devices. Aggregators and gateways in an edge computing model provide a buffer and initial analysis of operationalized data from standard zones or zones involved with care. The data aggregator interfaces with multiple transmitters, aggregates the data from many sources, and either performs a simple analysis even filtering for transmission to the cloud based on use case (e.g., for health it may be basic vitals on several patients), and transmits the aggregated, summarized, or vital data to the cloud to judge ongoing duty status. Operations on data at the edge enhance privacy, minimize exposure via raw data, and enable local reactions (e.g., notify the primary caregiver's device that a notification has expanded past the threshold). Note that this model also reduces latency and minimizes the use of data points beyond prescribed limits.

At the upper tiers of the architecture is the cloud infrastructure. The cloud infrastructure provides scalable and centralized platforms for processing, storage, and analysis of data. Cloud systems can accommodate enormous amounts of structured and unstructured healthcare data. Cloud systems also have sophisticated algorithms—AI and machine learning—that can identify patterns, make anomaly detections, and look for predictive insights. The back-end algorithms and models are agnostic in terms of how the results are delivered to end users through applications and dashboards that include mobile apps, clinician portals, or web dashboards. These applications display data in an understandable and actionable format through visualizations, alerts, and recommendations tailored toward patients' needs and the user's needs as they relate to healthcare providers within their workflows.

To conclude, security and compliance layers are essential to maintaining the security of sensitive medical data and trust in IoMT. In addition to end-to-end encryption, security identity management, user authentication, and compliance with HIPAA, GDPR, and local healthcare regulations, the security and compliance layer contains several key components. Therefore, security solutions need to maintain data confidentiality, integrity, and availability without compromising performance or creating negative user experiences.

In conclusion, IoMT architecture is not a single technology but a multi-tiered system organized for interoperability, scalability, and resiliency. Layered IoMT architecture provides seamless connection and functionality from sensor-level data capture through to secure cloud-based analytics and user applications. It is worth repeating that the architecture of IoMT is central to realizing the full potential of IoMT, as it empowers healthcare systems to provide more proactive, precise, and patient-centered care.

Real-World Applications and Use Cases

IoMT has applications in nearly every area of healthcare. It can facilitate a variety of use cases that improve patient engagement, enhance clinical workflows, and reduce costs.

- *Wearables and Personal Health Devices*: Devices specifically designed for monitoring heart rate, activity level, sleep pattern, and other measurements, such as smartwatches and fitness trackers, can be used by individuals to track their activities. Some of these devices detect atrial fibrillation or a drop in blood oxygen and notify individuals or care providers in real time.

- *Remote Patient Monitoring (RPM)*: Patients with chronic conditions, such as diabetes, hypertension, or heart failure, can be monitored continuously outside of the clinical environment. These connected devices can collect vital signs and notify the provider if an irregularity is identified, providing real-time intervention.

- *Smart Hospitals*: IoMT is being used in hospitals to refine care and ensure efficient use of devices and resources. Using smart beds, care providers can monitor movement and position adjustments automatically. RFID tags can be attached to any medical device to assist in locating equipment, collecting data on equipment use, and monitoring inventory.

- *Telemedicine and Virtual Care*: When equipped with connected diagnostic tools, such as digital stethoscopes or otoscopes, together with additional information about the patient, health professionals can offer real-time examination data to clarify assessment in continuing virtual consultations. In this case, the quality of the virtual consultation with digital tools can improve diagnostic accuracy.

- *Ingestible and Implantable Sensors*: Some IoMT devices are ingestible or implantable, meaning a patient swallows or has the device implanted. These may offer a slightly new way to keep track of a patient's drug adherence, digestive issues, and internal organ functioning.

Advantages and Outcomes

The Internet of Medical Things (IoMT) provides remarkable advantages impacting patients, providers, payers, and health systems.

- *Linked Care*: Continuous and remote monitoring creates opportunities for early detection and intervention, outcomes are progressive, and complications are reduced.

- *Cost Savings*: Reduced frequency of urgent hospital visits, and with effective management of chronic disease, there will be lower overall healthcare costs.

- *Operational Efficiency*: Automated method of data collection, intelligent scheduling, and real-time tracking of assets to enhance clinical work flows and reduce administrative burden.

- *Personalized Medicine*: IoMT devices can support unique treatment plans based on continuous physiological data.

- *Patient Empowerment*: The ability to access real-time health recordings encourages individuals to be active participants in their healthcare management.

However, IoMT also presents challenges. Following are the key challenges and considerations:

- *Security Risks*: Medical devices are attractive targets for cyber attackers, and the security of devices must be a priority.

- *Privacy of Data*: Continued collection and distribution of sensitive health information causes uncertainty in patient confidentiality and patient ownership of their health information.

- *Regulatory Compliance*: Devices must satisfy legislation such as HIPAA in the United States and GDPR in Europe, and a regulatory body such as the FDA must approve devices before they can be used.

- *Interoperability*: Different manufacturers create devices that communicate on different platforms; this is an identifiable barrier.

- *Data Management*: Values will need to be stored, analyzed, and interpreted meaningfully; IoMT devices are being used to collect health data at volumes never seen before and require infrastructure to manage.

Regulatory Landscape and Standards

As with many other industries, the IoMT industry and its devices are subject to strict regulations, and compliance will ensure safety and trust.

- *HIPAA (Health Insurance Portability and Accountability Act)*: It defines standards for the privacy and security of data in the United States.

- *FDA Guidelines*: It regulates the development, testing, and approval of connected medical devices.

- *GDPR (General Data Protection Regulation)*: It regulates data protection in the European Union.

- *ISO and IEC Standards*: It regulates quality (ISO 13485) and interoperability of devices.

- *HL7 and FHIR*: It supports exchanging data between electronic health systems.

By respecting these standards, manufacturers can determine that their devices are safe, trustworthy, and legal.

CHAPTER 1   GET STARTED WITH MICROSOFT SENTINEL AND IOMT

The Road Ahead: The Future of IoMT

While IoMT will undoubtedly thrive due to the advancements in technology and consumer demand for accessible healthcare, it can be hard to predict where IoMT is headed.

- *Artificial Intelligence*: AI will support and automate improved diagnostic accuracy, enhance the rigor of the clinical decision-making process, and extract patterns from large datasets.

- *Blockchain*: Will provide secure and transparent mechanisms to share data with all interested stakeholders.

- *5G Connectivity*: Will enable data in large volumes to be transferred in real time without latency.

- *Digital Twins*: Real-time data will be able to create a virtual model or representation of a patient to personalize the treatment path.

- *Precision Medicine*: Essentially combining genomic data with IoMT will allow for therapy with high levels of individualization.

The future of IoMT reflects predictive, preventive, and participatory health data, where technology serves to supplement human functionality, leading to improved outcomes. The Internet of Medical Things will support innovation to reconfigure the healthcare ecosystem to be more connected, preventive, and tailored to the unique needs of the patient. It can empower patients, enhance clinical decision-making, and increase operational efficiencies across the entire healthcare system. While challenges remain, accelerating innovations and regulatory frameworks will continue to allow for the proliferation of IoMT. As healthcare systems continue their digital transformation around the globe, IoMT will play a critical role in ensuring greater health and equity of experience.

As the Internet of Medical Things (IoMT) continues to disrupt healthcare, it will also bring with it multiple cybersecurity challenges.

In healthcare settings, the fusion of multiple connected devices, of cloud computing, and of data analytics will result in a tremendous expansion of the attack surface that cyber adversaries can take advantage of. The complexities of merging together these devices and environments come with the potential for the changes to make cybersecurity frameworks, technologies, and policy.

In this next section, we will examine the global cybersecurity landscape as it relates to IoMT. Several prominent threats, vulnerabilities, and regulations have recently arisen to protect data and devices in the healthcare ecosystem.

The purpose of this section is to examine the threats, vulnerabilities, and rules that affect IoMT systems, along with some recently developed solutions and practices.

The Expanding Threat Surface of IoMT

IoMT systems differ from traditional IT systems in that the devices exponentially increase the attack surface, with devices used in an uncontrolled open environment and with varying maturity of security. Further complicating the complexity of these systems is their embeddedness, extended lifecycle, and limited computational processing, where secure design and maintenance are challenging. Several factors, combined with their embedded nature, have allowed the IoMT to expose itself to an enormous number of cyber threats.

- *Device Diversity*: IoMT consists of thousands of device types and configurations with varying hardware, firmware, and communication protocols.

- *Legacy Systems*: Many hospital systems still deploy outdated software or utilize devices that the manufacturer no longer supports.

- *Interconnected Devices*: IoMT devices can share information over the networks, across other devices, and more commonly with cloud platforms, creating an enormous number of entry points.

- *Decentralized Data Flows*: Health data is generated and processed in multiple environments, including patients' homes, mobile apps, and public clouds.

These conditions make IoMT systems vulnerable and susceptible to a wide variety of cyberattack threats.

Common Cybersecurity Threats in IoMT

While the Internet of Medical Things (IoMT) presents exciting and revolutionary opportunities for modern healthcare, the new technology will also introduce a new range of cybersecurity vulnerabilities that place not just the integrity of the data but also patient safety in jeopardy. The interconnectedness of IoMT devices, their continuous data exchange, and their widespread application in various health environments provide a new lucrative target for cyber attackers.

Threats affecting IoMT systems range from financially motivated cybercrimes such as ransomware attacks to systematic intrusions by nation-state-sponsored cyber espionage or attacks on critical infrastructure. To effectively build defenses against these threats, it is essential to understand the diverse nature and combinatorial complexity of these threats.

There are several viable threat vectors in healthcare targeting IoMT systems. Often, the threats are opportunistic; sometimes, cybercriminals target IoMT in campaigns or adopt a persistent targeting approach against nation-state actors. Figure 1-2 depicts viable threat vectors in IoMT systems.

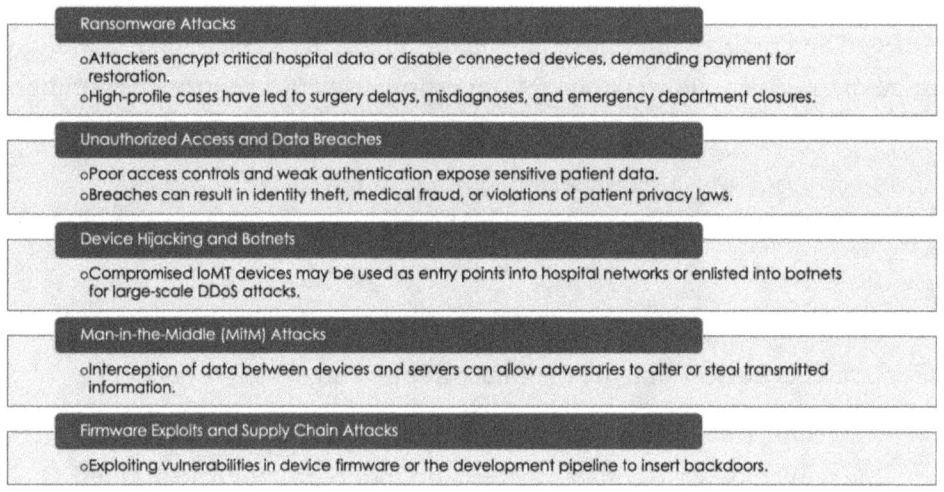

Figure 1-2. *Viable Threat Vectors in IoMT Systems*

Ransomware constitutes one of the most prominent threats within IoMT ecosystems. In ransomware attacks, bad actors encrypt key hospital systems or IoMT devices to keep them inoperable until a ransom is paid. Unlike conventional ransomware attacks in IT environments, however, ransomware attacks on IoMT systems can lead to the loss of life. When systems that control ventilators, infusion pumps, or patient monitors are disabled, patient care is irrevocably harmed. When these attacks have occurred in the real world, they have caused emergency rooms to shut down, have delayed urgent surgeries, and may have led to death. These attacks typically take advantage of aging or obsolete software, lack of segmentation within hospital networks, and unpatched devices—conditions that still exist in many hospitals.

Unauthorized access and data breaches are another primary threat vector of IoMT environments. Many IoMT deployments use weak authentication schemes or misconfigured access controls, exposing enormous volumes of personal health information (PHI) to breaches. Once breached, actors can steal patient records for personal identity fraud or insurance fraud or sell patient information on the dark web. Outside of the obvious reputational and financial damage, internal investigations into the breaches may result in penalties under regulations like HIPAA (Health Insurance Portability and Accountability Act) or GDPR (General Data Protection Regulation), particularly when an organization cannot prove adequate preventative measures were in place against breaches.

Device hijacking and asset enlistment to botnets are also risks to IoMT. In these types of scenarios, threat actors exploit vulnerabilities in connected medical devices, such as hospital-grade infusion pumps or remote monitoring tools, to gain access to internal networks. They can then use the compromised devices to carry out additional attacks or add them to large botnets to be used for distributed denial-of-service (DDoS) attacks. The well-known Mirai botnet, which targeted insecure IoT devices, highlighted how easy it is to weaponize poorly secured endpoints at scale.

Man-in-the-middle (MitM) attacks can be especially concerning in IoMT systems because there is a constant flow of data happening between devices, edge processors, and cloud servers. In an MitM attack, an adversary can intercept and possibly manipulate the data stream without the sender or the recipient knowing. This is a genuine concern when you consider manipulated diagnostic data, altered treatment parameters, or stolen credentials. For example, a hacker could change the dosage data transmitted from a specialized doctor's console to an infusion pump and have quite a damaging, if not lethal, effect on the patient.

An equally menacing threat is with firmware exploits and supply chain attacks. Firmware, the software embedded in medical devices and the systems used to create, manufacture, and distribute them, is not typically updated regularly. Many IoMT devices, especially legacy ones, often do not guarantee a secure boot-up. Malicious actors can inject malicious code during transit or provisioning, ultimately creating backdoors to devices that remain undetected in the firmware. Firmware attacks can exfiltrate data or enable remote use of the device while it's undetected, which can be especially pernicious when they do just this. Another aspect of the firmware threat is that if the firmware is compromised, a person's device could be at risk. Yet, nothing overtly would indicate that a compromise occurred for a million possible reasons.

Insider threats are among the underestimated and substantial hazards to be dealt with in the context of healthcare cybersecurity. Disgruntled and careless employees, including contractors or untrained staff, may willfully or wholly inadvertently compromise IoMT systems. Disgruntled and careless employees with privileged system access can bypass perimeter threats, act like malware by using a USB to implant malware, or manipulate the wider area to which the device connects. In specific healthcare environments, user access policies are either lacking or nonexistent. Staff often share credentials and take shortcuts to simplify their work, making it all but impossible to track these individuals.

Lastly, we have legacy systems and their interoperability and security challenges that permeate IoMT. Numerous hospitals/models still operate on aging infrastructures, never developed with threat models for cybersecurity in mind. This lack of a known attack surface poses risks when connecting or integrating its applications with established IoMT devices. Legacy software often lacks encryption, secure API capabilities, and access controls. The massive attack surface compromises the attempt to operationalize attacks against actors. The interoperability for patient care is essential, but it can have unintended consequences, such as poor security or risks that compromise quality assurance, when data passes through unsecured platforms or third-party applications.

As the fragmentation of device platforms increases, the growing threat model for cyberattacks on the IoMT ecosystem becomes more ambiguous, adaptive, and potentially malicious. The outcomes of IoMT threat hazards extend beyond data confidentiality, impacting operating continuity and compromising patient safety and public trust. The security posture for accountable technology in healthcare organizations, including IoMT devices, must adopt a forward-deploying security approach across multiple layers. This approach should be supported by practices that enforce security policies, provide training and testing for employee awareness, and continually remediate designs through ongoing monitoring to ensure maximum security.

Global Regulatory and Legal Pressures

Regulatory organizations throughout the globe are commencing to understand the substances of securing IoMT environments. Some examples:

- *United States*

  - The FDA requires medical device manufacturers to issue premarket and postmarket cybersecurity recommendations.

  - The 780 PATCH Act (2023) requires IoMT vendors to provide Software Bill of Materials (SBOM) and update capabilities.

- *European Union*

  - The GDPR provides significant controls on health data.

  - The Medical Device Regulation (MDR) requires cybersecurity to be included in conformity assessment procedures.

- *Asia-Pacific*

  - Singapore's Cybersecurity Labelling Scheme for Medical Devices (CLS-MD) promotes transparency.

  - Japan and South Korea's policies on device security have been included in more significant IoT and privacy norms.

- *Global Standards*

  - The ISO/IEC 81001 family issues identical practices for safe and secure health software and health IT systems.

  - The NIST Cybersecurity Framework needs to address healthcare environments.

While complying with these requirements is a compliance matter, complying with them as a verified process is a boundary requirement where strategy and structure regarding market access and strategy start.

Challenges in Implementing IoMT Cybersecurity

Even if there was more focus and attention on security, the challenges to implement it would still be reflected below:

- *Resources Are Not Available*: The device security is often limited by memory, processing power, or battery capacity. Devices may not have the memory, processing power, battery capacity, encryption, or antivirus software.

- *Different Security Maturity of Manufacturers*: The security maturity of device vendors varies considerably, especially with small manufacturers.

- *Operational Priority Over Security*: Hospitals are often more concerned with availability and performance than adhering to strict cybersecurity protocols.

- *Problems Relating to Management of Patches*: Devices that can be indefinitely operational (e.g., proprietary software and a piece of manufacturer-made hardware) are often unable to integrate patches easily and become completely obsolete in a short timeframe.

- *Lack of Standards*: Universal standards for secure communication and validation of devices in the IoMT ecosystem—there are no governing protocols to help integration.

Opportunities for Innovation and Resilience

The threat environment is vast but, at the same time, rife with opportunity for cybersecurity innovation across healthcare as a whole. Some of the unique opportunities include

- *Zero Trust Architecture*: With a "never trust but always verify" model, the IoMT developer can write the "verify" before letting any device, user, or access onto the network.

- *AI and Machine Learning to Identify Threats on Devices*: By taking the analytic approach to identify anomalies in device behavior or data flow that implies an intentional or unintentional compromise.

- *Blockchain for Data Integrity*: For example, decentralized ledgers may ensure tamper-free logging of medical transactions and audit trails for devices.

- *Embedded Security by Design*: Designing devices with encryption, secure boot, and secure firmware updates in the very design phase of the device.

- *Automated Patch Management*: There is an opportunity for cloud-based services to push patches virtually and securely to devices—e.g., without a universal touch as of yet, we can do a maximum firmware upgrade to a device, and it could take weeks or months (if you even get full updates) to circumvent gaps in vulnerabilities.

- *Cybersecurity Labelling*: By providing security labels and scores to offer transparency, buyers may understand what safety features exist within the medical devices.

- *Global Cooperative*: In sharing threat information across geographic boundaries, initiatives such as those from the World Health Organization (WHO) or INTERPOL are urgently needed.

Best Practices for Securing IoMT

Cybersecurity risks will exist in IoMT environments; however, stakeholders must adopt a multi-layered approach to circumvent back attacks:

- *Device Manufacturers*
  - Conduct threat modeling and pen-testing.
  - Block design for update mechanism and secure communications.
- *Healthcare Providers*
  - Implementing segmentation across networks and endpoint protection
  - Providing staff education campaigns regarding phishing, ransomware, and data handling

- *Policymakers and Regulators*
    - Implement minimum security standards for new entrants in the market.
    - Internationally harmonized cybersecurity guidelines from cyber protection groups
- *Patients and Consumers*
    - Understand that using personal apps in conjunction with professional devices will require regular updates.
    - Robustness of authentication and understanding policies for sharing data.

The confluence of digital health and cybersecurity raises challenges and opportunities in the healthcare sector. The promise of improved health outcomes with the potential for IoMT comes in contrast to the necessity to secure the growing, spiraling complexity of the digitally connected health space. Cybervictims are changing; therefore, cyber defenders must change too. By considering cooperation, responsible innovation, and forward-thinking regulation, a future of secure, resilient IoMT becomes an achievable goal. It is essential that all stakeholders—governments, providers, technologists, and patients—collaborate in establishing trust and safety in the foundation of connected healthcare.

Get Started with Microsoft Sentinel and the World of IoMT

The emergence of connected medical devices into healthcare, joined in unity of purpose and identified as the Internet of Medical Things (IoMT), has impacted the ways that medical data is gathered, stored, and analyzed. IoMT has provided the patient care world with tremendous possibilities, including improved outcomes and the utilization of wearables to monitor health parameters in real time, as well as connected diagnostic devices for vital sign checks. Unfortunately, the increase in IoMT devices has created new security challenges. Organizations must implement scalable and protectable security solutions to prepare for incursions such as data breaches, device tampering, and ransomware attacks.

CHAPTER 1   GET STARTED WITH MICROSOFT SENTINEL AND IOMT

This section's objective is to present Microsoft Sentinel as a practical and complete security information and event management (SIEM) solution on a cloud-based platform for the protection of critical IoMT spaces. While this chapter continues to explain how to get into Microsoft Sentinel in an IoMT space, it demonstrates how we are using Microsoft Sentinel to hunt, monitor, detect, and react to security threats in IoT-enabled medical devices. Microsoft Sentinel enables organizations to centralize the collection, analysis, and response of security data across their entire IoT and IT ecosystems, including IoMT devices, with comprehensive SIEM solutions. Never has advanced access control security been needed that is meant to function beyond the interconnectivity dilemma of IoMT networks, which are currently being issued across the world by healthcare providers to collect real-time patient data. Sentinel enhances their threat intelligence in real time by gathering security events from a large number of sources, including IoMT devices. In conjunction with machine learning, AI, and threat intelligence, the platform can identify anomalous behavior that suggests a potential security breach. With Microsoft Sentinel, health organizations can protect their IoMT ecosystems from continuous cyber threats.

Before you start using Sentinel for an IoMT environment, you must understand how to integrate it with IoT devices and systems. As part of this integration, Microsoft Azure IoT Hub creates a secure communication channel between devices and the cloud. Thanks to Sentinel's seamless connection to the Azure IoT infrastructure, it allows for real-time data collection and monitoring. With Azure's IoT Reference Architecture, organizations can visualize their IoMT ecosystem to identify critical security checkpoints, connect those points using Azure capabilities, and set up Sentinel to monitor the associated connections and devices. Using Sentinel's analytics and detection capabilities, health organizations can monitor the peace of mind of device health stats, better watch for security events, and respond quickly to incidents. The opportunity to hold significant amounts of data in the cloud means scalability is no longer a concern, and organizations can continue to monitor their security operation as their IoMT environments grow.

In addition to enhanced monitoring and detection capabilities for security incidents, Microsoft Sentinel offers robust automation and incident response features. These include powerful automated response functions within the technology. Depending on the parameters of a potential security threat identified in an IoMT network, Sentinel is capable of automatically starting a pre-configured playbook to contain the incident, limiting the environmental impact. With Azure Logic Apps, playbooks enable automated workflows that isolate compromised devices, alert security teams, and initiate device remediation. InfoSecurity teams can react to threats more quickly and with less business interruption to patient care and healthcare functions by leveraging automated response features and advanced analytics. The Sentinel solution also integrates with Microsoft Defender for Endpoint and expands its capabilities to detect and respond to threats across the healthcare ecosystem.

A unified security strategy is essential in the IoMT world. Microsoft Sentinel provides healthcare organizations with a unified view of their IoMT security posture, uniquely combining SIEM and Extended Detection and Response (XDR) to offer a 360-degree assessment. As the IoMT ecosystem continues to expand, cybercriminals are presented with more avenues for taking advantage of vulnerabilities. Therefore, healthcare organizations can leverage Microsoft Sentinel to be well-positioned to face the challenges, facilitating a secure and resilient patient care environment while protecting sensitive health information.

Microsoft Sentinel is a scalable, cloud-native SIEM that serves as an innovative, end-to-end SIEM and security orchestration, automation, and response (SOAR) solution. Microsoft Sentinel provides you with a 360-degree view across your organization to detect, investigate, and respond to cyberthreats.

Microsoft Sentinel leverages Microsoft's threat intelligence stream as well as yours and the power of AI to get insights, investigate, and detect threats and integrates first-class Azure services like Log Analytics and Logic Apps.

Eliminate the worry of increasing sophistication, increasing alert volume, and lengthy investigation and resolution times with Microsoft Sentinel.

Microsoft Sentinel Viewpoints of IoMT

Microsoft Sentinel plays an essential role in mitigating risks of unsecured and growing Internet of Medical Things (IoMT) devices. These devices, ranging from patient monitoring devices to infusion pumps and wearables such as health trackers, are indispensable in a healthcare environment but often have little in the way of built-in security controls. Microsoft Sentinel is a cloud SIEM/SOAR tool that supports healthcare organizations with continuously monitoring, detecting (via alerts and other indicators), and responding to threats on these devices. Additionally, it leverages the cloud to ingest massive volumes of data from thousands of endpoints and healthcare devices, allowing organizations to build a consolidated security posture with real-time visibility and incident response capabilities.

One of the strengths Microsoft Sentinel has for IoMT ecosystems is the ability to aggregate multiple data sources, like firewalls, endpoint protection systems, medical device logs, and Electronic Health Record (EHR) systems. This degree of integration allows for a single view into the security status of all health devices on a shared network. As telemetry is accumulated from multiple sources, Sentinel uses its native analytics rules and machine learning algorithms to determine anomalies, commonly associated with compromised medical devices or lateral movement in a hospital's network. For example, if a networked insulin pump starts talking to an IP address not observed previously, Sentinel would detect that activity and automatically trigger an alert.

The ability to orchestrate workflows and automate steps using Sentinel's SOAR capabilities is particularly beneficial for IoMT security. Healthcare organizations often have a limited number of security personnel and may not be able to respond to every alert manually. Sentinel allows you to build playbooks, or programmed workflows, that automatically react to certain threats in real time. For example, if a vulnerability is discovered and it appears on an ECG monitor connected to your network, the playbook could isolate that device from the network, notify the staff, and log the incident in your service management tool, such as ServiceNow. And it can do this faster than you can react, avoiding potential malware propagation or unauthorized access to your network.

Additionally, Microsoft Sentinel takes advantage of Microsoft threat intelligence, which is based on signals gathered from the entire global Microsoft ecosystem, including billions of security telemetry points from Windows, Azure, and Office 365. This threat intelligence enables Sentinel to better recognize attack patterns relevant to healthcare environments and IoMT threats, such as ransomware attacks on hospital infrastructure control systems or phishing attacks aimed at gaining access to medical device controllers. Health organizations can use Sentinel's dashboards and workbooks to graphically illustrate those threats and provide recommendations for response and mitigation.

Finally, Sentinel helps with auditability and compliance, critical issues with highly regulated industries such as healthcare. It helps make organizations more compliant with requirements such as HIPAA and HITRUST by providing logs of all security events and responses. Compliance dashboards can also be created to illustrate compliance with a combination of internal policies and external grants. As the adoption of IoMT matures and cybercriminal trends from the ransomware playbook appear to persist in attacking healthcare infrastructure in this new decade, Microsoft Sentinel is a robust, intelligent, and scalable defensive platform that will grow to meet the unique requirements and vulnerabilities presented in the healthcare setting.

CHAPTER 1   GET STARTED WITH MICROSOFT SENTINEL AND IOMT

Microsoft Sentinel for IoT

In today's world of digital transformation, organizations must ensure they are protecting themselves from cyberattacks now more than ever. With all the devices, users, and systems using your organization's network, it can be challenging to continually and comprehensively maintain security and compliance over an entire organization. However, the good news is that Microsoft Sentinel was created to be a budget-friendly security operations center for your organization.

Microsoft Sentinel is a cloud-based security product with advanced technology that provides a monitored security solution for your entire online space, regardless of the number of apps, devices, or data you create, use, or maintain. It is like having competent, non-expert security personnel that is omniscient, on alert, and monitoring your security posture over your organization's apps, in addition to the devices and the data used to store or manipulate it. In addition, if there is a problem, Microsoft Sentinel not only informs you about the issue but also identifies the specific situation, automatically takes action to respond to the threat, and helps you prevent attacks from being launched.

What differentiates Microsoft Sentinel from other security products is the use of AI and machine learning. Microsoft Sentinel processes a lot of data, identifying valid data while sorting out the noise. Microsoft Sentinel integrates with other software you likely already own, aggregating everything into a single security data view. Microsoft Sentinel enables you to provide surveillance over a small business or an enterprise-level organization, scaling with your organization to stay ahead in the battle against cybercrime.

Microsoft Sentinel is functional even if you do not view yourself as experienced in the fields of either cybersecurity or IT. Microsoft Sentinel can quickly get you started with preconfigured tools and take advantage of basic features to collect data, alerts, and automated responses to known threats. As you learn the foundation concepts from prior, you can always layer these components with your own rules and workflows based on your needs and situations.

In this segment, we will provide an overview of the key components of Microsoft Sentinel in a straightforward and digestible way.

Microsoft Sentinel is a formidable, cloud-based security offering designed to protect your entire organization. Please take note that it is a Security Information and Event Management (SIEM) and Security Orchestration, Automation, and Response (SOAR) platform. To put it simply, this means it can not only help detect cyberattacks but also investigate, respond to, and foresee them, all through intelligent technologies and automation.

Sentinel Cloud provides the technology with the tools, such as Log Analytics and Logic Apps, to take action within your security data. It uses artificial intelligence (AI) to assist in interpreting the data.

Sentinel Cloud can consume Microsoft's threat intelligence or import its own, or both, providing choices and flexibility.

As with the pace and sophistication of cyberattacks, security teams feel the mounting pressure to respond as these threats continuously come in from multiple sources they are trying to defend against.

With the pressure that Microsoft Sentinel offers towards prioritizing security alerts, associating alert events, and automating the mundane tasks, it is a path that the team can take to keep on top of the most pressing threats.

Sentinel is part of the Microsoft security set of offerings and can be leveraged without needing any special licenses to get started. It brings confidence through cloud infrastructure, rigorous processes, and controls that protect your data.

For service providers, Microsoft Sentinel also has the capabilities to shield numerous customers seamlessly. It does not make a difference whether you are protecting one company or hundreds; Microsoft Sentinel can scale to protect growth and evolution based on the needs it takes on.

Activate OoB (Out of Box) Security Contents

Within its SIEM offerings, Microsoft Sentinel provides built-in security content for security teams to collect data together, monitor activity, create alerts, investigate threats, respond to incidents, and integrate with any tools, platforms, and services.

Microsoft Sentinel has a wide variety of built-in content that can help security teams respond to and manage threats more efficiently. This is part of the SIEM capabilities, and it is intended to help you collect data, monitor your environment, create alerts, investigate incidents, hunt incidents, and integrate with anything else. Figure 1-3 is an image of OoB from Content Hub on the Microsoft Azure Portal.

CHAPTER 1   GET STARTED WITH MICROSOFT SENTINEL AND IOMT

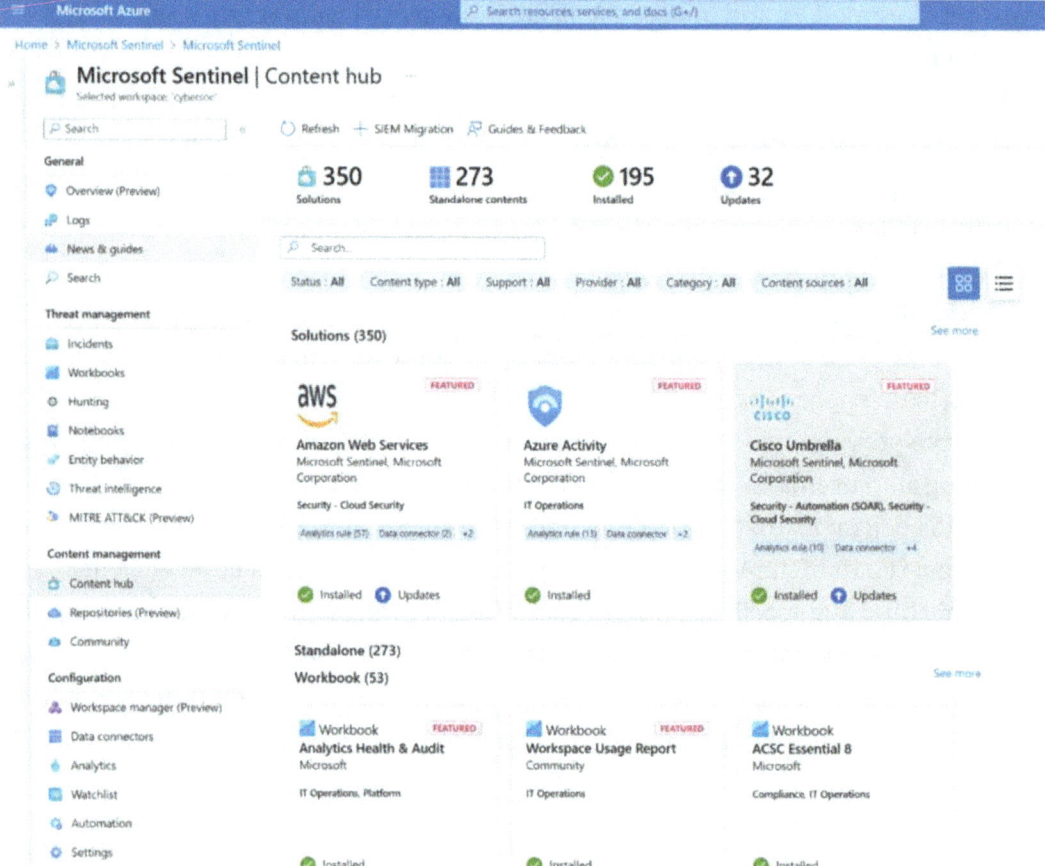

Figure 1-3. *Content Hub on Microsoft Azure Portal*

The available types of content in Microsoft Sentinel include

- *Data Connectors*: Data connectors will bring logs and data from another source into Sentinel so it can process the logs and data.

- *Parsers*: Parsers will assist in ordering and converting incoming data to a standard format in order to more easily utilize them throughout Sentinel's various tools.

- *Workbooks*: Workbooks will create visual dashboards and interactive reports for the user to view trends and other insights within their data.

- *Analytics Rules*: Analytics rules will generate alerts and group those alerts as incidents so that security teams can respond with more calibrated actions.

- *Hunting Queries*: Hunting queries will allow analysts to hunt for unknown threats before they affect them proactively.

- *Notebooks*: Notebooks will provide advanced data analysis and hunting privileges with abilities like Jupyter to allow more extensive investigations.

- *Watchlists*: Watchlists will allow you to add lists of important information, i.e., high-risk users or IPs, to be able to detect better and reduce unwanted alerts.

- *Playbooks*: Playbooks will allow automated workflows so you can respond quickly and consistently to threats utilizing Azure Logic Apps.

Microsoft Sentinel offers two styles of content: Pre-packaged solutions and end-to-end content collections built for specific use cases or sectors, as well as individual items that can be used independently based on your needs. The content Microsoft Sentinel provides can be used as is, natively out-of-the-box, modified for your ecosystem, or even your custom content to share with the community. This flexible framework allows Microsoft Sentinel to operate in many different security use cases and grow with your business.

Microsoft Sentinel Collects Data at Scale

Collection of data from all users, devices, applications, and systems—all users, all devices, all applications, and all systems that are either on premises or in the cloud. Figure 1-4 provides a summary of key capabilities available in Microsoft Sentinel for efficiently collecting data.

Figure 1-4. *Microsoft Sentinel Collects Data at Scale*

Microsoft Sentinel provides multiple data connectors or data sources that create real-time integration with various data sources. Microsoft Sentinel provides data connectors for Microsoft data sources such as Microsoft Entra ID, Azure Activity, Azure Storage, and more. Microsoft Sentinel also offers data connectors to data sources from non-Microsoft solutions that span an extensive range of both security and application ecosystems based on IIS mappings of non-Microsoft solutions. Microsoft Sentinel offers even more flexibility, allowing for data ingestion through standard event format (CEF), Syslog, and REST APIs. These data connectors can be explored and set up through the data connectors interface in the Microsoft Sentinel portal.

In addition to the data connectors provided by Microsoft Sentinel out of the box, the platform supports custom connectors that users can build as needed, provided a purpose-built data connector is available. Users can develop and deploy custom connectors, supported by Microsoft, to virtually create any data connector across their environments.

Microsoft Sentinel also utilizes data normalization to provide consistency across multiple data sources, whether they use ingestion time normalization, query time normalization, or other normalization methods. Data ingestion time normalization and query time normalization translate the data and map the data for defined datasets into a single, normalized schema so that queries, or correlations, or analyses across numerous datasets can happen more effectively with consistent, normalized schemas.

Microsoft Sentinel (Detect, Investigate, Respond)

Microsoft Sentinel is a cloud-native SIEM (security information and event management) and SOAR (security orchestration, automation, and response) solution. Microsoft Sentinel provides unique detection capabilities to allow the organization to detect threats beforehand within its digital environments. Microsoft Sentinel has the potential to collect security signals from a multitude of sources, including Microsoft 365, Azure, and on-premises systems. Utilizing its built-in AI and machine learning features, Sentinel can collect vast amounts of security signals and alerts from these sources to perform real-time analysis of ongoing events. Once the analysis has occurred, Microsoft Sentinel will identify anomalies, enabling it to detect attacks, such as logged malicious logins, lateral movement, privilege escalation, and malware activity, within the enterprise.

Microsoft Sentinel also provides rich investigation capabilities once the security team receives notifications of potential threats, so teams can quickly understand the extent and scope of an attack. Investigation is aided through visualizations such as interactive investigation graphs and incident timelines, whose representations allow the analyst to visualize the progression of the attack and see the assets, users, and points of entry that were affected in the attack timeline. Investigations also view consolidated events from different data sources, making it easier to investigate and reduce alert fatigue for incidents by grouping logically appropriate alerts.

Investigating incidents is a critical point of situational awareness and ongoing intelligence gathering. In addition to detection and investigation, Microsoft Sentinel provides unequivocally fast and automated response capabilities, enabling organizations to respond quickly and automate the process. Automated workflows known as playbooks are powered by Azure Logic Apps. Organizations can define workflows to contain incidents, including quarantining infected endpoints, locking out user accounts, or notifying incident responders. These custom automated workflows also reduced response times and potential harm, making them a critical component of any organizational cybersecurity solution. Figure 1-5 depicts threat detection capabilities.

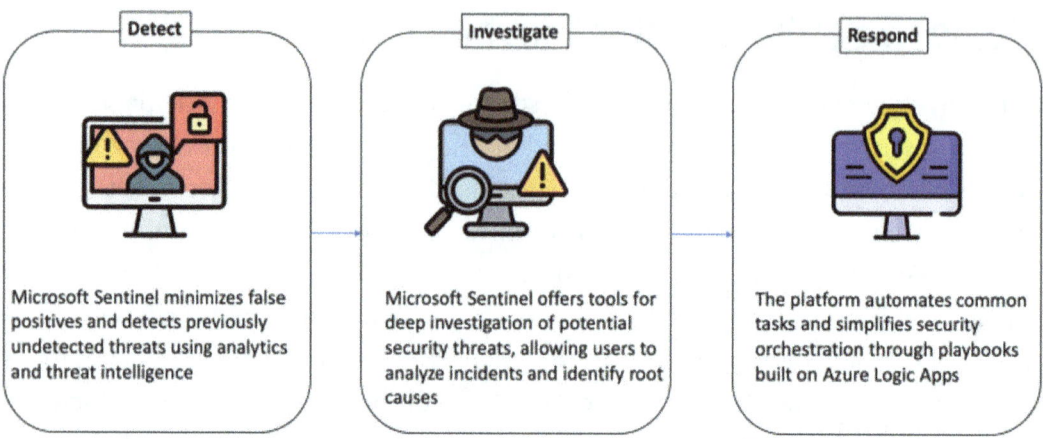

Figure 1-5. *Microsoft Sentinel Threat Detection*

Detect Threats with Microsoft Sentinel

The analytics capabilities offered through Microsoft Sentinel allow organizations to limit alert fatigue by reducing the number of alerts that need to be reviewed and investigated. Sentinel uses analytics that would enable related alerts to be grouped into incidents. This helps to call out real threats quickly. You can use the out-of-the-box analytic rules, or you can customize the analytic rules to your environment. Analytics rules, including behavioral analytics related to network activity, help identify anomalies by mapping regular network activity. Using low-fidelity alert correlations through different entities to generate high-fidelity incidents can help inform security practitioners and provide meaningful incidents.

Additionally, the platform provides integrated support for the MITRE ATT&CK® framework. Microsoft Sentinel ingests and analyzes data to find threats, provides monitoring and investigation, and offers an overview of activity. This includes how your environment is coordinated in terms of the tactics and techniques outlined in the framework. This allows organizations to acquire an overview of their security posture and potential gaps.

The threat intelligence integration in Microsoft Sentinel enables you to consume multiple intelligence sources and correlate relevant data to identify local threat activity. The additional context is a key part of the investigation that security analysts rely on to develop insights that support incident decision-making during investigation and response actions.

Watchlists are an additional feature that lets users associate outside data with events in Microsoft Sentinel. Examples of watchlists include high-value assets, former employees, and dedicated administrator service accounts. Once created, watchlists can be utilized within detection rules, threat hunting activities, searches, and automated response workflows.

In conclusion, Microsoft Sentinel has workbooks that provide interactive visual reports. Workbooks can also be created from scratch by using the different templates. After connecting a data source, I could look at immediate insights using workbook templates. Additionally, users can create their custom workbooks that suit their monitoring and reporting needs. Workbooks provide visualizations that enable teams to better understand patterns and trends that may need to be investigated in their environment. The specifics of Microsoft's Sentinel threat detection capabilities are outlined in Figure 1-6.

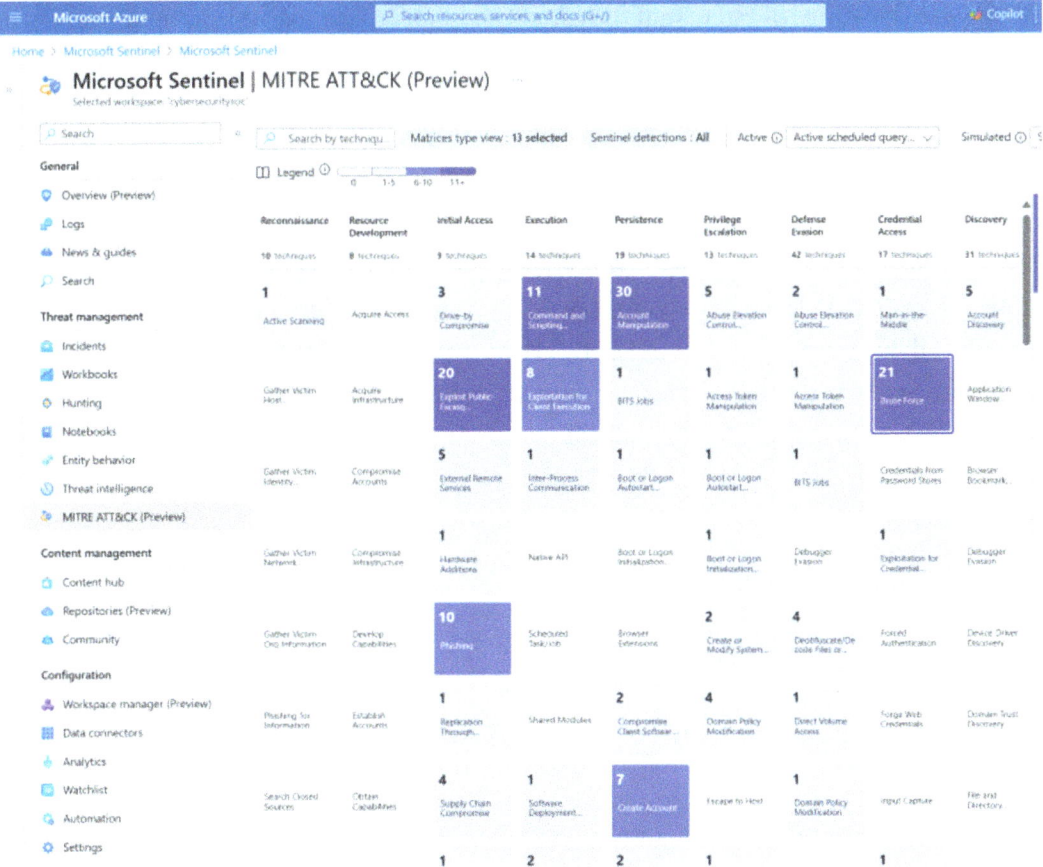

Figure 1-6. Microsoft Sentinel Threat Detection

CHAPTER 1   GET STARTED WITH MICROSOFT SENTINEL AND IOMT

Analyzing Threats with Microsoft Sentinel

The Microsoft Sentinel platform is designed to assist security teams in performing threat analysis in a fast and thorough manner. Utilization of artificial intelligence and advanced capabilities from a long history of Microsoft cybersecurity experience will assist investigators in understanding suspicious activity, assessing attack scope, and **identifying** root cause.

Next are the primary features that help to support threat analysis in Microsoft Sentinel.

Incidents

Sentinel groups related alerts into incidents, which allows you to see threats with a broader context. You can visualize the relationship between users, IP addresses, devices, and any other entities of interest in the interactive graph. The intent is to help you understand and analyze how the attack occurred and how it spread in your environment as well as your organization.

Hunts

Hunts are, in essence, a proactive search of your data to discover anomalous or damaging activity before the detection of an alert. Sentinel Hunts supports the ability to scan all data sources for threats. Sentinel's hunting capabilities utilize the MITRE ATT&CK framework to help drive your search. You can also translate your findings from a hunt to detection rules for future alerts.

Notebooks

Sentinel supports integration with Jupyter notebooks, which is commonly used as interactive applications for advanced analytics as well as machine learning. In laptops, you will be able to

- Perform custom analytics that are not available in Sentinel's built-in capabilities
- Create detailed visualizations, such as timelines and process trees
- Connect Sentinel data with other data sources, including local logs and 3rd party data

Sentinel's investigation capabilities provide both a broad understanding and a profound understanding of threats to act quickly against them.

Responding to Incidents Quicker—Automate That Which Is Essential

Microsoft Sentinel allows you to respond in a timely and efficient manner by automating repetitive tasks and simplifying your security tasks. Automation and orchestration have been designed to be scalable for Microsoft Sentinel, which allows you to keep pace with the threat landscape without being overwhelmed by the growing number of technologies.

Automation Rules

Automation rules allow you to smooth the incident response process by establishing a set of automation rules that dictate actions based on a series of conditions. Automation rules facilitate a centralized process for incident management, ensuring a timely and respectful response across your environment.

Playbooks

"Microsoft allow you to automate and orchestrate your threat response using playbooks containing a pre-defined series of activities. We allow you to run the playbooks on demand, or in response to an alert or incident, all governed by your automation rules. Playbooks are operationally run behind the scenes using flexible workflows that allow you to define logic and connect with the other systems and services in your environment."

It is common for platforms to implement automation frameworks, which can help reduce workload and incident response times and focus on what is important—keeping your organization secure.

Unifying Security Operations

As the complexity of today's digital environments grows (augmented by connecting IoT and IoMT devices), organizations require more than a sequential collection of tools to protect against complex attacks; they contend that security needs an integration of tools. The Microsoft Defender portal offers a comprehensive security operations experience, unifying essential security functions that would usually be arranged as tools, such as Security Information and Event Management (SIEM), Security Orchestration, Automation, and Response (SOAR), Extended Detection and Response (XDR), exposure management, cloud security, threat intelligence, and generative AI.

The Defender portal provides a single interface that integrates Microsoft Defender XDR, Microsoft Sentinel, Microsoft Security Exposure Management, and Microsoft Security Copilot, giving security teams a consolidated view for monitoring, detecting, investigating, remediating, and responding to cybersecurity risks, pre-, during, and post-attack, as well as providing organizations the opportunity to adopt additional Microsoft Defender services to build a robust and adaptive security posture that meets the needs of their specific digital environment—particularly important where IoT and IoMT devices exist and where traditional security controls are unlikely to exist.

The Growing Risk Surface of IoT and IoMT

The rapid growth of connected devices in healthcare and industrial environments, or what we broadly known as the Internet of Things (IoT) and Internet of Medical Things (IoMT), has further increased the risks organizations must defend and correspondingly increased the attack surface the organization must secure. Things such as patient-monitoring wearables, infusion pumps, industrial devices, HVAC, and other IoT devices are often outdated, lack even basic security controls, and are no longer governed by any traditional IT Organizations require a converged strategy for defending endpoints that provides visibility, proactive threat detection, and intelligent response in one experience.

Unified Security Begins with Microsoft Defender Portal

Microsoft is addressing this challenge by integrating all its best-in-breed security into a unified experience, the Microsoft Defender portal. The Microsoft Defender portal provides a single pane of glass for security teams to monitor, investigate, and respond to threats across their digital estate, including IoT and IoMT strategies. It enables security teams to integrate endpoint protection, extended detection and response (XDR), threat intelligence, and automation into a single plan, and it merges exposure management, allowing security teams to function quickly, positively, and without hesitation in their responses to threats.

Microsoft Sentinel: Cloud-Native SIEM for Total Visibility

Microsoft Sentinel offers robust, cloud-native Security Information and Event Management (SIEM) capability that applies end-to-end visibility to the data being gathered from a plethora of data sources, including IoT and OT environments. This comes with real-time analytics, correlation rules, and searches—empowering security analysts to detect suspicious user or device activity, investigate incidents, and hunt for threats from any device. The cloud-native, scalable architecture empowers security teams to effectively manage peaks in telemetry data from medical devices and embedded systems across critical care or operational environments.

Microsoft Defender XDR: Correlated Threat Detection and Response

Through Microsoft Sentinel, Microsoft Defender XDR (Extended Detection and Response) builds upon the security value of all Microsoft environments through fast and deep analytics of endpoint, identity, email, and network activity. Threat detection and response can be correlated through multiple vectors—for example, detecting lateral movement from a compromised medical device to sensitive patient records would be possible through XDR. Microsoft Defender XDR enhances team awareness and enables urgent mitigation actions to respond to threats through automated response playbooks, thereby reducing dwell time and potential harm in high-risk environments more effectively than most organizations' security teams could even comprehend—think about hospitals, research labs, etc.

Security Exposure Management: Proactive Risk Mitigation

Microsoft Security Exposure Management adds another critical capability to avoid defensive mitigations/responses after an attack or incident and to provide better insight into vulnerabilities and misconfigurations before exploitation. For instance, IoMT ecosystems cannot be trusted due to the firmware vulnerabilities and insecure defaults that are typically present. Security Exposure Management can provide nuanced visibility to get insight into the most significant security risk for each device. Remediation of the risk is based on validated threat intelligence and contextual understanding of the device itself to ensure leaders can improve security without bitterly impacting essential service delivery.

Generative AI: Moving from Data to Actionable Intelligence

A generative AI feature built into the Microsoft Defender portal solves the issue of information overload security analysts face by optimizing and automating security workflows, enabling analysts to respond faster and more efficiently. Analysts can ask questions/query complex data with natural language, receive summaries of their collected investigative content, or even receive responses to their requested remediation as if their requests originated from the Chakra app. At IoMT, where time to respond must be paramount, organizations often lack in-depth medical device security expertise. In such cases, generative AI can provide teams with much-needed insight to clarify the situation and instruct them to respond promptly and correctly.

Unified, Scalable Strategy for IoT and IoMT Security

Microsoft provides security teams with a unified strategy for security, IoT, and IoMT by integrating Microsoft Defender, Microsoft Sentinel, Security Exposure Management, and generative AI into a single portal. This unification enables security teams to optimize and automate security functions, working smarter, not harder, by combining intelligent and automated enterprise tools into an overall strategy for protecting an environment that traditional IT security approaches have often overlooked. Whether it is a smart hospital, research lab, or connected manufacturing floor, this combination of tools now allows your organization to shift from responding to incidents to proactively defending the integrity of your critical operations against modern operating threats, while protecting stakeholder trust, compliance, and operational continuity.

Framework of a Unified Approach to Security Operations

The modern security operations environment requires a complete and integrated approach through improved detection, investigations, and response to an ever-changing threat environment. Microsoft offers the Microsoft Defender portal as a response to this need for integrated security operations.

The Microsoft Defender portal provides a single pane of glass unifying essential security operations capabilities across your digital environment, which consists of

- Security Information and Event Management (SIEM)
- Security Orchestration, Automation, and Response (SOAR)
- Extended Detection and Response (XDR)
- Posture and Exposure management
- Cloud Security, Threat Intelligence, and Generative AI

As the security operations functions are unified, the Defenders portal includes different Microsoft security services:

- Microsoft Defender XDR
- Microsoft Sentinel
- Microsoft Security Exposure Management
- Microsoft Security Copilot

Through the integration of these Microsoft security services, organizations have a single point of contact to monitor, detect, investigate, remediate, and respond to cyber risks pre- and post-breach. This level of visibility simplifies the security operations experience and unifies security operations team members under a single operational framework.

Protecting Critical Assets Across the Enterprise

I'd like to take a moment to highlight for you that asset protection within the Defender portal occurs by leveraging services that protect identities, endpoints, cloud apps, email infrastructure, and operational technology (OT). Table 1-1 summarizes key capabilities and the associated Microsoft Defender solutions.

Table 1-1. *Key Capabilities and the Associated Microsoft Defender Solutions*

Capability	Microsoft Security Product
Detect and investigate threats to identity infrastructure	Microsoft Defender for Identity
Protect email, URLs, and Office 365 collaboration tools	Microsoft Defender for Office 365
Monitor and respond to threats on endpoint devices	Microsoft Defender for Endpoint
Extend protection to OT and IoT environments	Microsoft Defender for IoT
Assess vulnerabilities and device posture	Microsoft Defender Vulnerability Management
Govern and secure SaaS applications	Microsoft Defender for Cloud Apps

Table 1-2 summarizes key capabilities outside of Microsoft Defender XDR.

Table 1-2. *Offers a array of different service exist other than Microsoft Defender XDR*

Capability	Microsoft Security Product
Monitor non-Microsoft and on-premises assets	Microsoft Sentinel
Discover assets and assess risk exposure	Microsoft Security Exposure Management
Secure multicloud and hybrid environments	Microsoft Defender for Cloud

Simplifying Security Management

The Defender portal is a centralized point to monitor the organization's security posture. It integrates detection and incident response across services into a single consolidated incident queue that links incidents across applications. Doing so achieves efficiencies in triaging incidents and investigating threats, as an analyst can analyze incidents from the detection of identities, endpoints, cloud, and messaging and connect the dots from there. This enables analysts to

- Break down silos across identity, endpoint, cloud, and messaging secure services
- Use the shared context to understand and prioritize a high-impact threat

- Conduct proactive threat hunting across the enterprise
- Strengthening Risk Management and Attack Prevention

In support of being proactive to reduce risks, there are exposure and cloud protection capabilities across Defender products represented in the Defender portal, such as Microsoft Security Exposure Management and Microsoft Defender for Cloud. This allows organizations to

- Continuously discover and inventory assets
- Measure and track security posture in real time
- Leverage attack path analysis to discover vulnerable paths to critical assets
- Use exposure, vulnerability, or risk context to prioritize remediating vulnerabilities or exposure to reduce the attack surface

These capabilities contribute to an aligned risk management ethos by prioritizing exposure or attack surface reduction strategies for business-critical assets.

- Don't Delay the Detection of Threats and Response

Organizations need to focus on the metrics of time to detect (TTD)/time to respond (TTR) from any SOC. Defender portal provides improvement over these metrics through the analysis of

- High-fidelity correlation signals from the Defender products, Microsoft Sentinel, and Microsoft Security Threat Intelligence
- Security threat intelligence from global research teams at Microsoft
- Automated incident correlation and classification

When an active threat is identified, all automatic attack disruption mechanisms will trigger, such as

- Containing insecure devices
- Containing or restricting compromised user accounts
- Prevent users' lateral movement and vertical escalation

Limiting the attack to the contained scope has the potential to minimize damage and time to recovery.

- Increasing SOC Capabilities with AI

Microsoft Security Copilot is directly integrated into the Defender portal, bringing human and AI capabilities to enhance the SOC's service efficiency. With Microsoft Security Copilot, it will allow security teams to

- Summarize incidents and device data more quickly to get the full context
- Analyze script, files, or log to find the degree of malicious behavior
- Auto-generate automated Kusto Query Language (KQL) queries and incident reports
- Use the guided response workflow to remove any delays in remediating findings

The connective tissue between AI and SOC centers around reducing internal analyst fatigue, increasing accurate and trustworthy incident responses, and improving the efficiency of investigation timelines for related incidents.

Key Benefits:

- *Reducing Exposure and Making Better Use of Posture*: AI insights mainly cut through the chatter of the all-risks team with priority for all critical risk exposures and share actionable components for remediation.

- *Reduction in TTD + TTR*: The automated incident enrichment and its mapping to the MITRE ATT&CK framework chains to accelerate the speed of incident response following the strong and accurate identification of threats.

- *Positive Analyst Behavior*: Smart user prompts and contextual recommendations for action can now assist analysts in decision-making and closing incidents.

The Microsoft Defender portal has disrupted traditional SOC workflows by uniting tools, enabling intelligent integration, and leveraging AI for a prompt and accurate, individualized response to cyber threats. Everything from securing endpoints and managing vulnerabilities at scale to securing cloud workloads, the Defender portal provided everything with visibility and operational advantages to execute and secure in new, modern digital spaces.

Working with the Microsoft Defender Portal

In today's interconnected world, managing security for both cloud and on-premises environments can be challenging. However, Microsoft has a consolidated approach with the Microsoft Defender portal, a centralized, empowering location for security personnel to monitor and manage all threats, as well as respond to them. This discussion will cover the capabilities of the Defender portal, guiding you through how to enhance visualization and utilization, thereby improving threat investigation and security posture.

The Unified Security Hub

The Microsoft Defender portal is a single integrated platform for managing both pre-breach and post-breach security practices.

- For pre-breach security, the goal is to prevent identifying vulnerabilities, remediate vulnerabilities, and improve security posture continuously across your environments.

- When we discuss post-breach security, the structure is built to act. You will rely on threat detection, as well as investigate and respond quickly to potential incidents to protect your environment.

Key Services in the Portal

The Microsoft Defender portal is designed as a centralized security system that provides organizations with nearly all the Microsoft Security Services they need to monitor, manage, and respond to threats across and between their digital environments. It serves as a unified interface for managing both pre-breach and post-breach security actions, enabling security teams to spend less time assessing risk, diminishing their attack surface, and executing threat detection and incident investigation workflows, all while detecting threats quickly across their environments. The security solutions are

CHAPTER 1   GET STARTED WITH MICROSOFT SENTINEL AND IOMT

generally being used as an "added" service to improve your security, which is made from the integrated solutions with identity (which covers user/password and biometrics), endpoint (the devices we use), cloud (services such as Azure), email (to address multi-shaped data), and future functions built for threat hunting. The portal combines these tools as a whole package in a simpler format, eliminating the need to navigate multiple tasks across multiple services, as illustrated in Figure 1-7.

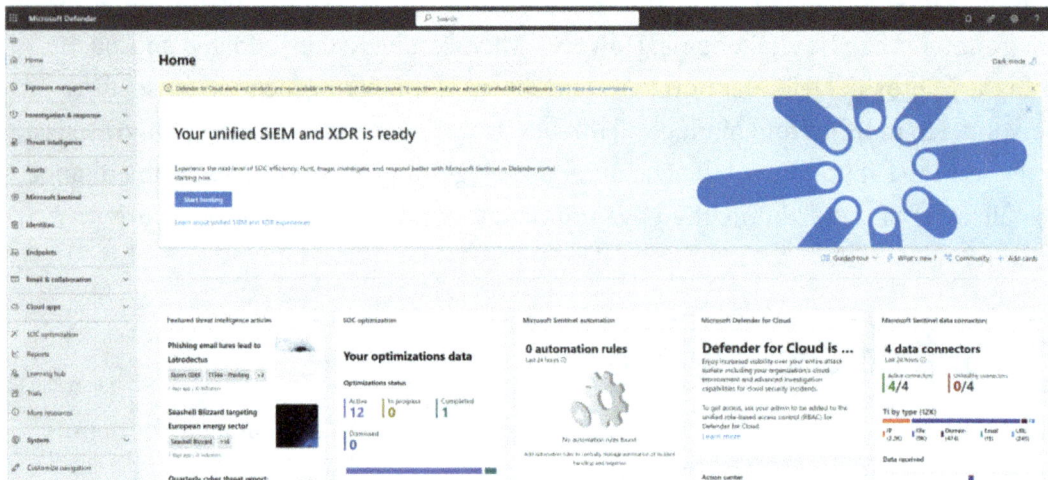

Figure 1-7. Microsoft Defender Portal

Defender XDR

Provides unified protection across your organization. Aggregates and correlates data from devices, identities, email, and cloud applications. You can identify threats, respond to incidents, and proactively hunt for vulnerabilities.

Sentinel

Automates the process of collecting and analyzing the massive amounts of security data. Essentially, it's an intelligent helper in identifying incidents and allows you to visualize your analytical data and improve security team operations.

Threat Intelligence

Determines a view (time limited) of threats out in the wild by aggregating from multiple intelligence feeds. The adversary's tactics, tools, and procedures/patterns are identified and therefore help you be more tactical.

Exposure Management

Extends risk visibility across your organization. You can identify your attack surface, find your weaknesses, and view your progress in closing those gaps.

Defender for Cloud

Helps protect cloud workloads across multiple cloud platforms. It identifies risks in your cloud infrastructure and provides recommendations that you can use to take action.

Getting Access

Access to the portal is restricted by roles and permissions, which include

- Access management categories, such as roles (Global Administrator) and roles (Security Administrator), are global roles.

- *Access Management Options*: These roles and security roles are custom roles that can provide more granularity of access management and permissions.

- *Access Management Approach*: RBAC (Role-Based Access Control) for managing permissions across services.

Navigating the Portal

The Home page is your starting point for many tasks. The page provides metrics about your current security status, active threats, and the alerts you received recently. On the Home page, you can also find other (more detailed) pages.

You'll also see other features such as

- Notifications allow you to know information about actions that are critical for you to take.
- Search helps you find tools, reports, or incidents faster.
- Guided tours of the product and notifications listing what's new help you to continue to learn and find new and valuable features.

Managing Security Exposure

The Exposure Management pages help you understand how vulnerable your organization is.

Some of the primary tools that you will use include

- *Attack Surface Map*: See all of your internet-facing and internal resources.
- *Attack Path Management*: Know what weak, exploitable points attackers may target.
- *Exposure Insights*: Look at the data available for critical vulnerabilities and risks.
- *Secure Score*: A numerical representation of your current security posture.
- *Data Connectors*: You can bring in third-party tools for deeper visibility and context.

Investigating and Responding to Threats

The Investigation and Response pages are there for you to utilize threats fully:

- *Incidents*: You can see and prioritize alerts being grouped, as each may represent coordinated attacks.
- *Alerts*: Review threat signals we pick up.
- *Advanced Hunting*: You can get more granular analysis of raw security data by writing queries.

- *Custom Detections*: Setting up custom queries to detect, investigate, and/or respond to certain behaviors.

- *Action Center*: View and approve your remedial actions.

- Submit suspicious emails, URLs, or files to be reviewed.

Deepening Threat Intelligence

The Threat Intelligence pages will allow you to access the following:

- *Threat Analytics*: See our reports and comparable information available on threats that are relevant to your environment.

- *Intel Profiles*: Information about attackers, tools, and vulnerabilities.

- *Intel Explorer and Projects*: Search threat data and files for investigations.

Managing Assets

In the Assets area of the product, you can monitor the following:

- *Devices*: Your device inventory, risk ratings, and start investigations.

- *Identities*: Who your users are and what accounts they have access to, and track privileged access to those accounts.

Improving Your Security Operations Center (SOC)

The SOC Optimization domain has recommendations for enhancing operational efficiencies and minimizing coverage gaps. It presents recommendations for the organization's threat landscape and configuration.

Reports and Trials: The Reports section covers all activities related to security; the Trials area is where you can assess new features or services before they become available.

Final Thoughts: The Microsoft Defender portal is more than a tool; it's your central command for protecting your organization from a digital-first world. If you get used to the portal's features, you will outpace threats, streamline operations, and safeguard what is essential.

Understanding Microsoft Defender XDR in the Microsoft Defender Portal

Microsoft Defender Extended Detection and Response (XDR) is a comprehensive, unified cybersecurity service that assists organizations to identify, investigate, and respond to complex threats across the enterprise. By integrating into the Microsoft Defender portal such that it functions as a unified threat management hub, Microsoft Defender XDR combines threat signals from many security components—including endpoints, identities, cloud services, email systems, and SaaS applications—into an efficient security service. In that sense, Microsoft Defender XDR simplifies security as it applies not only to security operations centers (SOC) but also to the more specific ways that SOC teams look at both identifying and understanding and mitigating cyber threats.

In essence, Microsoft Defender XDR combines a number of standalone Microsoft security services, each service operating on a specific piece of the attack surface. For example, Defender for Office 365 protects users from phishing and email threats, Defender for Endpoint (online or offline) provides proactive and reactive protections for devices, Defender for Identity uses Active Directory signals to detect identity threats and insider risks, Defender for Cloud Apps secures a cloud service and monitors for SaaS app usage, and if your organization uses Microsoft Sentinel, that integrates SIEM and SOAR into the entire detection and response pipeline with insights from Defender XDR.

Microsoft Defender XDR monitors an organization's environment for potential threats without doing anything on its own once detected. Unlike less sophisticated monitoring systems that treat every incident as a separate alert, if a potential threat is detected, Microsoft Defender XDR does not generate a new alert for that; it gathers related alerts and behaviors into a whole incident. The incidents offer a complete view of an attack's scope, timeline to attack, and affected assets. The majority of an organization's response depends on its understanding of threats; the incidents provide a vast amount of information tied to any behaviors your organization may need to prioritize a response. The dedicated incident queue allows users to view incidents, and the incident queue presents incidents in one place, with historical search filters and priority ratings based on the severity of the incident or alert. One of the best features of Defender XDR is that it can detect sophisticated human-led attacks, consisting of lateral movement that is mostly used in account compromises or ransomware attacks. This is accomplished by using deception technologies that deploy decoy assets. These decoy assets are designed to be convincing in how they are relevant to the organization but are not real assets, because they are designed to lure attackers into interacting with them, and once they begin to interact with them, defenders can generate a highly confident alert that has been released in the Defender portal. If an analyst utilizes the decoy assets effectively, then they will be able to bank on them as early warnings for in-progress attacks while also feeding their machine learning engines with highly accurate signals that use decoys for defense along the kill chain.

Not only can Defender XDR detect attacks, but it also provides the ability to disrupt them in real time through an automated response service. When a defender ping, or signal of malicious activity, is confirmed, the service can automatically isolate the compromised devices from the environment, disable a compromised user from signing into their accounts, or block a malicious URL automatically without the need for a defender to intervene. These actions are all predicated on some reliable threat signal correlated from millions of individual data points over billions of transactions and further refined through Microsoft's extensive threat intelligence processes and ecosystem.

Defender XDR also allows for a proactive defense approach by offering and training security analysts to utilize threat hunting in a non-linear methodology. Through the advanced hunting experience that integrates with Kusto Query Language (KQL), security operations center (SOC) teams can write complex queries to hunt for threat actors or for activity that is out of the ordinary or unattributed in the environment. If the SOC team is not overly familiar with KQL, then the portal will support them in writing queries with a guided interface or the use of templates. Security analysts can also write their own custom detection rules to create alerts or remediate specific behaviors, or indicators.

Lastly, with the automated investigation and remediation workflow in Defender XDR, organizations can lessen the burden on their security teams through automation of incident response. As incidents generate, the system assesses the entities involved, formats threat judgments, and maybe includes active necessary remediation steps: quarantining files, terminating malicious processes, isolating endpoints, etc. The automated actions provided within the toolset, together with investigatory summaries and pending items, are delivered through the Action Center in the Defender portal. At all times, this whole process, combined with direct ease of access for all potential actions, is very, very transparent, traceable, and manageable.

Overall, these capabilities make Microsoft Defender XDR an adaptive and smart option to be able to protect the modern enterprise against the ever-increasingly complex and coordinated cyberattacks—all via a single unified portal.

Unified Visibility Across the Organization

Possibly the greatest challenge with modern cybersecurity, to date, is handling the ongoing fragmentation in terms of tools and data sources. Defender XDR tackles this by providing a single view across all security events in a Microsoft ecosystem; security teams no longer pivot between multiple consoles or manually correlate security data. Instead, Defender XDR correlates telemetry from devices, cloud applications, identities, etc., into a single timeline of threats. This unification can reduce MTTR, from detection to analysis and remediation, optimally streamlining the efficiency of the SOC and maximizing exposure reliability. Investigating Context-Rich Incidents When an incident receives multiple alerts, Defender XDR provides more context than just the alerts; it provides correlation to help Security Operations Center (SOC) teams identify the "how" and "why" behind an attack. Each incident report contains context-rich information from the attack or the incident: entry point, any lateral movement, privilege escalation, and user(s) or system(s) involved. Context-rich investigation enables SOC analysts to think more strategically, focusing on root causes instead of symptoms, which helps them to more effectively contain the incident to mitigate risks and/or threats. When SOC teams are able to map incidents on the MITRE ATT&CK framework, they can use a common framework and share understanding of adversarial opportunities based on tried-and-true tactics and techniques.

Real-Time Collaboration and Workflow Collaboration

The process steps within the platform of Defender XDR were designed to support collaboration. Analysts have the collaborative capability to assign incidents to team members, comment in feeds, and document steps in the investigation in the same dashboard. The Incorporation of Teams and other collaboration tools also provides a seamless integration experience when security teams want to share conclusions or aggregate findings without having to take the team out of the workflow. Defender XDR integrates with IT service management tools like ServiceNow, as well as a security orchestration/automation platform, which can auto-ticket and auto-respond based on playbooks from the tools. Integrated processes and workflows close the deal for bringing detection and resolution together to more quickly neutralize risks and threats.

Cloud-Native Scale and AI-Powered Intelligence Defender XDR, as a cloud-native and powerful solution, can leverage Microsoft's enormous threat intelligence ecosystem and fuel augmented intelligence capabilities. Defender XDR signals are ingested daily from most global data sources, including Azure, Microsoft 365, third-party, and threat subscriptions, performing trillions of analyses on a daily basis. The power of a solution that operates at scale allows Defender XDR to keep pace and ultimately triage emerging risks faster than any traditional, siloed system. Defender XDR can ingest tremendous amounts of evidence while using built-in machine learning models to analyze traffic for patterns and expected anomalies and identify threats to provide surface-level insights on new or potentially unknown threats to the organization. With threat intelligence feeds, threat evidence and threat landscape updates are provided to Defender XDR in near-real-time. The ability to do this with significant scale is a trade secret and competitive advantage to Microsoft's solution and cybersecurity platform to allow organizations to leapfrog rapidly evolving cyber threats to stay ahead of the game.

Compliance, Reporting on Incidents, and Executive Dashboards Compliance and regulatory reporting are not solely tied to the threat detection and threat response capabilities of Defender XDR. The dashboard is also designed to support compliance and regulation, which is key as compliance is the cost of doing business. The Defender XDR dashboards support the need for built-in and pre-built compliance reports, audit trails, and restricted exportable summaries of data that can be utilized for internal audits, executive briefings, and/or submissions to regulators. The reporting functions help security leaders demonstrate due diligence by tracking incident response metrics and incidence of threats to identify trends of the organization's threat response program. Dashboards can be configured by the administrators to provide role-based permissions for different organizational stakeholders to access data aligned to their level of authority to support informed decisions from the dashboards and reports that are also aligned to accountability.

Unified Security with Microsoft Defender and Sentinel

Microsoft Defender includes a powerful, common cybersecurity platform. It functions by integrating multiple layers of protection into a single technical system. For example, integrating endpoint security, cloud and identity security, email safety, threat intelligence, exposure management, and SIEM (security information and event management) into a single, comprehensive program. Microsoft Defender leverages AI-powered defense, giving organizations the ability to identify threats sooner, respond quicker, and optimize their overall security operations.

CHAPTER 1   GET STARTED WITH MICROSOFT SENTINEL AND IOMT

Bringing Microsoft Sentinel into the Defender Portal

Microsoft Sentinel, Microsoft's cloud-native SIEM, is now integrated directly into the Microsoft Defender portal. Organizations can use Sentinel as part of Microsoft Defender XDR (Extended Detection and Response) or with Sentinel solo and Microsoft Defender as separate components. This integration creates a common experience for your security team working within both the SIEM and XDR ecosystems in concert to identify and respond to threats faster and more accurately.

If you are a regular user of Microsoft Sentinel inside the Azure portal, you should integrate your users with the Defender portal. This will grant your users a modern, unified environment with new features and enhancements to streamline and bolster your security operations.

Table 1-3 summarizes the key benefits of using Microsoft Sentinel in the Defender portal, with clear, reader-friendly descriptions.

Table 1-3. *Key Benefits of Using Microsoft Sentinel in the Microsoft Defender Portal*

Category	Benefit	Description
Streamlined Security Operations	Unified Incident Management	You can view and respond to all your security incidents from a simple queue. Whether an alert originated from Microsoft Defender or Sentinel, you manage everything in one spot, improving response times and lessening confusion.
	Entity Pages with Deep Context	Each alert or incident has rich, consolidated information about related users, devices, IP addresses, and Azure resources. Each provides more context about threats and situations you are investigating.
	Advanced Hunting in One Interface	You can run queries against all your security data (from Sentinel or any other Microsoft service) in one interface. No need to switch to different tools/tabs; you can save time hunting for threats. Security Copilot can help develop and improve KQL queries.

(continued)

Table 1-3. (*continued*)

Category	Benefit	Description
Smarter Threat Detection	AI-Powered Threat Detection	Artificial intelligence and machine learning are key capabilities that enable the quicker identification of real threats. Security Copilot uses its built-in cognitive scoring system to correlate, filter, and eliminate false positive alerts, thus enhancing signal detection for your team.
	Better Signal-to-Noise Ratio	Defender's Sentinel relies on high-quality alerts and correlated data. This ensures you rise to the top of your regular workload and reduces distraction from irrelevant signals.
Automation and AI Assistance	Security Copilot for Response	AI protocols can automatically summarize, develop incident reports, and analyze files and scripts to help suggest next steps—all in the Defender portal to keep you from jumping between tasks.
	Ready-to-Run Queries	Security Copilot helps you create or refine KQL queries while doing threat hunting, even if you aren't a KQL expert. This facilitates your proactive hunting faster and easier.
	Automatic Attack Disruption	Defender may have capabilities that allow for automatic disruption of attacker activity, including isolating compromised devices or accounts, thereby reducing the risk of waiting for manual action when high-confidence threats are detected.
	Case Management Tools	You can track and organize multiple alerts or incidents with related details and manage investigations or resolutions in a structured manner.

(*continued*)

Table 1-3. (*continued*)

Category	Benefit	Description
Enhanced Visibility and Risk Reduction	Attack Path Analysis	You can visualize attackers trying to move laterally across systems by exploiting existing vulnerabilities to help you find weak points before they are used against you.
	SOC Optimization Recommendations	You can receive targeted recommendations to optimize your Security Operations Centers (SOC), decrease risk exposure, and prioritize mitigation based on a risk's possible impacts.
Post-Incident Learning and Prevention	Tailored Mitigation Guidance	Once you have resolved an incident, you can receive personalized security recommendations as next steps to prevent a re-incident. These are aligned with Microsoft's Security Exposures Management approach.
Data and Cost Efficiency	Unified Data Access	Security teams should be able to use Defender XDR and Sentinel data from a single cohesive interface for respective analytics and investigative considerations without the challenge of duplicated data.
	Free Raw Log Hunting	While in preview, you can run advanced hunting queries against thirty days of raw logs for free, which means that when you are not ingesting that data into Sentinel, you are significantly lowering your costs while still enabling high-quality detection and monitoring.

While implementing Microsoft Sentinel from the Defender portal can create a more cohesive and compelling security event experience, it is important to note certain limitations, especially if you are using Sentinel on its own and it is not active with Microsoft Defender XDR. Advanced threat event reporting capabilities with Microsoft Defender: the Sentinel integration will provide a valuable security experience; however, some advanced functions are solely implemented with Microsoft Defender XDR switched on in the Azure Security configuration. One such example is Microsoft Security Exposure Management. Microsoft Security Exposure Management aims to minimize security risks. However, the assistance with attack paths and risk mitigation recommendations is only available when Defender XDR is enabled.

Another example is the Custom Detection Rules capability, which can be used to define the conditions for running alerts on a custom detection. The centralized Action Center helps centralize response actions and is only available when XDR is enabled. If your organization requires Microsoft Exposure Management or Custom Detection Rules and is interested in adopting the new Cloud Defender workflow for security operations, I recommend enabling Microsoft Defender XDR. This will allow you to access all the benefits of a unified security operation within the Defender portal.

Integrate Microsoft Defender XDR with Microsoft Sentinel

With ease, you can integrate Microsoft Defender XDR with Microsoft Sentinel and stream all Defender XDR incidents and advanced hunting events into your Sentinel workspace. Not only does this stream align both sets of incidents and events in the Defender and the Azure portals, but it also provides complete detail into every incident, including all the alerts, related entities, and likely practical context to easily triage and begin your investigation in Sentinel.

The incident will be updated in both portals, ensuring that any changes made are reflected in both. This two-way sync enables you to leverage the strengths of both types of investigations, incorporating both pieces of work into your investigations. You can also onboard Microsoft Sentinel directly in the Microsoft Defender portal for a more integrated security operations workflow.

There are two methods for integrating Microsoft Sentinel with Microsoft Defender XDR:

- *From Microsoft Sentinel*: You will consume data from Microsoft Defender XDR into Microsoft Sentinel by enabling the Defender XDR connector. You will manage and view this data through the Azure portal.

- *From the Microsoft Defender Portal*: You will integrate Microsoft Sentinel directly from the Defender portal and view the Microsoft Sentinel data and incidents alongside your Defender incidents, alerts, vulnerabilities, and other security insights. The integration requires that you onboard Microsoft Sentinel to the Defender portal.

Incident Correlation and Alerts

When you integrate Microsoft Defender XDR with Microsoft Sentinel, Microsoft Defender XDR incidents become visible and manageable directly in Sentinel. You now have a single incident queue for your entire organization, integrating the incidents from Defender XDR and all your other cloud and on-premise systems.

This integration gives your security team the ability to

- View incidents from multiple disparate sources and correlate them into one incident view.
- Leverage Defender XDR's advanced investigation tools and rich contextual data that exists in Microsoft 365.

Defender XDR automatically enriches and correlates alerts from multiple Defender products. This feature improves the relevance of alerts, decreases noise, reduces the SOC incident queue, and ultimately, increases the speed of response.

The Defender products where alerts are grouped and sent to Microsoft Sentinel include

- Microsoft Defender for Endpoint
- Microsoft Defender for Identity
- Microsoft Defender for Office 365
- Microsoft Defender for Cloud Apps
- Microsoft Defender Vulnerability Management

As well as alerts from other Microsoft services that are collected by Defender XDR, which include

- Microsoft Purview Data Loss Prevention
- Microsoft Entra ID Protection
- Microsoft Purview Insider Risk Management

Defender for Cloud Integration

The Defender XDR connector passes incidents from Microsoft Defender for Cloud to Sentinel, but to see the full alert and entity details for these incidents, you must also enable the Defender for Cloud connector in Microsoft Sentinel. Without this, the incidents may appear empty.

Incident Generation

Defender XDR not only collects alerts but also generates incidents by aggregating alerts into incidents, which it then automatically sends to Sentinel. This provides complete visibility and actionable insights across the security landscape.

Microsoft Copilot in Microsoft Defender

Microsoft Security Copilot combines the power of generative AI and human judgment, and through its support, helps SecOps teams detect, investigate, and respond to threats faster and better. It is integrated directly into the Microsoft Defender portal, providing practical support to key security workflows, including incident investigations, threat hunts, and real-time access to threat intelligence. With Copilot in Defender, security analysts can make decisions and take action more quickly, based on more informed data sources, with more confidence. This capability is offered to users who have access to Microsoft Security Copilot.

Security Copilot works in alignment with Microsoft's AI Principles and delivers responsible and secure use of AI technology across your organization.

Delivers the power of generative AI to your security operations, empowering security teams to work faster, more innovatively, and with more confidence. Copilot is easily integrated into the Microsoft Defender portal, acting as a real-time assistant for the security analyst by providing natural language insights, guided investigations, and automation to speed up requested threat detection and response.

Table 1-4 summarizes the key capabilities of using Microsoft Copilot in the Defender portal, with clear, reader-friendly descriptions.

Table 1-4. *Key Capabilities of Using Microsoft Sentinel in the Microsoft Defender Portal*

Capability	Description
Guided Incident Investigation	Condenses incidents, alerts, and prescriptive instructions for investigation and response.
Natural Language Queries	Permits analysts to ask security questions in plain language; Copilot translates those into the right queries.
Threat Intelligence Summaries	Presents threats with concise summaries, maps them to MITRE ATT&CK tactics, and identifies risks.
Automated Playbooks	Makes or integrates recommendations for automatic response actions, such as isolating devices or disabling a user.
Context-Aware Recommendations	Provides customized recommendations, taking into account the incident and your organization's security posture.
Enhanced Collaboration Support	Drafts incident reports and summary reports so security teams can better communicate with stakeholders.

Key Use Case of Microsoft Copilot in Defender

In today's cybersecurity climate, security operations teams are rapidly losing free time and feeling overwhelmed by the need to detect, investigate, and respond to threats efficiently around the clock. Microsoft Copilot in Defender presents a great use case around the ease of use of analyzing and responding to a threat through AI-powered assistants.

Copilot functions as a virtual security analyst by bringing together Microsoft's generative AI and Microsoft Defender into one solution. Copilot enables teams to drill down through large numbers of alerts quickly, correlate incidents across endpoints, identities, email, and cloud apps, and promptly reply with response actions. It saves time that is usually spent on manual triage by summarizing alerts, proposing next steps, and producing scripts for containment or remediation, all done through the security console.

The use case presented in Table 1-5 not only speeds up the response to a threat but also empowers less experienced analysts by enabling them to be onboarded faster and by making their decisions more consistent across the SOC (Security Operation Centre).

This means that organizations will benefit from lower dwell times, improved handling of incidents, and a stronger security operations approach.

Table 1-5. Key Use Cases of Using Microsoft Copilot in Defender

Use Case	How Copilot Helps
Responding to attacks	Promptly walks analysts through the diagnosis and containment of attacks.
Analyzing malware/scripts	Deobfuscates and evaluates scripts to detect potential malicious activity.
Evaluating devices	Summarizes device security posture and risky behavior in one view.
Assessing user risk	Provides insight into identity, including login actions and behavior anomalies.
Writing reports	Reduces documentation effort by auto-generating colorful, descriptive incident reports.
Hunting threats	Translates plain-language questions into KQL queries that are ready to run.
Making informed decisions	Summarizes last threat intel and potential exposure impact for quick prioritization.

Key Features of Microsoft Copilot in Defender

Microsoft Copilot in Defender presents teams with tools grounded in AI to increase threat investigation speed, minimize response complexity, and elevate decision-making.

Table 1-6 summarizes the key core features of using Microsoft Copilot in Defender, with explicit user-friendly descriptions.

Table 1-6. Key Features of Using Microsoft Copilot in Defender

Feature	Description
Expert-Like Incident Response	Copilot assists security teams in rapidly investigating attacks, assessing questionable files or scripts, and using appropriate mitigations to halt the attack or contain the ongoing incident.
Incident Summarization	For the more complicated incidents that triggered multiple alerts, Copilot summarizes the incident with a high level of conciseness: what happened, what assets were affected, and a timeline of the attack, which is provided automatically when an analyst views the details of the incident page.
Guided Response Actions	Copilot recommends attack-specific incident remediations to guide analysts in the most effective actions to take relative to the type of attack they are working to contain.
Script Analysis	Assesses obfuscated or potentially malicious scripts (like PowerShell commands) to reduce the length and complexity of an investigation to examine an attacker's behavior.
Device Summaries	Offers rapid assessment of devices associated with an incident, like their security posture, abnormal (or new) activity, vulnerabilities, and relevant information from Microsoft Intune.
File Analysis	Provides summaries of questionable files by showing detection results, certificates, API calls, and embedded strings, allowing them to assess the file's threat potential.
Identity Investigation	Delivers detailed identity summaries to help analysts recognize user risk, role changes, previous log-in behavior, and growth in device access history.
Incident Report Generation	Auto-generates detailed incident reports, including incident summary, actions taken, timestamps, and team members working on the event.
Threat Hunting Support	Enables analysts to engage in proactive threat hunting by generating precise KQL queries based on their natural language use.
Threat Intelligence Summarization	Bundles and summarizes relevant threat intelligence to help teams prioritize threat severity, recognize potential actors, and gain an understanding of levels of exposure.

To use Copilot in Microsoft Defender, verify that you have the proper license to use it in Microsoft Defender. Once it is known, the features will be accessible directly on the Microsoft Defender portal. The Copilot features are designed to help security teams work more effectively and faster, enabling them to operate at high speed with simple, natural language prompts.

In the portal, you can see the prompt suggestions that Copilot provides in the advanced hunting and threat intelligence locations. In advanced hunting, the prompts can help you write or improve KQL queries. In threat intelligence, Copilot can help you analyze scripts, files, and other threat indicators, too. The prompts are provided to help you navigate Copilot using the tool without prior technical knowledge or experience.

You can also provide your prompts by asking Copilot to summarize incidents, analyze files, or make recommendations. For example, you could provide a prompt such as "summarize incident 123 and give recommendations" or "what do the indicators in this script mean? Are they malicious?" Copilot's response will return the appropriate and actionable results. It can also be used to generate search queries, summarize alerts, and assist with investigations.

Your feedback is an essential part of improving Copilot results. All Copilot results are provided with a feedback option. You can mark the response as accurate, requiring improvement, or inappropriate. All options have an area where you can add comments describing your feedback, which will help improve results in the future.

Copilot was created with data privacy and security as its foundation. It respects the data handling and protection settings you defined in your organization, ensuring it can be used and kept secure according to your organization's terms.

Even though you might not see it, Copilot leverages built-in Microsoft tools (and not third-party tools) and plug-ins to collect and analyze information. This includes (but is not limited to) security tools from Microsoft that help identify and detect threats, enabling the processing of plain language prompts into advanced search queries. It is essential to allow those tools to do so so that Copilot can provide you with overall insightful and relevant information.

Microsoft Security Exposure Management

Microsoft Security Exposure Management is a proactive cybersecurity solution designed to help organizations discover, examine, and mitigate security risks before exposure. Exposure management identifies your weaknesses across your environment (e.g., misconfigurations, unpatched systems, vulnerable assets) before a threat has time to exploit them. Think of this as discovering weaknesses early. Exposure Management is integrated within Microsoft Defender, providing you visibility into your attack surfaces, identifying exposures with risk ratings, and providing you with prioritization recommendations for risk mitigation.

One unique aspect of Microsoft Security Exposure Management is that you can conduct continuous risk assessments. It can dynamically map exposures to real threat activity in the wild and help the security team understand how likely it is that the problem will be used against them and what the possible consequences of exploitation are. This much-needed context can help an organization see where it can afford to be remediating exposures vs. addressing what is likely to be exploited first. The platform also allows you to conduct attack simulations and breach and attack testing to test your defenses and readiness.

Microsoft Security Exposure Management enables organizations to utilize threat intelligence, vulnerability intelligence, and operational context to transition from a defensive to a proactive posture based on identified risks. This improves resilience and helps to mitigate successful cyberattacks from occurring in the first place.

Microsoft Security Exposure Management provides organizations with a complete view of their security posture across all assets and workloads, enabling them to connect the dots and enhance asset data with security context. This helps teams proactively manage attack surfaces, protect critical systems, and reduce exposure to attacks.

This will be useful for several roles in an organization, particularly

- Security and compliance administrators aiming to improve overall security posture as a core function!

- Security Operations teams and partners that need visibility across teams to effectively detect, investigate, and respond to threats

- Security architects are charged with addressing systemic issues that make security ineffective

- CISOs and decision makers who need an overarching understanding of the organization's exposure and risk to support strategy and investment choices

Security Exposure Management allows organizations to

Get a Coordinated Security View: The platform provides continuous discovery of assets and workloads, which the system organizes into a single, complete, up-to-the-minute view. The complete inventory shows the attack surface footprint, complete with on-prem, hybrid, and cloud features.

Manage and Investigate the Attack Surface: Users can assess and visualize how different systems connect and identify potential vulnerabilities. The solution maps devices, identities, machines, and storage onto it, utilizing an enterprise exposure graph for its mapping. Users can then query the graph to explore assets, understand exposure, and investigate threats. Users can also use visually oriented tools, such as an attack surface map, to enable teams to explore their environment and visualize risk space broadly.

Discover and Prioritize Critical Aspects: The Security Exposure Management platform allows security teams to set systems or define "critical" elements, enabling them to focus security efforts on systems critical to their operations and business continuity.

Understand and Manage Exposure Risk: Security Exposure Management provides information and posture data, offering insights that enable teams to take proactive actions against risk. This information includes security events, recommendations for fixes or improvements, benchmarking, metrics, and security efforts in delivery. The platform features threat intelligence to help organizations identify attack paths, which may include sequences of weaknesses that attackers can exploit in a particular user environment. The system runs several scenarios to identify chokepoints where multiple attack paths intersect, allowing you to focus your energies on the most impactful areas of protection.

Connect and Consolidate Security Data: The Security Exposure Management facilitates the integration of disparate data sources, thereby combining and analyzing security information from numerous tools, platforms, and applications. Using the Security Exposure Management integrated data model helps teams develop more profound insights and efficiencies and improve security operational effectiveness.

CHAPTER 1   GET STARTED WITH MICROSOFT SENTINEL AND IOMT

Microsoft Defender for Cloud

Microsoft Defender for Cloud serves as your security control tower for your cloud, tracking everything that you have—from your Azure resources to workloads running in AWS, Google Cloud, and on-premises, too. It enables you to understand your real risks, remediate those gaps, and proactively address threats, all from a single solution.

The most significant single value it brings is the ability to help you gain an overall cloud security posture. Similar to a fitness tracker, it monitors your cloud environment for adherence to current security best practices and common industry standards, as outlined by CIS, NIST, and others. You are alerted if something is not configured correctly, like a storage bucket or an open port. It tells you what that is and how to fix it. The same goes for the "Secure Score," which tells you what you are doing well and how to measure and improve upon it. Another significant advantage is how it protects your workloads. Whether you are using virtual machines, containers, databases, or serverless apps, Defender for Cloud applies intelligent analytics and Microsoft's global threat intelligence to identify suspicious behavior. It does not simply tell you that you have a problem but instead protects you and mitigates it. It also works closely with Microsoft Defender for Endpoint to provide you with protection across the cloud and is integrated into the underlying device.

And is it the best part? It is not limited only to Azure. Defender for Cloud can also help you protect your workloads across multiple clouds. You can even monitor your AWS and Google Cloud workloads with Defender for Cloud. It connects to these clouds, pulls their telemetry, and displays it all within one single dashboard. Compared to switching between interfaces to cross-correlate data, this approach offers significantly more value, allowing you more time to focus on protecting your organization.

Defender for Cloud is also forward-thinking. It uses ML to detect anomalous behavior, such as users logging in from unusual locations or scripts requesting privilege escalations. When it detects something suspicious, it can kick off an incident response or send it to Microsoft's Sentinel tool to begin a more scoped and engaged investigation and response.

The compliance reporting component has significant pre-built dashboards, out-of-the-box, to validate regulatory compliance scope across various standards. For example, PCI-DSS, ISO 27001, and GDPR. The dashboards provide a comprehensive view of your cloud environment's compliance status, including how it compares to the established measures. They also guide you on remediation steps, making the preparation for a potential synthesis audit less overwhelming.

Defender for Cloud has also considered your DevOps pipeline. It can be easily integrated into the CI/CD pipeline as well as your Infrastructure as Code templates, so you can remediate any security issues before your applications even go live. This approach, dubbed "shift-left," integrates security into the development lifecycle, rather than treating it as a post-thought process, thereby enabling the development of applications at the speed of business and security.

Microsoft Defender for Cloud also integrates seamlessly with Microsoft Defender XDR and gives a unified security experience for your entire organization. The integration provides alerts of cloud incidents and alerts directly in the Microsoft Defender portal—to provide them with everything they need in a unified approach to protect cloud workloads, devices, and identities.

Security teams can piece together the complete picture of an attack by linking alerts together and examining what happened, where, and who was involved. Automatically linking and correlating alerts (and incidents) across these realms signifies a substantially more efficient and responsive approach to seeking threats, connecting the dots, and taking action faster than ever.

Enhanced Investigation Experience in Microsoft Defender XDR

Microsoft Defender for Cloud works seamlessly with Microsoft Defender XDR to create a total security operations experience. Without any effort or additional processes, Defender for Cloud communicates with WhatsApp. Using Microsoft Defender XDR, security alerts and investigation of incidents mark a significant increase in visibility, detection of threats, and speed to respond by aggregating the cloud alerts and incidents into a secure interface. Security teams will gain a better understanding with deep contextual data across cloud environments, devices, and identities, and every investigation will take place from the same interface.

Below Table 1-7 demonstrates the key capabilities available as part of this integration, which shows how incidents, alerts, and threat data from Defender for Cloud are processed and displayed in Microsoft Defender XDR, and will probably make better frictionless detections when there is a correlation between the instance, alerts, and threat data.

Table 1-7. *Key capabilities showing how Defender for Cloud data integrates with Microsoft Defender XDR for better threat detection*

Feature Area	What It Does
Incidents	- All incidents from Defender for Cloud are visible in Microsoft Defender XDR.
	- You can find cloud resource assets in the incident queue.
	- The attack graph includes cloud resources, which show the relationship to the attack story.
	- The incident page has an "Assets" tab that lists the cloud resources involved.
	- Each virtual machine has its page, which shows all ties to alerts and activities.
	What about incident duplication with other Defender tools?
	- There is no incident duplication with the other Defender tools.
	- There is no duplication of alerts from the other sources in the Defender XDR alert queue, which contains all alerts.
Alerts	- Alerts even show the cloud platform where the alerts came from—Azure, AWS, or GCP, etc. Another incentive is in the "Asset" tab; all alerts show the related cloud resource.
	- Here, all incident alerts in the tenant are unique and tracked independently.
	- Aren't Defender alerts duplicated from other Defender sources?
Alert and Incident Correlation	Defender XDR brings links, alerts, and incidents together automatically—security teams can see the full picture of the attack sequence across cloud environments from several related alerts and incident facts after incident and alert prevention and protection have taken place.
Threat Detection	Defender's smart mapping between virtual/cloud resources and endpoints improves detection by enabling security teams to more easily assess, classify, pinpoint, and center attention on threats and groups of threats as they arise.
Unified API	Defender for Cloud alerts and incidents is now available through XDR's public API, which enables exported alert data to be imported into any system through a unified API.

Microsoft Defender XDR guards your organization on multiple fronts: devices, email, identities, and cloud apps. Now, with Microsoft Defender for Cloud fully integrated into XDR, your organization's cloud infrastructure obtains deep visibility and protection, just like your devices and identities. Now, your teams can investigate virtual machines, containers, and any cloud resources they require with no adjustments to their tools, ultimately improving efficiency, continuity, and a precise operational flow.

All alerts and incidents from Microsoft Defender for Cloud, including multicloud alerts from Azure, AWS, and Google Cloud, are fully integrated into Defender XDR. You will see these cloud assets in the alert and incident queues, distinguishable and categorized with other alerts and incidents. The virtual machines will also maintain their detail page with all relevant alerts and activity.

To make the management of alerts and incidents even smoother, Microsoft Defender for Cloud alerts and incidents are now fully part of the public Defender XDR APIs. As a result, your organization can export security data and ingest it into another system using a single standard method. Only specific high-priority alerts will be surfaced to reduce noise and enable your teams to focus on meaningful work.

Through advanced hunting, you can now create queries to scan over all your individual cloud, device, and identity data, all in one place. Microsoft Defender for Cloud alerts and audit logs are included in these repositories, enabling your teams to identify suspicious activity, such as control plane misuse or unauthorized processes in the event log, in real time. They can then develop custom detections tailored to their specific cloud environments.

If your organization is using Microsoft Sentinel and integrates Microsoft Defender for Cloud as standard through Defender XDR, you can take measures to prevent alert duplication. Microsoft recommends using the tenant-based data connector and disabling the previous subscription-based connectors. The rules and automations can also be adjusted to help manage and action your alerts, allowing you to keep your incident queue relevant and actionable.

Microsoft Defender for IoT

Operational Technology (OT) is the unique systems (both hardware and software) that analyze and regulate industrial production in vital sectors such as manufacturing, energy, utilities, and pharmaceuticals. Microsoft Defender for IoT is created uniquely to protect OT environments and is available through the Microsoft Defender portal, which provides security for industrial networks, devices, vulnerabilities, and threats, and allows organizations to ensure operational continuity, safety, and resilience from cybersecurity risks.

CHAPTER 1 GET STARTED WITH MICROSOFT SENTINEL AND IOMT

Microsoft Defender for IoT is a purpose-built security service for Internet of Things (IoT) and Operational Technology (OT) environments that provides organizations with visibility into their industrial and connected devices with real-time threat detection and threat information with strong integration into the existing IT security platform.

Table 1-8 summarizes the key core features of using Microsoft Defender for Internet of Things with clear, reader-friendly descriptions.

Table 1-8. Key Features of Using Microsoft Defender for Internet of Things

Feature	Description
Comprehensive Protection	Secures industrial systems and IoT or OT devices with 1-100+ protocol support and managed deployment for multiple vendors.
Real-Time Monitoring	Monitors air traffic and device behavior passively, allowing you to identify anomalies without disrupting operations.
Asset and Vulnerability Management	Automatically discovers and inventories all connected devices, identifying vulnerabilities for risk rankings.
Threat Detection with Intelligence	Differentiates between known and emerging threats while searching for risk using machine learning and continuously updated threat intelligence.
Flexible Deployment	Supports rapid, agentless, and agent-based deployment, as well as passive mode deployment, to maintain zero disruption to critical processes.
Seamless Integration	Integrates natively with platforms (e.g., Azure Sentinel, Splunk, or ServiceNow) to create a unified IT and OT security operations center.
Regulatory Compliance	Includes built-in reports and industry frameworks (NIST, IEC 62443, etc.) support to achieve compliance with industry-wide regulations.
Scalable and Adaptable	Scales with the growth of the enterprise and the shift in the needs of the network topology or security.
Supports Security Awareness	Provides visibility to demonstrate human-provoked coverage gaps, enabling user training to improve targeted development.
Data Protection	Guarantees the encryption of sensitive data in transit and at rest, while enabling secured data flows from environment to environment.

As industrial environments evolve toward increased connectivity, it is essential to secure OT (Operational Technology) and IoT (Internet of Things) infrastructure solutions. Microsoft Defender for IoT was developed to address the unique cybersecurity issues in these environments by providing advanced visibility, monitoring, and threat detection capabilities, and assisting organizations in protecting their industrial systems without disrupting or compromising critical operations. Defender for IoT will strive to address the primary use cases to achieve enhanced asset visibility, minimize security risks, deliver real-time threat detection, and sustain regulated compliance. These capabilities afford IT and OT security teams the ability to proactively manage security in complex and varied environments.

Table 1-9 summarizes the key domains of using Microsoft Defender for IoT with comprehensive and reader-friendly descriptions.

Table 1-9. Key Domains of Using Microsoft Defender for IoT

Domain	Description
Real-Time Monitoring and Detection	Continuously observes all device and network activity to proactively detect threats and limit the chance of any interruptions to operations.
Asset and Vulnerability Management	Provides total awareness of all connected devices, including vectors to target weaknesses of the OT/IoT environment.
Integrated Security Architecture	Provides centralized security management by tying together IoT/OT intelligence with existing enterprise security tools.
Advanced Analytics and ML	Utilizes AI to recognize sophisticated, multi-phased attacks that can cross both IT and OT borderlines.
Compliance and Governance	Supports organizations in fulfilling auditing and compliance requirements and generates complete compliance reports.
Scalability and Flexibility	With scalable deployment options based on the organization's needs and a broad set of use cases.
Security Awareness Enablement	Issue reports and alerts highlighting training events that can enhance human-centric security habits.
Data Security and Privacy	Protects sensitive information leveraging advanced encryption standards at all levels of operation.

CHAPTER 1   GET STARTED WITH MICROSOFT SENTINEL AND IOMT

Planning Best Practices for Unified Security Operations

Security professionals need a clear and organized approach for bringing together detection, response, and visibility of threats anywhere in the cloud and on-premises. Microsoft Defender has an ecosystem—Defender for Endpoint, Defender for Identity, Defender for Cloud, and XDR—where these services give you a centralized security operations environment. It takes thoughtful organizing to realize its full potential.

Following outlines, the 10 planning foundations we will address, along with basic definitions for each area. The planning foundations can bring you to structural levels to create a secure, scalable, and intelligent defense against threats within the Microsoft Defender portal.

- *Determine Security Objectives*: The first step is to understand your security objectives and set measurable targets, such as decreasing your mean time to detection (MTTD), improving compliance, or lowering your high-severity incident rate. Be sure to take your organization's industry, risk tolerance, and business goals into account to establish what success looks like in security operations. You should also make sure your objectives align with your overall IT and business strategy.

- *Inventory Assets and Determine Scope*: Develop a comprehensive and clearly defined inventory of digital assets that require protection. This digital asset inventory will include cloud infrastructure (Azure, AWS, and GCP), virtual machines, containers, databases, endpoints (Windows, macOS, and Linux), identities (Azure AD), and SaaS platforms (e.g., Microsoft 365 and Salesforce), and possibly additional inventory depending on your organization. Utilize auto-discovery of resources from Microsoft Defender for Cloud and other integrations to automatically identify and onboard all resources. Additionally, make sure you're including internal systems and third-party systems.

- *Consider Defender Plans Options*: Microsoft Defender products are modular. Assess your needs and only enable the plans that you need to ensure you get the best cost and coverage. For example, Defender for Endpoint for EDR, Defender for Office 365 for email, Defender for

Cloud for CSPM and CWP, Defender for Identity for monitoring on-prem AD. Review your licensing (Microsoft 365 E5, A5, and Microsoft Defender for Cloud plans), and ensure that subscriptions to the plans have been assigned and activated per resource.

- *Create Role-Based Access Control (RBAC)*: The most basic form of access control is essential. Assign department-specific access: security analysts require access to incidents and hunting tools; security architects will require access to configuration visibility, and compliance officers will require posture and reporting information. Utilize Azure RBAC, or Defender XDR Unified RBAC roles, to only provide access to the information users need to perform their work. Avoid assigning Global Admin roles unless required. Wherever you can, segment access by resource group, subscription, or management group.

- *Configure Centralized Monitoring*: Use the Microsoft Defender portal as your main console for alert triage, threat investigations, and incident management. Connect Defender for Cloud to the Defender XDR platform to utilize alerts across workloads. This provides Security Analysts with a single interface view containing alerts and incidents from endpoints, email, cloud workloads, identities, and IoT. Use the correlated incident timelines and asset graphs to visualize the attack's kill chain and facilitate faster investigations.

- *Enable Automation and Customize Workflows*: Reduce analyst friction/fatigue via using Automation Rules and Playbooks. For example, route incidents based on severity, suppress known false positives, and generate notifications in Teams or Slack. Use Logic Apps to automate remediation, e.g., isolation of endpoints, password reset of credentials, or dispatch alert notifications to 3rd party ticketing tools (ServiceNow). Customize the automation based on your team's maturity and workflows.

- *Leverage Threat Intelligence and Advanced Hunting*: Defender provides integrated global threat intelligence integrations to enrich detections. In addition to using the service, enrich detections through personalized threat hunting using KQL queries in advanced hunting. Use the included tables for deviceEvents, CloudAuditEvents, and IdentityInfo to query suspicious activities. Regular threat hunting maintains active and proactive detection of stealthy or polymorphic attacks that may elude automated detection and remediation options. Use saved queries and scheduled detection to evaluate recurring risks regularly.

- *Compliance and Reporting*: Many organizations are regulated by standards, including GDPR, HIPAA, PCI-DSS, and ISO 27001. Utilizing Defender for Cloud, leverage the Regulatory compliance dashboard to see configuration posture compliance with regulations. Monitor Secure Score, practice recommendations to improve organizational posture, and generate audit-ready reports for internal and external stakeholders. As needed, expand to Microsoft Purview to enrich data classification and governance.

- *Conduct Response Testing with Simulations*: Simulate and test your organization's configuration through simulated attacks (such as phishing, credential theft, or lateral movement) with Microsoft Attack Simulation or other paid or free, comprehensive red team tools. Additionally, run table-top exercises to validate alert routing and escalation paths, as well as validate timing for remediation. Ensure and validate that incident response workflows and automation rules function as intended. Use these exercises to observe misconfigurations and/or gaps in coverage and visibility.

- *Create a Feedback and Improvement Loop*: Security Operations is an ever-evolving ecosystem. Schedule regular reviews to assess the effectiveness of alerts, incident timing, workload, and feedback from SOC analysts and stakeholders, aiming to improve rules, detections, and automation efforts. Review cues and updates in the Microsoft Defender roadmap and implement new services available to achieve your organization's goals. Own your security configuration and think of security as a living system, and maintenance or continual tuning is key to resilience.

Above is a helpful framework for security planners, builders, and SOC leaders as they seek to maximize their investment in Microsoft Defender. By taking a deeper dive into each area—from asset discovery and access control to automation and compliance—you will build a foundation from which to grow high-performing, unified security operations capabilities, ready for current and future threats.

Planning Your Deployment

When you plan your unified security operations, the first essential step is to understand the range of services available to you within the Microsoft Defender portal. Figure 1-8 illustrates Planning your Unified Security Operations Deployment

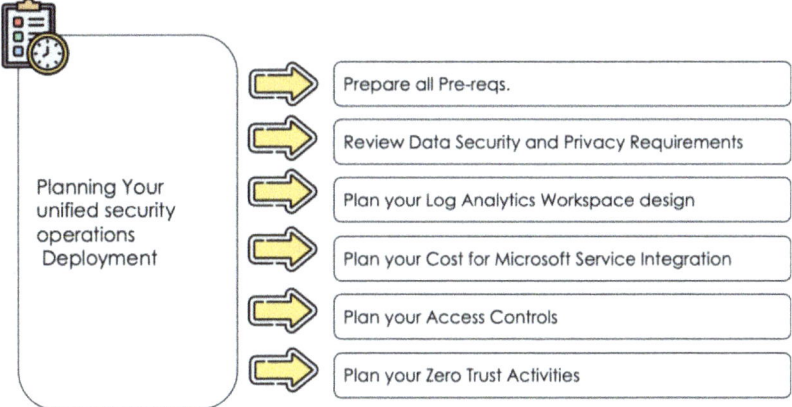

Figure 1-8. Planning Your Unified Security Operations Deployment

The Microsoft Defender portal is the landing place for many services, bringing together a suite of formidable security capabilities, specifically Microsoft Defender Extended Detection and Response (EDR) and Security Information and Event Management (SIEM), Microsoft Sentinel, Microsoft Security Exposure Management (SEM), and the AI-driven Microsoft Security Copilot. Collectively, these services enable a unified and holistic method for managing and responding to security threats across your environment.

Before you get started, it's worth identifying which services would fit best within the needs of your organization. Appropriately, if you want to do at least the bare minimum, deploying Microsoft Defender XDR and Microsoft Sentinel would fit the bill. Both services work together to monitor and protect environments from Microsoft, as well as non-Microsoft solutions, in the cloud and on-premises (whether hybrid or non-hybrid). This broad scope will help keep your security operations integrated and cohesive without leaving blind spots.

In addition to these minimums, the Defender portal provides a range of niche services that primarily focus on endpoints, identities, email, and cloud applications. Each service offers an additional level of protection and more support for defending against increasingly sophisticated cyber threats from many possible attackers. Table 1-10 lists examples of Microsoft Defender XDR services to investigate.

Table 1-10. Microsoft Defender XDR Services to Investigate

Service	Description
Microsoft Defender for Office 365	Protects your email, links, and collaboration tools against phishing, malware, and other malicious threats.
Microsoft Defender for Identity	Detects threats targeting both on-premises Active Directory and cloud-based identities like Microsoft Entra ID.
Microsoft Defender for Endpoint	Monitors and protects devices, detects breaches, and automates threat response on endpoints.
Microsoft Defender for IoT	Provides discovery and security monitoring specifically designed for Internet of Things (IoT) devices.
Microsoft Defender Vulnerability Management	Identifies assets and software, assesses vulnerabilities, and tracks device security posture.
Microsoft Defender for Cloud Apps	Controls and protects access to SaaS cloud applications, securing your data and user activities.

Apart from Defender XDR, the Azure portal also offers several other security tools that may not be included in your Defender XDR subscription. Table 1-11 lists examples of additional tools not included in your Defender XDR.

Table 1-11. *Additional Tools in Microsoft Azure*

Service	Description
Microsoft Security Exposure Management	Offers a unified view of your security posture across assets, enriching asset data with actionable security context.
Microsoft Security Copilot	Leverages AI to deliver insights and recommendations that empower your security operations teams.
Microsoft Defender for Cloud	Provides advanced threat detection and response for multi-cloud and hybrid environments.
Microsoft Defender Threat Intelligence	Aggregates threat intelligence data, correlating indicators of compromise with detailed actor and vulnerability profiles.
Microsoft Entra ID Protection	Analyzes risk associated with sign-in attempts, helping identify potentially compromised credentials or risky logins.
Microsoft Purview Insider Risk Management	Detects insider risks like data leaks and policy violations by correlating diverse risk signals.

You can implement a customized, multi-dimensional security strategy by combining and selecting some of these services based on your organizational priorities. This offers you a planned approach that not only enhances your security but also simplifies your operations by aggregating data, alerts, and response actions on a single platform.

Identify Data Security and Privacy Practices

Before leveraging Microsoft Defender services to create a unified security operation, it is essential to understand each of the data security and privacy practices for each service. Keep in mind that a few services contain the data security and retention standards as set by Microsoft Defender XDR and do not have separate policies.

Table 1-12. *Microsoft Defender XDR Identify Data Security and Privacy*

Security Service	Data Security and Privacy Summary
Required for Unified Security Operations	
Microsoft Defender XDR	Follows centralized data security and retention policies for threat protection and investigation.
Microsoft Sentinel	Includes controls for geographical data residency and regional availability of collected security data.
Optional Microsoft Defender XDR Services	
Microsoft Defender for Office	Inherits data security and retention practices from Microsoft Defender XDR.
Microsoft Defender for Identity	Uses dedicated identity monitoring privacy and data protection policies.
Microsoft Defender for Endpoint	Applies device-level data storage, retention, and user privacy safeguards.
Microsoft Defender for IoT (Enterprise Monitoring)	Adopts Microsoft Defender XDR's data security and retention framework.
Microsoft Defender Vulnerability Management	Aligned with Defender for Endpoint's storage and privacy controls.
Microsoft Defender for Cloud Apps	Provides standalone privacy practices focused on app activity monitoring.
Other Services Supported in Microsoft Defender Portal	
Microsoft Security Exposure Management	Defines specific rules for data freshness, retention timelines, and operational scope.
Microsoft Security Copilot	Applies generative AI-specific privacy and security handling mechanisms.
Microsoft Defender for Cloud	Implements structured cloud resource protection and data handling controls.

(*continued*)

Table 1-12. (*continued*)

Security Service	Data Security and Privacy Summary
Microsoft Defender Threat Intelligence	Utilizes Defender XDR's standards for data retention and threat intelligence storage.
Microsoft Entra ID Protection	Enforces retention and security policies for identity and access protection data.
Microsoft Purview Insider Risk Management	Governs internal risk monitoring and communication data under strict privacy rules.
Additional Microsoft 365 Governance	
Messaging Records Management (MRM)	Supports lifecycle policies and retention schedules for messaging data.

Planning Your Log Analytics Workspace Architecture for Microsoft Sentinel

When you enable Microsoft Sentinel in the Defender portal, you need to have a Log Analytics Workspace capable of supporting it. A single workspace may be sufficient in simpler environments, but additional workspaces can provide better granularity, cost management, and alignment with business or compliance requirements.

Here are some areas to consider when planning your Log Analytics workspace architecture:

- *Compliance Considerations*: What data residency or regulatory requirements do you have regarding the storage and processing of sensitive data?

- *Least Privilege Access*: How will you establish permission controls on sensitive data in Sentinel?

- *Data Segmentation*: You may use multiple workspaces to segregate environments, for example, production versus development, or business units.

Identifying Your Data Sources

Determining what data you wish to acquire into Sentinel is a critical first step in planning your Sentinel deployment. The types and volume of data that you want to obtain will directly influence your performance, visibility, and costs.

Start by reviewing your current estate, including any existing SIEM solutions. Identify which data sources are of the highest value for threat detection, investigation, and remediation.

While there are many different data sources, the recommended and familiar data sources are as follows:

Azure Services

If you're using Azure and leveraging diagnostic logs from Azure:

- Azure Firewall
- Azure Application Gateway
- Azure Key Vault
- Azure Kubernetes Service (AKS)
- Azure SQL Database
- Network Security Groups (NSG)
- Azure Arc-enabled servers

For ease and consistency, you may also set up automation, such as Azure Policy, to facilitate onboarding so that all the mentioned services are sending logs to your workspace.

Virtual Machines—On-Premises or Cloud Hosted

For virtual machines hosted on-premises or cloud-hosted, follow the below actions:

Using the Windows Security Events Connector, along with the Azure Monitor Agent (AMA), you will be able to collect server events using the Microsoft Defender for Endpoint integration. For Linux systems, you will use Syslog via AMA.

On-Premises or 3rd-Party Network Devices

If you use network devices or appliances that generate logs in formats such as CEF (Common Event Format) or SYSLOG, you can connect to these log sources using

- Syslog via AMA
- CEF via AMA

The connectors mentioned above will be used to collect the network and system activities for later analysis.

Planning for Costs/Budgeting

The Microsoft Sentinel pricing model is based on the amount of data ingested, with retention included in the cost model; therefore, budgeting is essential for your planning.

Consider the following when budgeting:

- *Data Ingestion Costs*: Estimate how many gigabytes of data are being ingested daily into the Log Analytics workspace.
- *Log Retention Policy*: Consider how long each type of log should be retained.
- *Automation Costs*: Include any Logic Apps or playbooks you want to use at the deployment.
- *Scalability*: Determine the forward enablement of data sources, and quantify upgrading analytical requirements.

Balancing coverage, performance, and cost will enable your organization to deploy a successful and sustainable solution.

Summary

In this chapter, we took a journey across the rapidly evolving terrain of the Internet of Medical Things; a paradigm shift in how we deliver, the way we operate, and how we secure healthcare. We started our journey with a baseline description of IoMT, decomposing its architecture, components, and the role it plays in enabling continual monitoring, intelligence-based decision-making, and ultimately patient-centric care.

We applied that knowledge pathway to the realm of cybersecurity for IoMT, which starts with an introduction to Microsoft Sentinel, a security information and event management (SIEM) and security orchestration, automation, and response (SOAR) solution enabled by the cloud. We examined how organisations can accelerate their adoption of Sentinel to monitor and secure connected medical devices, healthcare IT systems, and sensitive health data.

We examined how Microsoft Sentinel for IoT tackles the complex security challenges posed by IoMT devices. From identifying aberrant behaviour of medical endpoints to identifying telemetry that correlates to larger attack vectors, Sentinel's IoT capabilities provide valuable visibility and response capabilities to complex medical environments. This allows security teams to respond faster after threat identification and potentially limit the risk of lost data or impacted operations.

The chapter provided an overview of a Unified Security Operations Platform that combines the components of Microsoft Defender XDR, Microsoft Sentinel, Microsoft Security Exposure Management, and Microsoft Security Copilot into a consolidated and intelligent defence system. This was important in an IoMT context, as the unique challenge in healthcare is that we need to secure both industrial operational technology, clinical devices, and IT systems in an operationally cohesive environment, and this integration provides the basis for the collaboration.

The chapter concluded with best practices in planning a unified security operations strategy in healthcare environments. We reinforced key areas, including unifying the IT and OT teams, network segmentation, secure onboarding of IoMT devices, and using automation to reduce manual workload. We discussed that establishing transparent governance, compliance with regulations, and applying Zero Trust principles will build resiliency to support the future of healthcare security.

By the conclusion of this chapter, readers should be equipped to understand the IoMT ecosystem and have practical examples of Microsoft Sentinel and the full Microsoft Defender suite to apply in securing their healthcare environments against modern cybersecurity threats.

CHAPTER 2

Architecting and Deploying Microsoft Sentinel

With the rapid changes to the cybersecurity landscape, organizations are facing threats that are ever more sophisticated. Organizations will require a more advanced, complex, and adaptive defensive environment to face future threats. Microsoft Sentinel is a cloud-native security information and event management (SIEM) and security orchestration, automated response (SOAR) platform that allows security organizations to intelligently detect, investigate, and respond quicker than ever before to threats.

In this chapter, we will discuss the foundational and advanced capabilities of deploying and maintaining Microsoft Sentinel to achieve an effective security posture. We will first cover some foundational concepts of a Zero Trust security model implementation with Sentinel, beginning with the foundational understanding of identities being strictly needed and limited assets needed in a digital workspace for protection. We will also cover best practices for planning and architecting Sentinel workspaces and tenants to ensure scalability, performance, and compliance with various security policies and regulations.

As organizations migrate away from legacy systems, they will find migration to Microsoft Sentinel to be essential to their mission. We will cover those journeys in detail here to help work through the complexities of a security transition from legacy systems to Microsoft Sentinel. As effective data collection is paramount to security ownership and views, we will also discuss optimizing the cost and performance of the data ingestion piece. Also, there will be a discussion on integrating commerce systems and services that provide external threat intel as an aid to detection. We will also discuss the value and methods for ingesting and automatically enriching that data.

Effective log management remains at the core of all security monitoring solutions, and we will cover those strategies from a retention, analysis, and compliance perspective. To aggregate and normalize the disparate contents of log files, we introduce the Advanced Security Information Model (ASIM) and some basic data normalization paradigms that can help with detection and investigation workflows. Along with ASIM, there will be a discussion of User and Entity Behavior Analytics (UEBA), which includes machine learning to determine when anomalous activity may be indicative of an insider threat or a compromised account.

As security solutions become more complex, we propose utilizing Microsoft Sentinel's Copilot feature. Microsoft Sentinel's Copilot is AI-powered to provide suggestions, automation, and insights that ultimately empower security architects to make better and faster decisions. By the end of this chapter, you should understand the following:

- *Implementing Zero Trust with Sentinel*
- *Designing and Architecting Workspaces and Tenants*
- *Migrating to Microsoft Sentinel*
- *Optimizing Data Collection in Sentinel*
- *Integrating Threat Intelligence*
- *Effective Log Management*
- *Data Normalization and ASIM*
- *User and Entity Behavior Analytics (UEBA)*
- Utilizing Copilot for Security Architects

Implementing Zero Trust with Sentinel

Zero Trust is an innovative cybersecurity strategy based on the philosophy that no user or device, either inside or outside an organization's network, should be implicitly trusted. Zero Trust does not rely on perimeter-based controls (like firewalls) that treat internal systems as safe; instead, it adheres to the principle of "never trust, always verify," ensuring that every access request is authenticated, authorized, and encrypted before being granted access. Access is not trusted simply because a device is connected to the network or because a user has logged in once. Zero Trust encompasses continuous verification, identity verification, access controls, and monitoring to ensure that the right people and devices have access to the correct data at the right time.

In the realm of the Internet of Medical Things (IoMT), where medical devices are perpetually connected and transmit sensitive health information, Zero Trust is crucial. Hospitals and healthcare providers rely on using IoMT devices like insulin pumps, patient monitors, imaging tools, and innovative infusion systems to provide care while also tracking patient health in real time. Often, these IoMT devices exist outside of existing IT protections, are built with limited cybersecurity features, or may not have cybersecurity features at all. If one connected device gets hacked, it has access to the entire network, which not only puts patient privacy at risk but also patient lives. Meanwhile, IoMT systems also use and manage protected health information (PHI), which is regulated, meaning that a single breach can lead to serious legal and financial consequences. A zero trust approach requires that every user and device prove that it is safe and authorized before engaging with clinical systems or patient data—this inherently reduces the risk of unauthorized access or cyberattacks taking place that could impede care delivery.

Implementing a zero trust model in an Internet of Medical Things (IoMT) setting takes a carefully planned stepwise approach that includes both technical controls and their coordination with clinical workflows. Since the nature of healthcare includes sensitive data and life-critical systems, we need to be certain that security does not impact patient care. Here are some of the considerations for designing a Zero Trust architecture specifically for IoMT:

- *Asset Discovery Is the First Step*: You need to know what devices, users, and systems are connected to your environment. You should develop an accurate and real-time inventory of medical devices (e.g., infusion pumps, heart monitors, and imaging systems), clinical applications, and healthcare workers that are accessing or utilizing them.

- *Strong Identity and Access Controls Must Be Applied*: You should enforce multi-factor authentication (MFA) for all users (clinicians, administrative users, and IT staff) and further utilize role-based access controls or attribute-based access controls so that users will only access data or systems that pertain to their role.

- *Network Segmentation Will Limit Threats*: Micro-segmentation should be used to isolate IoMT devices into secured segments or zones. Operations associated with critical functions should be separated into segments or zones from those related to general IT applications (e.g., email and web browsing terminals). This inhibits attackers' ability to perform lateral movement across the systems if any one device is compromised.

- *Define and Enforce Access Policies*: Define specific security policies and designate who or what can communicate with each device or system.

- A nurse may see patient vitals but may not change the firmware on a nursing station. These policies should be dynamic and context-aware, based on factors such as device health, user location, or time of day.

- *Constantly Monitor Behaviors and Log*: Use real-time monitoring and analytics solutions like SIEM (Security Information and Event Management) and XDR (Extended Detection and Response). Keep an eye out for compromised devices by monitoring network activity, device behaviors, and login attempts.

- Using behavioral baselining to identify anomalies, for example, the outside blood pressure monitor suddenly tries to use the internet.

- *Device Posture Improvements*: Ensure medical devices are upgraded, patched, and configured securely, wherever applicable. Block devices that don't meet minimum device security clearance from having access to clinical networks.

- *Protect the Data at All Times*: Encrypt all sensitive data, while at rest (stored on a device) or "in transit" (in movement between devices or systems). Apply data loss prevention (DLP) rules to prevent unauthorized individuals from sharing patient data. Label and classify data to apply stricter controls to more sensitive information. If a medical device behaves suspiciously, we can automatically isolate it from the network. By integrating Layer Zero Trust with your security orchestration tools, we can respond to incidents more effectively.

- *Regularly Review and Improve*: Zero Trust is not a once-in-a-lifetime configuration. Audit security policies, access controls, and the inventory of devices regularly. Use threat-hunting scenarios to run drills and demonstrate that your organization is prepared.

Implementing a Zero Trust architecture with an eye toward patient safety and effectiveness can help healthcare organizations avoid cyber threats while ensuring patient safety and efficacy. The end goal is to create a secure environment that allows only trusted users, devices, and actions—that's it—without any assumptions or blind spots.

Making Zero Trust Work in Healthcare

Even though Zero Trust provides good protections, deploying it in the healthcare environment has some hurdles. Many older medical devices may not support modern security features, such as encryption or frequent software updates. Even when a security change does not directly affect the medical device or its patient treatment, changes to settings can disrupt clinical workflow, particularly in patient care, and must be ensured to avoid interruptions. Certain vendors and different medical devices inevitably cause difficulty in deploying a single policy for all devices. However, the advantages of Zero Trust are clear: patient safety, protection of medical data, and compliance with healthcare regulations. As health care becomes further digital with wearables, telemedicine, and AI-driven diagnostics, Zero Trust exposure decisions are essential to health care organizations' ability to fend off cyber threats. At the same time, they continue to deliver safe, effective, and trusted care to patients.

Common Challenges in Healthcare Environments

- *Legacy Devices*
  - Many medical devices were manufactured with no consideration of modern cybersecurity.
  - Some devices cannot be patched, cannot be updated, or cannot be configured even to perform secure/authenticated access.

- *Operational Sensitivity*
  - You have the potential to affect clinical workflows when changing settings on specific devices or may even affect patient care timing in some instances.
  - Security updates and downtimes may interfere with the timeliness of treatment, especially life-saving treatment.
- *Devices and Vendor Lock-In*
  - Each healthcare facility may refer to devices from many vendors—with many doing slightly different things; it makes it complicated to apply consistency in what we are trying to do.
  - Lack of standardization makes it difficult to apply consistent policies.
- *Lack of Visibility*
  - Your IT team may not have complete visibility of each of the connected medical devices.
  - You may have shadow IoT devices connected without consent (connected outside your knowledge).
- *Deferred Budgets and Resources*
  - Smaller hospitals may not have the budget, tools, or staff to adopt any full-fledged Zero Trust implementation.
  - With competing priorities, it's common that little will delay security priorities.

Real-World Steps for Implementing Zero Trust in Healthcare

Taking a structured, multidisciplinary approach to enabling Zero Trust in healthcare is of utmost importance. The first crucial step is to establish a unified governance model. That is, a cross-functional team consisting of IT and security professionals, clinical engineers, and risk or compliance officers. A clearly defined role and responsibilities for each member of the Zero Trust team are essential to ensuring that Zero Trust strategies are implemented in a coordinated manner throughout the organization.

A practical place to start is to focus on high-risk devices first, meaning devices that have access to sensitive patient data or have direct patient contact. Specific medical devices must take precedence over others, such as infusion pumps, imaging systems, and ventilators.

Network segmentation protocols must also be established initially. For example, IoMT devices should be logically separated from general-purpose IT networks like administrative systems and staff email. The use of VLANs, firewalls, and SDN (software-defined networking) technology is helpful to construct rigid boundaries and enforce some form of controlled communication between the zones.

To minimize unauthorized access, identity management is a key consideration. Organizations must enforce strong password policies and expect all users to adhere to multi-factor authentication (MFA) practices at every user level. In addition, the principle of least privilege must be applied, meaning users can access only the necessary data required to perform their job function, which reduces the organization's attack surface.

To monitor and detect threats in near real-time, continuous monitoring and behavioral analytics must be employed. Security Information and Event Management (SIEM) and Extended Detection and Response (XDR) tools can generally be used to detect suspicious activities across systems. Creating alerts as part of the solution to identify unauthorized access and anomalous behavior can also give organizations the ability to identify and mitigate potential breaches.

Hardening a medical device to point an exploitable vulnerability envelope to a much smaller surface area is the process of essentially locking it down. The steps involved in this process include turning off unused services, changing default passwords, closing unnecessary ports, and turning off physical ports such as USBs and radios. In some cases, it may be prudent to consider turning off any IoMT functionality altogether if not required for current use.

All IoMT traffic should be evaluated by secure inspection tooling to keep malicious traffic from entering your organization. This includes security gateways, proxies, or firewalls. By utilizing Deep Packet Inspection (DPI) and anomaly detection solutions, hidden incongruities in IoMT can be uncovered, revealing potential dangers in responses that may have only one-way data flow, where data cannot be trusted.

Organizations can mitigate further vulnerabilities with a well-defined admission policy thoroughly implemented and audited. The admission policy should establish security requirements for devices in the cyber market, including communication with health systems, minimum-security standards, current patch levels, firmware versions, and certification by reputable vendors. A device compliance and designation assessment tool, such as Network Access Control (NAC), can determine such needs as well as deny access or admit the device to the organization's network or operations.

The most protected data will need to be handled holistically. All patient data needs to have an encryption mechanism regardless of use case. All needed communication should have Transport Layer Security (TLS) and IPsec associations to prevent communications from being exploitable across the networks of traffic and all possible sources of data loss or exfiltration when a compromised health system may be engaged.

One of the critical aspects of implementing an incident response plan is that Zero Trust strategies should be integrated into it. The challenges presented in IoMT incidents, whether in device hijacking or ransomware, are exacerbated by the fact that one issue can masquerade as another from a device security and usage standpoint, submitting the documentation as devices with unintended consequences that protect information from a compromised organizational system. Wherever workflows with containment mitigation actions can be performed through device isolation, choosing to do so through automation of the system may allow organizations to respond more quickly to incidents by leveraging broad protocols, processes, and technical requirements.

Organizations need to give themselves the agility to carry out regular risk assessments to understand mitigation from evolving threats. Performing vulnerability scans and penetration tests on documents specific to healthcare environments is a part of this process, as is updating the threat model to reflect the organization's unique threat landscape.

People remain one of the most critical components of a Zero Trust strategy for security. Staff training and awareness programs with a frequency of reinforcement need to be structurally reliable pathways for deploying staff training. Understanding the foundations of Zero Trust and the secure use of devices, along with the awareness that one staff member's vigilance could impact organizational security, is crucial.

Working collaboratively with medical device manufacturers enables a healthcare organization to gain a deeper understanding of a device's capabilities, vulnerabilities, and awareness through regular firmware updates and vulnerability disclosures. This collaboration also facilitates requests for vendor support to explore remote device management alternatives.

Agility with continuous improvement can allow for sustained focus and success. Organizations should be doing continuous audits on usually timed intervals to review access and audit logs, behavior policies, conferences and verifications of the device or platform can reflect and confirm compliance and other pertinent regulations, frameworks, best practices and standards, to verify compliance to national and international rules and standards on observe veteran regulations/regulatory measures such as the American governmental HIPAA guidelines and others of the terms of industry, code-of-conduct guidelines of service such as standards coditive, guidelines of code as stipulated by a respect standards such as NIST, ISO, an ISO/IEC standard, HITRUST, and the Health Sector Coordinating Council to ensuring the organization and sector compliance are robust.

The final recommendation from each of the focus areas outlined is to continue to evolve and develop the security policy based on feedback. The steps carried out that planned work could be agreed as usable and not lost in protection or positions of security, or continue to review policy with parties affecting new policies, to employ stakeholders, clinicians, and relevant staff to discuss value and share experiences, could affect security stakeholders, not just the use of devices, but to recognize and provide some level of understanding and suggest an active collaboration with experts or early risk assessment judgement based on incidence, who will remain vigilant.

With these well-defined, actionable steps, healthcare organizations can successfully navigate the complexity of securing IoMT ecosystems. A Zero Trust solution, when implemented with attention to usability, device limitations, and clinical needs, significantly lowers risk while adhering to the highest standards of patient safety and care quality.

Enhancing Cybersecurity Resilience with Microsoft Defender XDR and Sentinel

Organizations in today's threat landscape are constantly challenged by a wide range of increasingly sophisticated, persistent, and complex threats. To defend against evolving threats, security teams must adopt tools that contribute not only to the identification and investigation of threats but also to response automation and policy enforcement. In this section, we will discuss how Microsoft's integrated offerings (Microsoft Defender XDR and Microsoft Sentinel) can be used in tandem to help improve and mature your organization's security posture. We will also discuss how these tools enhance threat detection time, response time, and an organization's Zero Trust architecture.

Understanding Microsoft Defender XDR and Sentinel

Microsoft Defender XDR (Extended Detection and Response) is a cloud-powered platform that allows organizations to collect, correlate, and analyze a variety of threat signals across the Microsoft 365 services. Whether being sourced from users, endpoints, email, or applications, Defender XDR gives your organization a consolidated view of its security landscape and can provide intelligent detection and response actions automatically.

Microsoft Sentinel is a cloud-native SIEM (Security Information and Event Management) and SOAR (Security Orchestration, Automation, and Response) solution. It ingests signals from across the organization's entire digital estate (including both cloud and on-premises environments). It provides strong analytics, significant threat detection capabilities, and automation to help security operations teams.

Defender XDR and Sentinel can be used in tandem to provide security teams with an end-to-end security solution that supports early threat detection, fast investigation, and automated response across all areas of your organization's digital estate.

Integrating XDR and Sentinel: A Unified Defense Strategy

To get quicker incident responses and more intelligent automation, organizations can integrate Microsoft Defender XDR with Microsoft Sentinel. This allows the advanced detection capabilities of Microsoft Defender XDR to be aligned with the orchestration and automation capabilities of Microsoft Sentinel, which can elevate the organization toward a proactive defense strategy. By deploying these two products together, the combined security capabilities span multiple domains, such as identities, endpoints, emails, and cloud workloads, to provide more comprehensive threat visibility and coordinated response activities.

The MS Defender XDR and MS Sentinel integration helps with analyzing correlated signals across multiple Microsoft 365 and Azure services so that threats can be accurately detected with cross-domain telemetry; respondents to be automatic and respond to threat alerts, t, by triggering an automated playbook, as needed, reducing human intervention; and better visibility of the entire enterprise environment, and centralizing threat hunting and investigation within a single pane of glass.

Once correctly set up, Sentinel can leverage Defender XDR signals to trigger alerts, automate responses, block harmful traffic, or quarantine suspicious entities, thereby decreasing the overall time for detection and response, as well as limiting the impact.

CHAPTER 2 ARCHITECTING AND DEPLOYING MICROSOFT SENTINEL

Reinforcing Zero Trust with Defender XDR and Sentinel

Microsoft's Zero Trust architecture is based on three core tenets: verify explicitly, least privileged access, and assume breach. The combination of Microsoft Defender XDR + Microsoft Sentinel embodies the three principles of zero trust and acts as a concrete way to operationalize zero trust across the organization.

Microsoft's approach to Zero Trust is rooted in three core principles:

- Verify Explicitly
- Use Least Privileged Access
- Assume Breach

Figure 2-1 depicts Zero Trust with Defender XDR and Sentinel. Let's explore how Microsoft Defender XDR and Sentinel support each principle.

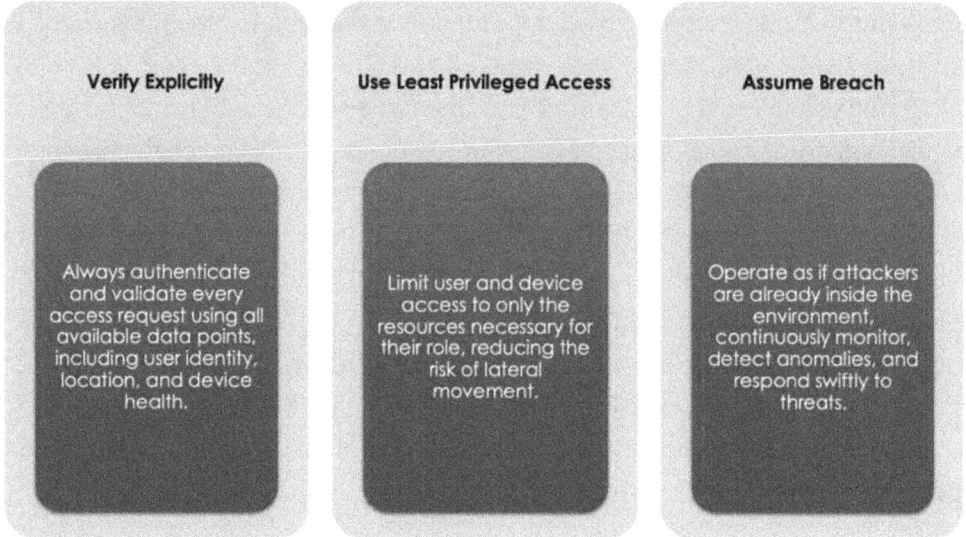

Figure 2-1. *Microsoft Zero Trust Principle*

Verify Explicitly

Microsoft Sentinel continuously ingests and analyzes telemetry from a wide array of users, devices, applications, and cloud workloads to ensure that access decisions are based on factual, real-time data. Defender XDR complements Sentinel through empathy and machine learning by combining risk signals across domains and correctly identifying anomalies and threats. With the signal from Defender XDR of suspicious behavior, including abnormal logins and documents accessed directly or indirectly, Sentinel can facilitate an automatic response to the inattentive behavior through investigation or active threat response, including blocking a login, isolating a compromised device, or escalating the incident to your security operations (SecOps) team. The combination of automated incident response through Defender XDR will enable stronger access decisions with better context for investigations and faster automatic incident response.

Use Least Privileged Access Controls

We know least privilege principles work well, right? Another method for implementing the least privilege principles is using continuous monitoring and adaptive access controls. Sentinel is an operation outlier for identifying unusual or inappropriate activity using the User and Entity Behavior Analytics (UEBA) engine. The UEBA engine will be alerted when a user attempts to access data or documents that are outside of the regular activity of a specific user. While Sentinel is assessing and analyzing user activity, the Defender XDR can access risk signals from Defender XDR to identify risks associated with Microsoft Entra ID Protection. Golden signals will be made available for you, and should your access controls be Conditional Access, they will be available to influence decisions about risk during Conditional Access. Together, organizations have the opportunity to develop a continuous monitoring principle that will fully identify each user's calculated risk, provide comprehensive decision-making using threat intelligence models, and establish a reactive system that will locate misuse and/or compromises early.

Assume Breach

The third process assumes a breach and that during the operating system, breaches come before incident response. Microsoft Defender XDR enables organizations to proactively scan user endpoints, applications, and cloud workloads for vulnerabilities that will provide indicators of compromises. Microsoft Sentinel correlates telemetry and risk signal data to recreate and verify complex attack patterns, including lateral movement and data exfiltration. Sentinel and Defender XDR mean early threat detection and threat response options for arrests based on early identification. Sentinel and Defender XDR can isolate infected devices, pause user accounts, and initiate threat hunting operations workflows and procedures at your local, national, and international operations in a rapid time. Organizations can always assume breach and maintain the operations model for covert threats, providing a constant cost advantage with the increased opportunity of exploiting the detections.

Organizations can leverage Microsoft Defender XDR and Microsoft Sentinel to build a usable and practical security operations platform. Your organization's zero trust principles will be reinforced through these technologies, strengthening your detection and response capabilities as well as providing a proactive, automated, and resilient security approach tailored to the ever-changing threats of today.

Implementing Microsoft Sentinel and Defender XDR

A unified security operations methodology allows organizations to effectively manage, monitor, and respond to threats across a variety of environments from a single platform. The integration of Microsoft's Defender portal with Microsoft's Defender XDR, Sentinel, and other custom apps and services provides organizations with a single pane of glass through which they can view their security posture as completely as possible. This unified experience enables security teams to detect, respond to, and remediate security alerts and incidents, regardless of their location (e.g., on-premises, cloud, or hybrid infrastructure).

To realize the full potential of a unified security operations model, organizations must implement a well-defined deployment model that consists of planning, configuring role-based access, integrating data, and enforcing security and compliance controls based on Zero Trust principles.

Planning and Prerequisites

Before implementing Microsoft Defender XDR and Microsoft Sentinel, it is vital to lay the groundwork. First things first—it is crucial to have a clear security operations plan that lays out your detection, response, and compliance goals. Next, design one or more Log Analytics workspaces to handle the expected log volume and set data retention appropriately. You will also need to plan for costs—ensure you review how you will allocate Microsoft Sentinel resources, as costs will rise with the ingestion of more data. You will need to identify which components of Microsoft Defender you need for your environment based on your threat landscape and infrastructure. You should also map user roles and access privileges based on the principle of least privilege. This will help with your deployments and is also recommended in terms of security. Determining these elements ahead of time will minimize operational risk and prepare your organization for an effective and scalable rollout.

Implementing Components of Microsoft Defender XDR

Microsoft Defender XDR utilizes an integrated approach to threat protection across many security domains, often considered the foundation of a responsive and intelligent incident detection and response strategy. Implementations of Microsoft Defender XDR typically begin with Microsoft Defender for Identity. Microsoft Defender for Identity monitors identity signals and user behavior to identify compromised credentials. The next step in YDR implementation involves Microsoft Defender for Office 365, which protects your channels of communication, such as email or collaboration tools, from phishing, malware, and other advanced threats.

Once deployed, Microsoft Defender for Endpoint is implemented as the next step, as it provides many capabilities for real-time threat detection and remediation of issues on your endpoint devices. There are optional add-ons available to help with device-level protection around vulnerability management and IoT monitoring. Microsoft Defender for Cloud Apps provides greater visibility and control through user activity and cloud applications. Microsoft Entra ID Protection analyzes sign-in attempts using AI to provide a risk assessment while maintaining access security. When used together, these services represent layers of defense that account for ever-changing threats while following the Zero Trust principle.

Expanding Security with Defender for Cloud and Security Copilot

Microsoft Defender for Cloud secures workloads in hybrid and multicloud environments, expanding its protection to platforms such as Azure, AWS, and Google Cloud. Defender for Cloud secures compute, storage, containers, and other cloud-native assets, and its signals can be shared with Defender XDR for a unified threat detection experience. Specify the core cloud environments and deploy Defender for Cloud access in a simple stepwise fashion, beginning with the core cloud environments and scaling out as applicable to additional workloads.

Microsoft Security Copilot further extends security operations and serves as an AI assistant for the Security Operations Center (SOC). It automates repetitive processes, speeds up threat analysis, and provides prescriptive remediation steps. There is less required human effort with faster response times, allowing your security analysts to focus on strategic threats versus operational noise.

Configuring Microsoft Sentinel for Detection and Analytics

Log Analytics workspaces must be established as part of the Microsoft Sentinel deployment process. They should be created or selected under a dedicated security resource group, which allows governance and visibility controls to be implemented. Then, onboard Microsoft Sentinel with role-based access control (RBAC) through Azure. Specific roles, such as Sentinel Reader, provide fine-grained access permissions and understanding from the Zero Trust perspective and implementation. Next, establish processes for health monitoring and audits to ensure system integrity and detect unauthorized changes. Load content packs to provide exemplary rule deployment and connect your data sources to ingest telemetry from Defender components and services. Enable User and Entity Behavior Analytics (UEBA) to detect anomalies based on behavior. Additionally, data retention policies must be configured to meet regulatory obligations and facilitate historical review.

Optimizing Analytics and Threat Detections

Once you complete your deployment, you must also optimize Microsoft Sentinel to ensure maximum detection and response abilities. Enable analytics rules aligned with your organization's risk profile, and then analyze the data sources to prioritize them. You can reduce false positives by adjusting thresholds for anomaly detection, which will allow your SOC to concentrate on valid threats.

Once the Microsoft Threat Intelligence (TI)-based rules are enabled, you can correlate the alerts generated with known malicious indicators, and you can identify gaps and correlate the detections with the behavior of your adversaries by completing the MITRE ATT&CK crosswalk. When working with Defender XDR, ensure you do not have duplicate alerts if you enable both systems to generate incidents automatically. This could impact your incident response process, maintaining clarity with alerting.

Role Management and Secure Access

Access controls should always align with your organization's access policy. Users in Sentinel should only receive roles that meet their task function's maximum need. To achieve this, roles should be explicitly assigned to Sentinel at the resource group level, thereby maintaining your governance processes. Ensure that you limit access to sensitive logs, security settings, and threat intelligence to prevent privilege misuse and limit insider threat risks. Mitigating risk through effective role management not only improves your security posture but also ensures accountability across your operation.

Changing Security Operations with Unified Tools

Implementing Microsoft Defender XDR and Microsoft Sentinel as a unified security operation platform has radically improved the detection, investigation, and response of organizations to threat events. Providing visibility, speed, and automation to the security lifecycle. Enabling Microsoft Sentinel's data capabilities and cloud-based orchestration has your security operations posture using a structured, role-conscious incline, and with a Zero Trust mindset, your SOC will become agile, machine-intelligent, and stronger against modern cyber threats—while still being compliant and inline across all of your data sources.

Implementing Zero Trust with Microsoft Sentinel and Defender XDR

The Zero Trust security model is based on continuous verification, least-privileged access, and proactive threat response. When integrated with cloud and hybrid environments, especially those that include IoMT or enterprise networks, Microsoft Sentinel and Microsoft Defender XDR add the capability of continually detecting, investigating, and responding to incidents in real time.

For organizations with Microsoft security capabilities, using Sentinel and Defender XDR creates a potent offering to implement Zero Trust security concepts across users, devices, apps, and workloads.

Table 2-1 provides a comprehensive overview of the factors supporting the implementation of Zero Trust, utilizing Microsoft's security tools, including device control, threat hunting, incident response, and cloud workload protection.

Table 2-1. *Microsoft's Security Tools Inventory*

Capability/Feature	Description	Product
Automated Investigation and Response (AIR)	Streamlines alert triage and remediation to reduce alert fatigue and response time.	Microsoft Defender XDR
Advanced Hunting	Intuitive, query-based hunting tool able to analyze more than 30 days of raw data to identify potential threats.	Microsoft Defender XDR
Custom File Indicators	Helps stop, contain, or mitigate the impact of malicious files using threat intelligence, and blocks the execution of malicious files.	Microsoft Defender XDR
Cloud Discovery	Investigate the use of cloud apps by building a usage profile using Defender for Endpoint traffic logs.	Microsoft Defender for Cloud Apps
Custom Network Indicators	Allows or blocks the ability to connect to IPs, URLs, or domains relating to threat intel you either created or imported.	Microsoft Defender XDR
Endpoint Detection and Response (EDR) Block Mode	Remediates threats on endpoints, even if Defender Antivirus is passive.	Microsoft Defender XDR
Device Response Capabilities	Isolates compromised devices or collects forensic data for later review, on or off the network.	Microsoft Defender XDR
Live Response	And can even provide shell access for an analyst to devices in real time to contain and assess the threat.	Microsoft Defender XDR
Secure Cloud Applications	A DevSecOps tool to secure applications and pipelines in multicloud environments.	Microsoft Defender for Cloud
Improve Your Security Posture (CSPM)	Used to identify misconfigurations and provide recommendations in the event of a breach.	Microsoft Defender for Cloud
Protect Cloud Workloads (CWPP)	Able to defend workloads including containers, VMs, storage, and databases.	Microsoft Defender for Cloud

(*continued*)

Table 2-1. (*continued*)

Capability/Feature	Description	Product
User and Entity Behavioral Analytics (UEBA)	Monitors users, IPs, and device behavior to identify insider threats or abnormal behavior that might indicate there is a problem.	Microsoft Sentinel
Fusion	Provides an AI-based correlation engine that allows the detection of complex multi-staged attacks called Advanced Persistent Threats (APTs); can provide mTAM (Multi-layer Threat Assessment Model) capabilities.	Microsoft Sentinel
Threat Intelligence	Integrates Microsoft and third-party threat intelligence to create context for the incident data being reviewed.	Microsoft Sentinel
Automation Rules	Can automate incident response across your incident types and customize rules to transform manually handled cases into playbooks.	Microsoft Sentinel
Anomaly Rules	Can detect patterns that indicate unusual behavior based on rule templates that leverage ML.	Microsoft Sentinel
Scheduled Queries	Comes with built-in rules (rule library) to detect suspicious chains of activity in log data from devices.	Microsoft Sentinel
Near Real-Time (NRT) Rules	Combines rules that operate in high frequency (for example, in 1 minute) so you can investigate unusual activity in near real-time.	Microsoft Sentinel
Hunting	Provides guided threat hunting with built-in queries to help locate advanced threats in your organization.	Microsoft Sentinel
Microsoft Defender XDR Connector	Windows logs and incident data sync between Defender XDR and Microsoft Sentinel.	Microsoft Defender XDR + Sentinel
Data Connectors	Provides both tools to ingest logs and telemetry data from various sources into Sentinel for visibility and analysis.	Microsoft Sentinel

(*continued*)

CHAPTER 2   ARCHITECTING AND DEPLOYING MICROSOFT SENTINEL

Table 2-1. (*continued*)

Capability/Feature	Description	Product
Content Hub Solution—Zero Trust (TIC 3.0)	Microsoft has provided templates in the form of a workbook, rules, and a playbook set that align with Zero Trust and TIC 3.0 frameworks.	Microsoft Sentinel
Security Orchestration, Automation, and Response (SOAR)	Can automate threat response at scale with playbooks and orchestration flows across your environment.	Microsoft Sentinel
SOC Optimization	You will be able to eliminate data noise while identifying gaps in coverage that will make your security operations centers more effective.	Microsoft Sentinel/ Defender Portal

Designing and Architecting Workspaces and Tenants

When designing a Log Analytics workspace in Azure Monitor and Microsoft Sentinel, the design considerations you make can significantly affect both the operational efficiency and cost of the system. For many organizations, a single workspace will be sufficient. However, it is often the case that larger or more complex organizations will utilize multiple workspaces, designed to offer the organization the most benefit.

This section will walk you through the design considerations needed to develop your workspace architecture and to decide if a single workspace or multiple workspaces make sense, based on your technical, operational, and organizational factors.

Single Workspace

A single tenant, or single workspace of Microsoft Sentinel, is where all monitoring data from different resources within the tenant is imported into a single workspace, regardless of their Azure region. Figure 2-2 depicts the architecture of a single tenant.

CHAPTER 2   ARCHITECTING AND DEPLOYING MICROSOFT SENTINEL

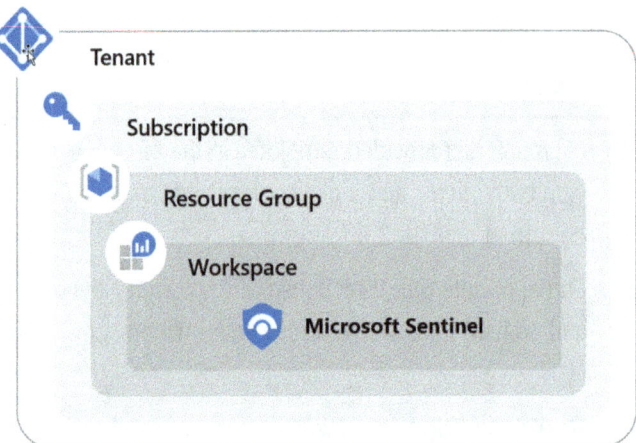

Figure 2-2. *Architecture of a Single Tenant*

While a single workspace may reduce complexity from an operations perspective and allow for centralized visibility, it also introduces two primary design considerations:

- *Bandwidth Costs*: Since the logs are being collected from resources in different Azure regions, the data needs to traverse Azure Regions to enter the workspace. Depending on the number of log entries and frequency of telemetry produced, cross-region logs may incur additional bandwidth billing.

- *Data Residency Requirements*: An organization may have strictly enforced regulatory or compliance policies that dictate that data must reside in specific regions. In instances where this is true, directing logs to a workspace in another area would violate the requirements, hence invalidating this design for a centralized workspace.

Consequently, while a single workspace for a tenant organization will often improve operational efficiency, the design also needs to consider the costs imposed and regional compliance requirements before establishing a design rationale.

Multiple Workspaces

Log Analytics workspaces in Azure serve as a containment strategy to collect, store, and analyze telemetry data from multiple sources (Azure resources, on-premises resources, and third-party sources). In many enterprise use cases, the nature and state of the operational, regulatory, or organizational requirements necessitate multiple workspaces. For instance, various business units, regions, or security teams within an enterprise may require data separation due to compliance obligations, internal access policies, or company directives to share costs. Figure 2-3 depicts the architecture of a multiple-tenant workspace.

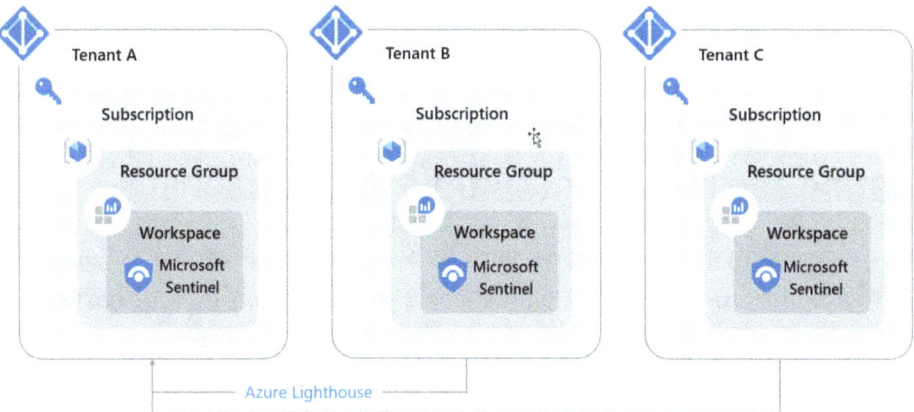

Figure 2-3. *Architecture of a Multiple Tenant*

Using multiple workspaces, teams can better maintain a separation of concerns. Each workspace can have its own data retention requirements, roles/access controls, and cost allocation. This unitary structure is particularly beneficial in multi-tenanted or multitenancy structures (e.g., multiple departments in a university) or larger extended organizations (like multinational companies), where having data flow to and from a centralized workspace may reduce efficiencies or create data privacy compliance issues. Sometimes, it also separates workspaces, but it is easier to maintain Role-Based Access Control (RBAC). In situations where workspaces correspond to various business units, projects, or teams, you can assign access controls to the team responsible for the workspace that corresponds to their project or business unit, thereby preventing the onboarding of unwarranted or irrelevant data. Separating workspaces is also a way to simplify obtaining granularity in financial accountability while only associating costs with the more specific departments or projects.

However, using multiple workspaces also has disadvantages. For instance, configuring the various steps to correlate and query data across workspaces, such as using Azure Lighthouse for cross-workspace queries or data forwarding, requires additional effort. This is because these tasks leverage workload options beyond telemetry data, which are not readily achievable within your Log Analytics workspaces.

Suppose the organization has mature security analytics tooling (like Microsoft Sentinel and others). In that case, they can often deploy their security analytics solutions in a single or central workspace while still being able to collect telemetry (via data connectors) from other workspaces or aggregate the visualizations with multi-workspace views. Although separating workspaces can increase flexibility and scalability over time, adequate planning for governance, consistency, and responsiveness in incident response workflows is crucial to avoid introducing new visibility problems within your organization.

Evaluating the Need for Multiple Workspaces

Over time, as your environment grows, various business and technical requirements can lead you to establish more than one workspace. Considerations include cost savings, regional regulations, data ownership boundaries, and access control.

When you are administering a Microsoft Sentinel workspace that is outside your Azure tenant, like in a customer or partner tenant, you can have a multi-tenant architecture using Azure Lighthouse.

Azure Lighthouse allows you to provide secure delegated access, so you can manage Sentinel workspaces in other tenants without needing to authenticate into each tenant one at a time. This provides an effective management capability with clear lines between different environments.

Once access is enabled with Lighthouse, the decisions about how to configure the workspace in each tenant, either in a central or distributed manner across regions, are not affected. You still will assess data residency, bandwidth costs, retention, and how your organization is structured for each tenant.

Table 2-2 lists the key criteria that need to be assessed when designing your workspace architecture. Each criterion is subsequently outlined in detail so that you may make educated design decisions relative to your environment.

Table 2-2. Design criteria for Multiple Workspaces

Design Criterion	Use Multiple Workspaces If...	Additional Inputs
Operational vs. Security Data	You have a security team that wants a standalone environment, or you do not want Sentinel pricing to apply to all operational data. Integrating Azure Monitor and Microsoft Sentinel into one workspace improves the visibility of data and ultimately the spectrum of correlational data. However, if you have a security team that wants isolation, or if you wish to avoid Sentinel pricing applied to operational log data, then it is worthwhile to operate separate workspaces. However, integrating an increase in sign-in workspaces will help fit in commitment tiers and lower costs when ingestion is high.	You have a security team that wants a standalone environment, or you do not want Sentinel pricing to apply to all operational data. Integrating Azure Monitor and Microsoft Sentinel into one workspace improves the visibility of data and ultimately the spectrum of correlational data. However, if you have a security team that wants isolation, or if you wish to avoid Sentinel pricing applied to operational log data, then it is worthwhile to operate separate workspaces. However, integrating an increase in sign-in workspaces will help fit in commitment tiers and lower costs when ingestion is high.
Multiple Azure Tenants	You operate across separate tenants (for example, for individual customers, business units, or partner-managed environments). For the most part, resources only push telemetry into a workspace in the same tenant. If you are managing multiple tenants for workloads (this is often the case with the MSP or enterprise group), then there will need to be at least one workspace per tenant. You may also plan on using Azure Lighthouse to provide ease of multi-tenant management.	You operate across separate tenants (for example, for individual customers, business units, or partner-managed environments). For the most part, resources only push telemetry into a workspace in the same tenant. If you are managing multiple tenants for workloads (this is often the case with the MSP or enterprise group), then there will need to be at least one workspace per tenant. You may also plan on using Azure Lighthouse to provide ease of multi-tenant management.

(*continued*)

Table 2-2. (*continued*)

Design Criterion	Use Multiple Workspaces If...	Additional Inputs
Data Residency (Regions)	Your organization has geographically or regulatory-bound data. For example, the US, the EU, and the UAE. Workspaces are also region-bound. If there are compliance aspects that dictate your data must reside within a region, you will need to plan for one workspace per region. In terms of the egress charges for cross-region data, they are generally minimal but can be reviewed in the Azure Pricing Calculator.	Your organization has geographically or regulatory-bound data. For example, the US, the EU, and the UAE. Workspaces are also region-bound. If there are compliance aspects that dictate your data must reside within a region, you will need to plan for one workspace per region. In terms of the egress charges for cross-region data, they are generally minimal but can be reviewed in the Azure Pricing Calculator.
Data Ownership	Separate business units or subsidiaries want to maintain ownership and access to isolated data. The creation of separate workspaces allows for the separate governance of multiple entities within the organization, which is beneficial concerning governance, privacy, and decentralized ownership. This is ideal when one subsidiary has its own IT and security team.	Separate business units or subsidiaries want to maintain ownership and access to isolated data. The creation of separate workspaces allows for the separate governance of multiple entities within the organization, which is beneficial concerning governance, privacy, and decentralized ownership. This is ideal when one subsidiary has its own IT and security team.

(*continued*)

Table 2-2. (*continued*)

Design Criterion	Use Multiple Workspaces If...	Additional Inputs
Split Billing	You need to track costs by department, project, or external client (e.g., chargeback). Azure Cost Management provides views by workspace. If that depth of granularity is still not ideal for you, separating across workspaces can allow you to better separate costs by billing entity. You could also have a chargeback model based solely on log queries for each subscription or resource group utilization.	You need to track costs by department, project, or external client (e.g., chargeback). Azure Cost Management provides views by workspace. If that depth of granularity is still not ideal for you, separating across workspaces can allow you to better separate costs by billing entity. You could also have a chargeback model based solely on log queries for each subscription or resource group utilization.
Data Retention Policies	The type of data, tables, or compliance zones dictates retention. You can configure retention by table for a workspace. However, if you need dissimilar policies for tables or services, it's advisable to have separate workspaces. For instance, security audit data requires a much larger retention than a performance log, which is within compliance limits.	The type of data, tables, or compliance zones dictates retention. You can configure retention by table for a workspace. However, if you need dissimilar policies for tables or services, it's advisable to have separate workspaces. For instance, security audit data requires a much larger retention than a performance log, which is within compliance limits.

(*continued*)

Table 2-2. (*continued*)

Design Criterion	Use Multiple Workspaces If...	Additional Inputs
Ingestion Commitment Tiers	You want to consolidate ingestion volumes to take advantage of volume-based pricing costs. Consolidating ingestion to a single workspace will help you get into Microsoft's daily utilization tiers when applicable. This will reduce overall ingestion costs, or if the workspaces are in dedicated clusters, you can share those tiers within and across tenants or regions, if that is an issue. The 100GB/day tier can make a significant difference in costs.	You want to consolidate ingestion volumes to take advantage of volume-based pricing costs. Consolidating ingestion to a single workspace will help you get into Microsoft's daily utilization tiers when applicable. This will reduce overall ingestion costs, or if the workspaces are in dedicated clusters, you can share those tiers within and across tenants or regions, if that is an issue. The 100GB/day tier can make a significant difference in costs.
Legacy Agent Limitations	Your Linux servers are running the legacy Log Analytics agent, which supports only one workspace. In contrast, Windows agents can connect to multiple workspaces. However, the Linux legacy agent does not have this feature. You could move those Linux machines to be Azure Monitor Agent (AMA)-capable agents or accept the limitation of having to use only one workspace per separate Linux environment.	Your Linux servers are running the legacy Log Analytics agent, which supports only one workspace. In contrast, Windows agents can connect to multiple workspaces. However, the Linux legacy agent does not have this feature. You could move those Linux machines to be Azure Monitor Agent (AMA)-capable agents or accept the limitation of having to use only one workspace per separate Linux environment.

(*continued*)

Table 2-2. (*continued*)

Design Criterion	Use Multiple Workspaces If...	Additional Inputs
Data Access Control	You need granular access control down to tables or RBAC roles. RBAC at the resource and table levels provides the necessary controls over who can access what resources. You could use the table-level RBAC to filter out security logs from users who are not business users while providing access to operational logs. Alternatively, you could use separate workspaces to compartmentalize data that, on some level, simplifies access models.	You need granular access control down to tables or RBAC roles. RBAC at the resource and table levels provides the necessary controls over who can access what resources. You could use the table-level RBAC to filter out security logs from users who are not business users while providing access to operational logs. Alternatively, you could use separate workspaces to compartmentalize data that, on some level, simplifies access models.
Resilience	You want to maintain the business continuity of the deployments of workspaces in the event of regional Azure outages. A multi-region powered workspace deployment will support data availability in disaster scenarios. Also, while you can prioritize getting as much ingestion volume duplicated for cost containment in the subscription factor, please remember some dependent resources (e.g., alerts, workbooks) don't move or failover automatically. It may be a good idea to archive the ARM templates you use in DevOps for recovery.	You want to maintain the business continuity of the deployments of workspaces in the event of regional Azure outages. A multi-region powered workspace deployment will support data availability in disaster scenarios. Also, while you can prioritize getting as much ingestion volume duplicated for cost containment in the subscription factor, please remember some dependent resources (e.g., alerts, workbooks) don't move or failover automatically. It may be a good idea to archive the ARM templates you use in DevOps for recovery.

There is no single decision that is correct for designing your workspace architecture for Azure Monitor and Microsoft Sentinel; it requires a thorough analysis of the size and needs of your organization from a regulatory perspective, team structure, and cost-optimized model. Start simple, then build it with intent and clarity using the markers and guidance.

Managing Workspaces Across Multiple Azure Tenants: Strategy Overview

In enterprise-level or service provider scenarios, organizations frequently manage multiple Azure tenants, whether for different internal business units, different subsidiaries, or external customers. Microsoft Sentinel and Azure Monitor provide flexible architecture models for multi-tenant capabilities.

Common entities in this area include Managed Service Providers (MSPs), Independent Software Vendors (ISVs), and large multinational enterprises. These environments include models that require centralized teams to access and operate across workspaces in various tenants, where each Azure tenant could be governed by different security, compliance, and billing models.

To allow cross-tenant monitoring and administration, Microsoft offers three main approaches:

- *Distributed Architecture*: Each tenant has its own workspace, with cross-tenant access managed in either Azure Lighthouse or guest accounts.

- *Centralized Architecture*: A workspace in the provider's tenant receives logs from multiple tenants.

- *Hybrid Architecture*: Hybrid model of the previous two—each tenant has their own local workspace, while selected or aggregated data can be pulled up into a main workspace to perform analysis or reporting.

Table 2-3 compares these three strategies based on key operational, security, and scalability criteria.

Table 2-3. *Key Operational, Security, and Scalability Criteria of Workspaces*

Criteria	Distributed Architecture	Centralized Architecture	Hybrid Architecture
Workspace Location	One workspace for each customer tenant	Single workspace in service provider tenant	Workspace by tenant + central workspace
Log Collection Scope	All resource types (VMs, PaaS, SaaS, and Azure services)	VM and Azure PaaS only through diagnostic settings	Select logs or aggregated metrics from distributed tenants.
Admin Access Method	Azure Lighthouse or Entra B2B guest users	Full access through service provider tenant	Azure Lighthouse or APIs/scripts for central synchronization
Customer Data Isolation	High—Separate workspaces, and have data policy and billing isolation.	Low—All customer data is in a shared workspace	Moderate—Operational workspaces are isolated while centralized data is aggregated
Customization (Retention, RBAC, and Pricing Tiers)	Per customer workspace—Full access flexibility	Shared by all customers (same retention, tier, and region)	Per tenant workspace + custom synchronization to central workspace
Cross-Tenant Analytics	Challenging across a lot of workspaces (> 100) because of the query scale limitations	Easy—All in one place	Central workspace allows for optimized summary analytics
Operational Overhead	High—Onboarding and managing many tenants is very complex	Low—Easy to have single central management	Moderate—Need for an added integration mechanism
Scalability for Querying	Limited—Cross workspace query performance starts degrading after ~100 workspaces	High—All customer data is in one workspace	The central workspace was optimized, but initial data collection adds complexity

(continued)

Table 2-3. (*continued*)

Criteria	Distributed Architecture	Centralized Architecture	Hybrid Architecture
Billing Ownership	Each customer pays for their workspace and usage	The service provider owns all billing	The customer pays for their own workspace, but the provider owns the costs to the central workspace
Use Case Suitability	MSPs needing customer isolation and full monitoring	SMEs or internal teams wanting simplicity	Enterprise-scale MSPs or ISVs requiring deep detail reporting and independence of tenant

Additional Considerations

- *Azure Lighthouse*: Recommended for MSPs and central teams to securely manage multiple tenants without switching accounts or guest identities having to refer to users from other tenants.

- *Log Query API and Ingestion API*: Automation of centralized queries and logs into multiple centralized workspaces.

- *Data Retention Strategy*: Retention strategy set by workspace; centralization makes for easier long-term retention strategies but comes at the cost of flexibility/access to older logs.

- *Power BI*: An excellent option for reporting across aggregate data from multiple tenant workspaces without the need to move logs.

Migrating to Microsoft Sentinel

The sophistication of cyber threats that organizations are facing is demanding that businesses secure scalable, intelligent, cloud-native security solutions as quickly as possible. Microsoft Sentinel, as a modern Security Information and Event Management (SIEM) and Security Orchestration, Automation, and Response (SOAR) solution, provides a robust platform for centralizing threat detections, investigation, and response across your enterprise, regardless of your hybrid, cloud, or on-premises strategy. The overall shift to Microsoft Sentinel is a strategic shift to leverage artificial intelligence, automation, and integrated threat intelligence to transform your decision-making processes around security operations. Migrating to Microsoft Sentinel allows security teams to centralize logs, recognize relationships between alerts from various sources, and orchestrate incident response all within one unified interface in the Microsoft Defender portal.

However, migrating to Microsoft Sentinel is not simply a lift and shift of your existing tools and processes. Careful planning around the environment components intended for migration, your organization's strategic business objectives, compliance requirements, budget, and legacy systems is required to make appropriate decisions regarding your planning and processes. When transitioning away from a legacy SIEM, migrating to a single log source from multiple log sources, or scaling your cloud security posture, migration often catalyzes opportunities to refine, modernize, and automate security operations in the technology environment.

Table 2-4 lists the key approach stages of a successful migration to Microsoft Sentinel.

Table 2-4. Approach of Migration to Microsoft Sentinel

Approach Stage	Description
Assessing Current SIEM Capabilities and Data Sources	Review your current SIEM solution to gain insight into its strengths, weaknesses, and current data ingestion operational processes. Make a note of critical log sources (e.g., firewalls, identity and access systems, endpoints, cloud services, etc.), any volume spikes or trends, and any use cases that must remain or improve in Sentinel. This process is carried out to inform scoping and priorities for the migration process.
Defining a Target Architecture for Sentinel Workspaces	Design the future state of your Sentinel deployment. Their connected plans include establishing a workspace model (centralized vs. distributed), tenant considerations, regions of preference, and how integration works with Microsoft Defender and any other tools. Part of this phase also involves addressing architectural uniformity about organizational, regulatory, and multicloud considerations.

(*continued*)

Table 2-4. (*continued*)

Approach Stage	Description
Designing for Performance, Compliance, and Cost-Efficiency	Optimize workspace configurations for performance, expandability, and legal compliance. You will need to implement retention policies to capture the right commitment tiers, thereby understanding future ingress and storage costs. This should be done while considering data residency laws at the regional and access level, as well as ownership boundaries.
Planning and Executing Data Ingestion from Diverse Sources	Select and onboard data connectors based on the required priorities. This includes native Microsoft connectors (Microsoft 365, Microsoft Defender, and Azure), third-party security appliances, and on-prem infrastructure. Where needed, consider Log Analytics agents, Azure Monitor, or using custom ingestion processes with APIs and Logic Apps.
Implementing Detection Rules, Workbooks, and Playbooks	Translate security use cases into Sentinel-native solutions: deploy analytics rules (for alerting), workbooks (for dashboards and visualizations), and playbooks (for automatic responses using Logic Apps). Use Microsoft's rule templates and customize or use a portion of them, considering any risks your organization might have.
Validating Success Through Incident Response and Reporting	Test and refine incident management workflows. Ensure you are producing actionable alerts, triaging incidents properly, and that automation response processes are working as expected. Produce reports and dashboards that are meaningful to track performance, coverage, and efficiency improvements across your SOC.

Phases of Migration

Moving to Microsoft Sentinel is an essential step in modernizing a security operations center (SOC) and is critical to preparing an organization for advanced cyber threats. Microsoft Sentinel is a cloud-native security information and event management (SIEM) and security orchestration, automation, and response (SOAR) solution. Microsoft Sentinel provides automation, scale, and depth of threat analytics that security teams can take advantage of. Organizations need to adopt a structured, phased approach that will help facilitate a straightforward and effective migration period. Figure 2-4 depicts the four required phases—Discovery, Design, Implement, and Operationalize—and an overview of the key activities and deliverables in each phase.

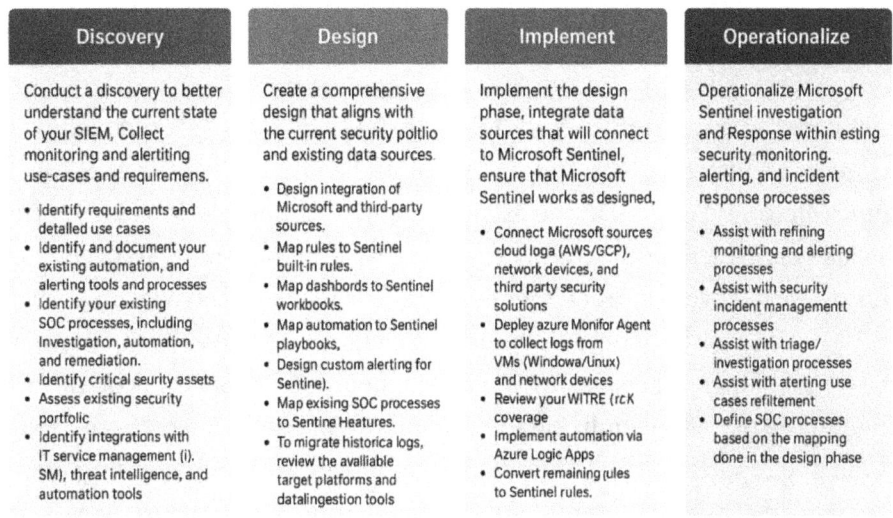

Figure 2-4. Phase of Migration to Microsoft Sentinel

Phase 1: Discovery

The program begins with the Discovery phase, where organizations work with their current SIEM to conduct a comprehensive assessment of their SIEM environment. The main objective is to gain a thorough understanding of the current environment, including all operational and technical dependencies. During the Discovery phase, teams identify the security requirements, use cases, and SIEM use cases that presently drive any monitoring and response workflows. They document existing tools, scripts, and configurations for the monitoring, alerting, remediation, and automation, as well as document existing processes of SOC analysts for detection and response.

This includes identifying critical security assets (high-value servers, endpoints, databases, workloads running in the cloud, etc.) that will be monitored continuously. Security architects will also review their broader security portfolio, looking for integration points such as IT Service Management (ITSM) platforms, threat intelligence feeds, and any custom or third-party automation tools.

Discovery phase deliverables include the project plan document, current-state analysis report, business and technical requirements documentation, and a complete list of monitoring and alerting use cases that will be migrated to Sentinel.

Phase 2: Design

After understanding the current environment, in the Design phase, organizations will develop the architecture that governs the centralized security processes that will now include Microsoft Sentinel in the existing security technology landscape. The teams will also plan the ingestion of Microsoft-native and third-party data sources during this phase to ensure correct integration. Security teams can also analyze their existing SIEM rules against Sentinel's built-in analytics rules to establish commonality in detection capabilities. Likewise, historical dashboards from previous platforms are represented in the same way, utilizing the capabilities of Sentinel workbooks to maintain visualization and reporting. The automation of reporting and dashboarding is an essential consideration in this stage. Current remediation and response workflows map to Sentinel playbooks, with Azure Logic Apps orchestrating automated tasks. Any custom alerting functionality is created to meet the specific needs of the client. Security teams also examine legacy SOC processes and map them to Sentinel capabilities to create an organized, repeatable operational outcome.

If historical logs must be maintained, the team will decide on options for migrating that log data into Sentinel. The team will focus on ingestion methods, retention costs, and compliance methods.

The Design phase concluded with design workshops documented, solution designs created, and integration plans that span ingestion methods, automation, and custom alerting logic.

Phase 3: Implement

With a validated design, the next phase, Implement, focuses on implementing the migration plan. This will include the technical configuration of Microsoft Sentinel and the onboarding of Microsoft or third-party data sources. Initial onboarding will focus on establishing connections to native Microsoft platforms, first connecting Azure, then Microsoft 365, along with other cloud providers such as AWS or GCP. On sharing security components and operations, network devices, endpoint detection tools, and third-party security platforms will be integrated into the Sentinel ingestion pipeline.

Before collecting system-level logs, the Azure Monitor agent will be deployed to Windows and Linux machines to enable Sentinel ingestion with the telemetry from all relevant endpoints in real-time.

Phase 4: Operationalize

The final phase, Operationalize, addresses the intent for Microsoft Sentinel to be part of the organization's daily security operations. The SOC team will continue to refine the overall monitoring and alerting workflows to be in alignment with the new telemetry being ingested into Microsoft Sentinel and the latest detection logic that is being put in place across all use cases. These workflows and detection logic will ultimately refine incident response processes without losing valuable detection processes and integral options afforded by Sentinel automation.

Support will be provided to the analysts about tuning alert thresholds, validating incident correlation logic, and tuning response playbooks. The SOC team will have time to become accustomed to the new system and its capabilities. There are numerous review materials at the analysts' disposal across the Microsoft community of use cases, blogs, courses, and review sites for ongoing operational continuity and improvements. The SOC team provides a structured approach to align and adjust triage and investigation processes and workflows with identification, investigation, and hunting via Sentinel.

The overall objective will be to leverage all of Sentinel's advanced features, including its investigation tools, to achieve faster incident response and reduce alert fatigue.

Critical to the success of the Operationalization phase, the SOC team will need to finalize and document operating procedures built from our mappings and process design through previous phases. This will not only allow for the institutionalization of the demonstration to the operational phase but also toward achieving long-term sustainability of the designated operation. The key deliverables achieved will be the finalized documentation of the configuration of Sentinel, including all workbooks, playbooks, custom alerts, and KQL (Kusto Query Language) queries developed for both hunting and incident correlation.

Achieving the Sentinel Advantage

Moving into Microsoft Sentinel is more than a technical deployment. It is a strategic move from one security operations model to a wholly different model. During the incremental and deliberate phases of Discovery, Design, Implementation, and Operationalization, any organization can minimize operational risk during the transition. This unique receptiveness throughout the phased SOC development process allows the SOC to take advantage of the agility associated with cloud-based ideas optimally, demonstrated through advanced analytics and detection automation, which was the foundation of the Microsoft Sentinel design.

With the appropriate organization-backed support on capability building and expertise to carefully plan and create an SOC development strategy, the transformation to Microsoft Sentinel will take security operations into a modern, responsive, intelligence defens e platform of the future.

Optimized Data Collection

The optimization of data collection regarding Microsoft Sentinel is crucial to impact cost-effectiveness and operational effectiveness as a security operations center (SOC). Microsoft Sentinel is a cloud-native SIEM that operates on a pay-per-ingestion pricing model, so it is imperative to maximize the quantity and quality of data being ingested. The first step is determining which data sources will help meet your threat detection objectives. Not every log is useful: many logs may be redundant, infrequently used, or, depending on the quantity of data that can be ingested, wasted resources. After determining your priority and high-value telemetry usage, it is critical to keep the overall cost of data ingestion in line with the security impact.

If you consider data collection optimization techniques, one such method is to use Sentinel's data connectors effectively. Microsoft Sentinel has native data connectors for many Microsoft and non-Microsoft platforms. Sentinel also provides many, if not all, of the data connectors with built-in filters/settings to give teams more control over the amounts and types of data that will be sent to the workspace. An example of utilizing the bandwidth allotment is the onboarding process for Office 365 logs. When an administrator is onboarding the logs from Office 365, there is an option to configure filters to only onboard specific workloads, such as Exchange Online, SharePoint, or any other workloads you want to collect telemetry from, eliminating the ingestion of

CHAPTER 2 ARCHITECTING AND DEPLOYING MICROSOFT SENTINEL

less critical telemetry. Configuring diagnostic settings in Azure Monitor using Azure Diagnostics enables teams to selectively send their preferred metrics or logs when using resources like Azure VM, Azure SQL, or Key Vaults, thereby avoiding the transmission of unnecessary data.

Another optimization use case involves examining Basic Logs and Archive Logs for long-term retention at a lower cost. Not every log data has to be queried in real time and/or repeatedly (unless it's related to compliance). You can transfer less critical data to a lower-tiered data retention option, enabling on-demand access when required. This means that not only can you reduce your ingestion costs, but your long-term retention costs will also be lower. Log sampling could also be done, where you report only a sampled portion of verbose logs, for example, DNS logs or proxy events. If you lack patience for slow queries and/or your threat detection requires more diplomatic decisions than negotiation, it is easier to stay on top of adequate ingestion volume versus affordability versus visibility.

Automating data collection can also enhance data collection optimization when implemented correctly. Sentinel will allow you to create Log Analytics workspace data collection rules (DCRs) to control data flows and transformations before ingestion. Your DCRs enable teams to apply filters, transformations, and conditional logic, only ingesting the data they need. As a bonus, policy retention combined with schedule data purge policies means that teams trying to develop "knowledge" won't keep unnecessary storage records along with their data anyway, which directly improves both cost and performance.

Lastly, you should incorporate an ongoing evaluation and tuning of your ingestion strategy to ensure it is on track. This involves auditing your log volume, ingestion cost, and query patterns periodically. Sentinel's built-in cost analysis tools and usage reports functionality enable SOC managers (those with complete data control) to identify which data source and/or table is consuming the most resources. Based on the SOC manager's value in data sources and data control, the team can adjust collection settings, discontinue connector usage, and consolidate data sources simultaneously, provided the data sources were relevant in a previous context. You should keep in mind that the data source you ingest should be sustainable, practical, and pertinent to distinguish impact from external events, industry trends, and friendly-faced threats, considering the evolving socio-political landscape.

Best Practices for Data Collection in Microsoft Sentinel

Effective data collection is crucial when using Microsoft Sentinel because it directly impacts both the quality of threat detection and the eventual cost. It's essential to be strategic in the data you collect to effectively take advantage of Sentinel without weighing down your workspace or overspending on data collection and storage. Deciding on the data you want to collect, filtering, and ultimately, making sure the data is aligned to your organization's monitoring goals is crucial. Figure 2-5 depicts the four best pratices—Prioritizing and Filtering Log Data, Handling Special Data Collection Scenarios, Working with Custom and Operational Logs, and Collecting from Cloud and Endpoint Sources.

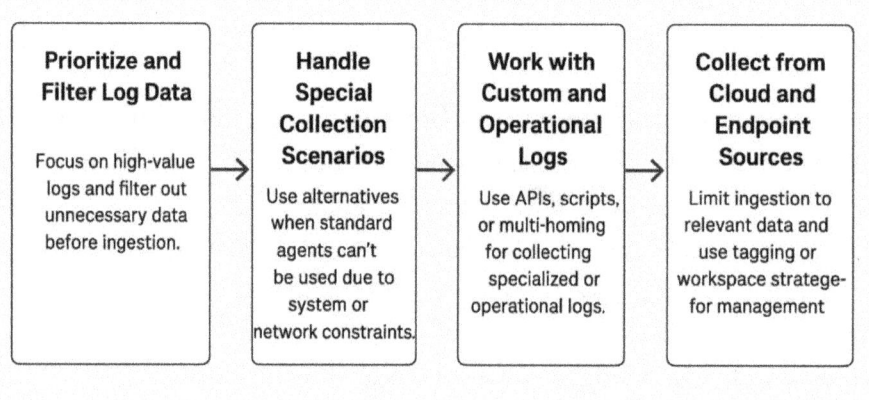

Figure 2-5. Best Practices for Data Collection in Microsoft Sentinel

Prioritizing and Filtering Log Data

When optimizing data sources and the ingestion of log data, the first step is to determine what logs are valuable or useful. Not all logs are created equal; some turn out to be noise, while others can become a critical piece of security insight. Creating rules to embrace or accept an inclusive plan of action for log visibility, reducing your ingestion size by only accepting high-value data—such as firewall traffic, authentication logs, endpoint alerts, and identity-related events—helps maintain visibility into your environment while also reducing the ingestion size.

Filtering log data within your data sources should happen close to the beginning of the pipeline. There are options to filter logs and reduce ingestion size, such as properly configuring your agents, like the Azure Monitor Agent, to collect specific events from Windows and Linux computers, as well as using other tools like Logstash to modify or remove log content before it reaches Sentinel. This may be necessary for systems that produce a lot of content in logs (Syslog/CEF), and the filtering happens on local systems, but there are limitations for presentation formats. And finally, if you filter logs or make custom-formatted logs, as opposed to semi-structured logs, or use Logstash, don't expect certain built-in features (i.e., if you change logs to custom formatting to retain data in different data models) to work with features such as machine learning or entity behavior analytics. Each time you change a log (or reformat) to a custom format in a custom way, you have to include this change in rules and workbooks manually.

Handling Special Data Collection Scenarios

Sometimes an organization cannot make use of standard agents and connectors. Network structures, system functionality, or custom logging requirements may force the situation. For instance, if an organization cannot install agents to stop or collect logged data, alternatives such as Windows Event Forwarding or Syslog forwarders for Linux machines can be used to collect event data in a centralized and secure manner. When your systems operate in air-gapped or restricted environments, where they cannot access the public internet, consider collecting logs via the Log Analytics gateway to gather logs securely without compromising external exposure or visibility. In some environments, you may need to tag data by region, department, or environment to enable better filtering and analysis as required. Tagging can often be accomplished at ingestion by injecting metadata, such as resource IDs, using tools like Logstash or other deployment templates. When the data is tagged, separate workspaces can be created for the various departments or tenants to allow for better separation and access control. Still, in some situations, this only increases ingestion costs.

Working with Custom and Operational Logs

All environments produce custom logs that are not easily organized into standard logs, either. Some examples of custom logs may be logs from third-party applications, internal tools, or specific monitoring agents. Collecting this type of data may involve API-based ingestion, PowerShell scripts, or simply placing logs into an observed directory. These methods can be effective but generally depend on developer work to ensure that the data is structured as needed, ingested accurately, and possibly structured in a way that is supportive of the analytic capabilities of Sentinel and its analytic models.

If there is a need to distinguish operational logs (i.e., system health and performance) from security logs (i.e., authentication failure), some examples of where you need to collect the log files so that you can determine in Sentinel which operational logs correspond to security violations. In this case, Sentinel supports multi-homing to multiple workspaces through the Azure Monitor Agent. This means you can send data from a machine to various workspaces, allowing for neat separation and analysis based on log type.

Collecting from Cloud and Endpoint Sources

There are also considerations for organizations deploying endpoint detection solutions or for those with multiple cloud environments. Data from Microsoft Defender can be obtained using built-in Sentinel connectors. Logs and/or other extended EDR telemetry are preferably obtained via Windows Event Forwarding. Each cloud platform, such as AWS or GCP, can use connectors. It's best practice to bring in only what you need; however, tagging and resource enrichment of the cloud data upon ingestion can assist with tracking by cloud ingestion origin. The adage, "if you ingest it, you own it," applies to these enhancements, so be careful about the addition of tools that potentially lead to costs around processing and storage.

When monitoring Microsoft applications, such as MS Office telemetry (Teams usage) and phishing reports, you may be combining the use of out-of-the-box connectors with scripts or API endpoints that allow you to ingest and relate raw event data holistically. Suppose you are supporting a large or federated environment. In that case, you may develop a custom workspace strategy and use tags or grouping incident entities to maintain context across employees, departments, or tenants.

Understanding Data Connectors in Microsoft Sentinel

Within modern security operations, the value of an organization's SIEM system is tied to the amount and quality of data ingested. Microsoft Sentinel operates as a cloud-native SIEM and SOAR solution to easily integrate multiple data sources in hybrid and multi-cloud environments through the engagement of data connectors for the rapidly growing catalog of connectors.

This section will discuss the definition of data connectors in Microsoft Sentinel, detail their types and use cases, and describe their role(s) in security monitoring and threat detection.

What Is a Data Connector?

In Microsoft Sentinel, data connectors are predefined or configurable mechanisms that allow Sentinel to collect data from public or private systems. Data connectors are leveraged to bring logs, telemetry, events, and alerts into Azure Monitor's Log Analytics workspace, where data is processed and analyzed by Sentinel.

Data connectors are the key component of defining a monitoring strategy for Sentinel and are the bridge between Sentinel and the asset or service being monitored. This could include user sign-ins from Microsoft Entra ID (formerly Azure AD), alerts from third-party firewall appliances, or threat intelligence from a provider. Data connectors enable standardized, secure, and efficient data collection processes. The Purpose of Data Connectors

In Sentinel, data connectors are essentially ways to ingest and collect security data from an unlimited number of different environments. The key roles for data connectors are

- To aggregate security visibility from Microsoft and non-Microsoft environments.

- To normalize data into a compliant schema to support analysis and querying.

- To support automation for investigation and incident response workstreams.

- To enable data correlation across multiple sources to be able to raise alerts for advanced threats.

Connectors are the first step to reliable data ingestion and thus usable, meaningful detections, alerts, dashboards, and incident response.

Types of Data Connectors

Microsoft Sentinel has a great range of connectors available to support all types of data sources, including cloud platforms, on-premise servers, Software as a Service (SaaS), and network devices. There are further data connectors categorized in Table 2-5.

Table 2-5. Types of Data Connectors

Connector Type	Description
Microsoft-native connectors	Collect telemetry not only for Microsoft services (i.e., Entra ID, Defender, and Office 365), but also from sources like AWS, Cisco, Palo Alto Networks, etc.
Third-party connectors	Integrate standardized protocols (such as firewalls, IDS/IPS, and appliances).
Syslog and CEF connectors	Use "prebuilt" templates as an integration tool, whether it uses polling or API calls. Little to no custom code required
Codeless Connector Framework (CCF)	Integrate custom-managed or unsupported sources using Azure Functions, Logic Apps, or REST APIs.
Custom connectors	Collect telemetry not only for Microsoft services (i.e., Entra ID, Defender, and Office 365), but also from sources like AWS, Cisco, Palo Alto Networks, etc.

Every type of connector is meant to give you flexibility and scalability to match data ingestion to business needs.

Common Use Cases

Data connectors facilitate a wide range of security and operational use cases, including:

- *Identity Monitoring*: Collecting sign-in and audit logs from Microsoft Entra ID to identify suspicious access.

- *Cloud Security Monitoring*: Ingesting GuardDuty and S3 WAF logs from AWS into Sentinel for multi-cloud visibility into workflow.

- *Email Security*: Building upon data from threat report providers like Mimecast or Proofpoint to better detect phishing.

- *Custom Applications*: Ingest logs from proprietary platforms or legacy systems using a REST API or Azure Function.

- *Threat Intelligence*: Enriching incidents with external threat feeds via TAXII or other commercial feeds.

These use cases demonstrate how connectors provide Sentinel with the necessary context to become a data-expanded SIEM platform.

How Data Connectors Work

The following list describes the steps involved in enabling and working with a data connector to onboard your data source:

- *Discovery and Selection*: To find the connector for your data source, search the Sentinel connector gallery.

- *Configuration and Authentication*: You will be required to configure the connector to your environment with the required credentials, API keys, or OAuth tokens. Many of the Microsoft connectors offer a guided setup experience to help you with this step.

- *Ingestion*: When successfully configured, the logs will start to flow into the Log Analytics workspace attached to Sentinel.

- *Normalization and Parsing*: The ingested data can be normalized to Microsoft's schema, utilizing schemas like ASIM (Advanced Security Information Model) that Microsoft built in for third-party systems. The data must be normalized so that you can easily leverage built-in queries, built-in detection rules, and built-in visualizations.

- *Utilization*: Analysts can now use the data to write KQL queries, build alerts, build dashboards, and start to enable automation through Sentinel's playbooks and analytics rules.

Benefits of Using Sentinel Connectors

Connectors provide a wide range of operational and strategic advantages:

- *Scalability*: Easily add dozens or hundreds of systems with little configuration.
- *Customization*: Ability to extend using Azure-native tools.
- *Ecosystem Integration*: Microsoft Defender XDR, Logic Apps, and third-party APIs are all integrated.
- *Security and Compliance*: Can be integrated into Microsoft Defender XDR and Logic Apps and can be connected with third-party APIs.

With the appropriate combination of data connectors, security teams can quickly realize the full capabilities of Sentinel as a unified solution for security monitoring.

Data connectors are the lifeblood of Microsoft Sentinel. They will allow you to take fragmented, siloed security data and change that into unified insights by providing a continuous flow of items into Sentinel's analytics engine. Data connectors form the foundation of an effective, scalable, and resilient SIEM deployment, whether your organization is plugging in Microsoft services, third-party platforms, or custom applications.

Integrating Threat Intelligence

Threat intelligence is critical for improving an organization's security posture. It gives organizations contextualized, actionable information about malicious activity, threats, and adversaries. Threat intelligence comes through Microsoft Sentinel as a cloud-native SIEM to enrich data, enable analytics, and automate reactions. This section examines how threat intelligence flows into Sentinel and how it gets implemented in the tool.

Threat Intelligence Integration: Overview

An overview of how threat intelligence is integrated into Microsoft Sentinel. At a high level, as listed below, this integration allows for

- The raw telemetry is to be enriched with threat indicators (IOCs).
- Real-time detection of known malicious entities.
- Automated responses based on threat classifications.
- Correlation of internal activity to some external malicious actor's behavior.

Table 2-6 lists the stages in the threat intelligence pipeline.

Table 2-6. Stages of Threat Intelligence Pipeline

Component	Role
Threat Intelligence Feeds	These include commercial, open-source, and community feeds like TAXII, Microsoft Threat Intelligence, and third-party providers.
Microsoft Sentinel	Central SIEM engine where threat intelligence is ingested and analyzed.
TI Connectors/API Ingestion	Data is brought into Sentinel through the Threat Intelligence—TAXII connector or via the Threat Intelligence Upload API.
Log Analytics Workspace	Acts as the central repository, storing all threat indicators and telemetry data from other sources.
Analytics Rules and Hunting	Uses threat intelligence indicators to create detection rules and queries that match against ingested data.
Investigation and Response	Sentinel provides workbooks, playbooks, and investigation graphs that help analysts understand the context and respond quickly.

Operational Use Cases

Post integration of threat intelligence, organizations will be able to

- Correlate logs for IPs, URLs, domains, and file hashes to known bad indicators.
- Trigger alerts for events that have matching indicators.
- Visualize threats in dashboards using specific workbooks.
- Automate response actions, such as blocking IPs or isolating endpoints, using SOAR playbooks.

Sources of Threat Intelligence

Microsoft Sentinel supports the ingestion of TI from a range of sources, including

- Microsoft Defender for Threat Intelligence.
- Commercially provided TI subscriptions (e.g., Recorded Future and Anomali).
- Open source intelligence feeds for TAXII.
- Custom/manual uploads via the TI API.

This range of sources provides security teams both breadth and depth in their view of the global threat landscape.

The integration of threat intelligence into Microsoft Sentinel will not only enhance the quality of detections but also evolve organizations from a reactive to a proactive defense posture. It gives SOC teams more insights that are timely, relevant, and contextual, thereby enabling them to take actions that will reduce the dwell times of threats.

Understanding Cyber Threat Intelligence (CTI)

In an ever-changing threat landscape, organizations must take a proactive approach toward developing a protective stance against digital technology systems. Organizations cannot simply rely on reactive knowledge; they require proactive knowledge that helps identify, mitigate, and respond to potential cyberattacks. Cyber Threat Intelligence (CTI) is a component that allows organizations to do just that.

Cyber Threat Intelligence is an umbrella term to describe the information that illuminates either current and/or impending threats against digital systems, users, and infrastructures. The CTI can provide a panoramic view of threat activity, such as reports that describe adversary motivation and capability, as well as fine details of compromise indicators, such as IP addresses, domain names, and file hashes.

The primary objective of CTI is to provide context to security operations, making it possible for security analysts or automated systems to recognize suspicious activity with context, properly attribute threats, and be able to respond to protect organizational assets as soon as possible.

Sources of Cyber Threat Intelligence

CTI can be gathered and disseminated in many different ways and can include many kinds of viewpoints and details about threats:

- *Open-Source Intelligence (OSINT)*: Publicly available threat data that is published by trustworthy communities and platforms.

- *Threat Intelligence Sharing Communities*: Groups of organizations sharing threat observations and attitudes to facilitate collective threat understanding.

- *Commercial Threat Feeds*: Vendors supply curated, paid, and sometimes actionable or timely threat intelligence.

- *Internal Investigations*: Threat indicators and patterns identified during your firm's own security encampments and incident response processes.

Types of Threat Intelligence in Microsoft Sentinel

In Microsoft Sentinel—a cloud-native SIEM and SOAR solution—CTI is typically employed via threat indicators, often known as Indicators of Compromise (IOCs) or Indicators of Attack (IOAs). Some of these indicators are observable objects, such as

- Malicious URLs or domain names
- Suspicious or known bad IP addresses
- File hashes related to malware samples
- Email addresses—or their user agents—related to phishing campaigns

This type of intelligence is also referred to as tactical threat intelligence. Typically, it is consumed within automated threat detection and correlation engines to identify and react to known threats at scale.

Threat intelligence can also include behavioral and contextual elements of threat actors, such as the Tactics, Techniques, and Procedures (TTPs) of attackers, the infrastructure they utilized to conduct their campaign, and the industries or victim profiles. In Microsoft Sentinel, the structured CTI is represented in the Structured Threat Information eXpression (STIX) format, which is a common and open standard for the representation and exchange of threat intelligence. STIX objects allow organizations not just to model observable data but also relationships across different threat objects, creating a complete picture of attacks.

When STIX-based threat intelligence is utilized in Microsoft Sentinel, it allows for:

- Better advanced alert correlation with actor behavior
- Fast threat-hunting in historical or live datasets
- Better context for incident investigation or response

Putting Threat Intelligence into Action in Microsoft Sentinel

To ensure that organizations obtain maximum value from CTI data, Microsoft Sentinel provides wrap-around capabilities within the Microsoft Sentinel environment for storing, managing, and better employing threat intelligence. Table 2-7 shows the high-level phases of the integration and operationalization of CTI to the Microsoft Sentinel environment.

Table 2-7. *Action List in Microsoft Sentinel*

Action	Description
Store threat intelligence in Microsoft Sentinel	Utilize threat intelligence from different platforms utilizing the built-in connector to gain threat intelligence from both third-party threat feeds and custom data sources using the Threat Intelligence Upload API, as well as external threat intelligence platforms, commercial threat feeds, or homegrown applications, utilizing either a direct API integration or regular ingestion of related data.
Connect threat intelligence sources	Utilize Sentinel's management interface to create new threat indicators either manually or using automated processes. Use tagging, organization, and contextual association of indicators with metadata to help provide clarity and make searching and understanding threats easier to navigate.
Create and manage threat indicators	Utilize Kusto Query Language (KQL) and search capabilities to navigate through imported CTI, and use workbooks to visualize the data and identify trends and patterns of threats.

(*continued*)

Table 2-7. (*continued*)

Action	Description
Query and visualize intelligence	Utilize analytic rule templates available in Sentinel, built-in analytics that leverage threat indicators to identify alerts of malicious activity, and automatically create and trigger security alerts or incidents based on configured iDetection and iResponse sensitivity levels.
Detect threats using threat intelligence	Utilize threat intelligence in proactive threat hunting queries to identify unknown and emerging threats in your environment.
Hunt for threats	Utilize contextual threat intelligence to help add context during investigations, understand attacker behaviors, prioritize response actions, and improve engagement with stakeholders.
Inform incident response	Utilize threat intelligence from different platforms utilizing the built-in connector to gain threat intelligence from both third-party threat feeds and custom data sources using the Threat Intelligence Upload API, as well as external threat intelligence platforms, commercial threat feeds, or homegrown applications, utilizing either a direct API integration or regular ingestion of related data.

Cyber Threat Intelligence is a critical layer for today's security operations. When merged with Microsoft Sentinel, CTI improves both administrative detection and response while empowering security teams to take informed and aggressive action. Whether coming from a global view or internal investigations, CTI transforms a raw telemetry feed into usable context, allowing organizations to stay ahead of threat actors.

Threat intelligence is only meaningful when it is actionable or automatically correlated with security events and used to inform detection, investigation, and response. Microsoft Sentinel, a cloud-native SIEM and SOAR solution, can connect with multiple threat intelligence platforms, allowing organizations to ingest, curate, and act on real-time threat indicators and contextual data from both internal and trusted external sources.

Organizations can integrate third-party threat intelligence solutions that enhance Sentinel's detection capabilities, improve alert quality, and inform more proactive threat hunting activity. Some integrations utilize specific connectors within Microsoft Sentinel, while others leverage Azure Logic Apps, the Microsoft Graph Security API, or custom ingestion methods like TAXII servers or REST APIs.

Table 2-8 summarizes the integration of some of the threat intelligence platforms with Microsoft Sentinel, the connectors used, and any additional interesting capabilities.

Table 2-8. *Threat Intelligence Platforms Integration Options*

Platform	Integration Method	Description
Agari Phishing Defense and Brand Protection	Built-in Sentinel Data Connector	Directly connect using the native Agari connector to track phishing threats and brand abuse indicators.
Anomali ThreatStream	Microsoft Graph Security API via ThreatStream Integrator	This option requires that you download the ThreatStream Integrator and connection extensions to send intelligence to Sentinel.
AlienVault OTX	Azure Logic Apps (Playbooks)	It utilizes Logic Apps to ingest threat indicators and observables from the OTX platform into Sentinel.
EclecticIQ Platform	Native Two-Way Integration	Provides enhanced threat detection and response by allowing two-way communication with EclecticIQ and Sentinel.
Filigran OpenCTI	Real-time Connector or TAXII 2.1 Server	It can send intelligence in real-time or via TAXII polling and receive structured incidents from Sentinel.
Group-IB Threat Intelligence and Attribution	Azure Logic Apps	This option utilizes Logic Apps to provide access to threat insights and actor profiling, ingesting them into Sentinel.
MISP (Open Source)	Threat Intelligence Upload Indicators API (via MISP2Sentinel)	Threat indicators can be pushed to Sentinel using the MISP2Sentinel utility found in the Azure Marketplace for ease of deployment.
Palo Alto Networks MineMeld	Microsoft Graph Security API	Indicators of compromised hosts can be sent to Sentinel using custom configurations of MineMeld; the setup configuration is described in "MineMeld Configuration."

(*continued*)

Table 2-8. (*continued*)

Platform	Integration Method	Description
Recorded Future	Azure Logic Apps (Playbooks)	The integration uses Logic Apps to deliver threat contextual intelligence to Sentinel workflows and analytic rules.
ThreatConnect	Microsoft Graph Security API	Integration of Sentinel uses the Graph Security Threat Indicators API; complete the integration using the official configuration guide.
ThreatQuotient ThreatQ	Microsoft Sentinel Connector	Integration with the ThreatQ-Sentinel connector allows bi-directional data exchange and automation capabilities.

By integrating a threat intelligence platform with Microsoft Sentinel, organizations can create a cohesive and responsive security ecosystem. Whether using a lot of sources from open threat sharing communities like MISP or commercial platforms like ThreatStream or Recorded Future, security operations teams have better visibility as well as the ability to act more rapidly and with accurate information. Each technology has its unique capabilities; however, they all combine to add value and purpose concerning building a more defensible position regarding a cyber event through intelligent and automated collaboration.

Effective Log Management

Log data collection, storage, and analysis are fundamental components of proactive threat detection and response in modern cybersecurity operations. A Microsoft Sentinel SIEM that runs on Azure, a cloud-native SIEM, allows organizations to centralize telemetry from hybrid, multicloud, and on-premises environments. But achieving success with Microsoft Sentinel relies on a well-thought-out log management strategy—not just data collection—that preserves data availability, optimizes analytical performance, and mitigates costs.

Organizations have to contend with creating their log management strategy in the context of a fundamental tension. They aim to collect as many logs as possible to achieve complete security visibility, thereby minimizing the cost and scale associated with managing large amounts of telemetry data. Microsoft Sentinel provides a structured approach to log ingestion and retention, allowing customers to configure their expectations around operational and cost limitations.

A significant element of Microsoft Sentinel's log management approach is organizing ingested data into two broad categories: primary security data and secondary security data. This categorization is informative when deciding how to store, retain, and query data and is a central consideration for the configuration of log storage plans in Sentinel.

Primary security data are log sources with a high degree of security value that are crucial for threat detection and operational monitoring, for example, logs used for near real-time analytics, correlation across multiple data sources, and security investigations. Examples entail logs that document the performance details of multiple antivirus or EDR platforms, authentication logs, audit logs, threat intelligence feeds, and external alerting logs. Primary data enables complex threat hunting queries, behavior analytics, and reporting on security at intervals. Since we need to use all of this data while performance and latency are paramount, primary data must be stored with the Analytics logs plan, which enables regular, discrete, and free access to this data.

Conversely, secondary security data generally refers to logs that are large and verbose but do not have any significant direct value to security detection on their own. However, this data is critical for investigation context and provides better insight into attack patterns in the larger context. Examples encompass proxy logs, Netflow, SSL/TLS certificate logs, IoT logs, and access logs from cloud storage products. These logs will be queried periodically for various purposes, including threat hunting, large queries, and enrichment during incident response. Secondary data is better suited to provide value through the Auxiliary logs plan, which stores data at a lower cost and with better accessibility, but at the expense of slower performance.

To support these distinctions, Microsoft Sentinel provides two log storage plans: Analytics logs and Auxiliary logs, which have set retention schemes and costs. The Analytics logs plan, designed for primary security data, will keep and store all logs ingested for 90 days by default (and up to two years). The Analytics logs are in what is called interactive retention, which enables frequent, unlimited querying of the log data at no per-query costs. After the data is kept for this period, it is moved to long-term retention, where it can be kept for twelve years. Long-term retention is much less expensive; however, accessing the data requires one of two options—a search job (which uses the background for retrieval) or a restore (which will return the data to an interactive status only temporarily, to be queried).

The Auxiliary logs plan, on the other hand, retains the data for thirty days for interactive retention, where, for instance, the storage costs are considerably lower. Plus, the query capabilities are limited with this dataset—you will have to deal with reduced performance (currently not knowing how fast it may go), you are charged for queries based on the amount of data scanned (which, with rate limiting, could become an expense), and these can only query 1 table at one time. However, organizations can establish summary rules for auxiliary data that determine the aggregate. When stored in the Analytics logs plan, they can then enable all analytic capabilities for a summarized dataset. When auxiliary data reaches long-term retention, it can only be retrieved through search jobs; it will not have a restore option like the analytics plan.

The most crucial point for a successful implementation is to develop a retention strategy that prioritizes the most valuable data based on its usage and storage type. Data logs should be evaluated based on their security intrinsic value, rather than the frequency of their access during warranted investigations or threat detections. The most vital logs, which serve as the basis for real-time incident alerts, reporting frequency, and behavior analytics, should be retained in the Analytics logs plan for a relatively lengthy period of interactive use (not more than a year). In contrast, potential logs that may still need to be reviewed in the future can still be helpful in the Auxiliary plan, to reduce costs and be kept for future investigative use.

Additionally, Microsoft Sentinel incorporates two retention states, or permanence, in both plan types for logs—interactive and long-term. The interactive state is activated immediately after data ingestion and depends on the plan's level of analytic access. This allows for quick searching in the Analytics plan and more economical access in the Auxiliary plan. When the interactive retention period expires, the data is moved to long-term retention, where it is stored for extended periods at very low prices, ensuring data preservation for at least 12 years. In the long term, access is limited to the initial ingestion of data into tables and structures, primarily to meet compliance requests and historical information needs.

To manage this effectively requires more than only storing the data; to be effective, the cost and volume of ingestion must be monitored to optimize connections while keeping amended log retention policies for both use cases for security and compliance with regulations, allowing organizations to properly issue data governance controls in Sentinel, like tagging, to make metadata visible and labelling controls, and RBAC, to ensure that access to logs is authorized and they can be easily found.

Ultimately, managing logs in Microsoft Sentinel involves protecting a dynamic lifecycle of activity, rather than a static experience. Successful aspects include the performance of data categorization and the selection of a limiting retention model, as well as the identification of rules-based analytical approaches to logs that are valuable for security at minimal costs. Securing this line of reasonable visibility without late-stage processes or long-time investigations allows the organization to primarily focus next on their appropriate threat detection and response, which illustrates that it is a good cultural value in the Microsoft Sentinel ecosystem.

Optimize and Increase Efficiency

In today's security landscape, organizations are required to retain vast amounts of log data for extended periods to support compliance, incident response, and threat hunting activities. While Microsoft Sentinel provides powerful analytics capabilities and includes 90 days of free log retention by default, retaining logs beyond that period in Log Analytics can become cost-prohibitive. To address this challenge, Azure Data Explorer (ADX) offers a scalable and cost-effective alternative for storing and querying long-term log data. By integrating ADX with Sentinel, organizations can offload older logs without sacrificing accessibility or performance. This section outlines best practices for implementing an optimized log retention strategy using ADX, ensuring organizations maintain visibility, compliance, and control while significantly reducing storage and analytics costs.

Implement a Tiered Log Retention Strategy

One of the most cost-effective approaches in Microsoft Sentinel is to differentiate between short-term and long-term log retention. By default, Sentinel provides 90 days of free retention within Log Analytics, which is suitable for immediate alerting, investigation, and compliance needs. However, extending log retention beyond this window within Log Analytics can become financially burdensome. Instead of retaining all logs in the same tier, organizations should offload older—but still valuable—data to a more cost-efficient solution like Azure Data Explorer (ADX), thereby preserving long-term insights without incurring high analytics costs.

Export Logs Efficiently Using Native Integrations

To seamlessly move data from Log Analytics to ADX, leverage Azure-native export methods such as the Data Export feature or streaming via Azure Event Hub. These services allow the continuous flow of selected log tables (like SecurityEvent, Heartbeat, or SigninLogs) into ADX. Automating this export process ensures that the pipeline remains resilient and real-time, allowing logs to be available in ADX as soon as they age out from Sentinel's analytics layer. This practice not only reduces storage costs but also helps preserve valuable historical telemetry that may be needed for audit or investigation purposes.

Automate Schema Mapping and Table Management

A key part of ADX integration involves mirroring the schema of Sentinel's native tables within the new ADX environment. Automating the creation of tables, data mappings, and update policies through scripting (e.g., PowerShell or ARM templates) ensures consistency, scalability, and reliability. This level of automation allows organizations to quickly replicate new log types and scale their ingestion policies without manual intervention. Automating these elements also minimizes the risk of schema mismatches, which can otherwise result in query failures or inconsistent datasets.

Integrate ADX Tables for Seamless Querying

Once logs are exported and stored in ADX, it's essential to maintain operational continuity by integrating ADX into Microsoft Sentinel's user interface. This can be achieved using the ADX operator within Kusto Query Language (KQL), allowing analysts to query external ADX tables as if they were native to Sentinel. This seamless integration enables security teams to perform threat hunting, retrospective analysis, and compliance reporting on extended datasets—all without migrating the data back into Sentinel. Ensuring your SOC team is familiar with querying across ADX and Log Analytics is a crucial enabler of this hybrid model.

Customize Retention and Lifecycle Policies

One of the key strengths of Azure Data Explorer is its flexibility in defining table-level retention and soft-delete policies. Organizations should tailor these settings based on regulatory compliance, operational relevance, and access patterns. For example, sensitive data might require a 365-day retention window with a soft-delete grace period for legal hold scenarios. By aligning retention policies with business and legal requirements, teams can enforce governance while maintaining control over storage costs. Proactively tuning these parameters ensures a sustainable and compliant log retention architecture.

Table 2-9 illustrates key best practices for designing and deploying effective log management in Microsoft Sentinel, specifically tailored for environments with IoT (Internet of Things) devices, including IoMT (Internet of Medical Things). This includes technical strategies and a practical example to illustrate the approach.

Table 2-9. Best Practices for Designing and Deploying Effective Log Management in Microsoft Sentinel

#	Best Practice	Description	Action Step
1	Classify IoT and IoMT Devices	Start by identifying and cataloguing your connected devices by type, device role, and criticality. This will help you customize your logging policies.	Use device management systems or Azure Defender for IoT to inventory devices (e.g., infusion pumps, smart thermostats, and ECG monitors).
2	Ingest Logs from IoT Gateways and Protocol Translators	Most IoT devices do not send logs directly. They will send their logs through gateways or via a protocol converter.	Connect logs from MQTT brokers, OPC-UA servers, or Modbus/RTU gateways into Azure IoT Hub and forward to Sentinel.
3	Enable Microsoft Defender for IoT Integration	You can use Microsoft Defender for IoT to monitor the behavior and anomalies of those devices without having to install any agents.	Integrate Defender for IoT with Microsoft Sentinel using the native connector to forward alerts and telemetry.

(*continued*)

Table 2-9. (*continued*)

#	Best Practice	Description	Action Step
4	Normalize and Enrich IoT Logs with ASIM	The Advanced Security Information Model (ASIM) can be leveraged to normalize your telemetry, enabling the detection of threats that cross your device types in a scalable manner.	Use the ASIM parsers and normalization for OT/IoT logs such as DeviceNetworkEvents and IotNetworkSessions.
5	Filter Noise and Prioritize Critical Logs	IoT telemetry can generate high volumes of logs that are of low value. Do not forget to filter out unnecessary data to save on the ingestion cost and mitigate alert fatigue.	Use Data Collection Rules (DCRs) and Log Analytics Workspace filters to ingest only high-value events (e.g., failed firmware updates and unauthorized access attempts).
6	Segment and Tag IoT Data by Device Type and Location	You can maximize your investigations and queries if the logs you are reviewing contain additional metadata (e.g., device category, physical location, department, etc.) and usage of those logs.	Add custom fields like DeviceType=ECGMonitor, Location=ICU, Department=Cardiology via transformation rules.
7	Correlate Logs Across IT and OT Domains	You can leverage (and cross-reference) the IoT telemetry with IT security incidents to help detect lateral movement and blended threats.	Use Sentinel's Kusto Query Language (KQL) to join IoT logs with identity, network, or endpoint alerts.
8	Monitor Log Volume and Retention	You should also be tracking your ingestion trends from IoT/IoMT-sourced telemetry. Be sure to tune your retention based on your compliance, diagnostics, and cost expectations.	Use the **Usage and Costs** workbook in Sentinel to monitor and adjust log retention settings per table or workspace.

(*continued*)

Table 2-9. (*continued*)

#	Best Practice	Description	Action Step
9	Visualize IoT Security Posture	You can create customized dashboards and workbooks using Power BI to stay informed about IoT device activity, identify anomalies affecting your connected devices, and receive alerts as needed from the IoT environment.	Use Sentinel Workbooks to create visualizations like device health heatmaps or protocol usage charts.
10	Conduct Drills Using IoMT Incident Scenarios	You can also simulate real-world incidents involving IoMT threats (e.g., malware spreading from a connected insulin pump) to test your ability to respond appropriately in the event of an alert being triggered.	Use sample data or MITRE ICS ATT&CK scenarios to validate that Sentinel correctly detects, alerts, and escalates anomalies.

Data Normalization and ASIM

Data normalization in ASIM (Advanced Security Information Model) refers to the process of taking raw security event data from multiple sources and converting it into a standard, predefined format. The standard format provides an advantage to security analysts and automated tools, enabling them to correlate, analyze, and identify security threats in heterogeneous environments with minimal data discrepancies. Explain why data normalization is needed in ASIM. Security data comes from many sources—firewalls, endpoint protection platforms, cloud services, ID providers, etc. Each source probably uses different field names, structures, and schemas.

For instance,

- A firewall log might have a user name as user_name
- A cloud app might use a username
- another source with a principalName

Without data normalization, regardless of the correlation, you will be forced to use source-specific queries, which will scale poorly and are difficult to maintain.

How ASIM Normalization Works

ASIM provides parsers, which are Kusto query functions used to progressively map raw data from Microsoft and third-party data to normalized schemas that ASIM defines. Each parser is for a specific data type (e.g., ProcessEvents, NetworkSession, DnsEvents, or AuthenticationEvents). This process consists of three steps:

- *Source Data*: Logs coming into Log Analytics or Sentinel from any connectors.

- *Parser Layer*: ASIM parsers read the structure of the source data and then translate the fields into a standard structure.

- *Normalized Schema*: The output is a virtual table with defined column names and data types that represent the data, no matter where it originated.

For instance, ASIMDns normalizes DNS logs, outputting a table representation that includes common fields such as DnsQuery, DnsResponseCode, and SrcIpAddr, regardless of the source (Windows DNS, Azure Firewall, or Cisco Umbrella).

The Value of Normalized Data in ASIM

- *Reduced Complexity for Detection Rules*: You only need one analytics rule to cover multiple data sources

- *Enhanced Threat Hunting, and Reduced Complexity*: Threat hunters will not need to manage complex queries; they will be able to write consistent queries across any question, creating a consistent query design

- *Optimized Aggregation, Scoring, and Visualization*: You can consider aggregating dashboards and querying tables using normalized data

- Streamlined enrichment and automation without concerns of adopting the raw schema

Data normalization is an outreach principle to ASIM to change telemetry from raw formats into a predetermined format without consideration of how complex a heterogeneous structure of the logs may appear. This implementation of normalization in ASIM allows telemetry to be normalized to reflect a standard schema, allowing consistent, scalable, and efficient operations in Microsoft Sentinel.

Everyday Use Cases for ASIM (Advanced Security Information Model)

By normalizing the information, ASIM averts the challenges of working with different types of security data in a new format. Which enables security teams and decision-makers to discover threats more quickly, craft queries more easily, and significantly enhance the value of interoperable content-sharing across security systems and applications, whether running in the cloud or on-premises networks. Table 2-10 illustrates what it means and gives an example.

Table 2-10. List Use Cases for ASIM

Use Case	What It Means	Example
Cross-source detection	ASIM enables detection of threats, utilizing data from multiple systems without the need to be concerned with where the data originates from or where you pulled it in from.	Detect brute force login attempts from Azure AD, Okta, and AWS all in the same rule.
Source-agnostic content	Once a rule or workbook is built using ASIM, it will work with any source that presents the same schema, even if added later.	A process event rule works with Defender for Endpoint, Sysmon, or Windows Event logs by default and automatically
Custom source support	Your own data sources can be mapped to ASIM while still utilizing Microsoft's built-in rules and analytics.	Your custom IoT logs can be normalized to ASIM to take advantage of existing ASIM detections.
Simplified queries	Analysts will not need to memorize field names for every source, as ASIM uses the same field names across all data.	Always use SrcIpAddr or UserPrincipalName in the query, no matter what you are querying or where the data originates from.

ASIM Components

Microsoft Sentinel's normalized schemas are predefined structures for specific types of security events that represent those events consistently and predictably. The schemas normalize common event categories, including but not limited to authentication, DNS activity, process creation, and network sessions. Each schema defines a collection of fields, including the column names for those fields and the expected formats for their values. These schemas and consistent column names enable easier query building, dashboards, and detection rules that work across data sources regardless of how the data was represented initially or structured.

Microsoft Sentinel performs the normalization through ASIM parsers, which are KQL-based functions that take the raw data from data tables such as Syslog, CommonSecurityLog, or custom logs. The ASIM parsers take the various tables and move the data into the required normalized format. There are many built-in parsers that you can get quickly and easily for familiar sources. The organization you support can deploy additional ASIM parsers or curate custom ones from the Microsoft Sentinel GitHub repository to extend or modify parsing logic, supporting custom log formats or specific source variations.

Once the data is normalized, you can use schema content (i.e., analytic rules, hunting queries, and workbooks) without having to rewrite or duplicate them for each respective data source. To illustrate this point, a detection rule written for the ASIM DNS schema will work regardless of the data coming from either Windows DNS, Azure Firewall, or a third-party appliance, provided the data was normalized using an appropriate ASIM parser. The significant benefit here is that the rule can be used independently of any single data source. This makes it simpler for you to manage and roll out new detection capabilities in Microsoft Sentinel across your environment without worrying about the specific data source.

Figure 2-6 provides a complete block diagram of how Microsoft Sentinel's Advanced Security Information Model (ASIM) framework works. The block diagram illustrates the flow of raw telemetry from multiple sources, via connectors, to layers of parsers that represent these sources. This process involves transforming data identity into normalized content for consumption through analytics, detection, and investigation. This layered architecture highlights the logical separation between ingestion, normalization, and consumption while demonstrating that the ASIM framework provides a standardized and scalable approach to working with heterogeneous security data. This visualization of the pipeline explains how Sentinel integrates large amounts of unspecified security data into coherent and actionable insights.

CHAPTER 2　ARCHITECTING AND DEPLOYING MICROSOFT SENTINEL

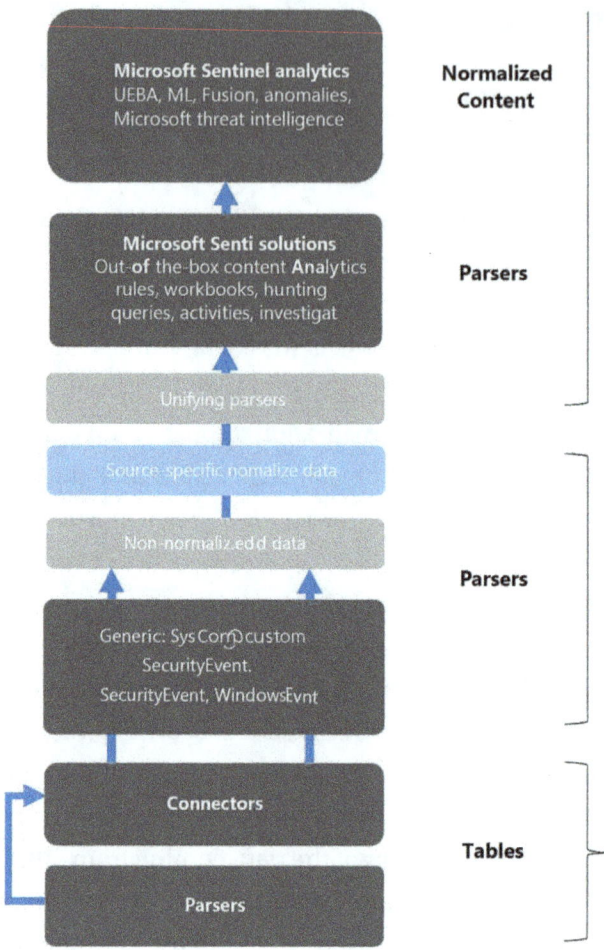

Figure 2-6. *Block Diagram of Microsoft Sentinel's Advanced Security Information Model (ASIM) Framework*

The Advanced Security Information Model (ASIM) is a core element of Microsoft Sentinel that provides a schema-oriented and standardized model for disparate security telemetry. In enterprises, security data can come from many disparate security and network systems: firewalls (Checkpoint, Cisco, and Firepower); antivirus (McAfee and Security Endpoint); VPN gateways (Cisco AnyConnect); identity providers (Active Directory, Azure Active Directory, and Crowdstrike); cloud platforms (Microsoft Azure and AWS); and the list goes on. These systems generate logs in proprietary or vendor-specific formats, presenting security analysts with a significant challenge: how to normalize, correlate, and query such progressively dissimilar data? ASIM responds to this challenge by defining a single schema for various security events and providing a series of KQL-based parsers to normalize and structure raw logs into records.

Conceptually, ASIM is not a storage model but instead a logical and semantic application at the time of query. ASIM does not require reingesting or reorganizing the data in the Log Analytics workspace, while it is utilizing Kusto functions, called parsers, to translate native logs into tables structured to ASIM metadata dynamically. As an example, if the user utilizes ASIM to query for DNS activity, ASIM provides a DnsActivity parser that takes the raw logs from a variety of sources (Windows DNS logs, Azure Firewall, third-party appliances) and maps them to a single schema. This means queries in ASIM are sourced independently, which reduces the complexity of the threat detection and investigation approach tremendously.

ASIM is especially valuable in large security operations centers (SOCs). In traditional SIEM deployments, when you write detection logic or threat hunting queries, each detection rule has to be written specifically for each log type and the structure of the data. Analysts can create reusable, modular KQL queries using a standard schema with ASIM, regardless of whether the logs come from a Palo Alto device, a Fortinet device, Azure, or AWS. This ability to reuse the same detection principles allows for a speedy deployment of analytic rules and content across customer environments, despite the heterogeneous log sources. An analyst can create a detection rule for lateral movement based on the network connections once, using ASIM's NetworkSession schema, and then deploy that across a myriad of customer environments with different firewalls and network monitoring tools.

ASIM also fits neatly in Microsoft's content ecosystem for Sentinel. Many of the solutions offered from the Sentinel Content Hub (threat detection packages, hunting packs, notebooks, etc.) are built on top of ASIM. This allows organizations to onboard content that works across data sources, assuming those data sources are ASIM-compliant. Microsoft continually adds new data types to ASIM, including process events, sign-in events, authentication logs, alerts, and cloud activities. ASIM's extensibility allows organizations to create parsers for their own data sources in a compliant manner.

ASIM is not just beneficial technically; ASIM increases operational agility and enhances data governance. Although security teams generally have time to wade through logs and do investigations, they often lose bandwidth when having to pivot between all data types and telemetry sources. If the logs are from ASIM, understanding their meaning is less of a concern, as it is not necessary to know how specific logs might vary based on predictable log structure, content, and intelligence. Just using ASIM already has the potential to reduce time spent on root cause analysis and time taken to respond to incidents. In addition, ASIM provides organizations an efficient way to map their detections and threat hunting attempts to adversary techniques by leveraging the MITRE ATT&CK framework and other threat modeling frameworks.

In short, the Advanced Security Information Model serves as a strategic enabler to modernize and scale security operations in Microsoft Sentinel by decoupling the detection logic from the raw log structure, providing more robust, maintainable, and transferable security analytics. ASIM is developing into the infrastructure of content-driven, intelligence-enabled SIEM deployments with dynamic parsers, rich schema documentation, and increasing native support across Microsoft and third-party connectors. ASIM has enabled organizations to convert fragmented telemetry into actionable security insights wherever possible with a standard, queryable structure.

Designing and deploying ASIM (Advanced Security Information Model) in Microsoft Sentinel requires an understanding of Kusto Query Language (KQL) and an architectural thought process focused on modularity, reusability, and performance. ASIM enables organizations to standardize and unify various telemetry data at query time using parsers, which can be either an existing or custom KQL user-defined function. The parsers convert the raw data from many connectors into a normalized schema so the analytics content and threat detection can behave consistently regardless of the source. This abstraction enables a product-agnostic experience, eliminating the need to worry about raw table names, such as Syslog or CommonSecurityLog. Queries can be made through any schema with interfaces like _Im_Dns or imAuthentication.

The architecture has two levels of parsers to deal with: source-specific parsers and unifying parsers. The source-specific parsers will read the raw logs from a particular product or data source. Say you have a Parser that normalizes DNS logs from Infoblox appliances. Each Parser has unique syntax, structure, semantics, and representation of the data coming from the source, above, where the Parser calls the source Parser, the unifying Parser aggregates to call multiple source-specific Parsers under a single schema. The unifying Parser provides the standardized interface that an analyst will use in their queries, such as _Im_Dns, _Im_WebSession, or imProcessCreate.

Microsoft Sentinel has both kinds of Parsers: built-in parts and workspace-deployed parts. Built-in Parsers are inherently present in every Sentinel workspace, and the metadata structure and the built-in content, such as analytics rules and hunting queries, are coupled. Implementing a built-in Parser has a fixed structure that the user cannot edit. The user can initiate workspace-deployed parsers or edit existing parsers, which may have been created manually or through deployment automation (e.g., ARM Templates). Applying a workspace-deployed Parser enables new Parser capabilities or support for a custom data source more quickly, but it does not integrate with the built-in content.

To maximize ASIM-based query performance, the Architect should design the Parser logic using filtering against parameters such as starttime, endtime, srcipaddr, or domain_has_any, such that normalization applies filtering beforehand to maximize performance processing time and improve results at scale. Adding filtering to the normalization step is especially relevant when indexing data in environments with high average data volumes. The parameters filtering should be included in the function signature. Within the parser logic, add conditional filtering only if provided, utilizing KQL constructs like iff, case, or has any to accomplish this. Developing custom ASIM parsers is a systematic development process starting with obtaining representative logs from the data source (preferably containing a range of behaviors, responses, and quirks in formatting). The logs can be compared against the schema (i.e., DnsEvent, NetworkSession, Authentication), for which the developer will want to develop two parser types per schema: a filtering parser that will allow users to filter the data before it is parsed at runtime, and a parameter-less parser that unifying parsers can reference. Parsing includes logic to perform parsing for strings, restricting fields with parse or extract, transforming values using a lookup table, or normalizing identifiers (MAC addresses, user names).

Performance optimization will be a constant concern while developing parsers. For this reason, filters should rely on native fields and the specialized operators, i.e., ==, has, or startswith. Avoid using regular expression iterations unless necessary. When renaming fields, always use project-rename to maintain performance and usage of the renamed fields. Use project-away to clean up any intermediate or overly large fields. Avoid the project unless building a standalone query, as this new query can potentially strip context away from existing fields.

Deploying parsers at scale will require an automation service and/or a version control system. The preferred option is to define each parser using a YAML template and to develop it into an ARM template using Microsoft's ASIM deployment tools. The YAML and ARM templates can be deployed across workspaces using Azure PowerShell or from the Azure portal. When working with environments that may leverage custom data sources or multiple tenants, this methodology will allow for consistent parsers and operational efficiencies by allowing DevOps-style parser lifecycle management.

Ultimately, ASIM architecture design in Microsoft Sentinel is about much more than coding KQL (Kusto Query Language). It affords a scalable, flexible model and a standardized means of normalization of security data. It unifies disparate telemetry sources into a single standard model, provides schema-based detection workflows for SOC (Security Operations Center) analysts, and lays the foundation for intelligent, automated, and cloud-centric security operations. An ASIM-aware architecture will enable security operations entities to effectively focus and maximize their potential multifaceted capabilities in Microsoft Sentinel when detecting advanced threats and/or supporting an investigation workflow.

Table 2-11 summarizes the lessons learned and best practices for building and deploying data normalization and ASIM in Microsoft Sentinel with an emphasis on IoT (Internet of Things) and IoMT (Internet of Medical Things) environments.

Table 2-11. *Lessons Learned and Best Practices for Building and Deploying Data Normalization*

Sl. No	Best Practice	Description	Action Step/Example
1	Identify IoT/IoMT Data Sources	Start by mapping all IoT and IoMT assets and identifying the logs they produce (e.g., syslogs, device telemetry, SNMP traps).	For IoMT: Identify data from connected infusion pumps, patient monitors, or smart imaging systems.
2	Use Appropriate ASIM Parsers	ASIM provides parsers for various data types like NetworkSession, DNS, Syslog, etc. Choose the right parser model that fits the IoT telemetry type.	Use ASIM's NetworkSession parser with firewall logs from the IoMT gateways.
3	Normalize IoT Logs Before Ingestion	If logs from IoT devices are unstructured, normalize them at the edge or via Azure IoT Hub/DPS before sending to Sentinel.	Use Azure Functions or Logstash to turn raw device messages into ASIM-compliant schemas.

(*continued*)

CHAPTER 2   ARCHITECTING AND DEPLOYING MICROSOFT SENTINEL

Table 2-11. (*continued*)

Sl. No	Best Practice	Description	Action Step/Example
4	Tag Data with Correct Normalization Schema	When ingesting data via custom connectors or event hubs, ensure the EventType and SchemaVersion fields match ASIM expectations.	For example, tag traffic from a hospital's IoMT VLAN as a NetworkSession, version 0.2.4.
5	Leverage ASIM-Supported Connectors	Prefer connectors that natively support ASIM or have pre-built normalization via solutions in the Content Hub.	Use the Defender for IoT (formerly Azure Defender for IoT) connector that includes ASIM normalization support.
6	Use Custom Parsers for Specialized Devices	If your IoT/IoMT system uses a proprietary format, develop custom KQL parsers aligned with ASIM schema standards.	Create a parser to match HL7-based telemetry logs from smart ECG monitors to the Heartbeat schema.
7	Validate Normalization Using ASIM Queries	Use sample ASIM KQL queries to validate if your normalized data is usable in detections, hunting, and workbooks.	Use the imNetworkSession or imHeartbeat functions to verify correlation with Log Analytics.
8	Correlate IoT/IoMT Data with Other Entities	After normalization, correlate IoT events with user, device, and network context for incident investigations.	Correlate any anomalous activity from a smart IV pump to the applicable IP address and to the activity of a specific nurse's login.
9	Continuously Monitor Parser Performance	Monitor performance and usage of ASIM parsers, and update them as schemas evolve.	Implement some type of alert mechanism for log parsing failures, or if ASIM required fields were missing from logs of your own design.
10	Document and Govern Custom Mappings	Maintain a version-controlled repository of your custom ASIM mappings, especially for regulated sectors like healthcare.	Implement a GitHub repo or SharePoint tracker to maintain an audit log of any changes to your IoMT parsers.

User and Entity Behavior Analytics (UEBA)

Detecting internal threats—such as compromised users, malicious insiders, or stealthy attackers—has always been one of the most complex problems in cybersecurity. Many traditionally used approaches rely on manual investigation, which involves reviewing an abundance of alerts, correlating across logs, and conducting time-consuming threat hunting. Advanced threats, in particular (zero-day exploits, targeted attacks, and persistent threats), nearly always fall through the cracks, exposing organizations to significant security risks.

We added User and Entity Behavior Analytics (UEBA) to Microsoft Sentinel to remove some of that challenge. UEBA applies machine learning to identify abnormal behaviors across your digital environment with the features of Microsoft Sentinel. When Sentinel ingests data from multiple, interconnected sources (e.g., firewalls, endpoints, identity publications, and cloud services), Sentinel builds behavioral baselines for each entity in your environment. Entities include users, IP addresses, devices, hosts, and apps; baselines are built over time and by comparing against peer groups. When an entity's activity deviates from its baseline, Sentinel can help to identify that deviation.

When Sentinel UEBA detects anomalous activity—whether it's an unexpected login from a different country, excessive access attempts to resources, or uncharacteristic use of computing resources—Sentinel will flag this anomaly for further examination. Even more interestingly, UEBA also evaluates the sensitivity/significance of the asset accessed or used. It can identify the related peer group for the entity and provide estimates of the estimated impact (often referred to as "blast radius") if that asset were compromised. This first-party intelligence enables security teams to prioritize threats and respond to what matters most.

By removing the uncertainty from behavioral analysis, UEBA minimizes the overall workload for security analysts. Instead of having to sort through false-positive and low-confidence alerts, analysts will receive rich-contextual, high-confidence alerts coming from UEBA that will enable faster and more effective investigation and response times. The crux of the solution is to perform rapid threat detection and rapid threat handling.

Security-Driven Use of Behavior Analytics

Microsoft Sentinel's UEBA implementation takes inspiration from modern analytics frameworks for security and implements an "outside-in" approach based on looking at behavioral analytics using three perspectives:

Use Cases

Sentinel makes detection decisions based on real-world attack stories with the MITRE ATT&CK framework as a guide. We examine how entities (users, hosts, etc.) are involved in attacks as victims, attackers, or pivot points, and then apply this knowledge to prioritize log data that is most pertinent or useful.

Data Sources

Sentinel fully supports native integrations with Microsoft cloud services and third-party cloud services to allow additional sources of enriched visibility. Data is not selected based on quantity; it is selected based on fit with particular threat detection use cases.

Analytics

At the center of UEBA is machine learning. Sentinel relies on various machine learning techniques employing unsupervised learning to find anomalies based on behaviors over time, location, devices, and frequencies related to peers. Through multiple forms of contextual evidence, the analyst can define and take action on suspicious events.

Understanding Behavior with Entity Context

Behavioral analytics is only as good as the context for that behavior. Microsoft Sentinel works to build out extensive entity profiles to utilize in behavioral analytics using identity information from Microsoft Entra ID (formerly Azure Active Directory). Bi-directional synchronization and storage of information are also performed to sync with on-premises Active Directory, using Microsoft Defender for Identity (currently in preview). The behavioral analytics data becomes increasingly richer using these items for anomaly detection. When it comes to hands-on analysis, analysts can access this identity data in the following ways:

- Through the Azure portal, from the Log Analytics workspace, using the IdentityInfo table.
- In the Microsoft Defender portal, using Advanced Hunting queries.

With the combination of identity context, machine learning, and a focus on anomalies that matter, UEBA in Microsoft Sentinel enables your security team to find and respond to advanced threats like never before.

User and Entity Behavior Analytics (UEBA) is a security function that leverages machine learning, advanced analytics, and behavioral modeling to understand when users and entities are acting unusually or irregularly in an organization's IT environment. In Microsoft Sentinel, UEBA is helpful in scenarios where teams want to be able to detect advanced threats, such as insider threats, compromised accounts, or advanced persistent threats (APTs), which are likely to be missed by traditional security controls. While traditional security controls rely largely on static rules or known signatures, UEBA attempts to detect anomalies associated with actions outside of what is considered to be "normal" by understanding what is "normal."

UEBA's Role in Threat Detection

Microsoft Sentinel uses UEBA functionality to provide an additional layer in its threat detection ecosystem. UEBA contains an extensive amount of telemetry from various sources, such as logs from endpoints, network devices, cloud services, applications, etc. UEBA uses log telemetry to provide behavior profiles for users and entities within an organization. When an event or group of events occurs that is significantly different than a user's established behavior profile, UEBA will show that as an activity of interest. The importance of UEBA lies in its ability to enable organizations to detect emerging threats in near real-time, even when no threat indicators or signatures were previously detected.

The Way UEBA Models Behavior

Using sophisticated statistics and machine learning algorithms, UEBA in Microsoft Sentinel will build baseline behaviors and adapt them over time as user behavior and entity behavior change. UEBA uses many dimensions to segment normal, including (1) user log-in time; (2) time to log into user accounts and systems; (3) time spent accessing elements within systems (accessing one system or interface within a system multiple times or for substantially more time than months or periods prior); (4) devices used to access (a change in the device used for access); (5) direct and indirect communications; and so on. This baseline behavior becomes refined and more accurate over time within UEBA, as continual configuration variance will result in lower false positives, which will help with accurately detecting possible malicious behavior.

Detecting Insider Threats and Compromised Accounts

A key, terrific aspect of UEBA is that it will detect both insider threats (users with malicious intent) and compromised accounts. For instance, if a user typically accesses files only during work hours but then comes in very late at night and downloads large amounts of sensitive data or accesses systems they had never accessed previously, UEBA will alert. Similarly, if an external attacker breaches a legal account, they often act like the usual user they compromised, except for some changed behavioral patterns. The alerting at an early point can reduce damage and prevent data breaches.

UEBA Is More Than Just Users

Although users are the primary basis for monitoring, UEBA checks for and attempts to model user behavior and group relationships with other entities, such as, but not limited to, devices, applications, and the network infrastructure and elements. For example, suppose a device spontaneously starts communicating with unusual external IP addresses, or an application starts accessing data based on a behavior different from what would be normally expected. In that case, it might be a sign of a compromise. The ability of UEBA to analyze the behavior of entities in connection with the activities of users provides a richer understanding of security posture to help uncover complex multi-stage attacks.

Integration with Microsoft Sentinel's Security Operations

UEBA alerts in Microsoft Sentinel integrate with the overarching security operations workflow and provide security analysts with rich context. When UEBA identifies an anomaly, it generates an incident or an alert, enriched with additional telemetry and threat intelligence, helping to ensure that the analyst is looking at the bigger picture when assessing the potential impact of remediation. Ultimately, after an incident or alert is raised by UEBA, the security analyst can use Sentinel's advanced workflows, workbooks, playbooks, or automated response actions to investigate the alert and develop a hypothesis on how to resolve and remediate the incident. The integration of UEBA into this overall response workflow means that UEBA findings are effectively incorporated into the investigation, threat hunting, and remediation process.

Reduced Alert Fatigue Using Intelligent Analytics

A central pain point in security operations is alert fatigue, where teams are overwhelmed by mostly false-positive alerts. Alert fatigue occurs because security analysts are deluged by alerts, which are too many events without appropriate context. The intelligence UEBA capability of Microsoft Sentinel addresses alert fatigue by using context and correlation on events before raising an alert. Because UEBA understands the expected behavior of a user or entity within an organization, it will filter out benign anomalies and draw its attention to the actual anomalous and suspicious activity. This approach allows a security team to focus its response efforts and enhance efficiency and effectiveness in the threat management lifecycle.

Continuous Improvement

Because UEBA is a dynamic application that constantly learns and adapts to changing entity and user behavior, its functionality is designed to adapt to the introduction of new applications and devices, as well as changing business processes. As the organization introduces new business processes, applications, and devices, UEBA's operational models update with that eventuality, thus maintaining the accuracy of detection over time. Furthermore, Microsoft Sentinel will periodically improve the underlying analytics and machine learning models used by UEBA whenever emergent trends by threat actors are detected or the research community identifies new concepts. The organization using Sentinel can constantly improve and enhance its capability to identify possible threats in its environment.

In Table 2-12, best practices are presented for configuring and using Microsoft Sentinel's UEBA (User and Entity Behavior Analytics) to ensure accurate and actionable findings, as well as constructively maintaining the wider security architecture perspective of your organization:

CHAPTER 2   ARCHITECTING AND DEPLOYING MICROSOFT SENTINEL

Table 2-12. Best Practices for Configuring and Using Microsoft Sentinel's UEBA

Sl. No	Best Practice	Description	IoMT Example
1	Inventory and Categorize IoT/IoMT Devices	To get started, it is first imperative to identify all IoT and IoMT devices, their log types, communication protocols, and data formats.	Catalog infusion pumps, patient monitors, ventilators, and imaging devices across hospital networks.
2	Ingest Device Telemetry via Trusted Pipelines	If the telemetry from the IoT and IoMT devices is being routed through any of the following mechanisms (Azure IoT Hub, Event Hubs, and Log Analytics agent), it can be secured and normalized.	Stream ECG device logs via Azure IoT Hub and forward them to Sentinel using a diagnostic pipeline.
3	Normalize Telemetry Using ASIM Parsers	Then the correct ASIM schema will need to be applied, determined by the log types of the devices (e.g., DeviceProcessEvents, NetworkSession, and Heartbeat), in order to obtain standard querying and analytics.	Map infusion pump alerts to the DeviceProcessEvents schema to track execution anomalies.
4	Tag Data with Metadata and Schema Version	When issuing tags (EventType and SchemaVersion), they need to be correct for the schema type and version in order to be usable by ASIM queries and detection rules.	Tag telemetry from a surgical robot as DeviceProcessEvents with SchemaVersion = 0.1.3.
5	Develop Custom Parsers for Proprietary Devices	When there is no native ASIM support, KQL-based parsers can be developed to normalize the proprietary formats to the ASIM schemas.	Build a custom parser to normalize HL7 or DICOM output from smart MRI scanners into the Heartbeat schema.
6	Correlate IoT Data with User and Network Context	Once the IoT logs are normalized with the addition of identity, IP, and session data to enrich the information and provide better situational awareness and investigation.	Correlate suspicious changes on an infusion pump with login activity from nurse stations.

(*continued*)

Table 2-12. (*continued*)

Sl. No	Best Practice	Description	IoMT Example
7	Test with ASIM Functions and Sample Queries	You should always validate that your normalized IoT or IoMT data is usable and validate the normalization you have made leveraging the built-in ASIM functions (imDeviceProcessEvents, imNetworkSession, etc.).	Run imDeviceProcessEvents on normalized telemetry from connected oxygen monitors to detect outliers.
8	Use Microsoft Defender for IoT Integration	For OT and healthcare IoT, you may consider integrating Microsoft's Defender for IoT for deep packet inspection and auto-normalized logs for your IoT devices.	Integrate network-layer logs from hospital VLANs via Defender for IoT into Sentinel for anomaly detection.
9	Govern Custom ASIM Mappings	Be sure to have documentation and a version control process for anything developed, like a custom parser, or when you extend a schema, even in a compliance-driven industry.	Track custom mappings for IoMT logs in a governance repository, noting parser versions and audit trails.
10	Continuously Improve Based on Feedback and Threats	As often as is practical, review normalization logic and update schemas as devices evolve to align with emerging threat models.	After a real-world alert involving a compromised IV pump, refine the parser to detect new behavioral patterns.

Utilizing Copilot for Security Architects

In today's cybersecurity operations, defenders are challenged to assess and respond to ever-increasing threat types and volumes. Security analysts and security practitioners are not the issue; as a function of the nature of security operations, previous tech scope regarding solutions assumed deep technical knowledge and time spent conducting investigations. If security operations are a manual process, and highly scripted manual run tasks are the outcome, we can apply this visualization to any job requiring deep knowledge, for example. Doctor, pilot, stop there. When we consider the evidence of incidents in this threat landscape, we all agree that Security Copilot would enable

CHAPTER 2 ARCHITECTING AND DEPLOYING MICROSOFT SENTINEL

more effective use of security operations staff time. Security Copilot seeks to provide a fundamentally driven, artificial intelligence-backed way for security operations personnel to operate at machine speed/scale.

Security Copilot is an intelligent assistant that integrates with Microsoft Sentinel and other key security tools in your organization. Security Copilot enables defenders to augment their analysis of incidents, create queries, comprehend signals, and help generate insights, all of which can enhance your security workflows. Notably, *any* security workflows and processes can be accelerated, optimized, and include more security roles in a process leveraging Security Copilot.

Table 2-13 illustrates that Security Copilot was designed to support defenders in critical security operations and its use cases.

Table 2-13. Use Case for Security Copilot

Use Case	Purpose
Investigate and remediate threats	Summarizes complex incidents in an automated fashion, with step-by-step instructions for triage and response.
Build and run queries	Translates natural language to technical Kusto Query Language (KQL) scripts, so anyone can conduct advanced threat hunting or script analysis.
Assess organizational security posture	Provides a 360° view of possible threats with prioritized observations and recommendations for improving overall posture.
Troubleshoot security and IT issues	Synthesizes relevant logs and telemetry to bring about root cause determination and recommendation for resolution.
Manage and define policies	Aids in drafting new policies, incorporating the policies with existing rules, and identifying contradictions.
Configure secure workflows	Provides guided steps for defining levels of secure access, which will help mitigate misconfiguration and susceptibility.
Generate reports	Produces clear and customized reports for different stakeholders in a summarized incident presentation of risk and mitigates.

Security Copilot works with the incident data and logs that Microsoft Sentinel already collects, enriching the context of any security investigation. It continues to enhance the incident response process by evaluating user prompts, contextualizing them with relevant information from inventory, and producing responses based on known and unknown authoritative internal and external sources. The loop of prompt evaluations, data enrichment, and personalized recommendations ensures that any resulting data is contextually appropriate and operationally relevant.

Security Copilot is available as a standalone application and is designed to integrate with existing security tools. Security Copilot can be directly accessed as an application or within the Microsoft Sentinel investigation view. Security Copilot interacts conversationally, allowing for natural language prompts from the analyst. For example, prompts such as "Summarize this incident," "Create a hunting query for lateral movement," or "Compare access policy X to policy Y" would return meaningful outputs in seconds—tasks that would have been time-consuming to accomplish for a person analyst with an appropriate level of expertise.

The functions of Security Copilot can also be enhanced through plugins, which are modular connectors that pull in even richer context through alerts, logs, vulnerability, threat intel sources, and internal policy documents. The plugins could consist of both native security tools and third-party systems, providing a rich base context with relatable insights across the enterprise.

For example, in the case of a malicious PowerShell script being detected, Security Copilot has the potential to

- Translate that script into plain language
- Identify the related MITRE ATT&CK techniques
- Produce a KQL query for searching similar behavior
- Provide recommendations for automation and response options
- Deliver a report for both SOC teams and executive communications

All of which means you get an orchestration of AI-driven reasoning, real-time access to intelligence, policies, and logic for responding, enabling Security Teams to work faster, smarter, and with greater confidence in their actions. Security Copilot takes security from being solely a reactive process and transforms it into a more proactive activity. This, of course, represents a shift of security from a siloed specialist endeavor to a more collaborative function across the organization.

Security Copilot integrates deeply with Microsoft Sentinel, providing a force multiplier for security analysts, architects, and decision makers. Security Copilot accelerates the entire detection and response lifecycle, using intelligence and automation to speed up the cycle.

Integrating Security Copilot with Microsoft Sentinel

Security Copilot, when integrated with Microsoft Sentinel, allows security teams to accelerate investigation and response efforts powered by AI-driven natural language interaction. Users can ask questions, summarize events, and construct hunting queries in a conversational interface.

Security Copilot offers an independent, standalone experience in which analysts engage the security environment using a chat-like interface. Microsoft Sentinel data provides context and enhances the experience in which a security analyst can gain visibility into incidents, alerts, and queries in their organization's telemetry.

The Core Capabilities of the Integration

Microsoft Sentinel integrates with Security Copilot in the following two ways:

- *Unified Incident Context*

    When used with Microsoft Sentinel alongside Microsoft Security solutions like an extended detection and response (XDR) platform, there is unified incident information available for Security Copilot. Incidents gathered from Microsoft Sentinel together allow an analyst to assess threats in one view across endpoints, identities, cloud workloads, etc.

- *Plugin-Based Functionality*

    Microsoft Sentinel offers dedicated plugins to Security Copilot in the conversational interface. The plugins allow a user to:

    - Convert natural language prompts into Kusto Query Language (KQL), allowing even those with lesser technical skills to create complex hunting queries.

    - Summarize incidents and get context from Sentinel alerts and logs.

    - Engage with Sentinel content like analytics rules, incidents, tables, etc., in guided AI prompts.

These integrations enable defenders to ask questions like "Show me anomalies in failed logins over the past 48 hours" or "Summarize all high-severity incidents impacting Azure resources" and receive succinct, actionable responses from licensed Microsoft Sentinel data.

Security Copilot and Microsoft Sentinel together enable analysts to reduce investigation times, increase accuracy in querying, and result in more effective incident response with the reductive power of simplicity and natural language.

Table 2-14 identifies the most essential best practice considerations for designing and deploying Microsoft Security Copilot in Microsoft Sentinel, with a unique focus on IoT/OT security and IoMT (Internet of Medical Things) environments. This outlines practical activities and an example related to health care/IoMT.

Table 2-14. Best Practice for Designing and Deploying Microsoft Security Copilot in Microsoft Sentinel

#	Best Practice	Description	Action Step	Example (IoMT)
1	Enable Security Copilot for Security Operations	Use Security Copilot to assist in threat analysis, investigation, and incident summarization in Sentinel.	Ensure Security Copilot is connected to Sentinel and has access to the necessary Log Analytics workspaces.	Copilot summarizes a sudden spike in device communication from an infusion pump to an unknown IP.
2	Connect IoT/OT and IoMT Device Data	Integrate IoT/OT devices using Azure Defender for IoT, and forward data to Sentinel.	Use built-in connectors to ingest IoT security alerts and telemetry.	Ingest data from smart medical devices such as patient monitors or insulin delivery systems.
3	Build a Device Inventory Knowledge Graph	Ensure all IoT/IoMT devices are classified and modeled as entities for Copilot context.	Use Microsoft Defender for IoT to automatically classify assets by device type, role, and communication pattern.	Copilot identifies that an ECG machine is communicating outside its defined subnet.

(*continued*)

Table 2-14. (*continued*)

#	Best Practice	Description	Action Step	Example (IoMT)
4	Leverage Natural Language Queries for Anomaly Investigation	Use Security Copilot's natural language interface to ask complex questions about device behavior.	Use prompts like "Show unusual behavior from hospital-connected devices in the last 24 hours."	The analyst asks, "Why did the MRI scanner connect to a non-medical IP overnight?"
5	Incorporate Threat Intelligence for IoT-Specific IOCs	Use threat intelligence feeds related to IoT/medical threats (e.g., FDA, MISP IoT feeds).	Connect TI feeds in Sentinel and allow Copilot to cross-reference indicators in the investigation.	Copilot detects that a known ransomware IP is attempting to scan connected surgical robots.
6	Automate Incident Summarization and Recommendations	Use Copilot to auto-summarize IoT security incidents and suggest mitigation steps.	Create playbooks that trigger Copilot-generated summaries and remediation guides.	Copilot summarizes a lateral movement attempt starting from a compromised blood analyzer.
7	Enable Entity Enrichment with Context	Enrich IoT entities with metadata (location, device owner, and criticality) to improve Copilot outputs.	Tag assets in Defender for IoT and sync with Sentinel's entity map.	Copilot prioritizes a critical ICU ventilator over a lab sensor during triage.
8	Use Prompt Engineering for Consistency	Standardize prompts and Copilot workflows for IoT/OT analysts.	Maintain a library of validated prompts specific to medical or industrial devices.	Example prompt: "List IoMT devices with abnormal DNS requests over the past 48 hours."

(*continued*)

Table 2-14. (*continued*)

#	Best Practice	Description	Action Step	Example (IoMT)
9	Deploy Role-Based Access for Copilot Usage	Control who can interact with Security Copilot in regulated environments like healthcare.	Use Microsoft Entra ID (Azure AD) to restrict Copilot actions by role (e.g., IoT SecOps, Compliance Officer).	The healthcare technician role is limited to viewing summaries, not triggering response actions.
10	Review and Train Copilot Using Historical IoT Cases	Use real incidents to improve Copilot's effectiveness by refining prompt and output quality.	Feed validated cases into Copilot and tune queries based on what worked well.	Use a past case of malware on a smart thermometer as a reference for anomaly detection patterns.

Summary

In this chapter, we discussed the foundational and advanced principles necessary to develop, deploy, and tune Microsoft Sentinel as a modern intelligent security operations platform. Each module shared the recommended practices and architecture necessary to improve an organization's detection and response capabilities.

We began with Zero Trust adoption and emphasized the paradigm shift from a perimeter-based approach to identity-first, least-privilege, and micro-segmented methodologies. Microsoft Sentinel is a crucial enforcement and visibility layer in an organization's Zero Trust strategy, particularly as organizations move to continuously monitor the behaviors of users accessing assets and enforce dynamic, risk-based policies for that access.

The chapter then discussed ways for readers to design and architect Sentinel workspaces and tenants around performance, governance, scalability, and multitenant use cases. We shared considerations on workspace boundaries, data sovereignty, role-based access, and a future-oriented design toward enterprise readiness.

Next, we tackled the strategic and operational steps for migrating to Microsoft Sentinel, including ways to assess existing SIEM, ways to onboard data, ways to recreate detection content, and ways to plan, assess, and validate incident handling processes to ensure as much continuity as possible during migration to Sentinel with minimal security blind spots.

CHAPTER 2   ARCHITECTING AND DEPLOYING MICROSOFT SENTINEL

We then moved to optimize data collection, where we briefly discussed how very deliberately choosing log sources, filtering, and enrichment can dramatically reduce costs while maximizing security value. In particular, we focused on the precept of ingesting high-fidelity data, prioritizing and finding connectors, and extracting the maximum value from incoming data using ingestion methods according to use cases and threat models.

We covered ingestion of threat intelligence as a force multiplier for native analytics within Sentinel. We explored using threat intelligence to combine, correlate, and enrich your telemetry data with external threat indicators. This supports using real-time enrichment and automation through enriched telemetry to be able to detect known threats and emerging threats.

We moved into managing logs effectively, where retention policies, tiered storage strategies, and ways to architect workspaces all play a part in business customer agility while maintaining privacy compliance. Making smart storage decisions ensures data availability for investigations while providing the organization with an option for avoiding unnecessary cost inflation.

Focusing on data normalization and ASIM (Advanced Security Information Model), we honed in on managing diverse data in a common schema to enable scalable and reusable analytics. Leveraging ASIM, we were able to make correlations across types of data, develop content more easily, and make our detection rules more portable and flexible.

We transitioned to User and Entity Behavior Analytics (UEBA): utilizing behavioral deviations to reveal unseen threats. Employing machine learning, Sentinel's UEBA capability can identify insider threats, lateral movement, and compromised accounts by profiling and characterizing normal behaviors and identifying deviations that exist with context.

Finally, we introduced Microsoft Security Copilot for security operations, introducing artificial intelligence tools and capabilities across all of our levels of users who perform this work. Security Copilot enhances productivity for both architects and analysts through natural language queries, automated incident summaries, and guided remediation for complex environments (e.g., IoT and healthcare service delivery (IoMT)).

Combining the material before you present an opportunity to apply a comprehensive framework that focuses on the design and development of a resilient and intelligent SOC using Microsoft Sentinel. If you put these practices into motion for detecting threats sooner, responding rapidly, and transforming security operations at the speed of today's threat landscape, I think you will find peace of mind.

CHAPTER 3

Engineering Microsoft Sentinel for Security Operations

In the rapidly changing threat landscape, security engineers need to shift from reactive defensiveness to proactive threat detection and threat response with the use of intelligence. Having said this, this module will provide you with the road map to operationalize Microsoft Sentinel in an enterprise environment. It outlines both foundational and advanced components necessary to utilize Sentinel as a comprehensive security operations platform, rather than a monitoring tool. Then it transitions to the advanced aspects of AI analysis, data reporting, and visualization.

The first session will dive deeply into how Microsoft Sentinel equips engineers with threat intelligence feeds to enhance alerts with context for improved situational awareness. You will learn how to utilize and manage the watchlist feature within Microsoft Sentinel, enabling dynamic investigations and improving access control logic. Next, we will transition into one of the keys of Microsoft Sentinel, the Kusto Query Language (KQL), which is the foundation of all Microsoft Sentinel analytical queries, and help you develop the competencies to extract valuable insights from the enormous amounts of telemetry information available.

From there, we will move into analytics rule development to identify complicated attack patterns and then transition into the domain of Security Orchestration, Automation, and Response (SOAR). This involves building automations or playbooks that will save time in your incident response work while alleviating the analyst fatigue associated with repetitive tasks.

CHAPTER 3 ENGINEERING MICROSOFT SENTINEL FOR SECURITY OPERATIONS

Through playing with the examples, you will learn how to create workbooks and visualize your data, providing real-time visuals for security leaders and stakeholders that show what you are achieving in a very easy-to-understand format. Finally, we will introduce you to an emerging practice for enhancing your Security Operations Center (SOC) by focusing on improving workflows, team collaboration, threat hunting maturity, and potentially incident management.

Whether you are deploying Sentinel for the first time or you are about to customize it after an initial setup, this module will help you drive outcomes in your Security Operations work using practical and recommended approaches.

At the end of this chapter, you should understand the following:

- Microsoft Sentinel for Security Engineers
- Leveraging Threat Intelligence
- Creating Watchlists in Sentinel
- Developing Content with KQL (Kusto Query Language)
- Building Effective Analytics
- Security Orchestration, Automation, and Response (SOAR)
- Workbooks, Reporting, and Data Visualization
- Optimizing the Security Operations Center (SOC)

Microsoft Sentinel for Security Engineers

As organizations ramp up their digital transformation and shift workloads to the cloud, the demand for a modern, adaptive, and intelligent security monitoring system is apropos. Microsoft Sentinel is a system that enables organizations with a single cloud-native platform designed to give cybersecurity engineers the visibility, intelligence, and automation they need to secure cloud-based environments. In this chapter, we will highlight ten core capabilities within Sentinel that every security engineer needs to perform good cloud security.

The first core capability, and arguably the most important, is data ingestion from a variety of cloud sources. When log and telemetry collection across identity providers, compute platforms, SaaS services, and edge devices is incomplete, the cloud environment becomes dark. Sentinel can ingest even the most unstructured data at scale from Azure, Microsoft 365, AWS, GCP, and on-premises systems, which allows security engineers to perform deep dives with complete visibility of latency when analyzing cloud environments. Suppose data pipelines are misconfigured across any one of the applications, including inconsistent logs or no logs at all. In that case, security engineers may be blind to threats such as lateral movement, credential abuse, or misconfigured assets until the breach has occurred.

The second core capability is analytics rule development. Security engineers must develop and tune behavioral rules that detect threat detection indicators by patterns, anomalies, or known indicators. Sentinel provides pre-configured rule templates right out of the box, and it also allows for custom rules to be created using KQL. Security engineers who fail to dedicate time to creating and tuning detection rules will be overwhelmed by false positives or worse, miss real threats entirely. Detection rules in Sentinel are the nervous system of threat visibility; without detection rules, Sentinel becomes passive instead of proactive.

The mastery of an effective threat investigation starts with the need for knowledge of KQL. This query language is behind every search, rule, workbook, and investigation in Sentinel. Engineers familiar with KQL can quickly analyze incidents, correlate information across systems, and expose hidden attack routes. When KQL proficiency is not available, threat investigations are cumbersome and manual, and we risk not being able to contain many threats before the threat actors move deeper into the network.

Security orchestration and automation (SOAR) is another critical discipline. Playbooks enable real-time incident response automation, including isolating endpoints, blocking IPs, and sending alerts. Engineers need to create workflows that align with SOC processes while still automating as much as possible. Automation helps reduce burnout for teams and ultimately decreases threat dwell times if an incident does arise.

Threat intelligence must also be considered for augmenting raw data with context. Sentinel will accept structured threat intelligence feeds and allow organizations to map indicators of compromise (IOCs) from threat intelligence feeds to telemetry received. Engineers can leverage threat intelligence relative to known bad actors and also contextualize alerts to third-party sources. Without strong integration of threat intelligence, analysts are left to determine if an alert is serious or credible and waste precious hours investigating false leads.

Watchlists are a tidy solution for lists of sensitive users, VIPs, critical assets, or known bad actors. Engineers can leverage watchlists in their detection rules to force special handling for those entities expanded in their watchlists above. Suppose engineers are unaware of watchlists beyond standard contingency planning. In that case, the organization will receive one-size-fits-all alerts, lacking the business context that special users or systems require to serve as valuable detection signals. This compromises detection accuracy and the prioritization of an initial response. Operational oversight and communication through reporting and dashboards are crucial for executive engagement. Engineers are consistently challenged to design dashboards that assess and summarize active threats, detection coverage, incident response capabilities, and SOC KPIs. Good, meaningful, and useful visuals displaying these metrics are essential and an effective vehicle for leadership buy-in, compliance reporting, and operational capabilities. When dashboards provided by their engineering or data science teams to mitigate risk and protect their company from specific cyber threats are missing, risk and cyber defenses become invisible to business leaders.

Another vital aspect of surveillance and threat monitoring is incident case management. Microsoft Sentinel enables security engineers to group alerts into incidents containing built-in investigation capabilities. Engineers need to organize, prioritize, assign, and track the lifecycle of incidents. Without proper case management, security operations often find themselves scrambling to find critical alerts, doubling their workload by investigating the same alerts, or delaying action due to a lack of proper oversight, which may have led to missed early warning signs of their organization being targeted by attack campaigns.

Hunting and anomaly detection are often part of the advanced capabilities within security that SOCs plan to implement, but they are a critical skill set for proactive defense. Engineers shouldn't wait for alerts; instead, they should persistently hunt for subtle signs of compromise, using built-in or custom KQL queries to gain new intelligence from the data and inform better security decisions. If security engineering adopts a reactive approach to security, it is already behind the attacker. Therefore, hunting is necessary to evolve into a more predictive defense mode, leveraging known attacks and identified intelligence to anticipate future threats.

Lastly, the final—and probably the most overlooked—capability is continuous tuning and optimization. Monitoring Microsoft Sentinel's relative performance continuously is a core skill; understanding what alerts and which rules need suppression, what data sources are creating too much noise, and what relative detection gaps exist will be a daily task for engineers. If your security engineers stop monitoring your security information and event management (SIEM) solution, Sentinel will become stale, meaning it will produce limited output. The threat landscape is constantly evolving—potentially rapidly—and so must your SIEM.

If you fail to implement the ten essentials described in this chapter, you are putting your organization at risk and creating operational inefficiencies. Unmonitored assets, poorly written rules, slow intervention times, and limited visibility are the very conditions that cyber attackers are looking for. A materially low level of detection capability in Microsoft Sentinel does not simply mean you will not detect threats. Still, your organization will be lulled into a false sense of security and believe that Microsoft Sentinel is supported as intended. When it's removed from the engineers' active management and consideration for Microsoft Sentinel maintainers as a living and breathing surveillance system that you will actively monitor and manage, this will result in late detections for your organization, prolonged recovery times after incidents, and, all too often, reputation and financial consequences.

When security engineers treat their Microsoft Sentinel platform purely as a strategic tool within the operational context of a defensive posture, they are taking a combined approach of detection as well as implementing automation, intelligence, and visibility to the process of detection. Queries and alerts are now transformed for tangible improvements to do the same work but faster—to now make informed, smarter decisions. In a world that continues to adopt a cloud-first mentality, Microsoft Sentinel is the new de facto modern security architecture to build from. Security engineers will need to consider themselves architects, not just engineers.

In the current world of cybersecurity, security engineers are defensive guards of the digital infrastructure. The role involves being constantly aware and making quick decisions, often from the perspective of evaluating high volumes of security data. This chapter has focused on guiding security engineers to develop a greater appreciation of their work, leveraging Microsoft Sentinel, which is a modern cloud-native SIEM and SOAR solution designed specifically for current threat landscape challenges.

Understanding the Role of Microsoft Sentinel

Microsoft Sentinel is much more than a collection of logs. It is an intelligent, scalable tool designed to detect, investigate, and respond to threats in real time. It collects your data from all parts of your environment, whether Azure, Microsoft 365, on-premises infrastructure, third-party security tools, or operational technology systems, and puts it in one place for visibility and analysis.

For security engineers, using Sentinel means you don't have to worry about connecting data from multiple dashboards. Sentinel gives you one pane of glass to see alerts, correlate present and past events, investigate suspicious activities, and automate actions taken when threats are detected.

Connecting Data Sources—The First Step

At its core, Sentinel relies on data. As a security engineer, your job starts by linking the appropriate data sources via automated data connectors that are native to Sentinel. When working with data connectors, check the proper sources such as the following:

- Identity and access logs (think Azure AD)
- Device logs (think Microsoft Defender for Endpoint)
- Network devices (think firewalls, VPNs)
- Applications (think Microsoft 365, AWS)
- Custom data (think syslog, Common Event Format—CEF)

Choosing the right data connectors enables Sentinel to have a clear and unobstructed look into what's happening in your environment. Even Sentinel provides recommendations that may be beneficial in deciding what log sources pose the most significant risk and thus should be prioritized in a data connector.

Detecting Threats Through Analytics Rules

As soon as sources of the appropriate data start flowing into Sentinel, you can pursue the next step as engineers: to build analytics rules, which allow you to specify what types of various behaviors should trigger an alert. Examples of behaviors could include:

- Unusual sign-ins from an unknown location
- Multiple failed attempts to log back in a short time
- A user downloading sensitive data in large amounts

There are many readily available templates for rules, including built-in rules that uncover threats through Microsoft's global threat intelligence. When creating alerts via queries, you can customize the rules or build your alert templates using Kusto Query Language (KQL).

KQL Capabilities for Security Engineers

KQL (Kusto Query Language) is the primary query language used in Sentinel for searching and analyzing data. As an engineer, learning KQL unlocks a door to a superpower where you can

- Perform detailed investigations of incidents
- Hunt threats that may be hidden
- Implement custom visuals using dashboards
- Generate alert rules and anomaly detections

Anyone with some familiarity with SQL or scripting will find KQL not challenging to learn. Furthermore, leveraging KQL's extraordinary capacity, even simple query operators can provide valuable insights into various situations using raw log data. For example, KQL can be utilized to look for failed logins, file accesses, or command-line activity that accompany known attack patterns.

Automating Your Response with Playbooks (SOAR)

One significant ability associated with Sentinel's capabilities is the ability to utilize SOAR (Security Orchestration, Automation, and Response) functionality associated with playbooks. Engineers can construct playbooks, which are automated workflows used to respond to specific alerts utilizing built-in triggers.

Playbooks can

- Then send email or Teams alerts straight to you as the analyst that an alert was received.
- Block users or IP addresses situationally, in real time.
- The playbook can open a ticket in your ITSM utilitarian workflows.
- The playbook can trigger the collection of enrichment data using threat intelligence.

This takes a majority of the task on your shoulders or analysts, and automates the action to take on the alert for additional analysis, and will chiefly pose an advantage with all alerts for your situational analysis and responses, particularly in environments wishing to minimize the delay of producing incident responses in high-volume subject areas.

Workbooks, Watchlists, and Threat Intelligence

Security engineers can also use workbooks to create visual dashboards and reports to track KPI metrics, monitor threats, and share that information with lead staff. The dashboards are interactive, and you can customize them even further using KQL queries.

Another powerful feature, available to all security engineers, is the ability to create watchlists. A watchlist is a list of suspicious users, devices, or IPs that could be relied on later during alert rules and investigations. For example, a watchlist of highly privileged accounts could help if it were to be discovered that they were behaving anomalously.

Sentinel is also able to integrate with threat intelligence feeds, which would allow alerts to be enriched with intelligence during an alert, such as whether an IP was known to be associated with a botnet or a phishing campaign. This can help security teams prioritize alerts based on known adversary threats.

Building a Smarter SOC

Security engineers play a critical role in building a smarter modern Security Operation Center by utilizing their security knowledge and the power of automation, analytic, and intelligence leveraging Sentinel. When Sentinel is combined with Defender for Endpoint, defenders will be able to detect more sophisticated threats earlier, respond faster, and utilize valuable modern new ways to operate more efficiently.

- Reduce false positives by tuning analytics rules.
- Proactively search for threats before they escalate using built-in hunting queries.
- Collaborate and work with analysts using case management and investigations tool.
- Report on the results using the dashboards and workbook

This section chapter has given security engineers the knowledge and skills to operationalize Microsoft Sentinel. Covering connecting your SIEM with data, detecting threats, automating a response, investigating incidents, and reporting on results, all from one centralized, uncomplicated, and single-orientated environment.

With Sentinel, engineers are more than defenders; they will be environmental enablers of Security intelligence, automation, and ongoing protection.

Reinventing Security Operations with Microsoft Sentinel

The rapidly evolving cybersecurity threat environment has placed extreme pressure on organizations to almost immediately change how they protect their digital environments in a way that is also cost-effective and agile. Traditional tools and legacy Security Information and Event Management (SIEM) solutions become expensive to maintain, more complex to scale, and are not built to provide the intelligence we needed to make decisions when responding to sophisticated attacks. Microsoft Sentinel is a cloud-native, AI-driven security information and event management designed for the future of cybersecurity.

In this section, I will explain how Microsoft Sentinel is reinventing SOCs to assist security teams in responding to more complicated problems more effectively, more quickly onboarding new platforms and integrating, applying automation intelligently, and using systematic detection processes, and active response.

A New Class of SIEM for a New Class of Threats

Microsoft Sentinel and SIEM, but the SIEM is designed as a cloud-based solution that can change immediately to coordinate across complex hybrid environments. Sentinel not only provides intelligent and flexible data management, but it also allows every organization to take action immediately, rather than trying to blindly mitigate a cyber incident with ineffective tools.

Today's security teams work with disjointed and fragmented tools, wading through hundreds of alerts and limited visibility of their environment. Microsoft Sentinel takes user data, enriched data, and automating workflows to give trusted intelligence, allowing defenders to see their environment and providing defenders immediate actionable intelligence needed to urgently get from detection to response.

Key Features That Distinguish Sentinel from the Competition

- *Fast Implementation with Easy Migration*: Security engineers will no longer struggle with a purposely complex migration from older SIEM systems. Microsoft Sentinel has powerful tools that allow automatic and seamless migration. These tools allow data to be configured seamlessly into the platform while keeping the underlying security configurations and operations at the same time, with few exceptions. This allows for a speedy onboarding process so that teams can start realizing value without delay.

- *Increase Security Coverage Across Digital Estate*: Microsoft Sentinel has a fast-expanding ecosystem comprising over 350 connectors that allow easy ingestion of data from varying sources (identities, emails, endpoints, cloud, applications, and network services). This variety of data being ingested provides security teams with visibility across their infrastructure for a comprehensive description of their environments and coverage to detect and respond to threats on all their critical assets.

- *Speed Up the Detection and Response Process with AI*: Speed is imperative when it comes to cybersecurity. Sentinel's correlation engine handles the burden of converting raw alerts to actionable incidents by allowing the security team to identify and resolve those alerts with low noise. With integrated AI, such as Security Copilot, teams are provided with the incident summary, the impact of the incident, and the implications of assigned tasks to remediate. All this information enables teams to identify, respond to, and remediate incidents more quickly, thereby shortening the time cycles for incident management.

- *Address Any Use Case with Broad and Diverse Resources*: Microsoft Sentinel has a large and very active community behind it. Security teams benefit from a wealth of detection rules, playbooks, dashboards, and analytic templates. With thousands of configurable resources to draw on, engineering teams can rapidly customize the platform for production purposes across a vast variety of use cases, i.e., compliance monitoring, insider threat detection, phishing response, and more.

- *Accelerate Investigations with Security Copilot*: Investigating complicated attacks takes valuable time and effort. Security Copilot uses generative AI to summarize incident timelines, correlate events across systems, and extract root causes. These capabilities can save analysts 75-85% of their time and keep them focused on the critical part: resolving the incident faster while having clarity on the threat vector.

- *Automate Repetitive Use Cases*: One of Microsoft Sentinel's key integrations of automation is at the core of Microsoft Sentinel. It automates everyday tasks in the workflow of security operations, from log analysis and alert triage to orchestrating actions after executing a script. By automating these processes, security operations teams can reduce the day-to-day workload of the department and allow skilled analysts to devote their high-value efforts to activities such as proactive threat hunting and long-term planning.

Although today's cybersecurity landscape has changed dramatically, many organizations continue to rely on outdated or niche SIEM (Security Information and Event Management) products that can't fulfill the challenges of modern threats. Unlike modern SIEM products, legacy platforms are typically very siloed in their processes, rely on heavy manual effort to analyze threat data, and lack the built-in automation, intelligence, or ease of use to detect and respond to developing attacks. These organizational vulnerabilities lead to alert fatigue, limited visibility, slow time to value due to heavy operational costs, and ultimately, holes in the organization's defense posture.

Microsoft Sentinel eliminates these barriers within cloud-native, AI-powered solutions that consider the complexities of today's IT environments. It takes machine learning, built-in automated workflows, end-to-end data collection at cloud and server scale, integrated threat intelligence, and integrated tools seamlessly across platforms to deliver a unified security operations experience that makes daily work easier and improves threat detection and response times at a lower cost. Organizations that shift to Microsoft Sentinel will be able to modernize their SOC to meet today's and future threats. Table 3-1 illustrates the comparative view of traditional SIEM versus Microsoft Sentinel.

Table 3-1. *Comparative View of Traditional SIEM Versus Microsoft Sentinel*

Category	Limitations of Traditional and Niche SIEM	What You Get with Microsoft Sentinel
Operations and User Experience	- Silo between tools - Time-consuming, needs regular updates - Complex workflows, difficult to learn	- There is a single, built-in, and unified experience - Integration into Microsoft Defender (XDR) - Simple to use; no specialization needed.
Threat Detection	- False positives - Manually investigate - Limited view of threats - Slow response time	- AI-powered detection and correlation - Integrated threat intelligence; enriched alerts - Investigation faster and more accurate.
Automation and Investigation	- Minimal automation - Excess analyst work - Only think reactively	- Security Copilot for AI-assisted response - Threat hunting based on machine learning; investigating alerts proactively.
Cost and Scalability	- High infrastructure and licensing costs - Additional costs for modules and functionality - Difficult to scale	- Cloud-native for cost-effectiveness - Easily scale as needs grow - Lower TCO.
Deployment and Integration	- Slow to onboard and integrate - Limited cloud and 3rd-party tooling and automation - Limited prebuilt use cases	- Plus, there are 350+ curated connectors for cloud, hybrid, and on-prem systems; codeless custom connectors; a large library of detection rules and playbooks.
Innovation and Vision	- Slow product updates - Not a strong investment in AI and research - No clear long-term roadmap	- Rapid innovative deployments with AI and machine learning at the core - Supported by 10,000+ Microsoft experts in security - Advanced threat intelligence and GenAI leadership.

Building Blocks of Sentinel's Modern Security Model

To appreciate how Sentinel is a holistic security strategy, it is helpful to examine its design in four related but separate building blocks:

- *Collect and Optimize*: Data is the bedrock of security. Sentinel is built with connectors and data normalization processes to allow organizations to easily ingest data from all sources of logs and telemetry throughout their digital estate. Sentinel is designed for organizations to elevate and manage data without breaking the bank with flexible data tiers and cost-optimized data storage.

- *Monitor and Detect*: Sentinel's analytics engine continuously monitors all the ingested data, looking for patterns of malicious activity. Large-scale threats can be quickly identified, and our machine learning and user/entity behavior analytics (UEBA) components look for subtle signs of emerging threats. To build on this, threat intelligence is integrated into monitoring to provide critical context and intelligence insights about known indicators of compromise (IOCs).

- *Respond and Investigate*: In the case of detected threats, Sentinel cuts the time-based response to threats by enabling security teams to get to work. Incident response workflows can be executed through automation rules, while the Security Copilot provides constraints for real-time decision-making, potentially adding depth to the investigation. By combining these capabilities, Microsoft Sentinel can improve organizations' metrics for mean time to remediation (MTTR), while enhancing SOC performance-related efficiency with the workflows added as defined processes.

- *Visualize and Improve*: Useable dashboards and visual insights permit "live" access to monitoring the security posture, as well as providing SOC leaders with a toolkit to control what is important, decide on objectives, specify key performance indicators, and realize opportunities for improvement—and in some instances Microsoft Sentinel even offers potential "daily" recommendations about utilizing your data more optimally and creating greater efficiency against your investments.

CHAPTER 3   ENGINEERING MICROSOFT SENTINEL FOR SECURITY OPERATIONS

The Numbers Tell the Story

The organizations that use Microsoft Sentinel as a capability enhancement and want to see a better outcome for the security function also experience material business outcomes:

- 44% decline in total SIEM-related costs by removing needed infrastructure investments and overall operational expenditures for the organization.

- 85% decrease in human investigation labor through automation, enabling SF, ESI, and AI-related human investigation and knowledge.

- 79% fewer false positives, allowing staff to make time available for the real extraordinary threats.

- 35% decline in the probability of a breach due to increased visibility into threats through faster response time.

- 93% faster ingestion of new data sources with our plug-and-play connectors.

The numbers tell the story not just of a platform built for performance, but more of a platform engineered for a sustainable, evolving security transformation.

Future-Proofing the Security Operations Center

With Microsoft Sentinel, organizations are not just implementing a new SIEM to replace an older generation of SIEM. Organizations are deploying a new, intelligent, scalable SIEM as a model to approach security in the future. Microsoft Sentinel aligns with the principles of modern security practices: Zero Trust, proactive defense, threat-informed defense, and continuous improvement.

Microsoft Sentinel enhances the capabilities of security teams by providing a platform that automates what can be automated, nourishes detections with real-time intelligence, and frees up human investigation expertise for higher-impact tasks.

Microsoft Sentinel is the next generation of operating security operations center capabilities. Informed by being a dramatically cloud-native platform, using artificial intelligence to detect sophisticated and complex threats, and enabling the seamless integration of cloud applications, allowing a new security operating system with scalable intelligence and system automation. Whether you are transitioning off an established legacy SIEM platform or establishing the foundational capabilities to build an SOC capability, Microsoft Sentinel delivers all the tools, insights, and flexibility an organization will need to prevail and thrive in today's cyber combat battlefield, and for security and operations engineers and SOC leaders, it is much more than a platform; it is a strategy around a future-ready resilient security.

Leveraging Threat Intelligence

Threat intelligence is knowledge, based on evidence, about existing or emerging cyber threats; i.e., threat intelligence encompasses information like malicious IP addresses, domains, file hashes, attack patterns, indicators of compromise (IOCs), and threat actors' behaviors. Threat intelligence provides teams with information about what attackers are likely to do, who they are, how they operate, to what ends, and how to mitigate/respond to their attacks.

Threat intelligence provides an organization with the means to transform raw data into actionable insights, leading to more brilliant, faster, and more effective security decisions. It's no longer just knowing that something bad happened; it's understanding what happened, why it happened, how it happened, and most importantly, what to do about it.

What Does Microsoft Sentinel Do to Manage Threat Intelligence?

Microsoft Sentinel helps organizations consolidate, manage, and take action on threat intelligence in an automated and scalable way. Sentinel has a specific threat intelligence module as well as the ability to facilitate both manual and automated ingestion of threat intelligence (TI) data from both internal and external data sources.

The following are uses of Microsoft Sentinel for threat intelligence:

- *Threat Intelligence Platform Integration*: Sentinel enables integration with threat intelligence platforms, such as TI feeds (STIX/TAXII), partnerships with Microsoft Defender Threat Intelligence, Anomali, Recorded Future, or MISP. Security engineers can bring curated indicators of compromise (IOCs) into Sentinel without effort.

- *Custom IOC Uploads*: Teams can upload their IOCs manually through the Sentinel UI or automate ingestion through APIs. This allows users to leverage either internal threat research or intelligence from regional Computer Emergency Response Teams (CERTs) or Managed Security Service Providers (MSSPs).

- *Threat Intelligence Table (ThreatIntelligenceIndicator)*: All threat indicators are recorded in a dedicated log analytics table, allowing security teams to leverage the same KQL to correlate intelligence with all alerts from within their connected environment.

- *Rule Enrichment and Matching*: Sentinel can enrich security events and alerts with threat intelligence data in real time. For example, if an outbound connection from a firewall log is identified in a TIs feed as a known threat actor, the Sentinel will trigger an alert.

- *Notebook and Automation*: Threat intelligence can be applied to hunting notebooks and playbooks. For example, create a logic app that runs automation on Sentinel to block domains with the same indicators as the malicious campaign or actor.

- *Visualization and Tracking*: Engineers can change threat intelligence from static data and embed it into their ongoing operational resource. They can create dashboards and workbooks to monitor threat intelligence hits, campaign activity, IOCs expiries, or actor-based behaviors.

Value of Threat Intelligence for Security Engineers

For a security engineer, threat intelligence is invaluable because it enables them to move from incident detection and response to active threat prevention in the SOC function. Here are a few examples of how:

- *Detection Accuracy*: Providing contextual threat intelligence enables security engineers to reduce false positive alerts by overlaying known threat indicators, helping them prioritize real-world threats.

- *Fast Investigation and Triage*: Alerts enriched with threat intelligence provide immediate context to security engineers, allowing them to determine if they are assessing part of a threat actor's known campaign or responding to a live threat.

- *Threat Hunting*: Threat intelligence allows security engineers to create more contextual threat hunting queries. Instead of sifting through massive datasets, hunts can now be driven by precision rather than extensive analysis.

- *Automated Response Decisions*: Playbooks can be written to utilize TI to make dynamic decisions. For example, a playbook can escalate only alerts that are confirmed by a TI feed and auto-close everything else.

- *Operational Readiness and Threat Awareness*: Intelligence enhances the overall operational readiness of the SOC by providing security engineers with immediate threat information visibility. Security teams can adjust analytics rules, harden their defensive posture, and provide operational briefings.

- *Strategic Defence Building*: Intelligence isn't only about threat actors today. Security engineers can examine trends, look at TTPs from actors, and leverage geopolitical indicators to develop long-term security strategies that align with threat trends. Microsoft Sentinel turns threat intelligence from a static list of indicators into a living, dynamic system that interacts with your security data in real-time. For security engineers, this means greater insight, automation, and confidence in defending cloud-first environments. It allows teams to detect smarter, respond faster, and stay ahead of adversaries—not just reacting to attacks but anticipating them.

Cyber threat intelligence (CTI) is the body of knowledge that allows individuals and organizations alike to understand current and emerging cyber threats. It conveys critical information regarding adversaries, such as adversary intent, adversary methods, adversary infrastructure, and adversary observed behaviors, which organizations can then use to develop defensive methods.

CTI can come in many forms. Sometimes, CTI comes in the form of detailed reports elaborating on the motivations, infrastructure, and techniques employed by threat actors. Other times, CTI comes in a more granular form, and the most common, tactical CTI, consists of lists of malicious IPs, domains, URLs, file hashes, and other digital badging that signal the presence of malicious activity. Commonly referred to as indicators of compromise (IOCs) or indicators of attack.

Organizations rely on cyber threat intelligence (CTI) to provide context to abnormal behavior. This context eliminates the need for security engineers to respond to any abnormal signal unthinkingly. It enables them to quickly validate whether this abnormal event is indeed part of an identified attack campaign. By providing context, the cycle time between detection and action is decreased while improving decision-making and response accuracy. Cyber threat intelligence is made feasible through public open-source threat feeds, intelligence-sharing communities (ISACs), commercially aggressive intelligence providers, and even insights aggregated from internal investigations.

In Microsoft Sentinel—a SIEM (security information and event monitoring) solution in the cloud—the integration and use of cyber threat intelligence is dynamic and can facilitate automated detection, enrichment of alerts, and investigation workflows utilizing data-fed insights. The most common type of threat intelligence used in SIEM is tactical intelligence, which can be IPs, domains, file hashes, and URLs (do not forget the URLs, etc.). These indicators are often the low-hanging fruit utilized in bulk writing rules for surveillance of malware, phishing campaigns, command-and-control infrastructure, and more.

Microsoft Sentinel utilizes not only tactical intelligence but also strategic and operational levels of threat intelligence. Threat actor tactics, techniques, and procedures (TTPs), the kinds of infrastructure they use, and what kinds of targets they will select. This is where Microsoft Sentinel utilizes STIX (Structured Threat Information eXpression) as a consumable standard for these complicated threat objects. STIX enables interoperability among threat intelligence platforms, allowing analysts to visualize specific threat objects and their connections relationships to and across each.

This broader layer of intelligence will show security engineers not only a single independent threat but also the full context of an attack campaign, so security can enable informed incident response, threat hunting, and risk assessment in multiple review phases.

To effectively consume threat intelligence in Microsoft Sentinel, security teams work through an ongoing three-cycle lifecycle.

Combining and Handling Cyber Threat Intelligence

With the features of Microsoft Sentinel, you can feed the data from any number of sources, platforms, and subscriptions into its workspace, using built-in data connectors, via third-party APIs, or through manual upload. In addition, you can introduce structured threat data (STIX/TAXII), interpreted structured threat data, or custom-built source intelligence, such as Microsoft Defender Threat Intelligence, which means you can create a central repository of threat intelligence across your organization for use in a variety of ways across analytics and automation. Once you have ingested that threat intelligence, it can be managed through the Microsoft Sentinel interface, and you can do several things, including

- Query and search intelligence with KQL
- Aggregate related threat artifacts by applying rules, tags, or relationships
- Use workbooks to present visualizations on trends, concordance, or actor activity

This third layer of management will help ensure your threat intelligence is relevant, clean, and supports your organization's detection strategy.

Using Threat Intelligence to Detect and Respond

With threat intelligence fully integrated, you can assume Microsoft Sentinel will take care of automatically correlating incoming telemetry and will be able to accomplish requests, including

- Detection of abnormal and/or known malicious behavior
- Trigger alerts and incidents through built-in rule templates or custom KQL
- Enrich existing hunting efforts and provide contextual information to investigators
- Provide data-rich insights into notebooks, reports, and dashboards

By embedding CTI within your detection and response workflows, Microsoft Sentinel transforms passive CTI analysis into an active cybersecurity capability. This practice connects knowledge to action, resulting not only in the detection of more threats but also in enhanced efficiency and effectiveness of your overall cybersecurity capability.

Connecting Microsoft Defender Threat Intelligence to Microsoft Sentinel

As a Security Operations Analyst, your job is to improve your organization's ability to accurately detect and respond to threats. One of the most effective ways to do this in Microsoft Sentinel is by providing trusted and reputable threat intelligence. Microsoft Defender Threat Intelligence (MDTI) gives you curated and validated Indicators of Compromise (IOCs) from both public open-source intelligence and Microsoft's own threat research. You can then link this feed to Sentinel, which gives you even more threat data to improve analytics, alerting, and investigation workflows.

Your manager has assigned you the task of setting up this integration to help make your SOC more capable. In this section, you'll work through the full installation process for the threat intelligence solution and set up the Defender Threat Intelligence data connector.

Step 1: Install the Threat Intelligence Solution from the Content Hub

Before you can connect any data feed, the threat intelligence solution must be installed within your Microsoft Sentinel workspace. This solution enables the ingestion and operational use of threat data from MDTI.

Follow these steps to install the solution:

1. Open the **Azure portal** or the **Microsoft Defender portal**.
2. Navigate to **Microsoft Sentinel**.
3. Under the **Content management** section, select **Content hub**.
4. In the search bar, type **Threat Intelligence**.
5. From the search results, select the **Threat Intelligence** solution.

6. Click on **Install/Update** to begin the installation.

7. Wait for the installation process to complete. This typically takes a few minutes.

Once installed, Sentinel is ready to accept threat intelligence feeds from Defender Threat Intelligence.

Step 2: Enable the Defender Threat Intelligence Data Connector

With the threat intelligence solution in place, your next step is to enable the actual data connector that links Sentinel to Microsoft Defender Threat Intelligence.

Here's how to do it:

1. From the **Azure portal** or **Defender portal**, return to **Microsoft Sentinel**.

2. In the **Configuration** section, select **Data connectors**.

3. In the search bar, type **Defender Threat Intelligence** to locate the connector. You'll see options for both **Standard** and **Premium** versions.

4. Click on the connector and select **Open connector page**.

5. On the connector page, click the **Connect** button.

6. Wait for the status to update from "Not Connected" to **Connected**.

Once the integration is completed, a data stream will begin flowing into your Sentinel workspace, and high-fidelity IOCs will become available to be used in analytic rules, hunting queries, incident enrichment, and automated response.

In enabling the Microsoft Defender Threat Intelligence connector, you have now granted Microsoft Sentinel high-fidelity, real-time, curated threat indicator feeds. The IOCs in these feeds include domains, IP addresses, URLs, and file hashes seen in known attacks and campaigns. Sentinel is using this data to discover valid, matching activity in your environments and to serve you alerts associated with confirmed high-confidence threats.

Using Microsoft Defender Threat Intelligence in conjunction with Microsoft Sentinel not only increases threat detection accuracy but also reduces investigation and triage times. You'll be able to become more intelligent, responsive to changes, and resilient to cyber threats as they continue to evolve with the right foundation in place.

Connecting the TAXII Threat Intelligence Connector in Microsoft Sentinel

Integrating STIX/TAXII Feeds for Enhanced Threat Detection

Microsoft Sentinel natively supports threat intelligence ingestion via the industry standard TAXII (Trusted Automated eXchange of Intelligence Information) protocol. Using both TAXII 2.0 and 2.1, security teams can automatically ingest structured threat indicators (such as IP addresses, file hashes, domains, and URLs) from trusted TAXII servers into the Sentinel workspace.

This ingestion allows security analysts to improve detection rules, automate alerts, and add external verified and recent threat data to ongoing threat hunting processes.

Setting Up the Threat Intelligence—TAXII Connector

To configure and enable the TAXII connector in Microsoft Sentinel, follow these straightforward steps within the Azure portal:

1. Open the **Azure portal** and navigate to **Microsoft Sentinel**.

2. From your selected Sentinel workspace, go to the **Data connectors** section.

3. Locate and select the **Threat Intelligence – TAXII** connector from the list.

4. In the preview pane on the right, click on **Open connector page** to access the detailed configuration interface.

Entering Configuration Details

On the connector configuration page, provide the required information to establish a secure connection with your TAXII server:

- *Friendly Name*: A display name to help identify the server connection within Sentinel.

- *API Root URL*: The base endpoint of the TAXII server.

- *Collection ID*: The unique identifier for the specific TAXII feed (or collection) you wish to connect.

- *Username and Password*: Authentication credentials, if required by the TAXII server.

Once all the necessary information has been entered, click **Add** to enable the connection. Sentinel will begin retrieving threat indicators from the configured TAXII server.

Managing Connected TAXII Servers

When the connection connects, Sentinel displays a list of all the TAXII sources configured. For each listed source, you can view metadata like the last indicator received time, which allows you to verify that the data ingestion is working properly.

In order to manage a server configuration (e.g., remove or edit a feed), use the ellipsis menu (⋯) at the end of the row for the server.

By connecting a TAXII server to Microsoft Sentinel, you've improved your threat detection with structured intelligence updates from external sources. Now the analytics, alerts, and investigations you perform using Sentinel are supported by the latest threat data, providing all the needed insight necessary to build a formidable defense posture, all based on insights from threat activity around the globe.

Connecting Microsoft Sentinel with the Threat Intelligence Upload API

Organizations frequently utilize Threat Intelligence Platforms (TIPs) to gather and aggregate threat intelligence data from various commercial, open-source, and internal threat data sources. If you want the ability to put this threat data into action within Microsoft Sentinel, you can leverage the Threat Intelligence Upload API—an API-based ingestion path that allows custom STIX-formatted threat objects to be ingested into your Microsoft Sentinel workspace directly.

By utilizing the API ingestion path, advanced security teams will be able to upload their sourced intelligence—including IPs, file hashes, domains, and full actor profiles—into Sentinel's analytic engine from the security team after a proper disposition. API ingestion does not utilize data connectors, so configuration through the UI is not required, giving you the flexibility to completely automate your ingestion process in a modern stack/architecture with the security use case in mind.

The Benefits of the Upload API

The Structured Threat Information Expression (STIX) is the industry standard to describe cyber threat data. The API was purpose-built to accept these objects, which can include not simply indicators of compromise (IOCs) but also contextual information about threat actors, TTPs (tactics, techniques, and procedures), malware families, and attack patterns. This allows security teams to import rich, structured intelligence into Microsoft Sentinel—rather than simply matching indicators.

Prerequisites Before Getting Started

To use the Upload API successfully, please ensure the following prerequisites are satisfied:

- *Permissions to the Sentinel Workspace*: You must have read and write access.
- A registered Microsoft Entra application (formerly Azure AD).
- The Microsoft Sentinel Contributor role assigned to your application at the workspace level.

Step-by-Step: Setting Up the Threat Intelligence Upload API

Step 1. Register a Microsoft Entra Application

To authenticate and send data through the Upload API, start by registering an application in Microsoft Entra.

- Navigate to Microsoft Entra ID ➤ App registrations.
- Create a new registration and note the Application (client) ID.
- Generate a Client Secret under the Certificates & Secrets tab and save it securely.

Roles such as Application Administrator, Application Developer, or Cloud Application Administrator have the necessary privileges to perform these tasks.

Step 2. Assign Permissions to the Application

Once your app is registered, it must be authorized to access the Sentinel workspace:

- Go to Azure portal ➤ Log Analytics workspaces.
- Select your Sentinel workspace, then navigate to Access control (IAM).
- Click Add ➤ Add role assignment.
- Choose Microsoft Sentinel Contributor as the role.
- Under Assign access to, select User, group, or service principal.
- Search for your app by name and assign the role.

This step grants your application the required access to post threat intelligence directly into Sentinel.

Step 3. Configure Your Threat Intelligence Platform or Application

Now that your Entra application is ready, configure your TIP or custom app to begin sending data. You will need to provide the following values:

- Application (client) ID
- OAuth 2.0 token (generated using your client ID and secret)
- Microsoft Sentinel Workspace ID

Enter these values in your platform's configuration where appropriate.

When you complete all the above configuration and setup, you can send your objects in STIX format to the Upload API endpoint. Once your submission is sent, Microsoft Sentinel will ingest the data very shortly thereafter.

Validating Ingestion and Watching STIX Objects

When submitting, it can take a few minutes until the data starts showing up. You can validate ingestion by

- Navigating to Microsoft Sentinel
- Opening the threat intelligence page from the menu
- Looking at the ingested STIX objects and their details

From here you can begin using that intelligence for analytics, detections, hunting, and enrichment across the data sources you have connected.

The Threat Intelligence Upload API provides a flexible, powerful option for advanced security teams that are looking to bring curated, high-value intelligence into Microsoft Sentinel. It supports the entire STIX data model and provides an API that is easily automated. This provides the opportunity for organizations to build a truly proactive and intelligence-led SOC.

Whether you are sourcing from commercial TIPs, building your own intel pipeline, or collaborating and consuming threat data from threat-sharing communities, this integration will work to ensure your threat data becomes part of a living defense framework. Actionable, contextual, and adaptive to the threat environment.

Using Threat Intelligence Indicators in Microsoft Sentinel Analytics Rules.

Turning Threat Data into Real-Time Alerts

Threat indicators (malicious IP addresses, domains, or file hashes) are a rich source of insights into when and how to identify and respond to possible security threats. In Microsoft Sentinel, you can create analytics rules that leverage threat indicators to react automatically to suspicious activities in your environment. A properly configured analytics rule continuously scans the ingested data for indicators of known threats, generating alerts or incidents based on configured thresholds if found.

What You Need Before You Start

Before you can use threat indicators in analytics rules, ensure the following exists:

- Threat indicators are present in your Sentinel workspace. You can gather threat indicators from threat feeds, third parties, manual entry, or a bulk upload (e.g., CSV).

- Relevant data connectors are connected and sending logs to your Sentinel workspace. For example, if you're going to match IP indicators against Azure subscription events, you'll need to connect the Azure Activity data connector.

- You have a rule template, or custom rule, that will correlate the threat indicators against event data. Sentinel has out-of-the-box templates to help get you started.

Creating a Rule That Uses Threat Intelligence

Now let's walk through configuring a rule that uses a threat indicator. One example is a rule that maps an IP address from threat intelligence against the Azure Activity logs, which would help to identify any behavior from known bad IPs.

Steps:

1. In the portal, go to Microsoft Sentinel and select the appropriate workspace.

2. From the menu, choose Analytics under the Configuration section.

3. Open the Rule templates tab to browse available rule templates.

4. Search for and select the template titled TI map IP entity to AzureActivity. This rule is prebuilt to match IP address indicators with Azure Activity events.

5. Click Create rule to launch the configuration wizard.

Understanding the Rule Logic

Once in the wizard, you will see that the core inner workings are already configured:

- *Query Logic*: The rule applies a KQL query that joins the ThreatIntelligenceIndicator table and the AzureActivity table by matching IP addresses.

- *Entity Mapping*: Sentinel is told how to understand things like IP addresses, user accounts, or URLs, so that incidents provide meaningful context.

- *Schedule*: By default, the rule runs every hour, checking the last hour's events, running in a subset of time in the past hour.

- *Alerting Criteria*: An alert will fire if any matching indicators are found.

You can either keep the defaults or customize them to fit your environment—for example, you can change the match window, frequency, and alert thresholds.

Defining Incident Settings and Automation

Next, move to the Incident settings section. Here, you can define whether the rule creates incidents, groups alerts together, and sets the level of severity.

You can add workflows, called playbooks, in the Automated response section. These are automated actions that will run based on alerts—an example could be to send notifications, isolate machines, or enrich alerts that have hints of more intelligence.

Playbooks are built using Logic Apps and are customizable to fit the way you want to operate.

To Finalize the Rule

After you have completed all of your settings:

- Click the Next button to validate the rule.
- If you validated successfully, click Create to turn it on.

In your Analytics, the rule will now show up under the Active rules tab and will operate according to the schedule you indicated.

Monitoring Alerts and Incidents

Once the rule is turned on, it will run continually looking for threats. When it finds a match, it will create a security alert. Alerts are logged to the SecurityAlert table and can be found in the Logs section.

Alerts from analytics rules create incidents that can be found in the Incidents section. Incidents are the backbone of the investigation workflow in Sentinel. That is where your SOC analysts will triage findings, conduct threat investigations, and respond.

IoMT is a connected network of connected medical devices, sensors, and healthcare IT systems that have emerged due to the rapid development of technology in healthcare. The IoMT can enhance patient care and operational efficiency through remote monitoring, but it also introduces a new operational risk: cyberattacks. Standard IT security models continue not to sufficiently meet all aspects of the vulnerabilities and complexity of medical devices. The focus of this chapter will be the MITRE ATT&CK® framework and its value in understanding, analyzing, and mitigating cyber threats for IoMT ease of operation for healthcare organizations.

What Is the MITRE ATT&CK® Framework?

The MITRE ATT&CK (Adversarial Tactics, Techniques, and Common Knowledge) framework is an internationally available, curated knowledge base of adversary tactics and techniques based on real-world observations. The MITRE Corporation created it, and it serves as a detailed, behavior-based model of post-compromise adversary behavior that can be used to develop particular threat models and methodologies for cybersecurity.

The ATT&CK framework is contrary to the traditional security models, which relate to indicators of compromise (IOCs) such as malware signatures. ATT&CK is oriented towards understanding the how and why of the attack while defining and categorizing adversary behavior in terms of:

- *Tactics*: The adversary's short-term (tactical) goals during the attack (the "why"). Examples of tactics are Initial Access, Execution, Persistence, Privilege Escalation, Defense Evasion, Credential Access, Discovery, Lateral Movement, Collection, Command and Control, Exfiltration, and Impact. For Industrial Control Systems (ICS), which are somewhat congruent with IoMT, there are additional tactics that would be relevant to consider, such as Inhibit Response Function and Impair Process Control.

- *Techniques*: These define the means that adversaries use to achieve their tactical goals (the "how"), and thus each tactic can have multiple techniques. For the tactic "Initial Access," the methods can consist of (but are not limited to) phishing, valid accounts, and so on.

- *Sub-techniques*: This is a finer-grained definition of how a technique can be executed.

- *Procedures*: This is an instance of how an adversary group may use a technique or sub-technique in an attack.

The ATT&CK framework is built upon matrices; the most commonly used is the Enterprise matrix, but MITRE also publishes the Mobile matrix and the ICS matrix. As there is no "IoMT" matrix or variations of IoMT, I have found the ICS matrix and elements of the Enterprise and Mobile matrices to be most relevant due to the nature of IoMT devices and their associations with enterprise networks.

The advantages of using MITRE ATT&CK:

- *Shared Language*: Provides a common language to describe threats and threat actors within the cybersecurity field and enables better communication and collaboration among security teams, consultancies, vendors, and stakeholders.

- *Adversary-Centric*: Adopting an adversary-centric viewpoint recognizes that the goal should not just be about blocking known threats but rather understanding adversary behaviors, in turn strengthening digital resilience, defense, and threat hunting.

- *Gap Analysis*: Organizations can map their existing defenses against known adversary techniques and then benchmark and identify gaps in their security and therefore weaknesses in their security posture.

- *Enhanced Threat Detection and Response*: When used by security operations centers (SOCs), threat operations and intelligence analysts can use the framework maps to triage alerts, enhance threat intelligence, and improve their overall detection and response strategies.

- *Red Teaming and Adversary Emulation*: Red teamers can use the framework to simulate a more realistic attack and evaluate how adequate specific controls, either technical or non-technical, are in an organization.

- *Risk Management*: The ATT&CK framework provides organizations with a systematic way in which to assess and prioritize risks based on real-world attack scenarios.

IoMT Security Challenges:

Before exploring ATT&CK's applicability, one must first appreciate the unique challenges of securing IoMT:

- *Device Vulnerabilities*: Most IoMT devices are low-powered, lack timely updates, and come with weak, almost non-existent, security features; therefore, implementing sound security practices or timeliness in patches is challenging for manufacturers.

- *Complexity of Ecosystem*: The healthcare environment has a broad and diverse range of devices from many manufacturers that create a highly complex attack surface.

- *Legacy Systems*: The use of legacy systems, often patchless by design, introduces vulnerabilities.

- *Data Sensitivity*: IoMT devices handle very sensitive patient data (Protected Health Information—PHI), making them prime for malicious threat actors seeking data or ransom.

- *Patient Safety Impact*: Engaging with a malicious IoMT device can not only affect patient health and safety; it has the potential to result in death.

- *Lack of Standardization*: The poor standardization across IoMT devices and protocols limits interoperability and implementation of more secure options.

- *Limited Visibility and Control*: Many devices don't support traditional security agents and monitoring tools. We classify these as "unmanaged," which creates "blind spots" for us.

- *Poor Network Segmentation*: Poor segmentation of networks in healthcare can allow attackers to laterally propagate from an IoMT device to other systems that are critical to the provider's operation.

Leveraging MITRE ATT&CK® for IoMT Security

When organizations integrate MITRE ATT&CK into their IoMT environment(s), they are not only employing an organizational framework for visibility, detection, and response capabilities, but they are also improving security overall. Here are some conceptual ideas to help organizations integrate the MITRE ATT&CK framework into their IoMT environment:

Asset Inventory and Mitigation Map

The first step is to gain complete visibility and "map" assets with accompanying capabilities, network connections, and information related to the data being processed. Once organizations establish an inventory of all assets, they will map the assets to respective ATT&CK tactics and techniques. For example, an infusion pump may fall under "Impair Process Control" (ICS Tactic) or "Data Manipulation" (Enterprise Technique).

Threat Modeling and Risk Assessment

Healthcare entities can examine adversary-centric threat modeling using the MITRE ATT&CK framework. First, identify common threat actors that would target IoMT and recognize what tactics and techniques they would commonly use. Next, consider the potential impact of attacks on specific medical devices and overall patient care, as well as the likelihood of such attacks occurring. This type of planning will help determine the prioritized exploitable vulnerabilities and will guide remediation efforts.

Gain Advanced Detection Capabilities

Building out the ATT&CK framework creates an opportunity for organizations to develop their detection capabilities and assess their detection efficacy. Security teams can:

Map existing detections: Evaluate existing security controls (i.e., intrusion detection systems, network monitoring tools within the organization, etc.) and begin the process of mapping those existing detections to ATT&CK technique(s) that they can successfully detect and take note of overall gaps in detection.

Build new detections: Develop impactful detection rules and alerts that leverage standard ATT&CK techniques applicable to the IoMT devices that organizations monitor. For example, suppose security teams are monitoring for unusual network activity or unauthorized access to a medical device control interface. In that case, they may encounter some everyday use of "Lateral Movement" or "Command and Control" in both cases.

Utilize IoMT-Specific Data Sources: Leverage IoMT data sources (i.e., device logs, firmware version history, communications patterns, etc.) and correlate that with SIEM data sources to increase ATT&CK detection capability.

Raise the Incident Response Rate

During an incident response, the incident response team collaborates as ATT&CK fractions and tactics/techniques, enabling them to hone in on and advance incident response analysis, containment, eradication, and ultimately recovery. Connecting and telling the story of an observed adversary activity using ATT&CK in many ways gives incident response teams the intuition to anticipate adversary activity after identifying the activity and provide ideas for future response playbooks.

Validation and Improved Security Control Measures

Organizations will need to routinely validate their security controls against ATT&CK techniques, which may include

- *Adversary Emulation*: Perform an exercise on real invasions of attacks, targeting the covering attacks established on ATT&CK techniques and actions to validate the IoMT security strategy and security operational resilience.

- *Red-Teaming*: Work with ethical hacking or the well-established expertise in exploring specific attack paths; known to engage ATT&CK techniques during their breach exercises.

- *Gap Repair*: Based on validation results, make appropriate efforts to repair as needed (i.e., network isolation, enhanced authentication controls, firmware updates and patches, anomaly detection, etc.).

Education and Awareness

All management commitment to ATT&CK has to be an organization-wide effort. Developing an organizational understanding of adversary tactics and techniques will not only strengthen security capabilities but also enable all stakeholders to contribute to a common culture that supports shared security objectives.

Creating Watchlists in Sentinel

Watchlists in Microsoft Sentinel are powerful tools designed to help security analysts in the management of reference data that can be used within the lifecycle of their threat detection and response responsibilities. Whether it is tracking high-value assets, managing lists for terminated employees, or enriching event data, some expanding references will invariably move to contextual identifiers in event data. Watchlists are designed to provide the security operations analyst with human interaction with structured lists of name-value pairs. The lists can be imported into the workspace, and for fast, low-latency queries, they can be cached and set for easy access. Watchlists provide security operations the flexibility to conveniently leverage them across detection rules, threat-hunting queries, workbooks, or automated response playbooks.

Enabling the use of watchlists within various security operations tasks can help organizations alleviate alert fatigue, enhance investigation possibilities, and improve the fidelity of their threat detection capabilities. As Cochrane noted, watchlists provide a direct link between processing raw telemetry and contextual contextuality. Watchlists are also an enrichment for data processing analysts who possess contextual organizational awareness to apply that knowledge to security signals or telemetry.

Practical Scenarios for Watchlist Use

In practice, the use cases, or scenarios, are infinite, as this tool is designed to allow the user to be flexible based upon their specific situation's needs for monitoring purposes. For example, in threat investigations, an analyst can use, import, or interact with an imported watchlist that includes a baseline of known indicators, such as a list of public IP addresses, file hashes, and a set of suspicious domains. Watchlist items can be imported in various file formats; however, for ease of use, we recommend CSV files. An example of this type of scenario is the ability to upload lists of known indicators, which can then be pulled in and incorporated to filter, correlate, or join event data in previously discussed sections.

A list of internal organizations referenced and safe harbor items would be more akin to knowledge about the organization. Examples again can be past employees who are terminated with elevated privileges within access controls or lists of previous (external) users whose rightful (expired) access to use the organization's systems has ended and should not be accessing any further. These lists can help build allowlists or blocklists, which can be called directly in analytics rules to improve detection and decrease noise.

Another robust use case is the creation of allowlists for known benign actions that might otherwise generate alerts. For example, analysts can mute alerts from automated scripts run from a known source of IP addresses or execution actions from trusted service accounts. In this instance, the security team can focus alerts around known-good behaviors and pay attention to actions that are truly anomalous or malicious.

Watchlists also help enrich existing logs with additional information to provide more contextual analysis. This enrichment is essential for analysts, as it enables them to pivot across datasets more quickly and with greater insight, which translates to increased efficiency overall in threat detection and response.

Important Considerations and Limitations

Watchlists are helpful, but there are some limitations and best practices to be aware of:

- *Naming Rules*: Watchlist names and aliases are initially defined as 3-64 characters. The name must start and end with any alphanumeric character. However, you can use spaces, hyphens, and underscores in the middle.

- *Inherent Intent*: Watchlists are designed primarily for reference data, not as recipients of high-volume datasets or data processing. They cannot replace the use of full telemetry or ingesting your logs.

- *Item Limits*: A Microsoft Sentinel workspace currently can have up to 10 million active items in a single watchlist in a single workspace. Deleted values aren't included in those limits. If workloads exceed those values, consider using custom log tables.

- *Retention Policy*: The Watchlist table retains data for 28 days. Be sure to take proper data lifecycle management into account.

- *Refresh Cycle*: The Watchlist refreshes at about 12-day intervals, which will also refresh the TimeGenerated field and its associated entries.

- *Workspace Level*: Watchlist management only occurs on a workspace level. You cannot use 'cross-workspace management' scenarios.

- *Local Size Limitations*: The local uploaded file has a provision for 3.8 MB. If the data exceeds this size, consider a cloud storage solution. You can still upload a file from cloud storage, provided it fits within the 500 MB file limit in terms of both structure and size.

- *KQL Criteria*: Columns and tables must meet KQL naming criteria. If properly formatted, you may see upload failures or query errors.

Creating Watchlists

There are many ways to create and group watchlists in Sentinel based on the size of the data and the format of the source data:

- *Local File Upload*: You can upload a CSV or JSON file (that has name-value pairs) directly into the workspace from your machine.

- *Cloud Uploads*: If your data set is large (up to 500 MB), you can upload your data file to your storage account in the cloud. Once the data file is uploaded, you can create a secure access URL (Shared Access Signature or SAS URL). This URL can be accessed by Microsoft Sentinel to securely collect the contents of your uploaded file and create the watchlist.

- *Watchlists with Templates*: Templates can be modified and used to create watchlists quickly. They also establish boundaries for consistent usage and outline the process for conducting and onboarding specific business reference data to the watchlist.

Once created, the watchlists can be used immediately as a table in KQL queries. Analysts can join it with other logs and use them in conditional logic for analytic rules, as a reference for workflows on automation designed to enrich onboarding incident engagement, or to trigger specific remediation activities.

Deploying Watchlists in Microsoft Sentinel

Watchlists in Microsoft Sentinel are a great feature that will allow you to correlate external data with the security events you have in your Microsoft Sentinel environment. You might have a list for critical company assets, people who have left the company recently, or some service accounts you want to watch closely. You can easily upload these lists as watchlists to add context to your security investigations and threat hunting activities. You can create watchlists by uploading a file locally or, in some cases, directly from your Azure Storage account for larger data sets. Microsoft Sentinel offers watchlist templates that can also add structure to your lists. For local file uploads, there is a limit of 3.8 MB, but for larger files (500 MB), you can upload them to Azure Storage. There are limitations with watchlists, so take time to understand them before you spend time uploading. Also, consider that the data written to the Log Analytics Watchlist table will only be kept for 28 days. Many of the playbooks, reports, and watchlist templates discussed in this article are in PREVIEW at the time of writing, which means that many of the features are still in development and may change. To learn more about the legal aspects of pre-release features, please refer to the Azure Preview Supplemental Terms, and the link will be in the additional links at the end of the article. Microsoft Sentinel is available in the Microsoft Defender portal, and users can access Microsoft Sentinel even if they do not have Microsoft Defender XDR or an E5 license. For information related to accessing Microsoft Sentinel in the Defender portal, please check the documentation.

Uploading a Watchlist from a Local Folder

The two primary methods for uploading a watchlist from your local machine (CSV file) are

- For a watchlist file you created without a template, enter the watchlist provisioned information.

- For a watchlist file created from the Microsoft Sentinel watchlist template, the Microsoft Sentinel Environment must already be provisioned, and this option saves time since Azure has prepopulated some information for you.

Uploading a Watchlist from a File You Created (Without a Template)

If you haven't used a Microsoft Sentinel watchlist template to prepare your file, follow these steps:

1. Navigate to Watchlists:

    a. In the Microsoft Defender portal, go to Microsoft Sentinel ➤ Configuration ➤ Watchlist.

    b. In the Azure portal, under Configuration, select Watchlist.

2. Select + New.

3. On the General page, provide a Name, Description, and Watchlist Alias for your watchlist.

CHAPTER 3   ENGINEERING MICROSOFT SENTINEL FOR SECURITY OPERATIONS

4. Select Next: Source.

5. On the Source page, you'll configure your data upload.

6. Select a Type for the Dataset: Choose a CSV file with a header (.csv).

    a. *Number of Lines Before Row with Headings*: Enter the number of lines in your data file that appear before the actual header row.

    b. *Upload File*: Either drag and drop your CSV file or select Browse for files to locate and upload it.

    c. *SearchKey*: This is a crucial field. Enter the name of a column in your watchlist that you anticipate frequently using for joining with other data or for searches. For example, if your watchlist contains server names and their corresponding IP addresses, and you often search or join by IP address, you'd designate the "IP Address" column as the SearchKey.

Note   If your CSV file exceeds 3.8 MB, you must use the instructions for creating a large watchlist from a file in Azure Storage.

---

7. Select Next: Review and Create.

8. Review all the information to ensure accuracy. Wait for the Validation passed message to appear, then select Create.

As soon as the watchlist has been created, you will receive a notification. It may take a few minutes for the watchlist to be fully processed.

Uploading a Watchlist Created from a Template (Preview)

You can use a Microsoft Sentinel watchlist template to create a watchlist:

1. Navigate to Watchlists:

    a. In the Azure portal, under Configuration, select Watchlist.

    b. In the Microsoft Defender portal, go to Microsoft Sentinel ➤ Configuration ➤ Watchlist.

2. Select the Templates (Preview) tab.

3. Choose the appropriate template from the list. Details of the template will appear in the right pane.

4. Select Create from template.

5. On the General tab, you'll notice that the Name, Description, and Watchlist Alias fields are pre-populated and read-only.

6. On the Source tab, select Browse for files and choose the CSV file you created using the template.

7. Select Next: Review and Create > Create.

Again, an Azure notification will confirm the watchlist's creation. Allow a few minutes for the watchlist to be fully available for queries.

Creating a Large Watchlist from a File in Azure Storage (Preview)

If your watchlist is large and exceeds 500 MB, you'll need to first upload your file to your Azure Storage account, where Microsoft Sentinel can read the data through a Shared Access Signature (SAS) URL. SAS URLs are URIs that contain a resource URI along with a shared access signature token, enabling secure delegated access to resources in your storage account.

Step 1: Upload Watchlist File to Azure Storage

You must first upload your large watchlist file to an Azure Storage account. If you haven't already, you will need to create a storage account. This storage account doesn't have to exist in the same resource group or region as your Microsoft Sentinel workspace. You can use AzCopy or the Azure portal to upload your CSV file.

Uploading Your File with AzCopy:

AzCopy is a command-line utility for high-performance data transfer to and from Azure Blob storage. To learn more, see information on uploading files to Azure Blob storage by using AzCopy.

If you don't already have a storage container, create one using the following AzCopy command:

```
azcopy make https://<storage-account-name>.<blob or dfs>.core.windows.net/<container-name>
```

Next, upload your file using this command:

```
azcopy copy '<local-file-path>' 'https://<storage-account-name>.<blob or dfs>.core.windows.net/<container-name>/<blob-name>'
```

Uploading Your File in Azure Portal:

If you prefer a graphical interface, you can upload your file directly through the Azure portal.

1. Go to your storage account in the Azure portal.

2. If you don't have an existing storage container, create a container. For public access level, the default "Private (no anonymous access)" is recommended.

3. Upload your CSV file to the storage account as a block blob.

Step 2: Create Shared Access Signature (SAS) URL

Once your file is in Azure Storage, you need to generate an SAS URL for Microsoft Sentinel to access it securely.

1. Follow the steps outlined in creating SAS tokens for blobs in the Azure portal.

2. Set the shared access signature token expiry time to a minimum of 6 hours.

3. Leave the Allowed IP addresses field blank (default value).

4. Copy the value for Blob SAS URL. You will need this in a later step.

Step 3: Add Azure to the CORS Tab

Before using your SAS URI, you must configure Cross-Origin Resource Sharing (CORS) in your storage account to allow access from the Azure portal.

1. Go to your storage account settings, and then navigate to the Resource sharing page.

2. Select the Blob service tab.

3. Add https://*.portal.azure.net to the Allowed origins table.

4. Select the appropriate allowed methods: GET and OPTIONS.

5. Save the configuration.

Step 4: Add the Watchlist to a Workspace

With your file uploaded and the SAS URL generated, you can now add the large watchlist to your Microsoft Sentinel workspace.

1. Navigate to Watchlists:

    a. In the Azure portal, under Configuration, select Watchlist.

    b. In the Microsoft Defender portal, go to Microsoft Sentinel ➤ Configuration ➤ Watchlist.

2. Select + New.

3. On the General page, provide the Name, Description, and Alias for your watchlist.

4. Select Next: Source.

5. On the Source page, use the following information to configure your data upload:

    a. *Source Type*: Select Azure Storage (preview).

    b. *Select a Type for the Dataset*: Choose a CSV file with a header (.csv).

    c. *Number of Lines Before Row with Headings*: Enter the number of lines in your data file that precede the header row.

d. *Blob SAS URL (Preview)*: Paste the shared access URL you copied in Step 2.

e. *SearchKey*: As before, enter the name of a column in your watchlist that you expect to use frequently for joins or searches.

After entering all the information, your page should resemble the provided image in the documentation.

6. Select Next: Review and Create.

7. Review the information carefully, ensuring it's correct. Wait for the Validation passed message.

8. Select Create.

It may take some time for a large watchlist to be created and its data to become available for queries in Microsoft Sentinel.

Developing Content with Kusto Query Language

Kusto Query Language (KQL) is a powerful way to get an understanding of your data. Think of it as a custom-built search engine for data. It will allow you to see patterns, identify anomalies, create statistical models, and much more.

KQL is designed to be simple, yet powerful. It allows you to query structured data (like a spreadsheet), semi-structured data, or completely unstructured data. KQL is an expressive query language, meaning it is relatively easy to read and understand what the query is trying to do. The language is also designed with an efficient way of writing the queries.

KQL is particularly capable of paging through telemetry data (data collected from systems), performance metrics, and logs of events (auditing of actions). KQL contains powerful capabilities for searching text, time-series queries, calculating or aggregating data, analyzing spatial information (e.g., geographical), and so on. It is uniquely capable of data exploration at depth.

The data you will be querying with KQL has a structure like a single database in a traditional database, i.e., a database with relations—databases, tables, and columns. If you have been using scripting/code or databases before, KQL will feel familiar. If not, don't worry! KQL is fairly intuitive, and you will quickly figure out how to write your own queries and start learning valuable insights for your organization.

In this section, the query language will be explained and, through examples, will provide practical exercises for you to begin to write queries. You can play with the environment and experiment in the query environment before you. To instruct yourself on how to use KQL, you can also look through tutorials on the common operators.

What Is a Kusto Query?

A Kusto Query is a request to process data and return results. KQL queries are always a read request—they are never write requests, and they will not alter or append data. Queries are written in free-text form, and KQL follows a "data-flow" model, which allows queries to be easy to read and create or automate in building. A Kusto Query can consist of one or more "query statements."

Queries search through data that is organized in a nested structure, similar to an SQL database, composed of databases, tables, and columns.

What Is a Query Statement?

There are three types of query statements that users work with in a Kusto query:

- A tabular expression statement
- A let statement
- A set statement

Each query statement is ended with a semicolon (;) and only impacts the query it is associated with.

The most common type of statement is the tabular expression statement. This means that both the data it has input to (input to) and the data it has returned (output) are in tabular or tabular dataset format.

Tabular statements will contain one or more operators. Each of the operators starts with a tabular input and gives tabular output. The operators are chained together via a "pipe" symbol (|). Each tabular dataset "flows" or "pipes" from one operator to the next. The dataset will be filtered, altered, and moved to the next operator each time.

Think of it like a funnel. You start with a tabular dataset in its entirety, and then as the tabs flow through the funnel operator, they are filtered, rearranged, and summarized. As the data "flows," each operator either remembers it or passes it on to the next operator. Because of this "flow," it is essential to order the operators in your query correctly. Ordering can affect both your results and performance. Ultimately, you will funnel down to a smaller and more specific output. Kusto Query Language (KQL) acts as the underlying language for data exploration, threat detection, and incident investigation in Microsoft Sentinel. For security professionals, being a proficient KQL "coder" enables you to develop more effective queries with the correct format and logic, leading to high-value queries that identify malicious activity, relate alerts to investigation logic, and automate the investigative process. In this chapter, we will incrementally look at KQL—from simple building blocks and data to more sophisticated analytical pieces, framing each more sophisticated piece with relevant real-world Sentinel use cases.

Kusto Query Language (KQL) is the underlying language for Microsoft Sentinel and other Azure services. KQL was developed to handle large amounts of data, primarily from streams of data from server logs, applications, and security tools.

KQL is known to be

- *Fast*: Aptly suited for real-time or near-real-time analysis
- *Efficient*: Concise syntax used to represent potentially complex logic in fewer words
- *Flexible*: Works well with both structured and semi-structured data.

Whether you need to analyze performance, investigate a potential threat, or examine behavior, KQL will be a practical tool for you.

What Can You Do with KQL?

KQL will be valuable to you regardless of your level of expertise. Understanding a few basic elements of KQL will allow for a simple way to examine your data, from raw logs to visualizing the outcome in plain language. Here are a few valuable things you can do with KQL:

- *Troubleshoot Issues*: Search through logs to help uncover a reason for failure or what happened during a critical incident.
- *Threat Detection*: Create your logic for alerts about suspicious activity.
- *Dashboard Building*: Use KQL queries to visualize in workbooks and dashboards.

- *Clean and Transform Your Data*: Edit or convert your data, or even filter it before analyzing or storing data.

- *Optimizing Your Storage*: Use data filtering to leave out non-relevant data about the data set you are analyzing, thus helping lower your storage fees.

All KQL queries are structured around a pipeline. The queries operate in a way that accepts the data and passes it through an ordered series of processing operators. The structure allows an analyst to manipulate their results iteratively using logical chains. A sample query with structure will look somewhat like this:

```sql
CopyEdit
Get Data | Filter | Summarize | Sort | Select
```

Each operator in this pipeline transforms the data and passes it to the next stage. This modular approach makes queries intuitive to write and easy to troubleshoot.

For example:

```kql
CopyEdit
SigninLogs                                    // Get Data
| where RiskLevelDuringSignIn == 'none'       // Filter
| summarize Count = count() by City           // Summarize
| sort by Count desc                          // Sort
| take 5                                      // Select
```

Each connector in the funnel performs some data processing before handing it off to the next step. This modular construction leads to intuitive querying and is generally easier to debug as you build the logic.

This query selected sign-in logs with no risk, grouped and counted the results by city, sorted them by the number of counts, and limited the results to five from the total number of cities.

Note Any line in a KQL query can also accept comments using double slashes (//), which is a helpful way to document parts of your logic for later reference.

Core Operators: Filter, Sort, Take, and More

Getting Data

Every KQL query begins by specifying the table to query. In Microsoft Sentinel, this might be a data source like SigninLogs, SecurityAlert, or Heartbeat. Table names are case-sensitive, so be consistent and precise.

```kql
CopyEdit
SigninLogs
```

Filtering: The where Operator

Filtering is typically your first transformation step. It helps narrow the scope of data early, which is crucial for performance.

```kql
CopyEdit
SigninLogs
| where TimeGenerated >= ago(7d)
```

You can combine multiple conditions:

```kql
CopyEdit
SigninLogs
| where TimeGenerated >= ago(7d)
    and RiskLevelDuringSignIn == "high"
```

Use and and or to combine conditions, and remember to order them to optimize performance—simple column checks should come before more complex comparisons.

Limiting: The take or limit Operator

To return a small subset of results, use take:

```kql
CopyEdit
SigninLogs
| take 10
```

This operator is useful during development when you want to test a query without loading too much data. Keep in mind that if used before sorting, take will return a random set of rows.

Sorting: The sort or order Operator

Sort your results to structure the data for reporting or prioritization:

kql
CopyEdit
SigninLogs
| sort by TimeGenerated desc

You can sort by multiple columns:

kql
CopyEdit
SigninLogs
| sort by TimeGenerated, Identity desc

Tip If sorting by just one field and returning the top results, use top instead. It combines sort and take for better performance.

Summarizing and Aggregating

The summarize Operator: **Summarize groups data and applies aggregation functions like count(), sum(), or avg().**

kql
CopyEdit
SigninLogs
| summarize Count = count() by City

This groups the sign-ins by city and counts the entries for each.

You can also aggregate multiple values:

```kql
CopyEdit
Perf
| summarize Count = count(), AvgCPU = avg(CPU_Usage) by ServerName
```

If you need to retain columns not used in aggregation, include them in the by clause.

Column Control: project, project-away, and extend

Selecting Columns with project

```kql
CopyEdit
Perf
| project ObjectName, CounterValue, CounterName
```

Only the specified columns are returned, in the listed order.

Removing Columns with project-away

```kql
CopyEdit
Perf
| project-away _ResourceId, MG, Type
```

This keeps all columns except the ones listed.

Adding Columns with extend

Create new calculated fields for analysis:

```kql
CopyEdit
Usage
| extend KBytes = Quantity * 1024
```

You can chain multiple extend operations:

```kql
CopyEdit
Usage
| extend KBytes = Quantity * 1024
| extend Bytes = KBytes * 1024
```

Working with Multiple Tables: union and join

Merging Tables with union: union allows you to combine multiple tables:

```kql
CopyEdit
SecurityEvent
| union OfficeActivity
```

You can tag the source of each row using withsource:

```kql
CopyEdit
SecurityEvent
| union withsource=SourceTable OfficeActivity
```

This creates a new column called SourceTable indicating where each row originated.

Joining Data Sets: Use join to combine related data from two tables:

```kql
CopyEdit
SigninLogs
| join kind=inner (
    SecurityEvent
    | where TimeGenerated >= ago(1d)
) on $left.UserPrincipalName == $right.AccountName
```

You can specify different join types (inner, leftouter, etc.), and it's good practice to keep the smaller table on the left for better performance.

Parsing and Transforming with evaluate

Evaluate allows you to apply advanced plugins or transform dynamic data types.

Example using bag_unpack:

```kql
CopyEdit
SigninLogs
| evaluate bag_unpack(LocationDetails)
| summarize Count = count() by city
```

Dynamic fields often store structured data similar to JSON. bag_unpack flattens these into columns, making them accessible for queries.

Using Variables with `let` Statements

let is used to define reusable expressions:

```kql
CopyEdit
let recent = ago(7d);
SigninLogs
| where TimeGenerated >= recent
```

You can also define subqueries:

```kql
CopyEdit
let highRiskSignins = SigninLogs
| where RiskLevelDuringSignIn == "high";
highRiskSignins
| summarize count() by UserPrincipalName
```

This method enhances readability and accessibility for complex queries when combining data sources.

Kusto Query Language is an important skill to learn for Microsoft Sentinel. From simple filters to more complex aggregations and joins, KQL provides analysts the power and flexibility to derive meaning from the large amounts of security data. Learning how to shape your query with proper filtering, summarization, and reuse of variables will allow for much better threat detection and incident response. Throughout this book, you will build upon these skills to write highly practical and actionable queries using your security telemetry.

Building Effective Analytics

With your Microsoft Sentinel environment now collecting telemetry from multiple sources across your organization, the next important step is threat detection. With security events generated as constantly as rain from a thunderstorm, Sentinel will help you find threats with detection mechanisms specifically designed for this purpose—your analytics rules.

Analytics rules utilize detection logic that scans your data for suspicious behavior and generates alerts if some event is determined to be unusual and/or dangerous. Alerts are grouped into incidents, providing meaningful context amongst related security events. In this section, we will examine how analytics rules work, the different types, and how to tailor them to meet the particular security requirements of your organization. Once notifications are grouped, analysts can investigate, respond, and automate parts of the response.

Analytics Rules: The Workhorse of Threat Detection

In Microsoft Sentinel, analytics rules are used to detect threats. These rules examine the collected data, analyze it for patterns, and generate alerts based on the values returned. Using prebuilt rules or Microsoft-curated detection logic based on real-world attacks, you can create your own custom rules or leverage prebuilt rule templates.

Analytical rules are categorized according to their function in the threat detection lifecycle.

Types of Analytics Rules in Microsoft Sentinel

Among Sentinel's rules, scheduled rules are the most common. These rules are set up to run on a schedule and examine data from a specified period. If a rule identifies several matching records above a threshold, an alert is triggered. In the event that several matching records are returned above a threshold you specify, the rule will trigger an alert. In the event that several matching records are returned above a threshold you specify, the rule will trigger an alert.

CHAPTER 3   ENGINEERING MICROSOFT SENTINEL FOR SECURITY OPERATIONS

Types of Analytics Rules in Microsoft Sentinel

- *Scheduled Rules*: Scheduled rules are the most common type of rule and the backbone of Sentinel's detection framework. These rules run at specific time intervals and inspect data from a specified time interval, known as the lookback period. If the query returns several matching records above a threshold you designate, the rule will trigger an alert.

    - The logic for scheduled rules leverages the Kusto Query Language (KQL), giving you powerful statistical and behavioral analysis capabilities. You can use existing templates as starting points or build your rules from scratch and have complete freedom to define what "suspicious" means in your environment.

- *Near-Real-Time (NRT) Rules*: NRT rules are a reduced version of scheduled rules but run at a much higher frequency—every minute. These rules are designed for time-sensitive detections that require immediate awareness. NRT rules are less flexible than scheduled rules in some ways, but because of their rapid execution, threat identification can occur faster.

- *Anomaly Rules*: Anomaly rules apply machine learning techniques to identify behaviors that vary from a baseline or expected range of behaviors. Anomaly rules do not trigger alerts as much as they log anomalous activities into an Anomalies table. Security teams can then reference the data assigned to an anomaly to add context to their investigations and prioritize future detections.

    - You cannot edit the out-of-the-box anomaly rules, but you can clone them, change the criteria, and run both the cloned rule and the scheduled rule at the same time to compare results before implementing a version of the cloned rule to production.

- *Microsoft Security Rules*: Microsoft security rules create incidents from alerts that are generated from outside Sentinel, but all are part of the Microsoft security ecosystem. The first two rules will allow Sentinel to treat external alerts like native incidents and will therefore help reduce your investigation time. If you have integrated Sentinel into one or more Microsoft portals or services that create incidents on their own, keep in mind that these rules may have been turned off to prevent incident duplication.

- *Threat Intelligence Rule*: This one is a special rule type that matches incoming event data—such as DNS queries, Syslog, or CEF logs—against known indicators (IP addresses or domains) associated with malicious activity. This rule is not customizable but contributes to another area of threat intelligence in your detection landscape and may help expose hidden threats with high confidence.

- *Advanced Multistage Attack Detection (Fusion)*: Fusion will detect multistage attacks that take place across multiple systems by using correlation and machine learning. Fusion will not rely on a single alert but will instead correlate multiple alerts and low-confidence signals and combine them into a high-confidence incident. Fusion is a background feature that runs by default and is not customizable; only one instance of the rule can exist.

- *Machine Learning Behavior Analytics*: This type of rule looks for anomalous login behavior based on user and geolocation, and especially those over SSH and RDP. These rules have been built to expose targeted or stealthy intrusions. These rules are also not customizable, but they do provide specific detection based on patterns of user behavior.

Rule Access and Permissions

Every rule in Sentinel has a permissions token associated with it, which enables it to continuously query the data it examines without requiring the user who created it to have workspace access. This design allows rules to run in isolation from an individual user role.

However, please note that if you are in a multiple-tenant or cross-subscription environment, such as those used by MSSPs, the rule will use the user credentials of the user who created it. If the user loses access, the rule will be turned off, and a health monitoring alert will be sent to your team.

This is an important safeguard to deny inadvertent disclosure of customer data and unauthorized access.

Indication from Detection to Action: Incidents

When a rule detects suspicious activity and an alert is generated, Microsoft Sentinel will automatically reference other related alerts and create incidents. Incidents are effectively case files that can provide context to security teams about the nature and scope of a potential threat, as well as information about the impacted resources.

Incidents can also be assigned to analysts, and they can initiate automated responses using playbooks. Orchestrating detection to response will assist organizations in reducing response times and overall risk exposure.

Microsoft Sentinel's threat detection engine is designed around analytics rules—useful and powerful tools that transform raw telemetry into insights, whether using scheduled queries, machine learning anomaly detection, or advanced correlation engines like Fusion.

Customizing rules, using built-in templates, and understanding the functionality of standard rule types with Sentinel will allow you to align it to your threat environment better.

Automated incident creation and automated responses will also ensure that your detection strategy is more efficient while still being effective!

Role of Threat Hunting in Modern Security Operations

Threat hunting is an advanced security discipline that goes beyond traditional alert-based monitoring. Rather than waiting for automated detections, threat hunting involves proactively searching for signs of compromise that may have slipped past initial defenses. Microsoft Sentinel offers a robust platform for threat hunting, combining powerful data analytics with strategic frameworks to help security teams identify and investigate suspicious behaviors across their environment.

It identifies, tracks, and eliminates malicious actors or compromises present in a system or environment. Security monitoring based on alerts relies on warning signs or automatic detection, while threat hunting seeks out potential compromises. As part of Microsoft Sentinel's hunting platform, it combines high-performance data disaggregation with well-thought-out methodologies to enable security teams to detect malicious behaviors across their environments.

Threat hunters are often part of a Security Operations Center (SOC) and serve as an important front line in locating threats that may be hidden—anomalies or behaviors that might never have warranted an alert but still arguably represent the first signs of an attack.

Launchpad for Discovery: Built-In Queries

Included with Microsoft Sentinel is a sizable collection of included hunting queries that give you a sturdy starting point for your investigations. This collection of queries allows you to sift through large amounts of log and event data across your environment that is identifying patterns or behaviors of known attack techniques.

The Hunting interface in Sentinel provides a centralized view of the hunting queries available. Microsoft provides the hunting queries for you by data source, tactic, and provider, which allows you to quickly narrow down and prioritize which queries are meaningful to your current investigation situation. You can favorite queries for easy future access and know that every time you visit the Hunting page, all queries on the page will automatically run again, keeping track of regularly recurring issues.

Best Practice: Use the included hunting queries as a baseline. Run them regularly and flag them to develop behavioral baselines in your environment, and find repeat incidents that may not trigger alerts appropriately. The framework for Threat Hunting: MITRE ATT&CK

Threat hunting requires structure, and Microsoft Sentinel has an excellent way to incorporate hunting with the MITRE ATT&CK framework structure.

MITRE ATT&CK assumes known adversary behavior is categorized into the "tactics" (the why of the attack) and the "techniques" (the how). The Sentinel teams intended to enhance offensive security tools hunting within Sentinel based on the model of real-world adversary playbooks.

In the Sentinel environment, you will find queries separated into sets based on ATT&CK tactics: initial access, persistence, lateral movement, etc. On the hunting page is a visual timeline that allows you to review and filter which tactics you want to select from and see interactive filtering.

Real-World Best Practice: When creating your threat-hunting methodology include ATT&CK by filtering your hunting queries based on tactics you know are targeting common gaps or emerging threats, and concentrate on tactics that are higher risk or capable of exploitation in the most recent incidents.

Managing and Modifying Hunting Queries

Each of the built-in queries in Sentinel is defined with contextual metadata to provide detail, including a description of the query, the tactics it targets, any entities targeted in the context of the query, and the query logic itself. Analysts can view and run these queries, and all queries can be customized from "able to the interface." So security teams can modify and create queries to their environment as they build their own baseline or face new emerging threats. For example, a built-in query for finding suspicious PowerShell usage might also be edited to reflect internal naming conventions or possibly have predefined filters for known, benign scripts. You can clone a query to edit and save as a custom hunting query to make use of again in future.

Best Practice: Edit queries to fit the unique parts of your environment within your organization. What might be normal in one environment, may be fairly anomalous in a different environment. The use of entity mapping provides another level of context and clarity to your query results.

Creating Custom Queries Using KQL

Although there are some built-in queries that analysts can use as a starting point, custom hunting queries are where analysts really become experts, as they are able to add a significant contextual layer that the analyst has on their local environment. Microsoft Sentinel leverages Kusto Query Language (KQL), an incredibly powerful open English-like query syntax for exploring data based off a high-performance engine that enables analysts to build robust and complex condition-based queries that hunt for specific indicators or behaviors.

Custom hunting queries will include a number of configurable pieces:

- Name and Description for reference and identification

- The KQL query

- Entity mapping for application of relevant identifiers (ex. IPs, users, hosts)

- Tactics and techniques defined for classification of query purpose and context

- Custom queries are also stored along with built-in queries, allowing for straightforward management and sharing with peers.

Best Practice: Foster a culture of hunting and crafting custom hunting queries in the SOC. Encourage appropriate peer review and version control of custom queries (even if this just means ensuring the query is not broken). You will also want to document custom queries to allow for minimizing reinventing the wheel for yourself as an analyst. I would suggest considering the advantage of keeping a repository of your organization's specific hunts as a component of your threat model.

Community Contributions and Continual Improvement

In addition to your custom queries and any of Sentinel's default queries, there is immense content available for threat hunting from the security community. Microsoft Sentinel has the capability to import and make use of queries discovered from third-party repositories. Community-sourced content can also include hunting queries that are good to go, playbooks, and detection rules that ultimately may be developed and reviewed by a community of expert thought leaders from around the world.

Best Practice: Periodically comb through community repositories when you have time to continue to refine threat detection coverage. If you identify queries you wish to use, always check for compatibility with your existing environment, data availability, and a goal to tune out false positive rates.

Practical Considerations for Threat Hunting Success

Another commonality with more advanced security practices is that threat hunting does require some discipline, documentation, and accountability relative to operational goals. Here are a few things to be mindful of

- Schedule regular hunting sprints where you may focus on areas of great value tactics or high-risk tactics.

- Collaborate and talk about the hunting outputs that relate to and align with incident response functional teams and detection engineering teams to progress ongoing investigations or enhance alerts in similar alerts.

- Create feedback loops and apply findings to improve detection rules. If you conduct a custom hunt that continually yields an anomaly, consider documenting it and converting it into an analytics rule.

- While threat hunting is a hands-on activity led by analyst experience, to be more efficient, using automated cron jobs to run queries on a set schedule or having dashboards set up with discovery context will really amplify your reduction of false positives and enhance your hunting efforts.

To summarize, Microsoft Sentinel will facilitate the thought processes of an attacker, allowing the analyst to act like a defender. Using both built-in queries and benefitting from the larger MITRE ATT&CK framework, as well as creating their own KQL logic to find things that may be invisible, can be very empowering. By applying a structured workflow to simplify and facilitate your process, as well as benefitting from contributions from the community above and beyond the analytic function of detection, threat hunting becomes a significant proactive and structured component of your defence-in-depth cybersecurity model.

Turning Data into Threat Intelligence

The current enterprise landscape is such that all systems, applications, and endpoints are regularly generating telemetry relevant to security. Microsoft Sentinel will serve as the "central nervous system" for your security operations, gathering and analyzing vast amounts of available data to detect signs of malicious behavior. The foundational detection capability is the analytics rule. Using configurable logic, analytics rules will examine incoming data to identify known patterns of compromise.

This section will provide an overview of how to use the analytics rules to detect the exploitation of a real-world vulnerability—in this case, the Apache Log4j exploit. It will describe the entire cycle of this exercise, from the implementation of a rule that provides an automated response when needed. In this process, we will highlight best practices and decision points that you will encounter, along with key concepts that you will see at various levels of analytics rules. You will likely find analytics rules to be a valuable fit for your future detection framework.

From Rule Templates to Detection Logic

Microsoft Sentinel provides existing rule templates for security teams to draw from. These templates have been written by analysts with a direct mapping to a known threat behavior. Using these templates gives security teams a good base from which rules can be written rapidly and customized as desired.

As an example, the exploitation of the Apache Log4j (Log4Shell) vulnerability is a significant security flaw that received considerable press globally. For the Apache Log4j (Log4Shell) vulnerability exploitation, Microsoft Sentinel provides a rule template that specifically provides a mechanism to detect one or more indicators of the potential exploitation of the Log4j (Log4Shell) vulnerability in your environment. The rule takes as input logs from multiple sources and surfaces suspicious user accounts and/or IP addresses as identifiable entities in your workspace, based on its detection of indicators.

To implement this, you should know where the relevant rule template can be found. Rule templates can be found in the Analytics section under the Rule Templates tab. A simple search for an appropriate keyword, such as "Log4j," finds templates of analytics rules explicitly related to that threat.

Understanding Rule Logic and Setting It Up

From that template, you can open it up in Sentinel's Analytics Rule Wizard and configure the rule logic, behavior, and automation. Each Analytics rule will have components you can configure:

- *Rule Name and Description*: This should be a clear naming construct that reflects the intent of the rule and your customizations.

- *Execution Settings*: Please indicate whether the rule runs immediately or remains disabled until you manually enable it.

- *KQL Query Logic*: The most valuable component of the rule. The Kusto Query Language (KQL) logic section is where the power of the rule resides. Specifically, this script will look for indicators of compromise from logs. You can enlarge the query or customize it based on your intentions to gain a deeper understanding of suspicious behavior.

Best Practice: When building rule queries, ensure the lookback period for historical search equals the query execution period. This prevents the data gap and provides a continuous understanding of the threat.

Enriching Alerts with Metadata

Analytics rules will automatically create alerts, but they will also enrich alerts with metadata and entities, giving them the relative context to be acted on. Sentinel enables mapping fields of the query output to known entities, like user accounts, user identities, IP addresses, hostnames, etc. It is critical for investigations that each alert provides structured context for using these mappings or fields.

You may configure additional custom details, which populate specific data points such as a timestamp or device ID directly in the alert body. This retains context and reduces any further querying during triage.

You can also dynamically customize alert names using placeholders. For instance, using a timestamp within the title of an alert helps analysts quickly distinguish between incidents.

Best Practice: Leverage alert enrichment to add relevant context within the alert, enabling quicker investigation and more precise response direction.

Scheduling and Thresholds

After logic and enrichment have been identified, running schedules and alerting thresholds are configured for the rule. These are items such as

- When to run the rule (e.g., run every 1 hour)
- Lookback time (e.g., looking back at 1 hour of data)
- Alerting threshold (e.g., only alerted if results > 0)
- Event aggregation (e.g., aggregate alerts from all events that matched)

The goal of alerts is to ensure timeliness and minimize noise. Rules that run too often at a very low alerting threshold may generate unnecessary false positives; as another example, rules that are too loose may omit potential fast-moving threats.

Best Practice: Start with conservative thresholds and iterate over time based on learned results and input from incident responders.

Incident Creation and Management

Sentinel offers outstanding flexibility in how each alert can exist separately or roll up to become an actionable incident immediately. An incident serves as a container storage for many potential events. The majority of detection rules will generate incidents by default. After an incident has been created, it can be assigned, tracked, and investigated all within the Sentinel portal.

If you want your organization to use a third-party incident management platform, Sentinel can be configured to route the alerts forward while preventing Sentinel from creating incidents.

Best Practice: For high-fidelity rules, turn on an incident creation option to tie together alerts into relevant units for investigation. Use tags and event categorization to fit into your triage workflows.

Automating the Response

Finding something may still be only half of the job. Automated response capabilities of Sentinel allow you to assign playbooks and create some basic automated rules directly from the rule configuration screen. For example, suppose you have an alert triggered from a Log4j event. The alert can then be tagged for visibility, emailed to a team, or even isolated using a security tool.

It's best to streamline easy-to-repeat and lower-risk tasks, such as tagging, creating tickets, or improving data, while leaving more complicated tasks like remediation to humans.

Reviewing and Publishing the Rule

- Now that all configurations are complete for building the rule, including logic, enrichment, incident behavior, and any desired automation, proceed to the review rule screen to verify that the rule is as expected. You can validate the rule and then publish it immediately or save it for a future publication.

- - Once the rule is published, it runs in the background according to schedule. The alerts generated from rule executions will appear on the Incidents page and can be searched, filtered, or further investigated.

Monitoring and Life Cycle Management

Just as the rules are operating, it will be important for your team to monitor the rules for performance. If a rule fails to run, Sentinel will provide health status, and detailed logs are available to determine performance issues.

- The rules are editable, disabled, and deleted from the Analytics page in Sentinel. Likewise, automation rules linked to alerts can also be edited or deleted if not required.

- **Best Practice**: Regularly review the rules you have set up in your environment to retire detections that are no longer valid, adjust thresholds, and consider the changes to the threat landscape in your organization.

- The potential for use based on your needs and business case for Analytics rules in Microsoft Sentinel convert large volumes of raw telemetry into usable and actionable intelligence. When starting from a template or custom queries, you can command your SOC to have real-time visibility to measure wherever the unmeasured continues to evolve as threats like Log4j exploits.

- By enriching alerts, adding automated response capability, and categorizing detections with incident reporting, Sentinel provides the ability not only to detect a threat but also to detect and respond to the threat quickly and in an organized manner. This is the essence of security operations today—where speed, clarity, and automation often determine reality vs. resilience.

Security Orchestration, Automation, and Response (SOAR)

The Internet of Medical Things (IoMT) is changing how care is delivered through connectivity of multiple medical devices and applications to provide a medical data-oriented connection; this spatial or hyper-connectedness increases the attack vectors for many devices and complicates security more than ever. The healthcare field has been traditionally reluctant to embrace automation, but SOAR platforms will play a key role in addressing these new cyber challenges by automating threat detection and automation followed by response across many devices, networks, and systems. In addition to growing cybersecurity issues here, given the ever-present challenge with patients' safety and privacy, the SOAR platforms can help lower the risk for security breaches of patient information or damaging services within the healthcare environment.

IoMT environments often employ legacy systems and proprietary and unique devices with an interface to internet-connected medical devices, like infusion pumps, radiology imaging machines, pacemakers, and a plethora of wearables and sensors. These devices and systems frequently do use standardized controls for security, and many are not even within the process of patch management. SOAR provides the necessary visibility and control to see this 'ecology' view across the medical cybersecurity environment by centralizing threat data from other IoMT. The SOAR medical platform combines with system events gathered from their Security Information Event Management (SIEM) systems, incorporating vulnerability scanners, endpoint detection devices, and network monitoring hosts to determine their risk posture and achieve a more usual environment for decision-making.

Another great benefit with SOAR in the IoMT areas is the promising protection from automation of routine security incidents and time-critical response actions. For example, when abnormal device behavior occurs, such as unusual communication patterns with an external IP or sudden spikes in network activity, SOAR can call on previous workflows to isolate the offending device, alert organizational IT staff, and begin some triaging without the need for any human action. In a healthcare environment, this type of rapid reaction is vital. Acting on an issue is more than just a detection event; time plays an important role, and even a short amount of time lost responding to or detecting a new hazard can compromise patient care or safety.

With few cybersecurity professionals having both healthcare and IoT knowledge, the importance of automation becomes greater. SOAR (Security Operations Automation and Response) platforms are useful in addressing the skills divide by standardizing the process of incident response for various types of incidents. Without automation, the expectation would be for highly specialized staff to respond to every case, but SOAR is designed to standardize these processes, allowing for identification and response all while allowing a team to scale their threat management in a busy distributed IoMT environment. By automating identification and response for repeatable tasks, such as log correlation, alert triaging, and policy enforcement, SOAR frees security functions to deal with higher-value, more complex investigative work.

Another area where SOAR adds significant value is compliance within the IoMT space. Healthcare organizations are closely monitored for compliance in terms of data privacy, integrity, and availability. SOAR can help automate reports, audit trails, and policy enforcement during an audit, ensuring every action during an incident is documented and accounted for within the framework of compliance. SOAR will help organizations make governance easier as well as reduce the possibility of legal and financial repercussions from any breaches.

Through the OWL form of coordinating alerts with workflows across the three organizational teams (cybersecurity team, IT operations, and clinical engineering), SOAR increases collaborative efforts between these teams. Security is not a one-man show, especially in hospitals where the security function demands cooperation involving people in medicine, IT operation, and government regulation. SOAR integrates workflows in a centralized system, reducing siloed communication between teams. Through coordinated workflows and collaborations, actions can be taken to collaborate across teams that are focused on a single security action, whether it is taking the medical device offline, communicating with the clinical staff, or performing a playbook to investigate network activity.

And with the ever-increasing sophistication of current cyberattacks in healthcare, from ransomware to data exfiltration, healthcare organizations will need a new form of evading the hazards of cyber intrusion. SOAR brings machine learning in addition to threat intelligence and contextualized awareness to each automated workflow functioning as a cyber defense in conjunction with organizational cybersecurity. The threat landscape in the IoMT is becoming larger, and SOAR will remain a valuable tool in securing the online infrastructure that delivers modern healthcare to the public.

In the current day SOC (Security Operations Center), acting against threats in a short timeframe is vital. The number of incidents and the complexity of incidents are only going to grow, and dealing with it all personally becomes inaccurate and inefficient. Microsoft Sentinel acknowledges this capability gap through automation and establishes automation rules—rules where centralized rule-based logic automates your threat response workflows. These automation rules provide the foundation for security orchestration, automation, and response (SOAR) strategy through Sentinel and will be key for a security team to still achieve the goals of reducing response time and improving the consistency and effectiveness of their work with existing resources.

Automation rules allow an organization to automate the workload to carry out common and subsequently repeating tasks at speed based on the organization's expectation, to ensure incidents are triaged, tagged, enriched, or fully resolved with minimum human intervention. This automated capability can be applied to individual incidents, groups of alerts, or categories of incidents to deliver a response returning speed and accuracy.

Components to Understand in Automation Rules

An automation rule in Sentinel consists of three key components:

1. *Trigger*: What will cause the rule to run? The trigger may be based on the creation of an incident, the update of an incident, or the generation of an alert.

2. *Conditions*: The criteria that provide more details about when the rule executes; for example, incident severity, the analytics rule name, tags for entities, changes in incident properties, and other metadata.

3. *Actions*: The actions the rule will perform automatically after a trigger occurs and if the conditions are met. Actions may include assigning incidents, applying tags, updating incident status or severity, or invoking playbooks when a more complex task is needed.

Incident Automation Versus Alert Automation

Most automation use cases can be more satisfactorily addressed at the incident level. An incident functions as an investigative container by grouping alerts that are related (in some way), the entities related to the incident, and analyst notes into a single view. Given that incidents are adept at adapting as alerts are tagged onto them (or as investigations progress), automating a rule at this level is conducive to more complete and contextualized responses.

Alert Automation may be appropriate in cases where incidents are not generated by analytics rules or when custom logic is required to establish whether or not alerts are sufficiently valid to warrant an incident. Alert automation can also be used for processes that provide enrichment, early notification, or pre-integration into a ticketing system external to any incident.

Triggers in Automation Rules

Triggers tell automation rules when to run:

- *Incident Creation*: The rule will run when a new incident is created either manually or automatically through analytics.
- *Incident Update*: Triggered by any change to an existing incident, such as severity changes, new tags added, new owner assigned, or a comment added.
- *Alert Created*: Triggered when a new alert is generated by analytics that does not end in an incident. Each trigger allows a set of condition types and can even be customized to issues or analytic rules.

Conditions for Rule Execution

Conditions are the element that determines if a rule will execute after it has been triggered. For rules based on incidents, it may look at

- Incident name/type
- Alert severity
- Tags (can evaluate individual tags or all tags)
- Entity presence or attribute values
- Changes to the incident properties (e.g., severity increased for an incident to have a specific user act)

As an example, a rule could check if an incident had a tag of "PenTest" with a severity of "High," and only then would it automatically close it.

For updates to incidents, there are evaluations of the state before the change and the state after the change, which allow for more specific and precise logic statements such as "Only act if severity increased to critical."

Establishing Automation Actions

Once the trigger fires and any conditions are met, then these actions may be

- Assigning the owner to the incident
- Changing the incident severity or status (i.e., from "New" to "Active," or closing it with a reason)
- Adding classification tags
- Adding tasks for analyst triage
- Running a playbook for advanced or external interaction

Each automation rule can include multiple actions, and you have the option to define the execution order.

Playbook and Advanced Automation

In cases where you need to integrate with external systems or perform complex multi-step logic, playbooks—which are built using Azure Logic Apps—can be called from automation rules. Playbooks can support tasks, such as

- Passing incident information to a ticketing platform
- Notifying analysts via emails or messaging platform
- Enriching incidents with external threat intelligence
- Making decisions based on third parties
- Automation rules can sequence multiple playbooks in the order you want them to execute and use them in conjunction with simple incident actions.

Managing Order of Execution

Automation rules are executed in the order you established. This order is important because the execution of a previous automation rule can impact the execution of subsequent rules. For example, if one automation rule lowers the severity of an incident, any automation rule that only ran for "High" severity incidents will not execute because its original condition of being "High" was changed. It is important to effectively manage rule order, especially with the combination of suppression, assignment, tagging, and enrichment.

Incident creation and update triggers execute in separate queues, but you may explicitly define the order of each automation rule within the same trigger type.

CHAPTER 3   ENGINEERING MICROSOFT SENTINEL FOR SECURITY OPERATIONS

Common Use Cases and Scenarios

Automation rules can be configured to satisfy many operational requirements, including

- *Incident Assignment*: Automatically assign incidents to specialists (i.e., for topic, origin, or severity).

- *Incident Suppression*: Automatically close known benign incidents or known test-related incidents (i.e., penetration tests) to reduce noise in your environment.

- *Task Automation*: Add repeatable steps to every incident with your work instructions to help guide analysts through the triage process or investigation process.

- *Tagging and Classification*: Tags may be added to incidents based on analytic rules, origin IPs, or entity details.

- *Time-Limited Automation*: You can assign enforcement expiration dates to temporary automation rules, such as for testing windows affected or assigned analysts.

Managing Automation Rules

You can manage automation rules across three of the main Sentinel views:

- *Automation Page*: You can view and edit, enable/disable, reorder, and create automation rules in one location.

- *Analytics Rule Wizard*: while creating or editing analytics rules, you can create automation rules, which can bind automation directly together with the analytics as you are defining the detections.

- *Incidents Page*: This view can be helpful to use when you want to create something that only ties to a specific incident or a very specific recurring incident (i.e., close just noisy incidents automatically).

When you create rules in different contexts, they will populate with relevant default configurations but may be modified to fit your workflows.

Exporting and Importing Automation Rules

Automation rules can be exported as JSON templates. You can version control them and create them as code! The export templates are portable across workspaces and even across tenants, enabling you to keep consistency in deployments that span environments (multi-environment) or the cloud (multi-tenant).

This capability helps support continuous integration and deployment (CI/CD) pipelines, enabling teams to manage Sentinel configurations via code and in keeping with infrastructure-as-code principles.

Multitenant Considerations

In a multitenant ecosystem, such as one managed by MSSPs, automation rules can run across tenants as long as the necessary permissions have been generated. Sentinel utilizes a managed service account to run playbooks, which must have access to the resource groups of these playbooks. This access can be within the same tenant or a partner's tenant.

Figure 3-1 design allows a service provider to run automation and playbooks in the client's tenant, or vice versa, for an organizational or compliance reason.

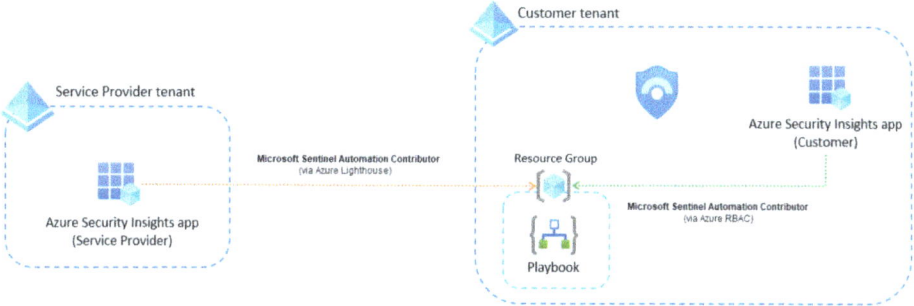

Figure 3-1. Multitenant Ecosystem

Automation rules within Microsoft Sentinel are essential for establishing a responsive and scalable SOC. Automation rules enable security teams to automate threat response at both incident and alert levels, optimize repetitive tasks, reduce alert noise, and streamline threat response across detection tools and external systems. When organizations define triggers, conditions, and actions, they manage the flow of execution and order, which shapes threat response activity and enables them to respond faster. Automated rules will improve response times, increase consistency, and enhance analyst focus on high-priority threats.

Automating Incident Response Through Playbooks in Microsoft Sentinel

Security operations centers (SOCs) operate in an intense landscape, where alerts and incidents rush in from multiple sources. As a result, speed and consistency are essential. As a built-in capability of Microsoft Sentinel, playbooks are a powerful method to automate incident response actions and decrease manual effort. Playbooks automate entirely those repetitive tasks, orchestrate multi-step, multi-account, or environment workflows, and improve the overall speed and reliability of security threat responses, allowing analysts to focus on high-priority investigations.

A playbook triggers a set of response actions when a specific set of conditions is met in Microsoft Sentinel. A Microsoft Sentinel playbook is built on Azure Logic Apps and will be triggered automatically for incoming alerts or incidents via connected automation rules. However, it can also be triggered manually on demand. For instance, if an alert indicates that the user account and computer have been compromised, a playbook could disconnect the device from the network and revoke the user's credentials before the SOC team has had the opportunity to start triaging the incident. Playbooks have value in four distinct but general stages of incident response—enrichment, orchestration, synchronization, and remediation. When playbooks can go into enrichment mode, they can gather and attach contextually relevant information to enrich the incident for investigation, such as threat intelligence or user activity logs. Playbooks in orchestration mode can notify the response team, create a collaboration thread in Microsoft Teams, or engage with third parties to orchestrate a response. Synchronization playbooks synchronize Sentinel to the ticketing platforms by creating or updating incidents. Remediation playbooks can take actions like disabling accounts, quarantining endpoints, or blocking an IP address.

To implement and manage playbooks, be sure to assign users to the Microsoft Sentinel system account with the correct permissions. Suppose you want to create or edit a playbook. In that case, it requires a role of Logic App Contributor or Logic Apps Standard Developer, depending on the consumption or standard logic app you've implemented. If you want to have playbooks triggered by automation rules, the Microsoft

Sentinel service account will also need access to the resource group in which the playbook is. This also adds additional security to the playbooks, as they may be triggered and actions taken without requiring elevation of rights specific to the user being granted. Microsoft Sentinel offers customizable playbook templates, which are prebuilt workflows that can help expedite the deployment of automation. Playbook templates are not actual playbooks, but they provide a foundation for customization and building unique automation logic. Playbook templates can be accessed through the Sentinel interface. They will also be updated periodically and provide guidance on best practices for workflow design. The scope of playbook templates is broad, with possibilities for alert notifications to more complex multi-step integrations with external platforms.

When a playbook is made or modified, it can be executed in two different ways: immediately or automatically with an automation rule, or manually from either the alert or incident page. Automatic playbook execution is dependent upon the parameters set up in the analytics or automation rules, such as alert type or severity level, which allows Sentinel to respond to threat activity in real-time. Manual execution enables the analyst to decide when or where they need to run a playbook according to their situational awareness and investigation workflow; this flexibility supports MEME-type workflows in both a proactive and reactive SOC.

In larger or more complex environments, Sentinel playbooks can trigger multiple scenarios, given multiple automation executions for one playbook. A single playbook may be associated with various analytics or incidents, which provides the possibility of broad and standardized enforcement of response policies. Playbooks can also be incorporated into CI/CD pipelines by exporting or importing them as JSON templates, allowing for version control, adjacent or centralized management, or reuse in multiple Sentinel workspaces. This capability enables the automation workflows to be reliably consistent regardless of process changes for security events and operational environments.

By successfully using playbooks within its SOC, an organization can improve the efficiency, accuracy, and speed of its actions. Automation can reduce the possibility of human error, enforce transparent or repeatable processes, and implement them in response to discovered threats. Playbooks can be used for various purposes, including blocking compromised users, alerting the correct team to escalate critical alerts, and adding external threat intelligence information to incidents. Microsoft Sentinel playbooks supplement any effective and responsive security operation.

CHAPTER 3   ENGINEERING MICROSOFT SENTINEL FOR SECURITY OPERATIONS

Workbooks, Reporting, and Data Visualization

After connecting your data sources to Microsoft Sentinel, the next step in developing a proactive security operations strategy is to visualize that data for real analysis. This is where workbooks come into play. Workbooks provide the user with an interactive and customizable platform for monitoring data trends, investigating anomalies, and producing meaningful insights from logs and alerts. Workbooks are used to turn raw data into visualizations, such as charts or tables, into rich visual reports, and help security teams make faster and more informed decisions. Workbooks are visualization tools built on Azure Monitor workbooks and customized for security scenarios in Sentinel.

You can create your workbooks from scratch and utilize templates to make a decent starting point for visualizing some types of security data. The templates usually come with solution packages and as standalone items in the content hub. Workbooks work like any Azure resource, and you can manage workbooks with Azure role-based governance (RBAC). For example, you can give viewers read access but allow contributors to build or modify content. Once created, a workbook is a permanent artifact in Sentinel, and the state is maintained in the resource group associated with your workspace so that it can be managed with other Sentinel resources.

Creating a workbook is simple, and you can do so from a blank canvas or with a preinstalled template. Templates provide a scaffolded starting point, often with visual components already laid out against original data prototypes. You can add filters, charts, and queries to the workbook that reflect your operational priorities, like bringing failed sign-ins to the forefront, aggregating incident counts, or showing trends over time for alert severity. It is usually best practice that any queries in the workbook leverage ASIM parsers, which enable a standardized, normalized approach across various log sources to ensure your audience is presented with visualizations that are scalable and consistent across the time series.

Microsoft Sentinel enables its users to save their workbooks as shared or personal reports, which provides flexibility around how each report is accessible throughout your enterprise. Shared workbooks offer functionality for multiple teams and are well-suited for dashboards used during threat-hunting sessions or daily stand-up meetings. Personal workbooks allow each analyst to develop individual style dashboards that fit their workflows. It is easy to switch between workbooks, and all workbooks can be duplicated with the "Save As" option, enabling experimentation with creating new analyses without concern for affecting the original.

One feature that helps improve the experience of workbooks is the option to pin a custom tile from Log Analytics to your Sentinel workbooks. These custom tiles provide you with snapshot visibility of key metrics, such as the number of alerts across a time series or failed login attempts by physical location. The workbooks can be refreshed manually or at automatic intervals based on your specifications. The refresh intervals can be set from every 5 minutes to every 24 hours, and the automatic refreshing of the visualizations is suspended while editing to avoid any unnecessary load.

Workbooks have many purposes and should be developed with the intended audience in mind. For example, a workbook designed for a network administrator will have a different appearance and objective based on firewall data and analysis of internet traffic versus an incident response supervisor dashboard focused on response times and incident escalation trends. Some organizations will also include workbooks that coincide with defined time-based review patterns, for example, conducting an hourly review of suspicious sign-in activity or conducting a daily review of escalated incidents. By considering the intended persona and frequency of design, every workbook will have a purpose in operations.

Advanced-level workbook users can also develop a query that tracks activity across multiple log sources. For example, one workbook could correlate new user additions from identity logs, and if they are added to high-privilege roles within 24 hours, it could indicate a compromise. These advanced visualization opportunities, powered by Kusto Query Language (or KQL), will help identify suspicious and concerning user behavior that will be more difficult to detect with traditional alerting methods. When developed, Sentinel workbooks can bring time-series data together from several different sources with sophisticated query logic, creating a foundation for proactive threat detection and accurate continuous monitoring.

Overall, Microsoft Sentinel workbooks enhance your SOC's ability to have contextually driven and empirically based analytical capability by creating, improving, and making actionable data visualizations. Whether you enrich reports and dashboards with dynamic charting components, automate regular reporting timelines, or correlate cross-domain activity to analyze deep threat activity, workbooks are a flexible and powerful means for understanding and interrogating the evolving security landscape.

Commonly Used Workbooks in Microsoft Sentinel

After completing the Microsoft Sentinel configuration and connecting your data and sources, visualizing that data is crucial for effectively understanding your environment and responding to potential threats. Workbooks fulfill this role by translating raw data into a structured format. The workbooks provide built-in dashboards and interactive reports to allow security analysts, admins, and engineers to monitor activity, risk factors, and operational effectiveness.

Microsoft Sentinel has a library of prebuilt workbooks that allow for many use cases, ranging from identity and access information to compliance reporting, incident triage, and data ingestion health. Those workbooks can be deployed as a solution (package) or added directly to the Sentinel interface, as they are available there. Once deployed, they are available in your environment for your use, either out of the box or customized to suit your day-to-day security operation needs.

Workbooks are most effective if they are based on the data you are actively collecting. For example, if you are collecting Microsoft Entra ID logs, installing the audit and sign-in workbooks will give you immediate insights into user activity and any sign-in anomalies. If you are working towards Zero Trust architecture, you may visualize specific Zero Trust metrics through the Zero Trust workbook.

Table 3-2 presents the workbooks in Microsoft Sentinel that are most commonly used, their use case, and any relevant solution or package information for rapid identification and deployment based on your goals for security operations.

Table 3-2. Microsoft Sentinel Workbooks

Workbook Name	Purpose	Solution Name
Analytics Health and Audit	Shows the status and changes of analytics rules.	Analytics Health and Audit
Azure Activity	Gives a full view of Azure user and system activity.	Azure Activity
Azure Security Benchmark	Helps assess cloud security against standard benchmarks.	Azure Security Benchmark
CMMC Compliance	Visualizes controls for cybersecurity maturity requirements.	CMMC 2.0

(*continued*)

Table 3-2. (*continued*)

Workbook Name	Purpose	Solution Name
Data Collection Health	Monitors how well your data connectors are ingesting logs.	Data Collection Monitoring
Event Analyzer	Simplifies Windows event log auditing and analysis.	Windows Security Events
Identity and Access	Shows trends and alerts related to user access activities.	Windows Security Events
Incident Overview	Summarizes incident details to support triage and investigation.	SOC Handbook
Investigation Insights	Offers tools and visuals for deep investigation into incidents and user behavior.	SOC Handbook
Cloud App Usage	Displays insights about cloud apps being accessed and by whom.	Defender for Cloud Apps
Audit Logs (Identity)	Shows admin actions like user changes and device activities.	Microsoft Entra ID
Sign-In Logs (Identity)	Highlights user sign-ins, failed attempts, and access anomalies.	Microsoft Entra ID
MITRE ATT&CK Mapping	Displays how Sentinel detections align with MITRE ATT&CK tactics and techniques.	SOC Handbook
Office 365 Usage	Tracks activity across Exchange, Teams, SharePoint, and OneDrive.	Microsoft 365
Security Alerts	Visualizes all security alerts generated in Sentinel.	SOC Handbook
SOC Efficiency	Helps SOC managers track performance, triage speed, and response metrics.	SOC Handbook
Threat Intelligence	Shows ingestion and matches for threat indicators across all data.	Threat Intelligence
Workspace Usage Report	Monitors data usage, latency, and cost metrics in your Sentinel workspace.	Workspace Usage Report
Zero Trust Dashboard	Provides visual metrics aligned with Zero Trust principles and architecture.	Zero Trust (TIC 3.0)

Every workbook is a unique dashboard that allows teams to explore information relevant to their role. Whether your role is related to operations, governance, threat detection, or compliance, these workbooks provide a great starting point. You will be able to customize them even more, such as by adding filters, tweaking queries, or creating new views, over time. These workbooks are vital in successful, visual-driven security operations in Microsoft Sentinel.

SOC Optimization Using Microsoft Sentinel for IoMT

The Internet of Medical Things (IoMT) will change the health care sector by connecting a range of devices, including patient monitors, imaging systems, infusion pumps, and wearable health trackers, to digital networks. IoMT comes with an increased attack surface that might raise pressing cybersecurity issues. To complicate matters, many of these devices are run on obsolete operating systems, have no inbuilt security, and are difficult to patch, which makes them prime targets for cyberattacks. To address the new complications of the risks, Security Operations Centers (SOC) are going to need to evolve. Microsoft Sentinel provides the intelligence, automation, and integration to make SOCs work in IoMT environments more efficiently.

Centralized Visibility and Unified Data Ingestion

The first means to improve efficiency for the SOC team is to bring together the telemetry from the many different IoMT devices and their infrastructures. Microsoft Sentinel gathers logs from hospital IT systems, medical devices, IoT security gateways, identity systems, and third-party monitors. Once ingested via data connectors within the Azure Monitor ecosystem, Sentinel provides centralized visibility into clinical and operational environments to reduce blind spots and provide a baseline for threat detection along complicated healthcare networks.

Threat Detection and Behavioral Analytics

The analytics within Microsoft Sentinel are essential for threat detection, especially in the particular environment of IoMT. It can detect anomalies in communications from a medical device, raising a flag for determining possible lateral movement or a command-and-control engagement. In combination with the User and Entity Behavior Analytics

(UEBA) extension and device behavior profiling, SOC personnel can easily determine what constitutes medical activity versus malicious activity they need to respond to. For example, suppose an infusion pump, for whatever reason, suddenly makes a file server request or starts generating internet traffic. In that case, Sentinel can mark it as suspicious even if the behavior is not signature-based or does not match other malware.

Automation Using Playbooks

Incident response time is crucial in a healthcare environment; if an analyst's response time is delayed, it can impact patient safety. Microsoft Sentinel allows organizations running a Security Operations Center (SOC) to operationalize incident response using automated playbooks, which provide computerized workflows powered by Logic Apps. The SOC can use playbooks to automatically isolate the compromised device, notify the incident response team, create the helpdesk ticket, perform a forensic snapshot, etc. An IoMT perspective suggests that automation can help remediate threats, minimize disruptions to patient care, and reduce alert fatigue among analysts.

Improved Threat Intelligence Integration

IoMT security must be proactive, and that means utilizing threat intelligence feeds specifically related to medical technology and healthcare infrastructure. Microsoft Sentinel can perform online ingestion of internal and external threat intelligence, which enables the SOC to historically correlate device activity against known indicators of compromise (IOCs) aimed at IoT and/or healthcare assets. Additionally, Sentinel can enrich alert data with contextual threat intelligence data to further accelerate prioritization and decision-making—it enables organizations to identify better-targeted incidents like ransom campaigns that may disrupt clinical workflows or data theft of patient information.

Incident Investigation and Root Cause Analysis

IoMT incidents typically involve clinical and IT teams, so investigations must remain precise and detail-oriented. Likewise, Microsoft Sentinel presents an enriched investigation module with entity mapping, timeline generation, and graph-based displays of activity. During an investigation, incident investigators can visualize how compromised devices interacted with other devices, how they moved, and how the incident affected the overall situation. In order to analyze root causes, report compliance information, and improve defenses to avoid similar future attacks, this holistic visibility is crucial.

Compliance and Risk Management

Healthcare is a heavily regulated environment that operates under standards such as HIPAA, GDPR, and HITECH. Microsoft Sentinel has workbooks and compliance templates to support a SOC's capability to monitor these configurations. These workbooks can provide a real-time view of access violations, unauthorized devices communicating, and abnormal audit trail activity. Also, through built-in reporting, SOC teams can produce audit evidence or retrospective analysis documentation to ensure regulatory mandates were met while protecting patients' interests.

Ongoing Improvement and SOC Maturity

Optimizing an SOC for IoMT is not a one-off event. This is a continuous process, and Microsoft Sentinel helps through advanced metrics, KPIs, and custom dashboards to promote a mature SOC. Examples of SOC metrics include mean time to detect (MTTD), mean time to respond (MTTR), alert volume, and analyst workload. These metrics can help an organization understand its gaps and improve workflows while aligning a SOC's efforts with clinical priorities. Sentinel also enables the use of simulation and threat hunting capabilities to keep security teams ahead of the evolving threat landscape.

Managing Device Diversity and Complexity in IoMT

In IoMT, one of the most significant uncertainties is the number and range of devices in use. The devices vary in terms of manufacturer, model, functionality, network behavior, and communication. Not all of them are built with cybersecurity in mind, and in many cases, there is little to no support for standard logging or agent monitoring. Microsoft Sentinel tackles this complexity of managing increasing data sources by supporting flexible ingestion methods. One of them is agentless collection from Syslog, integrations with APIs, or custom connectors that enable access to legacy or non-traditional devices connected to networks with minimal physical controls and restricted remote access, such as the medical Internet of Things (IoMT). Moreover, with Azure Lighthouse and Arc, versions of legacy and non-traditional devices could come under a single security oversight mechanism, whether an actual ventilator or some wearables that measure vital stats. In the sense of broadening threat detection, the use of Sentinel encompasses all devices, including the intended tether that doctors will use to monitor patients in hospitals, nursing homes, or anywhere else, such as RV-ing or camping around national parks.

Sentinel's advanced analytics capabilities provide the ability to normalize and correlate data from independent systems, allowing it to convert signals that are entirely fragmented into, essentially, stories of coherent security. In an IoMT environment, a typical story could be just a little more complex than if a device generates increased arousal traffic as detected in the diagnostic scanner, such as a routine scheduled update or indications of data exfiltration. Using built-in parsers and the Advanced Security Information Model (ASIM), security data from both traditional and non-traditional sources can be normalized so the strategies for managing threat data can be consistent for category queries. Moreover, such structured data enables more effective use of rule-building and cross-platform correlation strategies in the process of separating the standard, logical functionality of legitimate devices and associated functions from occurring malicious behavior in the exact servicing location.

Intended Use Cases for Healthcare Models

So, while enhancing and optimizing a SOC for IoMT is not simply to ingest more data, it is to aid in the development of unique use cases that represent the realities of clinical functionalities and expectations. Microsoft Sentinel enables you to develop a roadmap for creating custom analytics rules and detection content that supports healthcare workflows. Use case examples include scenarios where a nurse's workstation attempts to access medical image files outside of shift time frames or when the infusion pump communicates with an external source identified by an IP address. Scenarios like these can be constructed using Kusto Query Language (KQL) with context like user identity, device role, location, or patient ward assignment. By customizing detection logic for the unique operational environment of a healthcare facility, the SOC can reduce false positives and prioritize alerts that are more relevant to the organization.

Additionally, Sentinel can address clinical safety use cases when cybersecurity interacts with patient care. For example, a series of failed login attempts on a medical device that is connected to life-saving systems will not only represent a possible brute-force attack but also an immediate risk to the safety of patients. Sentinel can designate this type of event as a high-severity incident and route it through different incident response playbooks specific to critical-care devices so that Safety Operations is no longer working alone but is working as a partner with biomedical engineering and patient safety teams.

Integration with Existing Security and IT Ecosystems

Most healthcare organizations have SLAs (service level agreements) for SOC teams that require coordination with IT operations, biomedical engineering, network teams, and often external provider service teams. Microsoft Sentinel is designed to integrate into existing ticketing, messaging, and security platforms. This integration through Logic Apps can include the creation of incident tickets into ITSM (IT Service Management) systems such as ServiceNow, alerting Teams Channels for real-time collaboration, or updating network security tools to block or quarantine suspicious endpoints. Sentinel has an advantage in that it has integrations with vulnerability management platforms and CMMS (computerized maintenance management systems) for data to incident enrichment of device health, software version, and maintenance events, which are essential to the prioritization and triage decision-making process in an IoMT scenario. These integrations can organize the organization's response and facilitate the ability to coordinate workflows. For example, suppose an outdated medical device raises a red flag due to suspicious outbound communication. In that case, Sentinel can launch a playbook that requests IT to verify the device patching status, notifies the Clinical Engineering team, and automates network segmentation. The endpoint will be in a better position to evaluate the possible threat, and the centralized SOC will have better oversight on what the incident response may be without inhibiting the operator from performing patient care delivery.

Scaling Operations

Most healthcare networks are large and geographically dispersed across many regions or facilities. Within the context of an extensive health system, scientific approaches can be developed to develop the SOC, but consideration must also be made for scale and regional autonomy. Microsoft Sentinel supports both single-tenant and multi-tenant models for various health systems, including those with regional hospitals, clinics, and remote facilities, all managed under a single enterprise SOC. Organizations can apply a separate Sentinel workspace by region or by operating unit and still achieve one view of their work across each region using Azure Lighthouse. Local teams can have options to manage incidents in their environment, while the centralized SOC has oversight and can share relevant threat intelligence.

In addition, role-based access control (RBAC) enables administrators to set granular access control policies using roles, regions, and device types. It is critical to have this separation of duties in healthcare, as security operations must not just comply with privacy regulations but also the medical workflow. With A&O and reporting in a federated model, healthcare organizations can control their security posture at autonomy and scale with the growth of their IoMT environments.

Measure and Mature the Effectiveness of the SOC

Continual improvement is paramount to the optimization and maturity of the SOC. Microsoft Sentinel will point security teams in the right direction toward maturity and away from reactive defense. The SOC can define its metrics, create dashboards, and develop custom workbooks based on its performance metrics to measure response to key indicators, such as the time it takes to detect, contain, or mitigate incidents; the number of false positives reported within a review period; and its response to incident inefficiencies. Sentinel also includes built-in simulation capabilities that can be used as supporting tools during red or blue team exercises. By using the tools incorporated in Sentinel, healthcare environments can build improvement plans that are a process enabling them to identify gaps as appropriate and improve their incident response process.

This same approach supports well-established frameworks, such as NIST, MITRE ATT&CK, and Zero Trust, with the latter being the model healthcare is transitioning toward. Sentinel offers built-in support that enables healthcare organizations to map alerts and incidents to specific MITRE ATT&CK tactics and techniques, demonstrating how attackers are progressing and whether coverage is being conducted on all aspects of their progression. These steps and statements support a stronger defense-in-depth type of philosophy, where not only are detection capabilities essential, but also resilience and recovery. In the end, Sentinel enables SOC leaders to provide the data necessary

CHAPTER 3   ENGINEERING MICROSOFT SENTINEL FOR SECURITY OPERATIONS

to substantiate investment decisions in security, support compliance with regulatory practices, and promote new approaches to safer, smarter healthcare delivery in a highly connected healthcare world.

IoMT is changing nearly everything about how healthcare delivery capabilities are clinically executed, and this comes with security implications. SOC optimization in this environment is so much more than log collection and alerting; it requires intelligent automation, healthcare-aware analytics, seamless integrations, scalable operational models, etc. Microsoft Sentinel is an excellent platform to meet the above requirements. It provides the SOC teams with the capabilities to mitigate risks, be more efficient, and establish trust in the security posture for patients in a very connected world.

Summary

This chapter serves as a guide to how security engineers can maximize their use of Microsoft Sentinel in modern security operations. The chapter begins with an introduction to Microsoft Sentinel from a security engineer's perspective, outlining their roles in managing, maintaining, and enforcing responsibilities related to data connectors, log health and monitoring, and creating detection and automation rules.

Following the introduction, this chapter highlights how to use threat intelligence by consuming external and internal threat intelligence, mapping indicators of compromise (IOCs) into Sentinel, and using threat intelligence to support detection and hunting initiatives. There is also an entire section dedicated to the creation of watchlists, demonstrating how to use both static and dynamic datasets to improve analytics, detection logic, and context-specific alerts tailored to the organization's environment.

The following section provides practical guidance on creating content with KQL (Kusto Query Language), enabling readers to learn how to craft efficient queries for hunting, investigation, and custom detection. This then naturally flows into creating analytics. The section will review creating schedule-based rules, suppression, and behavioral detections to reduce false positives and improve the fidelity of detections.

The chapter also discusses some of the Security Orchestration, Automation, and Response (SOAR) capabilities in Sentinel, which explain how to encode your playbooks with Logic Apps, automate the triage process, and assist in pulling parts of your incident response process together. In conjunction with this, the cover cases module covers

CHAPTER 3   ENGINEERING MICROSOFT SENTINEL FOR SECURITY OPERATIONS

workbooks/data visualization, as well as how to build live dashboards and reports to provide visibility into security posture, incident trends, and potential threat actors, and associates with analytic pathways in timelines.

The final part of the chapter, which can be reviewed in a standalone way, will supplement your thinking to improve the Security Operations Center (SOC) to leverage insight in security operations from Sentinel, with topics related to case management mapping to best practices, encouragement to gain an understanding of some SOC metrics that combine analysis, and observations of continuous improvement cycles/practices. Additionally, it describes how threat modeling in the incident response process aligns with common frameworks, such as MITRE ATT&CK and NIST. These modules combine a full suite of skills for engineering privileged and intelligent security operations with Sentinel, based on the preceding planning, preparation, and process.

CHAPTER 4

Threat Detection, Investigation, and Response

In today's rapidly changing world of cybersecurity, a reactive stance no longer meets the need. To discover, investigate, and respond to active threats effectively, security operations must move towards a proactive, intelligence-led posture. The section Threat Detection, Investigation, and Response was created to provide security analysts with the practical skills, tools, and techniques to operate Microsoft Sentinel successfully.

We start by examining how Microsoft Sentinel enables security analysts to be successful by providing a single workspace for monitoring, investigating, and responding. We then move into building analytics rules that we craft to help us discover suspicious behaviors and patterns of activity based on a variety of data sources we have available to us. Furthermore, you will see the full life cycle of incident response, including managing security incidents, investigating alerts, live containment of incidents, and achieving some of the goals of an IR plan through response automation.

Kusto Query Language (KQL), a necessary skill for you as an analyst, is featured heavily throughout this section, as it applies to both reactive investigations and proactive threat hunting. Our detailed coverage of hunting styles and real-life examples will show you how to discover threats that may not have been caught with traditional detections. We also show you how to build basic threat intelligence into your workflows, offering extra context and detail to your detection and response efforts.

As AI-assisted operations become commonplace, we also introduce how embedded Copilot experiences can simplify everyday analyst tasks (like summarizing incidents or suggesting next steps) to make operational teams one step ahead of the adversary. Whether it's triaging alerts, building detection logic, or leading threat hunts, this chapter

CHAPTER 4   THREAT DETECTION, INVESTIGATION, AND RESPONSE

gets you ready to confidently perform the central tasks of modern security operations using Microsoft Sentinel.

By the end of this chapter, you should understand the following:

- Microsoft Sentinel for Security Analysts
- Crafting Threat Detection and Analytics Rules
- Incident Response Management
- Investigating Security Incidents
- Automating Incident Response
- Disrupting Attacks Effectively
- Using KQL for Analysts
- Hunting for Threats
- Hunting with KQL
- Integrating Threat Intelligence into Response Strategies
- Using Copilot for Security Analysts in the Embedded Experience

Microsoft Sentinel for Security Analysts

As organizations accelerate their digital transformation and migrate workloads to the cloud, they will increasingly need a modern, adaptive, intelligent security monitoring capability. Microsoft Sentinel fills that need for an organization through a centralized cloud-native platform that allows cybersecurity engineers the visibility, intelligence, and automation they need to protect their cloud-based environments. In this chapter, we will summarize ten fundamental capabilities that every security engineer needs to master to protect the cloud.

One of which is substantial data ingestion across various cloud sources. Without unifying log and telemetry collection across identity providers, compute platforms, SaaS services, and edge devices, organizations will fail to see their cloud environment in its entirety. Being able to ingest data at scale from Azure, Microsoft 365, AWS, GCP, and on-premise systems establishes a comprehensive viewpoint for engineers. Ingestion data pipelines that are poorly designed and inconsistent across numerous sources can create blind spots, which can expose an organization to risk without oversight over threats like lateral movement, credential abuse, or misconfigured assets.

An additional core component is building analytics rules. Security engineers will need to develop and tune behavioral rules that help identify threats based on patterns, anomalies, and known indicators of threats. Sentinel has analytics rules out of the box, as well as custom rules in KQL. Those engineers who enlist the use of detection rules without going through the effort to build and tune them will only risk overwhelming themselves with a series of false positives, or even worse, missing potential actual threats entirely. In this regard, detection rules will be the nervous system of threat visibility to their security operations teams and external stakeholders. In the absence of a detecting signal, Sentinel remains passive instead of being proactive.

Engineers need to be well-versed in Kusto Query Language (KQL) to conduct proper threat investigations. The KQL query language drives every search, rule, workbook, and investigation in Sentinel. Engineers learning KQL can quickly break down incidents, correlate across systems, and bring to the surface clandestine attack paths. Without KQL knowledge, threat investigations become slow and manual, with each step of the investigation process tying down the organization from timely threat containment.

Security orchestration and automation (SOAR) is also a vital discipline. Playbooks provide the ability for automatic, real-time response to an incident—isolating endpoints, blocking IPs, sending alerts, and so forth. Engineers should be able to build workflows that provide an easier path for SOC processes while lowering the dependency on human involvement. Without automation, the team faces burnout, or dwell time for threats increases, enabling attackers to pivot further into the environment.

Integrating threat intelligence helps provide context to raw data. Sentinel provides the ability to ingest structured threat intelligence feeds, as well as mapping Indicators of Compromise (IOCs) to telemetry. Engineers can use threat intelligence to tie together known bad actors and enrich alerts with external context. Without threat intelligence, analysts must rely on guesswork to assess the credibility, severity, or associated risk of alerts, which wastes time following false leads.

Watchlists provide an elegant mechanism to manage users of interest (sensitive users, VIPs, and critical assets) as well as known bad actors. Engineers can employ watchlists to trigger special handling of that entity in the detection rules. Without watchlists, engineers are bound to an all-or-nothing alert that cannot distinguish between the business contextuality of what a user/system/event is expected to be. This impacts the accuracy of alerts and diminishes the intended prioritization of response.

Operationally, workbooks and reporting serve as a function for oversight within the organization, as well as for broader stakeholder communications. Engineers need to develop dashboards that tell a story of active threats, detection coverage, incident response metrics, and SOC KPIs. Dashboards are not just nice to have—they are mission-critical to secure leadership support, compliance reporting, and operationalizing effectiveness. Without these insights, technology obscures significant aspects of cybersecurity from business consumers.

Another critical element is incident case management. Microsoft Sentinel enables alerts to be grouped into incidents (incident events) and utilizes context-sensitive and embedded investigation tools. Engineers should be expected to organize and prioritize incidents/cases, appropriately assign ownership, and track the lifecycle of cases. Incident case management and case management structures are critical components of the SOC life cycle; without them, SOC teams can lose track of alerts of considerable significance, allow redundancy, and/or disregard the early warning signs of attack campaigns.

Hunting and anomaly detection are often perceived as advanced areas; however, they are essential to proactive defensive efforts. Engineers should not solely rely on alerts to detect indicators of compromise or attack; instead, they should utilize advanced KQL queries (standard or custom) to hunt for subtle signs of compromise proactively. The delay in their occurrence or the fact that this type of cybersecurity alerting maker only reacts leaves security even further behind where attackers begin. Searching does bring security from a reactionary nature to a predictive defense nature.

Finally, continuous tuning and optimization are the most undervalued or understated skills of everyone who operates Microsoft Sentinel. Engineers should examine the overall performance of Sentinel on an ongoing or repeated basis: what alerts get to the engineer, what alerts are working, which suppression is more important, where do data sources generate noise, and where do detection gaps exist? If engineers examine all these practice areas and exclude continuous iteration, Sentinel will become stale. The threat landscape is evolving, and so is the other side of the wall. Not implementing these ten essentials is not just an inefficient use of their time; it also puts the organization at unnecessary risk. When assets are untethered, rules are weak, response times are slow, and visibility is poor, any organization is an ideal target for attackers looking for their next target. A broken Sentinel implementation not only means no alerts but also offers an organization a false sense of security. When your engineers start to view Sentinel as a system that is unnecessary and requires ongoing monitoring and strategy, the organization will suffer from prolonged detection and recovery times and may face significant reputational and financial impacts.

Security engineers who treat Sentinel as a strategic tool that is designed to link detection, automation, intelligence, and insight will enhance their security approach. This provides security engineers and the organizations they work for with greater outcome acceptability, while also enabling them to make more accurate and faster decisions. In a cloud-first world, Microsoft Sentinel is non-negotiable. It is the launch point for new security architectures, and security engineers are the architects.

In the modern cybersecurity world, the responsibility of security engineers is also vast and very heavy. The role requires self-awareness, quick decisions, and sifting through an abundance of security-related data. This chapter is intended to help security engineers use only the essentials of Microsoft Sentinel, a modern, cloud-based SIEM and SOAR designed to meet the complex threats of today.

Understanding the Microsoft Sentinel Role

Microsoft Sentinel does not operate like a log collection utility. It is an intelligent, scalable solution that is designed to detect, investigate, and respond to threats in the moment. Sentinel is designed to ingest all data from your environment, including Azure, Microsoft 365, on-prem infrastructure, third-party security tooling, and even operational technology. Sentinel supplies a filtered amount of data in one place for easy ingestion and analysis.

For security engineers, this means you can stop collecting data from various dashboards. Sentinel provides a single-pane view to monitor alerts, link events, investigate behaviors, and respond to threats, offering automated options for threat management.

Connecting Data Sources—The First Step

Sentinel lives and dies with data. As a security engineer, you must first establish the proper connections to data sources using the data connectors provided by Sentinel. Data sources include

- Identity and access logs (such as Azure AD)
- Device logs (like Microsoft Defender for Endpoint)
- Network devices (including firewalls and VPNs)

- Applications (including Microsoft 365 and AWS)
- Custom data (like syslog and Common Event Format—CEF)

Picking the right connectors ensures that Sentinel has a complete picture of what is happening in your environment. Sentinel will even provide recommendations to help you focus on the most critical log sources based on the threat coverage it can provide.

Detecting Threats with Analytics Rules

With data flowing, engineers can create analytics rules. The analytics rules will specify the types of behaviors that should raise an alert. For example:

- Unusual sign-ins from unfamiliar locations
- Multiple failed logins in a short period
- A user downloading large amounts of sensitive information

Sentinel already comes with several built-in rule templates, which include threat detections that Microsoft has pulled from existing global threat intelligence. These default analytics rules can be altered to suit your purpose, or you can write your own utilizing Kusto Query Language (KQL).

Power of KQL for Engineers

KQL is the query language used in Sentinel to search and analyze data. For engineers, learning KQL is like finding a diamond in the rough—it allows you to

- Investigate incident details
- Hunt for hidden threats
- Create dashboards
- Set alerts and anomaly detection

KQL is easy to learn if you have previous experience with scripting or SQL. Using a few simple queries, you could see under the hood. For example, using KQL, you can detect failed logins, view file-level access, and track command-line activity, which helps identify attack patterns for review.

Automating Response with Playbooks (SOAR)

One of Sentinel's best features is SOAR (Security Orchestration, Automation, and Response). Engineers can create playbooks or automated workflows that respond based on alerts. Playbooks can

- Alert logger analysts via email or Teams
- Block users or IPs in real-time
- Open tickets in ITSM solutions
- Pull enrichment data from threat intelligence sources

This frees up time for analysts to focus on investigation analysis at scale and speed when responding to incidents in a high-volume environment.

Workbooks, Watchlists, and Threat Intelligence

Security engineers can also use workbooks to build visual dashboards and reports. A great way to track KPIs, mark threats, and report out to leadership. Multiple dashboards can be queued, and there are interactive features, using KQL queries, that allow engineers to customize previews. Watchlists are another great feature. Security engineers can make lists of users, devices, or IPs to monitor deterministically, which can easily be referred to by alert rules and halted by investigations. They can create a watchlist of high-privilege accounts to review intermittently for abnormal behavior. Sentinel allows for threat intel feeds that help alert to contextual information if an IP is known to be associated with a botnet or phishing campaign. They can combine two identified actors from a conference call into a known threat and prioritize threat detection alerts. Additionally, they can group multiple alerts as a single actor from the two identified threats correlated to the event.

Building a Smarter SOC

Using Sentinel, security engineers can then be the drivers behind building a better, more innovative, intelligent, and proactive Security Operations Center (SOC). By leveraging automation, analytics, and intelligence, teams can take action by discovering, detecting, responding to, and recording practical actions to more reliably identify advanced threat-related events early and significantly reduce timelines and efficiencies.

Engineers can help continuously support security posture by

- Tuning analytic rules to decrease false positive cycles determines whether an event is a false positive or simply a nuisance.

- Leveraging built-in hunting queries can help teams discover threats before they become abnormalities.

- Collaboratively work with the analyst using case management on contextual review.

- Record results/findings using workbooks and reporting dashboards (dashboards can also be that report).

This section's chapter has introduced security engineers at all levels to the basic way, context, knowledge, and skills required to operationalize the Sentinel family within their organization. You have noted how to connect data, detect threat activity, initiate automated responses, investigate instances, and share reports, all from within a single integrated analysis platform. Within the Microsoft Sentinel space, engineers can grow a role beyond defender to become an enabler of security intelligence, automation, and continuous advanced security protections.

Reinventing Security Operations with Microsoft Sentinel

As cyber threats advance at an unprecedented scale, businesses face increasing pressure to protect their digital environments while scaling and maintaining efficiency. Conventional security tools and outdated SIEM (Security Information and Event Management) solutions cannot compete—they are inflexible, expensive to retain, and lack adaptive intelligence in the face of complex attacks. Microsoft Sentinel—a cloud-native and AI-enhanced SIEM—gives brave new security operations centers the solution they need.

This section will focus on how Sentinel has reinvented the modern SOC for security teams, enabling them to address fundamental security challenges. Everything from getting started rapidly with integrations to intelligent automation and detection of sophisticated threats, Sentinel gives modern-day security professionals additional tools to protect, respond, and scale.

A New Breed of SIEM for a New Breed of Threats

Microsoft Sentinel is not just another SIEM. Built inherently as a cloud-native SIEM for a diverse hybrid environment, Microsoft Sentinel combines strong artificial intelligence capabilities, flexible data management, and widespread integration with tools and services to enable organizations to defend against threats, rather than be forced to react after the fact.

Today's security teams lack the necessary tools and receive far too many alerts, making it impossible to fully understand the actual environment. It is difficult for security teams to connect tools and intelligence to take action, which is why Microsoft Sentinel enables security professionals to move out of a purely detection perspective to become proactive responders. Leveraging Microsoft Sentinel to collect and analyze data allows defenders to move edge to edge and take action as quickly and effectively as possible.

Key Innovations That Make Sentinel the Best

- *Accelerate Onboarding with Seamless Migration*: There is zero burden on the security engineer migrating away from their dirty legacy SIEM. Microsoft Sentinel offers advanced mechanisms that encode and refine all of the processes used to migrate to Sentinel. The methods established to enter your data, retain your configurations, and facilitate ongoing intake are executed in tandem. Onboarding teams can derive value from Sentinel in real time with little to no interruptions to their operational workflows.

- *Widen Visibility Across Your Digital Estate*: Microsoft Sentinel has a mature and vibrant ecosystem with over 350 connectors. Data ingestion into Sentinel is seamless, easy, and connected, no matter your identities, emails, endpoints, clouds, applications, and network services. Your data, no matter the source, translates to complete situational awareness across your organization and all its critical assets.

CHAPTER 4   THREAT DETECTION, INVESTIGATION, AND RESPONSE

- *Decrease Dwell Time with AI-Powered Faster Detection and Remediation*: In cybersecurity, time is of the essence. Sentinel provides advanced capabilities such as a powerful correlation engine that converts alerts into simple incidents, making it easier for a team to cut noise and focus on actual incidents. Built-in AI platforms, like Security Copilot, provide automatic summaries of the incidents and impacts and a guided remediation pathway, shorter incidents, and much faster response across the entire security landscape.

- *Address Any Use Case with a Comprehensive Resource Library*: Microsoft Sentinel is backed by a consistently updated and active community. Security teams have a vast collection of detection rules, playbooks, dashboards, and analytic templates available to them. With thousands of customizable elements, engineers can deploy the platform for a varied list of use cases (compliance, insider threat detection, phishing, etc.) in record time.

- *Enhance Investigations with Security Copilot*: Investigating complex attacks is often tedious, taking both time and resources away from critical security needs. Security Copilot uses AI to summarize timelines of incidents, correlate events across systems, and uncover root causes. By reducing the required manual work by up to 85%, analysts can resolve cases faster and with greater clarity about the full threat landscape.

- *Automate Routine Tasks to Enhance Efficiency*: Microsoft Sentinel exemplifies the purposeful application of automation within methods. With the many log analyses, alert triaging, script executions, and orchestration of responses, it is substantially more efficient to automate many tasks! This enables productive analysts to be timely in high-level activities, such as proactive threat hunting and strategic planning.

In an era of intense enterprise cybersecurity risk, many organizations remain reliant on abstract or niche SIEM solutions (security information and event management) to address emerging threats, or worse, legacy or siloed solutions that are becoming obsolete. As organizations migrate to hybrid cloud systems and environments that never exist on any "single silo" or perimeter, treating these ubiquitous but impotent biometric systems as a one-dimensional historical footprint of isolated human activity, much like an archival strip, will not provide adequate detection; ultimately, those organizations will never have any success in responding to a systemic attack. Given the small scale we see (MITRE ATT&CK is an excellent resource), organizations will continue to fall victim to alert fatigue, escalating operational funding, limited visibility, and an alarming time to value.

Microsoft Sentinel has all the core features necessary to integrate cloud-native with Multinational A. In today's multivariate IT environments, they will become the loudest competitor. The integration of built-in automation, machine learning, and scalable data collection, along with connecting security operations to threat intelligence, will significantly enhance the health, cohesion, and productivity of security operations and their workflows. The benefit of simple operations is the higher quality of threat identification, rapid resolution, and economic value of transitioning to Microsoft Sentinel cloud for a comprehensive SOC (Security Operations Center). Regardless of the version an organization starts with, it will put itself in a position to respond to current and future threats. Table 4-1 illustrates the comparative study between SIEM and Microsoft Sentinel.

Table 4-1. *Comparative Study Between SIEM and Microsoft Sentinel*

Category	Limitations of Traditional and Niche SIEM	What You Get with Microsoft Sentinel
Operations and User Experience	– Everyone is relying on tools that they're using in silos - Updates are frequent and take a lot of time and effort - Workflows are difficult and require extensive training	– Everything you require in one unified experience - Rich and seamless integration with Microsoft Defender (XDR) - A solution to empower any user; no special skills needed
Threat Detection	– Attention needed for too many false positives - Manual investigation is the only option - Lack of visibility or contextualized understanding of threats - Slow to respond	– Deeper threat detection and correlation powered by AI - Integrated threat intelligence to enrich alerts - More accurate and timely investigations with lots of context

(*continued*)

Table 4-1. (*continued*)

Category	Limitations of Traditional and Niche SIEM	What You Get with Microsoft Sentinel
Automation and Investigation	– Little automation - More work for analysts - Reactive only	– Security Copilot AI-based response tool - Machine learning (ML)-based threat hunting - Proactive investigations into alerts
Cost and Scalability	– Infrastructure and licensing are very expensive - Pay for different modules, add-ons, and features - Hard to scale	– Cloud-native and economical - Flexible and can scale with your requirements - Reduced total cost of ownership (TCO)
Deployment and Integration	– Time wasted to set up and integrate tooling - No support for cloud or other third-party tools - Limited prebuilt use cases	– 350+ pre-built connectors for cloud, hybrid, and on-prem systems - Codeless custom connectors - Broad library of detection and response playbooks and detection rules
Innovation and Vision	– Slow product updates - Investment in AI and resourcing is weak - No long-term roadmap	– Rapid innovation at the core with AI and ML - Backed by 10,000+ Microsoft security professionals - Leading threat intelligence and GenAI capabilities

Building Blocks of Sentinel's Modern Security Model

To understand how Sentinel aids holistic security, it is easiest to consider its architecture as having four building blocks that, while separate, interconnect:

- *Collect and Optimize*: Data is the currency of security. Sentinel enables easy log and telemetry collection across your digital estate using built-in connectors and normalization. With data tiers and optimized cost storage, organizations can ingest surplus data without the fear of rising operational costs.

- *Monitor and Detect*: Sentinel has an advanced analytics engine that is constantly monitoring data for patterns of malicious activity. As an example, machine learning detection models can embrace subtle but emerging anomalies using User/Entity Behaviors Analytics (UEBA). The thought examples of already integrated or interoperable Threat Alerts intelligence layers provide additional context and insights for patches or known "Indicators of Compromise" (IOCs).

- *Respond and Investigate*: Once malicious intent has been detected, Sentinel has the foundational capacity to provide security teams with the ability to respond and escalate in urgency. By rule, automation triggers incident response, while Security Copilot can provide real-time guidance and deep investigative support. The result is reduced "mean time to resolution" (MTTR) and elevated efficiencies within the operations of a Security Operations Center (SOC).

- *Visualize and Improve*: Custom dashboards and pictographic visualizations offer quantifiable and continuous insights into security posture. They enable SOC leaders to make informed decisions, track key performance indicators, and identify areas for improvement. Sentinel even provides daily recommendations to improve data and maximize ROI on security software.

Sentinel's Quantifiable Value

Overall, organizations that use Microsoft Sentinel do so from the perspective of competence and also improve business outcomes. Some quantifiable examples include

- 44% total SIEM cost reduction through reduced or non-existent infrastructure cost and operations efficiency.

- 85% reduction in investigative labor from automated incident investigation and AI-supported intelligence.

- 79% lower number of false positives that consume analysts' time to analyze real malicious intent.

- 35% reduced breach likelihood through increased visibility and ability to respond faster.

- 93% faster onboarding of data using "plug-and-play" connectors.

All of these outcomes are reflective of a platform that was built for high performance with sustainable security transformation.

Future-Proofing the Security Operations Center

Sentinel is not merely the replacement of an old SIEM; it is the acceptance of a more intelligent and scalable model for security. Microsoft Sentinel is designed within modern security principles: Zero Trust, Proactive Defense, Threat-Informed Response, and Continuous Improvement.

By enabling security teams to stay ahead of criminals, we can automate tasks where possible, provide detection strength through live intelligence, and emphasize areas where human expertise adds value.

Microsoft Sentinel is a next-generation security operation with a cloud-native platform, AI-powered threat detection capability, and an unrivaled means of flexibility, value, and sophistication. Whether migrating from an existing SIEM or building a SOC from a standing start, Sentinel has the highest level of available tools, insights, and options needed in the current cyber battlefield. For security engineers and SOC leaders, this is no longer merely a reactive platform; it is a strategic weapon that every organization should leverage for a future-proof security posture.

Crafting Threat Detection and Analytics Rules in Microsoft Sentinel

The foundation of Microsoft Sentinel's capability to detect, illustrate, and react to threats is reliant upon the rules for analytics detection and analytics response. This portion of the governance strategy will discuss building and tuning rules for analytics detection and response that will support security teams to detect threats early, minimize false positives, and then take actions with fidelity.

Microsoft Sentinel allows the analyst to create analytics detection rules using Kusto Query Language (KQL) with specific criteria to identify suspicious behaviors. Microsoft Sentinel will continually run the analytics rules against the source log data to support the security teams in identifying anomalies, finding malicious patterns, and identifying the known or unknown indicators of compromise. Several types of rules can be created, including scheduled rules, near-real-time (NRT) rules, Microsoft Security templates, and machine learning-based behavioral detections. Each rule type serves a specific detection purpose, such as identifying brute-force attacks, lateral movement, suspicious PowerShell execution, or insider threats.

There is a delicate balance to strike when creating the rules. Rules should be specific enough to limit alert fatigue as a result of false positives and broad enough to capture evolving threat landscapes. Microsoft Sentinel allows content tuning for each of the rules, such as frequency of rule invocations, thresholds for alerts, and entity mappings, to name a few. Rules can be enriched with threat intelligence, custom watchlists, and correlation across several data sources. Rules may also provide for incidents to be automatically created, including playbooks to trigger and enable an automated response within a greater security orchestration effort. As you continually review detection coverage and improve your rule logic, you can continuously adapt to a changing threat landscape and keep your environment safe.

Ultimately, the objective of building out analytics rules is to transform raw telemetry into actionable intelligence. With Sentinel's flexibility and scalability, organizations can now build a library of high-fidelity detections unique to their environment that will allow them to get ahead of threats.

At the core of Microsoft Sentinel's proactive defense capabilities is the analytics engine, which detects, surfaces, and escalates suspicious behavior across terabytes of security information and logs. Building threat detection analytics rules is a key task for security analysts and engineers, as it enables them to turn raw telemetry into actionable alerts. This is not simply about writing queries but building detections that are accurate, relevant, and robust against an ever-changing threat landscape.

Understanding Analytics Rules in Sentinel

Analytics rules are the fundamental mechanism in Sentinel for the detection of threats. An analytics rule monitors incoming log data and looks for identifiable patterns or indicators of potentially malicious activity. An alert is generated when a rule's condition is met. There are numerous variations of analytics rules supported in Sentinel to accommodate the many different detection needs:

- *Scheduled Rules*: Run according to a preset schedule (e.g., every 5, 10, or 15 minutes) to detect known behaviors through custom Kusto Query Language (KQL) queries.

- *Near-Real-Time (NRT) Rules*: Detect in low-latency situations to support critical detection scenarios that need near-real-time reactions.

- *Microsoft Security Templates*: Provide templates that are built by Microsoft based on Microsoft's own threat intelligence and security best practices. They are helpful for everyday use cases.

- *Fusion Rules (ML-Based)*: Track multistage attacks, lateral movements, and data exfiltration attempts, using machine learning and graph-based correlation to relate signals across many sources of data.

While each of the above rules has a different agenda when it comes to detection, you can tune them for your organizational operations and threat environment.

Establishing High-Quality Detections

Writing applicable detection rules stems from having an understanding of the threat scenarios you wish to detect. Credential theft, your move to persistence, and command-and-control communications—each scenario will have some behavioral traits that can be observed (e.g., through logs and telemetry). You want to understand what the behaviors are and observe these behaviors in your rules.

When writing detection rules, keep in mind the following:

- *The Clarity of Logic*: the KQL query within your rule must articulate your intended detection logic clearly, be easily understood, and be easy to maintain.

- *Data Source*: Sentinel's rules need to use the right data tables and fields based on the data source structure. Understanding how Azure AD, Microsoft Defender, firewall logs, and custom sources structure their data is required.

- *Entity Tracking*: For investigation and incident enrichment, rules should track entities (e.g., accounts, hosts, IPs, and URLs) successfully. This allows for incident groupings and the production of applicable timelines for entities.

- *Thresholds and Filtering*: It is reasonable to have your rules use logical thresholds and filters to help reduce some of the usual noise experienced. For example, the rule may only alert on multiple suspicious events within a short period.

- *Custom Fields and Parsing*: Sentinel has KQL parse, extract, and mv-expand functions to help extract additional fields from potentially unstructured or custom logs that may contain nested or custom fields.

Enriching Detections with Threat Intelligence

Microsoft Sentinel can incorporate threat indicators directly into analytics rules. Threat indicators can be a malicious IP, domain, file hash, or email address. One notable benefit of using threat intelligence is that you will be able to reference the above indicators dynamically in your logic. When this is adequately developed, a ruleset that captures threat intelligence should automatically generate alerts based on the data ingested into Sentinel, conforming to the indicators of compromise (IOC). This integration ensures that your detection logic evolves with current threat intelligence feeds, enabling proactive detection even before malicious activity causes harm.

Watchlists and Custom Lists

Another excellent value add that may be leveraged within analytic rules is watchlists. Watchlists are lists that you can create of essential/critical assets, users, applications, or IP ranges that you would like to watch more closely. When you run your logs against a watchlist, you can achieve many meaningful contextual alerts. For example, administrator logins from unexpected locations or sensitive file accesses from high-risk users.

Alert Fatigue

While comprehensive coverage for detectors is essential, you do not want to have so many alerts (especially false alerts) that it tires out your security resources. Therefore, tuning will be an ongoing process: frequently revisiting rule performance, lowering your thresholds, and grouping incidents to reduce false alerts will help all of your analysts focus on what is most important.

Some best practice recommendations may include

- Group alerts into incidents rather than individual alerts, so the investigation is less complicated
- Use allowlists to block known benign activity
- Use time-based thresholds for repeated actions (e.g., multiple failed logins within 10 minutes)
- Increase your detection fidelity by joining and/or unioning signals

Automation and Integrating with Your Incident Response Processes

All analytic rules can connect to automation workflows called playbooks. A playbook can take actions such as alerting your team, isolating endpoints, disabling accounts, or even adding context to the incidents. Since analytics rules can be ingested into an automation process, Sentinel enables you to respond to critical threats as they occur in real time, instead of relying on your team's response process.

Detection Rule Lifecycle

The rule creation process will typically follow a lifecycle similar to the one below.

1. Design and plan, to include the detection definition and scope of detection
2. Query development (writing and testing your KQL-based query) through the Logs blade
3. Rule creation (taking your tested query and turning it into an analytics rule with the Sentinel wizard)
4. Tuning and optimization, monitoring rule activity for false positives, and improved accuracy.
5. Maintenance and refresh continually revisit rules to ensure they appropriately represent the latest threat(s) in a continuously changing environment.

Continuous Improvement and Inter-Team Collaboration

The work of detection engineering should not be a one-off process. Threat adversaries are constantly changing, and your detections should also reflect that. Microsoft Sentinel supports content management solutions, including integrations with GitHub as well as CI/CD pipelines for rules, allowing teams to version control their detections, and in some cases, allowing for inter-team collaboration on detections. Improved quality processes, such as recycling templates, sharing detection patterns across your environments, and detection gap analysis, incrementally improve your maturity.

Creation and implementation of analytic rules in Microsoft Sentinel is both an art and a science. You need to understand threats, know what data exists within your environment, and write logic that is both efficient for performance and sufficient from a detection accuracy perspective. With purposeful analytic rules, the analytic rule engine becomes the heart and soul of your detections and operational processes. This enables you to extract security alerts that matter, improving your response time as an organization and enhancing your security posture. Improving and formalizing your analytic rules with signature insight and threat intelligence and automating your processes will keep your team agile from a threat perspective.

Understanding Incidents and Alerts in the Microsoft Defender Portal

The Microsoft Defender portal is a security operations hub that unites signals across the digital environment—endpoint, identity, cloud, network, and third-party sources—into a consumable source of action. This single pane of glass allows security teams to monitor, detect, investigate, and respond in a more timely and effective manner.

Two basic signals formulate the basis of the platform: alerts and incidents.

Alerts: The Frontline Signals

Alerts are the primary detection signals that are formed from security telemetry. They represent suspicious or malicious activity that was detected in the environment, such as credential dumping, malware execution, anomalous sign-in, or lateral movement. Alerts can be created through multiple detection mechanisms such as analytic rules, behavior analytics, and signature detections. While each alert alone has value, it only represents one concern, and in isolation, may not provide enough context to form the full story of the attack.

Incidents: The Complete Attack Narrative

To provide a more comprehensive context for the alerts, they are organized into incidents—containers that group alerts related to one another, forming a single investigation case. Instead of requiring the analyst to piece together everything scattered across different alerts, the system will automatically correlate the related alerts using machine learning and rule-based logic. This results in a complete picture of the entire attack campaign.

Incidents are created by intelligent correlation engines, which look at the timing, behaviors, entities involved, and the context of the threats. This process connects signals across multiple sources, producing a broader picture of adversarial activity. During an attack, the system consistently updates the incident folder with relevant alerts and evidence as new alerts come in.

Each incident is a context-enriched accounting of an attack.

- A timeline of events and alerts
- Techniques and tactics mapped against known attack frameworks
- A summary of all impacted users, endpoints, and resources
- Attack graphs that show the relationships and dependencies among the entities
- Details of automatic investigation and response actions that were enacted
- Evidence including malicious files, compromised accounts, IP addresses, and behaviors observed
- A written summary that narrates the incident

This repeatable structure allows analysts to rapidly view the totality of an attack, prioritize their response, and document their findings for potential reporting and compliance purposes.

Correlation and Intelligence in Action

The platform automatically creates incidents from related alerts, freeing the analyst from the manual work of sorting, correlating, and mapping threat alerts and artifacts to broader campaigns. This ability to automate the story-building process creates more efficient analysis, especially during the response to APTs, multistage intrusions, and concurrent attack vectors.

Furthermore, the correlation logic is continuously evolving through AI feedback loops and telemetry analysis, aiding in the detection of even obscure, previously unseen constructs and attacks, while still triggering incident building.

Alerts and Source of Detection Events

Alerts are ingested from an array of integrated security tools into telemetry pipelines. These include

- Endpoint telemetry from antivirus and endpoint detection tools
- Identity and access management systems
- Network security appliances
- Cloud-based infrastructure
- Application security and behavioral analytics
- Custom detections made through Microsoft Sentinel

Microsoft Sentinel provides a source for detection logic through log analytics rules, machine learning anomaly detection models, and threat intelligence integration. When Sentinel is connected to the Defender portal, raw logs and alerts generated by Sentinel rule engines become accessible for correlation and investigation via the Defender portal. This means you can easily correlate log events across multiple domains of log data, leveraging the synergy provided by the SIEM and XDR.

Investigation and Response Tools

The Defender portal includes many unique tools to facilitate efficient incident investigations and responses, including

Incident Management

Analysts can triage an incident based on urgency, severity, and organizational impacts. Through the incident view, an analyst may drill down into related alerts, event timelines, root causes of the incident, and remediation activities currently active.

Automated Investigation and Remediation

There are alert sources that support an automated investigation. When enabled, the system will be able to gather evidence, determine potential impacts, and facilitate containment and remediation actions without analyst involvement. This helps reduce mean time to respond (MTTR) to a high-confidence threat.

Attacks Disruption

As a platform, Defender can act at machine speed to disrupt attempts to perpetrate attacks. When high-confidence and confirmed threats are detected, a list of actions can be taken automatically. For example, based on disruption policies, the system can isolate devices, deactivate user accounts, or block traffic to contain the threat from spreading.

Sentinel Automation Rules

Sentinel contains automation rules to support the triage process of incidents and alerts. Automation rules can tag, suppress, assign, or close incidents based on the predefined logic. For instance, low-fidelity alert sources that are known safe can be auto-closed, while high-severity alerts can be escalated and assigned to teams.

Advanced Hunting

Using Kusto Query Language (KQL), analysts can search across their environments to ideally expose threats that aren't so obvious, follow the movements of attackers, or validate hypotheses of threats as they proceed. Guided query builders are used by people who want to hunt visually versus blank canvas KQL queries.

AI-Assisted Security Operations

In addition to these tools, AI can be incorporated to help analysts better operationalize workflows. Security Copilot-style tools can help analysts interpret alerts, summarize an entire attack scenario, or reach out with possible actions for remediation. These assistants can transform natural language questions into KQL queries, map out step-by-step incident responses, and assist with code-based logic to examine investigation logic, enabling even the smallest SOC to enhance its capabilities against threats.

A Unified Framework for Detection and Response

The Defender portal will have a unified experience that eliminates the silos often found in traditional security operations. It will help provide a cohesive framework for analysts to analyze, correlate, and act on signals in an efficient workflow, regardless of the source of the signals, whether they are detected from security events originating from Microsoft solutions or other third-party solutions.

The connected experience offered in the Defender portal we mentioned above will help focus security teams on faster, more precise, and less manual means of detection, understanding, and responding to threats, from first alerts to final remediation. This will provide a bridge between SIEM and XDR capabilities, offering the advantages of both in the visibility of a SIEM, along with the full response capabilities of XDR, all within a single pane of glass.

Managing Incidents in Microsoft Defender

Incident management is a core component of any modern security operations program. Managing incidents effectively in Microsoft Defender means more than just alert monitoring—it means managing security events in a way that is organized, repeatable, and coordinated by a level of clarity and consistency.

When a structured process is used to triage, investigate, and close incidents, security teams become more efficient and reactive, reduce risk and exposure by tracking incidents, and keep a clear log of activity that can later be audited and used to run reports for analysis.

CHAPTER 4   THREAT DETECTION, INVESTIGATION, AND RESPONSE

The Role of Incidents in the Security Workflow

In the Defender ecosystem, incidents are containers for events that provide security teams with a consolidated view of alerts. Incidents help security teams understand the context of closely related alerts and unfold them in a way that allows the team to understand and respond to an actual attack scenario as a cohesive whole, instead of disparate alerts each to be worked on separately. Figure 4-1 illustrates the high-level security incident management flow.

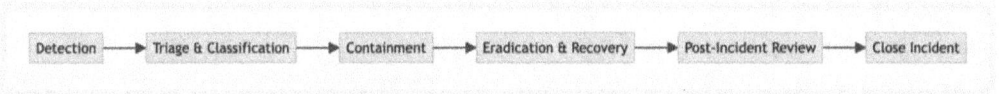

Figure 4-1. *High-Level Security Incident Management Flow*

Good incident management allows teams to

- Assign ownership and track accountability
- Adjust severity to account for real-world consequences
- Tag alerts for filtering and classification
- Update status throughout the investigative process
- Document conclusion and resolution details
- Export the incident records for reporting offline

Using incident management involves establishing a consistent workflow, improving communication, enhancing situational awareness and visibility, and ensuring the appropriate action is taken for each event.

Triage: Prioritizing Incidents to Determine When to Take Action

The declaration of an incident is the first step in working on any new case. In this stage, you'll receive or generate incidents, assign them to analytics, categorize the incidents appropriately, and tag the incidents so that they can easily be filtered or prioritized.

Assign Ownership

Incidents should be assigned to a person or team who will become responsible for owning the incident. Assigned ownership will ensure the incident is being addressed on an active basis. If ownership of the incident is escalated or transferred, it can be updated. Ownership of an incident also extends to any alerts associated with that incident, so whoever owns the incident also owns the complete investigation across alerts.

Setting Severity

Severity sets the potential impact of the incident and is usually associated with the worst alert within the incident. Once the security teams gather more context during their triage phase, they can update the severity. Typical severity tags include the following:

- *High*: Critical threats that require action
- *Medium*: Moderate risk with the potential for operational impact
- *Low*: No real impact but an early warning
- *Informational*: There is no immediate threat, but it serves as awareness

Applying Tags

Tags are an easy way to label and categorize incidents. Organizations can create custom tags for campaign names, department relevance, phases of investigations, or any other business-relevant identifiers. Tags can also be helpful filters when working your way through a large number of incidents in the queue.

Investigation and Resolution

After triaging the incidents, they will go into an investigative stage where analysts will make their observations of the investigation's complete scope and gather the supporting evidence that supports the selection of the correct resolution pathway.

Changing Incident Status

The incident state tracks the current stage of the investigation. Typical statuses are

- *Active*: The probe for new or ongoing incidents is currently functioning. This is the status of the initial investigations into incidents as they arise.

- *In Progress*: Investigation into an incident is ongoing.

- *Resolved*: Investigation into incident is complete, and any remediation activities have been completed.

When marking an incident as "Resolved," analysts are prompted to record the closure status by providing a summary of the resolution, a brief note of their findings, or actions taken.

Classification of Incidents

Each resolved incident needs to be classified to leverage historical analysis and improve detection capability in the future. Classifications may include

- *True Positive*: A confirmed threat, sometimes with a threat type label, e.g., malware, phishing

- *False Positive*: A benign activity mistakenly labelled as malicious.

- *Informational*: Expected or testing activity (e.g., red teaming or exercise).

Accurate classification improves detection capability over time and helps the organization focus on rule refinement and reducing noise.

Adding Investigation Notes

As an incident develops, analysts should log their investigative activities, insights, and thought processes. Adding comments and notes is also helpful for continuity when multiple analysts are working on the investigation, and it is good practice for subsequent audits and incident reviews.

Audit and Reporting

Effective incident management involves appropriate documentation and reporting, which is not possible without robust reports. The Defender application allows audit trails to be maintained and exported so they can be viewed offline or used in executive briefings.

Renaming Incidents

For accuracy, incidents can be renamed to reflect their context better (i.e., type of attack or affected assets). Custom naming allows for quicker identification and more precise navigation through the queue.

Reviewing the Activity Log

The activity log is a timeline that contains the history of all status changes, comments, classifications, and updates made in temporal order. Our detailed audit log for each incident is useful for post-incident review and compliance reporting.

Exporting Incident Reports

While not a required step, security teams may elect to export details of the incident to a PDF for documentation, ingestion into an email briefing, or as a means to review the incident offline. Reports usually contain the following sections:

Project

- Incident summary
- Attack chain and threat tactics
- Affected assets (devices, users, and apps)
- Related alerts and activities
- Comments, classification
- Visualizations (attack graphs and timelines)

This provides stakeholders with a greater understanding of the incident and the organization's response.

CHAPTER 4 THREAT DETECTION, INVESTIGATION, AND RESPONSE

Improving Efficiency Through Automation

Automation aids incident management to help streamline the processes involved in responding to an incident. The automated incident management capabilities supported by Defender and Sentinel are enabled by rules and playbooks that can be initiated by KQL queries or AI service automation. Notably,

- *Automatic Assignment*: Incidents can automatically be assigned/routed to assigned analysts based on criteria such as severity, source, etc.

- *Auto-Tagging and Triage*: Rules can apply tags, change severity, or suppress alerts when a known benign pattern is detected.

- *Integrated Playbooks*: Automation workflows can isolate devices, notify teams, let relevant parties know the context of an alert, or initiate remediation actions; it can be started directly from the incident creation.

It is a more efficient process from detection to remediation with incident management. When organizations establish a structured approach to triage, investigation, and remediation of incidents, it fosters a team-oriented approach to defending against the complexities of the threat landscape we see today. Using Defender to investigate with Sentinel's operational and data ingest and automation capabilities, security teams can evolve their incident management approach from a bargain basement reactive state of alert blindness to effective proactive containment.

With a level of maturity in the incident management process, organizations' Security Operations Center (SOC) will be competent to systematically, effectively, and decisively manage incidents: routinely confronted with the known threats, while other risk factors are factored against a backdrop of emerging, avant-garde threat vectors.

Investigating Security Incidents

Incidents, in Microsoft Sentinel, represent full investigative cases that hold all alerts, evidence, and entities related to potential threat actors or active attacks. Incidents are constructed by pulling in alerts created by analytics rules or ingested from sources of external security products. Each incident contains properties inherited from the alerts, such as severity, status, and associated MITRE ATT&CK tactics and techniques.

CHAPTER 4   THREAT DETECTION, INVESTIGATION, AND RESPONSE

Sentinel's investigative capabilities center around the incident details page, which houses all investigative features in an entire case management experience. Sentinel allows investigators and analysts to use one screen to examine the incident and evidence, review contextual information, execute hunting queries, assign incident ownership, and take responding steps. This layout allows security teams to standardize workflow processes, address the most pressing threats, and decrease the mean time to resolve (MTTR).

Before starting an investigation, it is prudent to establish your workflow. Sentinel provides a suite of tools to manage and record everything associated with your investigations. The potential tasks related to the incident can be viewed, and any relevant task can be added, enabling investigators and analysts to standardize their processes and avoid missing critical steps. In addition, an activity log is maintained for the incident that continuously tracks all of the incident's activity, including automation rules or analyst comments, allowing investigators to collaborate and hold each other accountable for documenting their investigation.

Interactive logging capabilities are another vital aspect of any investigation. Sentinel integrates Log Analytics into the incident view, enabling investigators to run KQL queries directly within the investigation. Whether you are tracking entities, pivoting through alerts, or validating hypotheses, querying logs in context is a huge productivity enhancement and facilitates a data-driven decision process.

Analysts can take a variety of actions directly from the incident details page. Playbooks can be run to automate response steps, such as containment or enrichment. New automation rules can be created to generate similar future incidents, and teams can coordinate through integrated communication channels. All of these actions can help analysts respond quickly and in a repeatable manner to evolving threats.

The incident page layout is designed to allow a full investigation. The left panel provides the high-level incident context: alert activity, evidence, and entities involved. Analysts can drill further into each alert or bookmark to see the logs associated with them and the kill chain techniques related to each. Additionally, the timeline provides a visual investigation tool to allow analysts to visualize the relationships between alerts and entities to facilitate intuitive navigation through complicated attack paths.

The body of the incident page includes two tabs: overview and entities. The overview tab includes widgets that facilitate a strategic view of the investigation. The incident timeline shows a flow of alerts and bookmarks in time order, which can help reconstruct attacker activity. The similar incidents widget enables analysts to view related activity across the environment, providing context that will likely help determine if there are larger attack campaigns as well. The Entities widget offers a complete list of all the involved entities—users, devices, and IP addresses—that can be investigated in more detail. Finally, Top Insights provides auto-generated insights based on curated queries and machine learning, with recommendations and threat context based on the observed behaviors.

The Entities tab expands the information in the Overview tab, providing a list of all the involved entities. Each list item includes not just brute identifiers but also activities and valuable insights based on known threat behaviors. Analysts can filter, search the list, review timelines of related events, and take actions on entities, such as putting them on threat intelligence lists or triggering automated actions.

One of the most potent tools for investigative work within Sentinel is the Investigation Graph. The Investigation Graph provides a visualization of the relationships between alerts, entities, and underlying evidence to assist analysts in understanding the breadth of the attack and identifying potential targets. Analysts can select entities on the graph to explore related alerts and pivot through exploration queries designed by cybersecurity experts. Investigators viewing the timeline feature within the graph can see how the incident has developed through time, which facilitates reconstructing the narrative of the attack.

Documentation is another pillar of effective investigation. Sentinel provides an activity log to support full auditing of each change made or comment added to the incident investigation. Analysts can add insights, remediation steps, or hypotheses in rich-text comments for collaboration across shifts and teams. Comments may also have links, formatted text, and references to external data to support reporting within the incident narrative.

As investigations conclude, the incidents can be resolved and classified accordingly. Classification provides the capability for the SOC to classify incidents as true positives, expected behavior, or false positives. This classification feedback will improve the accuracy of threat detections in future incidents, which can contribute to further developing the threat detection strategy.

The incident data may also be exported for reporting or archival purposes. The export function will create a structured document that contains all the incident details, including timeline markers, impacted entities, supporting evidence, and analyst actions. This document is helpful for audits, executive summaries, and compiling knowledge base documents.

During the investigation phase of incident response, Sentinel has enabled analysts to expand or narrow the direction of their inquiry. Analysts can add or remove alerts on the alert list based on relevance, and they can mark significant alerts using bookmarks through the investigation process. This ability to refine the investigation allows for an adaptive, iterative investigative approach that is required by the developing nature of cybersecurity threats.

In summary, Microsoft Sentinel has provided a holistic and adaptable investigation process. As security operations teams centralize available data, automate repetitive investigative steps, and analyze key incident components in detail, they can confidently investigate, come up with a clear and valid response, and focus on improving the organization's threat detection and response capabilities.

Alert Correlation and Incident Merging in the Microsoft Defender Portal

In today's security operations, an incident is seldom a solitary thing. One attack elicits many alerts for various systems, and learning the relationship between those alerts is vital in forming an accurate outline of the threat. Microsoft Defender features a powerful correlation engine that can automatically correlate related alerts into one incident, allowing the analyst to investigate the context of the incident.

When an alert is generated, either utilizing Defender's native detection systems or other combined data sources (such as Microsoft Sentinel), that alert is evaluated for its uniqueness and relevance. If the alert is distinct and not linked to existing incidents, it is the first alert for a new case the organization will investigate. On the other hand, if the alert has contextual similarities to other alerts that must be considered (common entities, overlapping time windows, evidence of shared attack vector), the alert will be measured against other alerts and will be grouped into an existing incident. The correlation logic is intended to diminish alert fatigue and expand the analyst's capacity to focus on valuable security stories.

When an organization's Microsoft Sentinel is connected to Defender, the correlation process considers alerts from Sentinel. Each Sentinel workspace is considered an independent source. Organizations can identify one Sentinel workspace as primary, allowing its alerts to be correlated with alerts from Defender's other services. Alerts from secondary Sentinel workspaces remain independent, and any incidents formed will be based on the distributed alerts from Sentinel itself. This architectural boundary offers an element of constrained correlation across diverse logging environments, especially in scenarios where multiple Sentinel workspaces are being used for segmentation or regional compliance. While the system uses automation to correlate alerts into incidents, analysts may at times find situations where this automation does not align with the operational needs. In such situations, analysts may manually reassign alerts. Alerts must be associated with an incident, so they may either be moved to an existing incident or assigned to a newly created incident. This manual action allows for some level of precision and refinement of the incident groupings—especially in complex investigations.

Incident correlation doesn't just happen at the initial group of alerts stage. Defender continues to stay aware of the state of alerts and incidents as they evolve over time. As an investigation unfolds, Defender may observe a greater level of relationships across incidents that were originally deemed as separate. When noticeable enough similarities are found—whether it be by common entities, shared kill chain, or overlapping artifacts—Defender will merge the shared incidents into one single case.

The merge process follows a set of internal criteria. Incidents are capable of merging if there are users, devices, or mailboxes involved in the incidents; if the incidents reference specific files or processes; if the incidents are consistent with instances of multistage attacks. For example, a phishing email incident could later be correlated to a lateral movement alert involving the same user account, resulting in them uniting into one case that accurately observes the entire attack chain. When incidents are merged, the contents of one incident (referred to as the source incident) are copied into another incident (referred to as the target incident), where the source incident is automatically closed and enabled as part of the target's investigative record. All alerts, entities, and tags from the source incident are moved into the target incident to maintain the total context of the investigation. Notably, comments and activity logs from the source incident do not get included in the target incident, but they are still accessible via the original incident records for audit and reference purposes.

As for the direction of the merge, which incident becomes the target incident, the platform determines which incident survives the process and remains active based on its logic for retaining the most complete and informative view. This process is automated, and analysts are unable to dictate which incident remains active as a result of the merge.

In some cases, incidents will not be merged automatically. If either incident is already closed, if the incidents are assigned to different individuals, or if they have different classifications or determinations (such as one being a false positive and the other being a true positive), the merge will be prevented. Unfavorable technical limits, such as surpassing the maximum number of supported entities or the use of device group segregation policies, would also prevent a merge from occurring.

In cases like these, you will be provided a manual merge capability. In these instances, the analyst could simply reconcile the conflicting conditions (e.g., unassigning one of the incidents) and then elect to do a manual merge. You can manually merge up to 5 (five) incidents at a time using the same rules that apply to automatic merges. A manual merge should ideally be used instead of simply moving alerts between incidents because it supports a more complete record of the investigative process, timeline, and related metadata.

The current model for incidents and merges in Microsoft Defender and Sentinel are cutting-edge approaches to incident management. By correlating related alerts and tracking automated and manual refinement, both models help security teams to clarify their incident investigations and decrease noise to solve threats more effectively throughout the organization's entirety.

Planning an Incident Response Workflow in Microsoft Defender

For any successful cybersecurity operation, the capability to rapidly and accurately react to cybersecurity incidents is paramount. Within the Microsoft Defender portal, incidents are groups of alerts that, when combined, tell the complete story of the incident. These incidents serve as the entry point for investigation and response, enabling analysts to track the progression of the attack, understand the scope, and take actions to limit and remediate any threat.

To help create a more organized and efficient way to respond to incidents, it is essential to develop a structured incident workflow chart. This delineates the process for analysts to follow as they work through the incident lifecycle, including triage, investigation, containment, eradication, recovery, and post-incident review. The Microsoft Defender portal contains tools and visualizations to support this model and a structured incident response workflow, allowing security teams to respond according to their level of experience and the maturity of the organization.

An efficient workflow begins with selecting the high-priority items from the incident queue. The first step in that process is triage, where analysts will filter the alerts by severity, time, and type of asset to assess which incidents need immediate reaction.

CHAPTER 4   THREAT DETECTION, INVESTIGATION, AND RESPONSE

Once an analyst identifies an incident, it should be handled appropriately, which includes assigning the incident to the analyst, altering the incident title if appropriate to describe the event better, and attaching any relevant tags or comments that will help organize and document the incident. In support of this initial triage process, analysts and incident response teams can set up automation rules that will automatically handle selected incident types. Automation rules are helpful for simple incidents that do not require a great deal of analysis, which frees up the analyst's time to focus on a larger, more complex, or high-risk incident/threat. When responding to an incident, the first step is to investigate the entire scope of the attack. Analysts should review the attack story (a contextual visualization that describes the overview of the attack, the severity, the source of detection, and the assets affected). Analysts can then review the alert details to drill down to understand the timeline, source, and behavior associated with the attack. Entities of importance, like impacted users, devices, or mailboxes, can be selected directly from the portal to see any related activity, alerts, and any associated metadata. The portal also differentiates alerts that were automatically remediated by an investigation from Defender.

Once the threat is understood, steps to contain it should be initiated to minimize its impact. This can include deactivating compromised user accounts, isolating affected devices, and/or blocking known indicators of compromise (e.g., known malicious IP addresses). After containing the threat, the organization should begin restoring its environment to its normal state. Systems should be recovered, and accounts can be reactivated after validating their integrity. Additionally, it must be verified that the threat has been eliminated.

Resolving the threat does not represent the end of the process. There remains a post-incident analysis process, which is the most crucial stage because it is where the most learning can take place. The team should aim to determine the nature of the attack, how it occurred, and its impacts. The organization can compare the attack against known threat patterns or current trends in attacks. There is also an opportunity to review the resolution workflow that was employed during the incident response and revise it as necessary to account for any learning. Playbooks, policies, and security programs may need to be updated to prevent recurrence or improve response capabilities in the future.

There may be different entry points into the workflow depending on the analyst's experience level. New analysts are provided with guided walkthroughs to cover the basic skills of incident analysis, remediation, and documentation. They are asked to focus on incident triage and proper classification and management practices, including renaming and assigning incidents, tagging, and adding comments. As they gain more experience, they will have opportunities to engage in advanced analysis or detection of threats, combat them, or carry out proactive hunting activities. More experienced analysts may also take advantage of identifying emerging threats and developing detections based on attack vectors related to current trends in threats.

The workflow will further evolve depending on roles within the team. For example, Tier 1 incident responders will focus primarily on triage and case management, which will prepare the Tier 2 analyst for the next step, which is more thorough analysis of evidence collection, alert correlation, and damage remediation, generally referred to as forensic analysis. The Tier 3 analyst, commonly known as a threat hunter/advanced analyst, would work on detecting threats proactively, identifying patterns of behavior, and performing deep correlations with threats. Tier 3s will also assist in developing and revising response playbooks, as well as conducting root cause analyses of threats. The security operations center manager also has a role in incorporating the use of Microsoft Defender into an operational architecture, which has to be integrated with the team's other workflows and operational/security objectives.

By providing a structured and role-based incident response workflow process, security teams should be able to utilize the Microsoft Defender portal in its entirety and present the ability to respond to incidents effectively, no matter the nature of the security incident. Structuring the incident response process provides opportunities for improving consistency, accelerating resolution time, improving the coordination of actions across roles, and ultimately enhancing the overall security posture of the organization.

Investigating Security Incidents Involving IoT Devices Using Microsoft Sentinel

It is challenging to investigate security incidents involving Internet of Things (IoT) devices due to their inherent nature. IoT devices are often very diverse, on a massive scale, and have limited visibility as they have differing levels compared to a traditional network device we are used to. Microsoft Sentinel is built to solve the challenges organizations face by allowing organizations complete visibility and one view of any incidents with IoT devices using centralized incident management, a different analytics engine (KQL), and automation. A workflow that organizations can follow will give a security operations team a starting point to address/respond to incidents, especially when events involve IoT assets.

CHAPTER 4   THREAT DETECTION, INVESTIGATION, AND RESPONSE

To begin the investigation of an incident dealing with IoT, telemetry from the impacted IoT devices needs to be ingested into Microsoft Sentinel. Typically, IoT telemetry is ingested into Sentinel via Azure IoT Hub, Azure Defender for IoT, or any custom connectors built by a company. Once telemetry is ingested into Sentinel, it normalizes the data and correlates/analyzes it to convert device behavior into security events. Alerts will be created by analytic rules looking for anomalies, known indicators of compromise, or suspicious behaviors in the IoT telemetry, such as devices communicating outside their normal behavior, lateral movement, or command injection behavior.

When an analytic rule generates an alert, Sentinel creates the incident automatically. The incident details tab is the first place an analyst will go to get familiar with the scope and nature of the security event they will be working on. When an alert is generated, it will be linked to an incident in Sentinel. When the analyst explores the incident, they will see the "Incident Overview" tab first. The "Incident Overview" tab summarizes alerts, affected entities, and timelines, providing a concise overview of what happened, when it happened, and which IoT devices were involved. An example of an alert may state that a sensor device had communications with external IPs, and that is indicative of unauthorized communication. As a response, an investigation must be conducted to determine if the sensor device was compromised or if it is being used as a pivot point for lateral movement. The next phase in the investigation will involve examining the alert details, including the detection logic that triggered the alert, the associated risk or severity level, and the MITRE ATT&CK tactics that have been mapped. Analysts may then move to the Entities tab, which will show devices, user accounts, or IP addresses that have some connection to the event or incident. Each entity can be reviewed further by looking at the recent activities and related alerts. Unique hostnames or device IDs usually represent IoT devices, and any anomalies related to the communications pattern, firmware, or behavior may be indicative of malicious activity.

If all of this is not enough, Microsoft Sentinel allows analysts to open the Log Analytics workspace directly from the incident view to run custom KQL (Kusto Query Language) queries to search for additional evidence. This is useful for IoT investigations in which threat actors might try to masquerade their activities amongst regular device traffic. For queries to identify indications of compromise, analysts may review failed authentication attempts, use of uncommon ports, or IP addresses identified as malicious. Analysts can search traffic logs to find beaconing patterns or to isolate protocol use that is not permitted.

Also useful when conducting visual investigations is Sentinel's Investigation Graph. Analysts can view alerts, entities, event sequences, and other relevant data in this visual framework. This is useful when investigating multi-stage attacks, attacks that span across multiple devices, or attacks that leverage IoT endpoints to allow lateral movement into a more extended environment. If assessed appropriately, it can indicate whether an incident is limited or if other resources are involved, recommending a rapid containment effort.

When an IoT device has been affected by a threat, an organization may need to disconnect the device or block relevant IP addresses, revoke device credentials, or deploy specific network rules to prevent further contact.

Certainly, Benoit (Sentinel) can create automated playbooks leveraging Logic Apps to make communications to operations teams, revise device settings, or open tickets in external systems.

As part of the resolution process, the analyst describes the cause of the incident, how it was identified, what evidence was collected, and how it was addressed within the incident case comments. For trend analysis, incidents can be categorized by tags (such as "IoT Malware" and "Unauthorized Access").

Finally, the importance of a post-incident review should be highlighted. Analysts should be able to determine if detection rules should be made more efficient, if additional telemetry sources could be onboarded to increase effectiveness, or if device configurations need to be reviewed or hardened. By viewing the incident in its entirety, teams will likely emerge with new lessons learned and thus improve on future response efforts to not only tighten response effectiveness but also adapt to IoT threats.

This workflow is why Microsoft Sentinel supports security teams in enabling them to investigate IoT-related incidents to an appropriate depth, speed, and accuracy to bring valuable visibility & control to one of the modern digital environment's most complex and vulnerable layers.

Automating Incident Response in IoMT Ecosystems with Microsoft Sentinel

The Internet of Medical Things (IoMT) has transformed modern healthcare by interconnecting medical devices, patient monitoring systems, and hospital infrastructure. While this enhances patient care and operational efficiency, it also significantly expands the attack surface. Protecting these critical medical systems requires not only real-time detection but also swift, automated responses to security incidents. Microsoft Sentinel enables such a capability by combining intelligent threat detection, built-in orchestration tools, and integration with medical IT systems.

The Role of IoMT in Modern Healthcare Security

The Internet of Medical Things (IoMT) has revolutionized healthcare by linking various medical devices, monitoring systems, and hospital IT resources. This interconnection leads to improved clinical outcomes, streamlined workflows, and real-time patient monitoring. This comes with an expanded attack surface, which means that protection for IoMT systems cannot be passive; they require real-time threat detection, as well as proactive, automated, context-relevant responses that ensure patient safety while remaining compliant with regulations.

Microsoft Sentinel provides a cohesive platform to help address this challenge. Microsoft Sentinel integrates intelligent threat detection with built-in orchestration tools and streamlined integration with clinical IT systems, enabling healthcare to monitor, detect, and respond to cyber threats intelligently and automatically.

Know the Specific Threats in IoMT Environments

IoMT devices have unique security challenges. Many of the devices rely on outdated operating systems, lack native encryption, and cannot be patched easily because they are used as clinical resources. This functionality creates a target for cyberattacks that ideally lead to unauthorized access and exfiltration of Protected Health Information (PHI) and mitigates medical procedures.

Unlike traditional IT assets, most IoMT devices are not endpoint protection agents and do not record comprehensive log files in standard formats. When there is no "endpoint" to deflect attacks, Microsoft introduced Microsoft Sentinel, which enables cybersecurity monitoring and detection through an impressive number of other telemetry sources, including firewall sources, DNS logs, NetFlow, and feeds from medical device inventories. Enhanced visibility into North America-wide suspicious behavior can be achieved through integration with platforms such as Microsoft Defender for IoT, which will improve visibility of devices performing suspicious activities, such as anomalous outbound connections, unauthorized malicious lateral movement, or simply erroneous device behavior on clinical VLANs.

Building an Automated Incident Response Process for the IoMT

An effective automated incident response process for the IoMT needs a deliberate, process-based approach. You will need a structured plan that follows a multi-phased approach. For example, the first phase involves onboarding the relevant telemetry and normalizing it to a proper state to work from.

Phase 1: Normalize Your IoMT Telemetry Using ASIM

Before you can embark on an effective detection or response process, you'll need to ingest and normalize the IoMT data using Microsoft Sentinel's Advanced Security Information Model (ASIM). Normalization enables consistent data consumption and reaction using detection rules and incident response playbooks. The data sources you'll be using include logs extracted from Defender for IoT, VLAN segmentation appliances, messaging from HL7/DICOM systems, images preserved on PACS (Picture Archiving and Communication System) servers, and so forth. All of these data sources have to be meaningfully mapped to ASIM parsers as well to feature interoperability throughout the detection pipeline.

Phase 2: Analytics Rules to Detect IoMT Threats

Next, you will want to customize the Sentinel analytics rules to fit the IoMT ecosystem best. Several examples of detection that would be pertinent to IoMT threats:

- Suspicious beaconing activity from devices (e.g., infusion pumps) pulling in unknown external IPs.

- Protocol violations (non-HL7 traffic) within clinical subnets.

- Unauthorized credential access attempts targeted at PACS or other radiology images.

- Use of USB devices on either medical imaging or other diagnostic systems.

These alerts need to generate high-fidelity incidents that will be enriched with device context, user identities, and network metadata (etc.) to support ongoing investigation and triage.

Phase 3: Automation Rules to Trigger Playbooks

Automation rules can act as filters to determine the decision point for triggering incident automation, thereby influencing incident response bias. Sentinel allows rules to be constructed based on severity, MITRE ATT&CK tags, incident entities, and source analytics rules. For instance, high-severity IoMT-tagged incidents can cause network isolation playbooks to invoke automatically. Or, if you detect lateral movement inside IoMT VLANs around the same time, this may require an escalation and response. With rules, you provide rule-based opportunities to ease triage and analyst workload, and departments can take action (e.g., containment) immediately without analysts having to perform any of these actions manually.

Phase 4: Create Logic App Playbooks for Response

Sentinel automation relies on Azure Logic Apps to orchestrate the response workflows created by playbooks. Playbooks can be configured to

- Quarantine IoMT devices via integrations with Network Access Control (NAC) or Software-Defined Networking (SDN) systems.
- Notify clinical engineering and cybersecurity in Microsoft Teams, SMS, or secure email.
- Create incident tickets in the hospital's ITSM system, such as ServiceNow.
- Run a custom PowerShell script to update firewall rules or access control lists (ACLs).

An example of a playbook, when detecting some suspicious DICOM transfers from an imaging device, may include the following actions:

- Extract the IoMT device IP and hostname.
- Query Defender for IoT (to get device classification).
- Notify the biomedical department for validation.
- Start NAC-based isolation.
- Append the Sentinel incident with specific device vulnerability and whether it had a history.
- Adding Visibility with Microsoft Defender for IoT.

Microsoft Defender for IoT is a vital integration point in this architecture. It delivers passive monitoring of more innovative medical devices with insights into vulnerabilities, behavioral profiles, risks, and the context of alerts. By attaching Defender for IoT to Sentinel, you can:

Extract device metadata, such as the device's OS version, vendor, and role.

Correlate alerts across labels and devices (e.g., an alert from an imaging system and the pieces of the clinical care unit on the same subnet).

- Identify potential origins or lateral spread of infections in real time.
- Automation playbooks can derive actionable knowledge from this data to determine whether to quarantine a medical device, notify, or escalate an incident.
- Adding Conditional Logic for Clinical Safety

Not all devices can be treated equally in an automation response plan. Some medical devices, such as ventilators or infusion pumps, are considered life-support devices and cannot be disconnected or otherwise taken offline without compromising patient care. As such, Sentinel playbooks must be designed to feature conditional logic that

- Will not automatically isolate Class I life-support devices.
- Will escalate incidents involving Class II and III devices to biomedical engineers or others for review.
- Will document all actions taken for audit and regulatory purposes.

Finding the right balance between automation and clinical considerations is a critical element to maintaining operational safety.

Continuous Monitoring and Optimization

All automation workflows should be reviewed and optimized by Sentinel Workbooks, and their audit logs should be reviewed as well. This data should include

- Playbook status: executed (success/fail)
- Time-to-respond
- Analyst overrides or escalations
- Change history and control validation

Security teams should routinely assess the feedback from SOC analysts and clinical operations, through their findings, to continuously fine-tune their automation logic to maximize precision, as well as help to ensure false positives are limited and new threat vectors have been acknowledged.

Example: Ransomware Attack Targeting Imaging Devices

Let's play through an example of the situation where Sentinel detects ransomware behaviors from an X-ray machine. During detection, the platform observes anomalous SMB traffic from the X-ray machine to a radiology file server. Now, an example of a fully autonomous workflow looks like this: a detection rule results in a serious incident; the automation rule initiates (triggers) a playbook for Defender for IoT; the device category is used as a Class II imaging asset; NAC disconnects the device from the network; the radiology team and biomed are alerted; a forensics copy of the traffic is saved; the incident is sent to the Tier-2 SOC Analyst for investigation and deeper analysis; and in under a few minutes, all of this is done to contain an incident while not compromising patient privacy nor disrupting care.

Streamlining Automation via Sentinel Capabilities

Microsoft Sentinel offers automation functionality in the automation rules and playbooks. Automation playbooks provide a deeper level of integration and more advanced workflow capabilities than automation rules. For more advanced, multi-step workflows, there is a deeper native integration to external systems via playbooks.

Automation rules will provide functions you can create that will trigger when incidents are made; after that, it reviews the agreed-upon conditions you defined (severity, title) and executes the agreed-upon actions, which can include adjusting the severity of an incident, assigning a specific team member or team, tagging the incident, and/or leveraging a playbook to initiate follow-up actions. Automation rules can be reused in many incident analytics rules and added in a specific order to define the execution and flow of actions.

Further Considerations with Playbooks and Automation Rules

Playbooks, created in Azure Logic Apps, enable additional actions, such as responding to an attack via threat containment, ticketing, or communication. Playbooks also support conditional branches, API calls to other services/apps, and Microsoft and other services. Automation rules/conditions can call a playbook when incidents meet their conditions.

- You can manage your automation rules in a few different ways in the Sentinel interface:
- *Automation Blade*: Single pane view of all automation across Sentinel
- *Analytics Rule Wizard*: Links automation rules with the specific detection rule you created
- *Incidents Blade*: Enables quick rule creation for common/repeat false positives.

All rules have a trigger (incident created), conditions (incident properties), and actions (status change, delayed triggered playbook execution). From there, you indicate if the rule has an expiration date (flagged for temporary) and execution order (using different rules for similar situations).

Strategic Use of Automation Tools and Playbooks

In practice, automation rules and automation playbooks will work most effectively together. The automation rule in this example assigned the incident and tagged it, while the incident was contained in a playbook triggered by the events previously highlighted via the automation rule—acknowledge or escalate for action. In a new milestone, Sentinel now supports both Logic App Standard and Consumption models, providing flexibility in managing execution and costs.

Shipping and deploying these capabilities will enable healthcare managers to respond promptly to IoMT threats while maintaining auditable outcomes, reduce the demand on analysts' workloads, and ensure a consistent (policy-driven) approach to managing and acquiring a hotel framework across their clinical environment.

Conclusion

The ability to automate incident response (IR) via Microsoft Sentinel is crucial to assisting hospitals or health systems to protect their IoMT ecosystems—via normalization of ASIM, leveraging Defender for IoT, and building playbooks concerning clinical safety and critical decision-making will assist a health organization to enhance their response time, curtail the expansion of the attack, and protect the patient experience. Improvements in layered and automated security will enhance the cybersecurity posture of clinical environments, aligning systems and universities with the realities of modern healthcare operations.

Disrupting Attacks Effectively

The Internet of Medical Things (IoMT) is an extension of the Internet of Things (IoT) that uses online computer networks to support direct and indirect workflows with capabilities that are almost anywhere. IoMT is the sum of the possibilities of medical devices and applications connected to healthcare IT systems. These devices vary considerably—everything from the incorporation of small wearables, part of the patient monitoring area of the device realm, to infusion pumps and imaging equipment. All these devices are crucial in patient care workflows. Still, by their very nature, each increases and modifies the threat models for cyberattacks that could compromise patient safety, confidentiality of patient information, and provision of care.

Internet of Medical Things (IoMT) devices typically reside in specific environments, such as medically supervised settings that do not permit frequent software updates or patches. These devices also rely on unique operating systems or have a long life cycle, considering the unique hospital regulatory environment around healthcare. Cyberattack disruption of IoMT systems is an increasingly important aspect of healthcare cyber resiliency.

Motivations of Attacks in IoMT

Motivations of common cyberattacks against IoMT look to

- Compromise patient data privacy and confidentiality by intercepting or exfiltrating sensitive medical data.

- Disrupt the functionality of the IoMT device and/or patient devices, which could harm the patient or interfere with the nature of clinical workflows by changing settings or injecting false data.

- Gain access to healthcare devices to establish a foothold inside their network for later lateral and privilege escalation.

- Utilize IoMT as part of a ransomware or denial-of-service attack that exacerbates existing service disruptions (e.g., ransomware crippling an entire hospital's operations).

Attacks on the above devices can be either non-wholesome interference (e.g., changing a setting) or outright killing the device by taking it offline entirely. Even the slightest interruption to critical care can provide false comfort to vulnerable patients, who require the healthcare system to implement reasonably practical cyber-resiliency defenses.

Attacks on the IoMT space must retain the capability to disrupt cyberattacks to be effectively mitigated. This requires a layered approach to thwarting the cyberattack while collaborating or coordinating with other healthcare organizations that prioritize information sharing. The provisions for developing effective disruption strategies involve the following principles:

- *Initial Detection and Timely Action*: The sooner suspicious behavior can be detected on an IoMT device, the better chance security teams have of taking mitigating action before other attacks can escalate.

- *Minimal to No Disruption of the Device's Function*: Disruption methods should maintain the operational requirements of the device since many IoMT devices are life-critical. For instance, even while isolating a device, the device must continue to function in its primary role as a patient monitor.

- *Segmentation and Network Protections*: Having a segmented network should limit the lateral movement of an attacker across IoMT devices and other systems. In general, micro-segmentation and zero-trust architectures can all help diminish risk.

- *Behavior Analytics*: Due to the profile-based nature of IoMT devices, most signature-based detection methods struggle to detect unknowns effectively. Behavior analytics help detect anomalies and provide alerts to possible attacks.

CHAPTER 4   THREAT DETECTION, INVESTIGATION, AND RESPONSE

- *Automated Action*: Once the attack is confirmed, the use of automation is critical to containing the attack. Automated actions might include surrounding devices, blocking malicious traffic, and turning off compromised credentials, among other measures.

- *Forensics and Investigation*: Disruption of an attack entails forensics data capture for investigation, root cause review, and compliance report.

Examples of Attack Disruption Techniques Found in IoMT

The following are examples of techniques used for disruptions and taking action on attacks to IoMT.

- *Device Isolation*: In addition to network segmentation, a baseline policy can be enforced to isolate any existing activity of possibly compromised IoMT devices, not only in a segmented manner but also in real-time, thereby isolating any moment-to-moment compromised activity.

- *Revoke Access*: Temporarily turning off compromised user or service account privileges enables the security team to halt any actions taken by the attacker in their compromised state.

- *Threat Intelligence Feed*: Utilizing a threat intelligence feed to block IPs and domain names associated with known attacker infrastructure can restrict IoMT devices from operating within normal parameters, mitigating the risk of data exfiltration vulnerabilities.

- *Auto Playbooks*: Organizations can make use of predefined response workflows, or auto-playbooks, to initiate a sequence of containment activities automatically. Improving response time and reducing human errors are vital benefits.

- *Traffic Filtering*: Organizations are contributing to the attack surface in IoMT with the addition of rippling malware directly from the Internet into IoMT before filtering the traffic. Organizations must inspect and filter network traffic to identify anomalies or known destructive patterns in the data, which will help block any command and control communications.

- *Firmware and Patch Management Alerts*: Organizations must be in a continual state of analysis and monitoring regarding patch and firmware status. Monitoring helps prevent attacks leveraging known vulnerabilities.

Challenges to Disruption of an IoMT Attack

- *Device Diversity and Legacy Systems*: Due to the heterogeneity of IoMT devices and the varied security aspects of each, the disruption attack tactics are difficult to exploit holistically.

- *Regulatory Issues*: There are legal or organizational healthcare regulations that can limit some types of automatic actions or require ICT teams to take manual action.

- *Lack of Visibility*: In some organizations, some devices have little to no logging or telemetry information at all, making it extremely difficult to detect or respond to an IoMT event.

- *Resource Constraints*: Many IoMT devices have low CPU and memory capabilities; therefore, if security controls are to be embedded, then it is imperative that such embedding occur with as much awareness as possible.

The Way Ahead: In-Use Disruption Attacks to IoMT Security Posture

For organizations to consider incorporating disruption actions into their IoMT ecosystem, they must also consider disruption attacks as a proxy for the patch management process typically implemented by a security program. It must invest equally in realizing and understanding assessments of its IoMT, the real-time detection behaviors, automating containment actions to devices, and analytics geared solely for monitoring and analyzing medical devices.

Collaboration among clinical, security, and ICT teams will help keep disruption actions on track, aligning with both patient safety and operational priorities.

MS Sentinel, Making Disruption Attacks Effective

Microsoft Sentinel is a cloud-native security information and event management (SIEM) and security orchestration, automated response (SOAR) solution. It provides an integrated platform to help organizations identify, investigate, and respond to threats in real time.

With Sentinel's scalable architecture and built-in intelligence, it is well suited to handle complex environments like healthcare, where IoMTs are connected devices that must be monitored for incoming alerts about security events and potential attacks, and where those attacks must be disrupted before they can cause harm.

Key Capabilities in Microsoft Sentinel to Disrupt Attacks

- *Comprehensive Data Collection*: Utilizing its integrated, scalable data lake, Sentinel ingests large volumes of data from endpoints, network devices, cloud resources, and IoMT devices. This enables correlation across different data sources to create an overall view of an organization's security posture.

- *Advanced Analytics and AI*: Sentinel's built-in analytics rules are powered by artificial intelligence and machine learning, making it capable of assessing threats related to suspicious behaviors, anomalies, and known attack patterns for all connected assets, including IoMT devices.

- *Automated Investigation*: Sentinel can automate triage and investigation of alerts with AI-driven playbooks to conduct incident analyses and surface actionable insights, reducing workload on security teams and speeding detection of attacks on IoMTs.

- *Automation and Orchestration*: Security teams can define playbooks (automated workflows) that contain actions like isolating devices, blocking IPs, resetting compromised credentials, or notifying stakeholders. When Sentinel detects relevant threats, playbooks are automatically triggered.

- *Threat Intelligence Integration*: Sentinel offers robust integration with threat intelligence feeds that provide real-time indicators of compromise (IOCs), allowing security teams to block or flag known malicious entities before intrusion can occur on their IoMTs.

- *Customizable Alerts and Incident Management*: Analysts can configure detection rules and automation workflows to their unique environment to ensure that IoMT devices receive tailored monitoring and disruption approaches.

How Sentinel Disrupts Attacks on IoMT

Microsoft Sentinel disrupts attacks on IoMT by monitoring abnormal device behavior through the use of machine learning and combining threat intelligence with network-based analytics. It can quickly take containment actions using playbooks to isolate compromised devices without impacting patient care. The actions taken in Sentinel are based on the full visibility we receive from Defender for IoT, allowing us to detect threats in their earliest stages, which minimizes impacts to clinical operations and patient safety resulting from a cyberattack.

- *Continuous Monitoring*: Sentinel is continuously monitoring IoMT logs and network telemetry for early warnings such as unexpected access patterns or device communication with suspect endpoints.

- *Automated Containment*: If a threat is detected, the Sentinel playbooks can automatically isolate or stop affected devices from communication to eliminate lateral movement.

- *Incident Correlation*: Sentinel correlates alerts from multiple devices and systems simultaneously, allowing for a complete overview of the attack scenario and the capability to prioritize incidents based on severity.

- *Fast Notifications and Collaboration*: Sentinel immediately notifies security contacts with comprehensive incident details, which facilitates speedier ongoing collaboration and response activities.

- *Continuous Improvement*: Sentinel has built-in post-incident analysis functionality that drives rule tuning, learning, and threat hunting workflows for future threat detection and disruption.

Building Disruption Workflows in Sentinel

To effectively disrupt attacks, build multi-level playbooks that accomplish the following:

- *Detection and Validation of Threats*: Use analytics and AI to detect anomalous IoMT behaviors and to validate an alert through several channels, i.e., the sensing data plus evidence of an anomaly from other sensors.

- *Production of Automated Containment of the Threat Event*: Types of actions can then be triggered based on the system alert severity and include instant quarantine or severing access of the device from the network.

- *Auto-enrich Investigation*: Automatically collect contextual information such as device profile, network health, network topology, and user profile information to support the human analyst.

- *Notify Responders*: Alert appropriate responders, including the incident response team, clinical engineering, and/or management as appropriate.

- *Remediation and Recovery*: Enlist with patch management or provisioning systems used to enable remediation work streams.

Protecting IoMT environments requires specific attention focused on attack disruptions, as IoMT has significant unique risks and operational limitations. Microsoft Sentinel is an essential partner in providing continuous network and log monitoring, rich analytical intelligence, and automated response orchestration designed to stop attacks very quickly and minimize operational impact.

With rich real-time detections of threats, AI assistance for investigations, and a set of pre-built playbooks, healthcare organizations will be able to protect their IoMT assets efficiently without sacrificing patient safety and IR compliance.

Using KQL for Analysts

Kusto Query Language (KQL) is a powerful, expressive query language designed to interact with extensive storage systems of data where your data is stored in the Azure Data Explorer service and is extensively used in Microsoft Sentinel. KQL was developed to efficiently extract, search, and manipulate data from extensive collections of logs and telemetry generated by your systems, applications, and networks.

KQL has many advantages over other languages, primarily in the context of time-series data and log analytics. KQL enables security analysts to craft queries that, within seconds, can search through millions and billions of records in extensive collections of logs and telemetry data, yielding valuable insights into activities, behaviors, and anomalies related to potential security incidents. With KQL, security analysts can use complex, rich syntax to develop dynamic data queries that perform filtering, aggregations, joins, pattern matching, statistical analyses, and even advanced machine learning algorithms that best suit their needs for security investigations and threat hunting.

The Importance of KQL Within Microsoft Sentinel

Microsoft Sentinel is a cloud-based Security Information and Event Management (SIEM) solution, as well as a Security Orchestration Automated Response (SOAR) solution, where it collects and stores massive amounts of security data from multiple sources: endpoint data from user systems, from network sensors, cloud applications, IoT devices, and the list goes on. The scale of the diversity of data sources and types indicates that automated alerts and simple dashboards, by themselves, are often not enough to investigate issues deeply or even to conduct proactive threat hunting.

This is why KQL is so vitally important; KQL enables security analysts to write queries tailored to their individual environment and security use cases. KQL provides the security analyst with the ability to slice and dice the raw data. For instance, if a suspicious alert comes in, this capability allows for detailed analysis. The analyst can write KQL queries to further enrich the alert's context, including network traffic, users, and activities occurring at the same time, as well as any other relevant information that would help determine if it is a real threat or a false positive.

Beyond investigating alerts, KQL enables ongoing optimization of detection by allowing analysts to create custom detection rules and notebooks. KQL can help support these activities as a hunting tool, identifying additional threats that automated tools, which rely on subtle patterns and longer timeframe behaviors, might miss. Also, KQL forms the basis for building automated investigations, adding more data to incidents, and creating reports—all of which are basic functions of a mature security operations center.

A Brief Understanding of the KQL Query Structure

The goal of the Kusto Query Language (KQL) is to enable users to explore, filter, and analyze data in a clean and structured manner. A KQL query is a request for read-only access; the result of the query fetches data and may transform it into results, but neither the KQL nor the execution engine has modified the underlying data. KQL is written in plain text and has been designed based on a data-flow model. This means KQL is intended to be readable in an intuitive manner, allowing users to compose KQL requests with minimal effort. They can also automate it with relative ease.

Using traditional query languages usually requires rigid nesting syntax, while KQL uses the operations that describe the data movements over the processing sequence. Regular KQL queries start with a data source (a log table or dataset) and from there, move the data through operations to filter, order, transform, and summarize to generate results. Every operation in KQL builds on the last one, distilling the dataset to achieve the intended outcome. To visualize, data moves through a funnel. The large aperture at the top consists of the complete raw dataset, as each query requires the data to move through more and more specific operations that are reapportioning it. The operations that are used are called operators. The operators operate one after the other. Each operator works off the previous operator's output, either eliminating irrelevant data or shaping the remaining data into a more useful data structure.

For instance, the original dataset may contain millions of log records. The first operation could filter these records by time range or event type, thereby reducing the number of records. In this first operation, you have filtered all data that is irrelevant to the investigation. The reduced data is now presented to the next operator in the query. Here, you may extract fields, summarize activity, join other data sources, etc. This process will continue through the operators until the last operation is completed, resulting in more relevant and significantly smaller data, now displayed in a tabular output.

The stepwise refinement enables KQL to quickly process potentially massive datasets, which can be many terabytes in size and have varying structures and sizes. This allows for the most selective filters to be applied early on in the query, reducing the strain on the latter operators and ultimately enhancing performance and clarity. Indeed, the shape of a KQL query is primarily influenced by its data processing cycle—reporting from extensive data, and through a progression of logical operations, you dig down to narrow insight. This provides KQL with not only a strong querying language but also an intuitive and helpful way to triage extensive data collections, like security logs and telemetry in Microsoft Sentinel.

CHAPTER 4 THREAT DETECTION, INVESTIGATION, AND RESPONSE

Best Practices for Writing KQL Queries in Sentinel

It is a skill every security analyst using Microsoft Sentinel should strive to cultivate: writing efficient, readable, and usable KQL queries. KQL can be an overwhelmingly powerful partner in your analysis; however, poorly constructed queries can also significantly reduce analysis performance with slow performance, excessive resource usage, or blind spots in your insight. Optimize your queries as much as possible by following best practices.

The first is to filter your data where possible as early as you can in your queries. The successful and efficient nature of subsequent operations improves as KQL is operating against the least amount of data, likely to achieve the analytics goal. For example, when you can filter by date/time range, specific devices, or specific event types at the beginning of your query, it dramatically reduces the extent of what KQL has to iterate over for the rest of your query.

The second is to project only everything you need, and do this purposely. Retrieving additional marker columns increases the amount of data that KQL iteratively retrieves, and consequently, the duration of the entire query execution time. KQL makes it easy to avoid projecting if you plan to execute it as is; however, projecting only the relevant fields streamlines your queries and clarifies what the results are supposed to represent.

Finally, to create meaningful metrics, use summarization and aggregation functions to summarize large-scale data. Instead of analyzing all events independently, it is usually more efficient to aggregate events based on essential characteristics such as user, IP address, or event type, as this allows you to identify patterns or anomalies in a much more efficient fashion.

Fourth, leverage KQL's built-in operators for dataset joining, such as inner join, left outer join, or union. These operators are crucial for correlating specific information across data streams. Still, they should be used with caution, as they can generate massive intermediate datasets or lose information relevant to the query.

Fifth, it's best practice to modularize and write queries for readability. As a rule of thumb, combining queries using the 'let' statement to separate complex queries into more digestible pieces is a good habit to adopt. It will make your queries easier to maintain and debug in their entirety and will provide a better experience for analysts managing and touching your queries in the future.

Sixth, keep query performance and cost in mind. Microsoft Sentinel charges based on the amount of data ingested and the resources consumed during query execution.

Therefore, the better your queries are, the better your cost will be, and the better your team's experience and responsiveness when investigating security incidents will be.

Seventh, make sure to test your queries using sample data, and double-check the output to ensure that it outputs as designed. Testing your queries gives you a chance to find logical errors early and will help you to improve the accuracy of your queries.

Eighth, use comments to describe the logic, purpose, and assumptions driving your query. Well-commented code is easier to share, review, and update as a team.

Ninth, use wildcard searches or pattern searching sparingly (or better yet, only when strictly required), as these can be very expensive and slow, particularly on massive datasets.

Lastly, keep learning, and utilize the vast supply of KQL documentation and examples supplied by the community. As KQL continues to evolve, new functions and features will be added to enhance functionality and usability in security analytics.

Kusto Query Language is a fundamental skill for any aspiring security analyst working in Microsoft Sentinel. With KQL, analysts can navigate complex information, see aspects that typically go unnoticed, and customize the data available for detections beyond the standard alerts. Any analyst needs to follow best practices while writing KQL queries so they can guarantee that they are performing not only effective investigations but efficient and sustainable investigations as well. In a nutshell, KQL enables an analyst to transform raw log data into usable intelligence that enhances an organization's security well-being.

Using KQL in Incident Management with Microsoft Sentinel

Incident management in Microsoft Sentinel is a critical aspect that allows security teams to comfortably detect, investigate, and respond to threats. If you are a security analyst or incident responder in Sentinel, one of your most powerful tools is the Kusto Query Language (KQL). This chapter explains the KQL aspect of incident management within workflows and efficiently applies KQL to security operations.

When an incident is formed, analysts will use KQL queries to

- Probe and investigate intentional and suspicious activity more deeply.

- Correlate data from many sources to better understand the scope and impact.

- Create custom detections and build analytics rules to detect similar threats in the future.

- Automate responses and provide evidence for reports for compliance.

Developing a comprehensive understanding of how to write and implement KQL can reduce the time required for an incident investigation and ultimately maximize confidence around the response.

How KQL Is Used in Incident Investigation

While Microsoft Sentinel raises an incident, Sentinel's incident can group multiple correlated alerts and logs that exhibit some form of suspicious behavior. To effectively investigate this incident, analysts must familiarize themselves with the raw data and develop appropriate queries for inquiry.

Here is how KQL can assist:

1. *Exploring Logs*: Analysts will write and run KQL queries against log data tables to identify specific evidence that is relevant to the incident, whether that be login attempts, file changes/modifications, network connections, processes being executed, etc.

2. *Filter and Correlate*. KQL allows an analyst to filter on a significant amount of data. That is, an analyst can filter a large dataset for specific criteria of their choosing, such as IP address, usernames, time frame, event type, etc. It is often valuable to combine data from different sources, as an attacker may utilize various tools/abilities, so understanding the entirety of the attack chain may be important.

3. *Timeline*: Both sorting and summarizing the events taking place put details chronologically so that we can effectively timestamp an understanding of how an attack unfolded over time or in sequential order.

4. *Customizations*: KQL allows for tailored queries to detect unusual or unexpected behaviors that the built-in detections/rules may miss, allowing for an expanded ability to cover detection measures.

CHAPTER 4   THREAT DETECTION, INVESTIGATION, AND RESPONSE

Steps to Use KQL in Incident Management

Step 1: Access the Logs in Microsoft Sentinel

- You can access the Azure portal to open your Microsoft Sentinel workspace.
- You can then select Logs to open the query editor.
- Then, depending on your data sources, you can select the different data tables, such as SecurityEvent, Syslog, AzureActivity, etc.

Step 2: Start with Incident Context

- You can use information from the incident details page, such as time range, affected user, and/or affected IP address.
- Filter on these known attributes to help quickly narrow down to relevant data when you start your KQL query.

    For example:

```kql
CopyEdit
SecurityEvent
| where TimeGenerated between(datetime(2025-07-01) .. datetime(2025-07-02))
| where Account == "compromisedUser"
```

Step 3: Refine and Correlate Data

- Combine data from multiple tables using KQL operators like join, union, and summarize.

    For example, to correlate login failures with network connections, you might write:

```kql
CopyEdit
let FailedLogins = SecurityEvent
    | where EventID == 4625
    | where TimeGenerated > ago(1d);
```

```
let NetworkConnections = CommonSecurityLog
    | where TimeGenerated > ago(1d);
FailedLogins
| join kind=inner (NetworkConnections) on $left.Account == $right.UserName
| summarize count() by Account, DestinationIP
```

Step 4: Visualize and Interpret Results

- Use project to select relevant columns and render to display charts or timelines.
- Example timeline visualization:

```kql
CopyEdit
SecurityEvent
| where Account == "compromisedUser"
| order by TimeGenerated asc
| project TimeGenerated, EventID, Computer
| render timechart
```

Step 5: Save Queries and Generate Analytics Rules

- You can save investigation queries to use again when needed.
- When queries generate investigation results of suspicious behavior with no further queries identifying the behavior, you can provide an analytic rule for a sensor to alert you automatically.

Step 6: Automate Response Actions

- You could combine KQL queries with Sentinel playbooks (built on top of Azure Logic Apps) to automate initiating responses such as isolating devices, alerting your team's attention, blocking IPs, etc.

Some Tips for Writing Good KQL Queries in Incident Management

- Always filter early on, such as narrowing time ranges, to help performance.

- Using let statements, making the queries modular, will help you with these more complex or pending queries.

- Comment on the query to help make logic more straightforward.

- Test the queries with sample data to confirm the correct result.

- Use anything built into Sentinel, such as tables or watchlists, to help provide more context to your investigation.

KQL is an essential skill for security analysts leveraging Microsoft Sentinel. It empowers teams to investigate an incident deeply, correlate separate data flows, and develop pre-emptive defenses where possible. By mastering KQL in incident management, businesses can decrease their risk by accelerating detection capabilities and enhancing response capabilities to improve their overall security posture.

Hunting for Threats

With the Internet of Medical Things (IoMT) significantly improving the way patients are cared for via real-time monitoring, diagnostics, and automation, there is a developing ecosystem of connected medical devices, including infusion pumps, pacemakers, MRI machines, and remote patient monitors. This means the interconnectedness of these devices and networks also creates a large attack surface, full of vulnerabilities. Detection mechanisms are insufficient on their own, as security analysts must now more than ever search for attackers to proactively reduce the chance of a compromise before it turns malignant. Threat hunting in the IoMT context cannot be optional; it holds clinical and operational demands beyond conventional threat hunting.

Why Hunt for Threats in the IoMT Environment?

The IoMT environment poses a distinct challenge because of the convergence of IT (Information Technology), OT (Operational Technology), and clinical technologies. This triad of convergence creates an unusual number of dependencies and flows of sensitive data. An adversary acting in this space poses a significant risk, not only of a data breach by an associate or vendor, but also of a direct threat to patients from compromised medical devices, further compromised clinical resources, and critical care outages. In addition to lacking appropriate security controls and logging capabilities, many medical devices are unconventional endpoints that can be ideal targets for adversaries seeking to minimize detection. Tracking and monitoring device alerts alone might not be sufficient; analysts will need to find anomalies using threat hunting procedures extending beyond alerts.

The Problems Associated with Reactive Security

SIEM (Security Information and Event Management) tools and EDR (Endpoint Detection and Response) platforms risk being valuable but inherently reactive, as detecting threats requires an indication of compromise (IOC), a signature, or a behavioral baseline. Bad actors targeting the healthcare sector are more advanced, often utilizing various advanced techniques, including living off the land, supply chain compromises, or zero-day exploits in proprietary device firmware. Without the threat hunting aspect, this process can happen without detection for long periods. Threat hunting can reveal these minor signs that most alert-based systems will not detect.

Adversaries Are After IoMT

Attackers are focusing on IoMT environments more actively because they can perceive these environments as weak and often have data or processes that can be extremely valuable to them. Threat groups like FIN11, UNC1878, and affiliates of Conti have laterally penetrated hospitals using ransomware as their delivery mechanism. As a way to move laterally across the network to establish their target, adversaries often will leverage IoMT devices as part of their payload, targeting these networks. Threat hunting provides a framework for analysts to recognize lateral movement and detect TikTok device function in isolation, thereby understanding the magnitude of a compromise. In some cases, threat actors may remain persistent until they find unmonitored devices, as these are the optimal launching point for both reconnaissance and data exfiltration.

Why Threat Hunting Matters for the Analyst

For analysts, threat hunting involves dedicating time and resources to actively hunt for previously undetected malicious activity. In IoMT ecosystems, downtime due to tampering can cost lives, so the stakes are higher. Prioritizing threat hunting is critically important to ensure that threat hunting is part of an organization's operational function and not an afterthought. Analysts can integrate threat hunting into their daily or weekly SOC workflow, thereby organically increasing their visibility and response capacity. In highly regulated areas, such as healthcare, proactive threat detection ensures compliance with existing requirements for vigilance, including HIPAA, as well as emerging governance standards, such as FDA guidance and other mechanisms that help organizations regulate the maturity of their cybersecurity programs.

Key Domains for Threat Hunting

A strategic set of focus statements is needed to guide ongoing threat-hunting efforts. Not all traffic or assets in IoMT environments are of equal importance or risk. When making your assessments, analysts should consider where they are most likely to find an active threat or where, if something were compromised, the compromise would be most impactful.

Areas of concern should be focused on

- *Network Behavior of Devices*: Any unusual connections made by devices to unknown IPs, or outside of the scope of intended communication, should be observed. Devices (e.g., CT scanners, infusion pumps) should only communicate through specific and predictable ports and IPs. Any change in this behavior should warrant a follow-up to determine if it is lateral movement or if the device is making command-and-control (C2) connections to outside networks.

- *Unpatched, End-of-Life Devices*: Many legacy devices that are still in use run critical OSs old enough to sweat. If you are not looking for these devices, they should be continuously scanned for exploitation attempts or suspicious behavior. Outdated OSs are easier targets for attackers than more "secure" or newer OSs. Systems running assumed obsolete OS have been the subject of numerous security incidents, and as they are still in use, it is likely for good reason.

- *Protocol Anomalies (i.e., HL7, DICOM, and MQTT)*: Since almost every medical device is connected to a network, the protocols they rely on are often prevalent, such as HL7 for health information exchange or DICOM for imaging. If you notice unusual payloads or malformed messages, check their bandwidth. If messages are not occurring on these protocols or are occurring at unusual bandwidth frequencies, they could be misuse or exfiltration.

- *Spoofing (Identity) Device Activity and Unauthorized Use*: Many threat actors would transition to masquerading as a trusted medical device or similar system to avoid network controls. In this type of forensic investigation, you should consider looking for duplicate MAC addresses or address conflicts on a VLAN that has a clinical purpose. When you conduct a hunt and see an asset that undergoes a context check, you may uncover unauthorized use.

- *Privileged Account Behavior and Account Access*: Frequently, technicians' accounts are prioritized by threat actors with privileged access. How an organization prioritizes threat analysis and hunting for privileged account behavior is critical, especially if obsolete assets are involved in maintenance, repair, or diagnostics. Analysts should consider whether a device was part of recent remote vendor access and compare its behavior to establish a baseline. You could see behaviors like logins from countries in which the organization doesn't have any employees or devices that are otherwise unexpected.

Using KQL to Hunt in Microsoft Sentinel: If you are working in Microsoft Sentinel and have everything else working (Defender for IoT, relevant healthcare accounts/connectors, etc.), you can query all the IoMT content you can. Analysts can write Kusto Query Language (KQL) queries on data received from IoMT-related telemetry, sitting on top of a powerful aggregation tool for analysis. HIQ queries would look for information such as

- New or rare external destinations from devices.
- Internal port scans originating from IoMT.
- Configuration changes are either sudden in inactive devices or occur over time after configuration.
- Suspicious remote desktop or command-line activity, targeting or originating from medical endpoints.

Role of Baseline Establishment

Before analysts can hunt effectively for threats, they must establish a behavioral baseline for each class of device. For every one of them, they will need to understand the normal traffic volume, regular communication partners, and typical usage patterns. For example, an innovative infusion pump may communicate with a medication database or a telemetry server. However, the threat hunter would look closely at anything that deviates from that norm, such as an infusion pump trying to connect to a workstation or an unknown IP. Part of the value of building out these types of profiles lies in their usefulness for anomaly-based hunting, where not just known threats, but even references to those known threats, present opportunities for the hunt.

How the Intelligence in Threat Intelligence Can Supercharge Threat Hunting

The ramp-up in experience when operating in threat hunting is more potent with something there to provide that additional boost. For instance, analysts can take tactical Indicators of Compromise (IOCs), such as malicious IPs and domains, and hunt with them through the environment. They can also take strategic threat actor profiles as leads to drive operational hunting. For example, suppose intelligence indicates there is an APT operationally targeting radiology infrastructure with a backdoor tool. In that case, the analyst can search for indicators of that tool or behavior as they relate to PACS systems and the diagnostic network.

Visibility of Devices Can Be Challenging; Potential Workarounds Are Available

IoMT threat hunting can be problematic because many devices lack telemetry, visibility, or logging capabilities. Unlike desks, laptops, or servers, IoMT assets may not have logs, or they may not support an agent to collect tags. In these cases, analysts will have some luck with passive network monitoring, traffic flow analysis, and behavioral intent. Other potential workarounds could be integration with Network Detection and Response (NDR) tools or deploying Defender for IoT sensors to offer valuable telemetry on otherwise opaque devices. Ranking Critical Device Types

Not all devices carry the same risk. Threat hunting procedures should be centered on prioritization:

- Devices tied to life-critical processes (e.g., ventilators and infusion pumps)
- Devices involved in patient imaging or diagnostics
- Gateways that connect clinical systems with enterprise networks
- Devices with access through remote support channels or public networks

By concentrating on these areas, security analysts can ensure they cover the highest-impact area first.

Collaborating with Clinical Teams on Hunting

Security analysts should collaborate closely with both clinical engineering and biomedical device teams. Any threat hunting initiative that may require the isolation or configuration for testing of devices requires thorough coordination with clinical teams to ensure patient care is not interrupted. Additionally, clinical teams can further assist by confirming whether any particular behavior is part of a recognized or validated workflow or if it may present an incident. Effective threat hunting in IoMT environments will require a complete cross-functional mindset.

Automating and Scaling Threat Hunts

Threat hunting is not only a creatively driven, manual process, but it can also easily be scaled. With Microsoft Sentinel, analysts can save their hunting query logs and convert those queries into scheduled analytics rules. Growing your hunting into detection puts your organization that much closer to a mature security program. Playbooks can also be used to automatically respond to threats and run workflows, including notifying a technician, isolating the device, or creating a ticket in the hospital's ITSM.

Creating a Threat Hunting Program in Healthcare

Finally, to be effective, attack hunting in IoMT must be built to support institutionalization as part of the cybersecurity program. This consists of

- Defining your hunting goals and targets
- Inventorying your IoMT assets
- Obtaining telemetry sources
- Briefing and training your analysts, considering the workflow and potential device profiles
- Developing and modifying your hunting playbook based on the lessons you learn

Having some structure to the process will help with consistency and provide a starting point to allow the hunting program to be flexible and adapt as the landscape of the threats continues to change.

Ongoing Education and Engaging in the Community

Given the rapid evolution of the threat landscape and available IoMT technologies, security analysts must adopt a broad mindset of continuous learning. Maintain active engagement in the healthcare ISAC community, engage in threat sharing as a group, and foster colleague relationships to reinforce security analysts' abilities. This will enable them to develop more diligent and thorough hunt scenarios based on collective feedback from a community that understands resilience.

Hunting for threats within the IoMT space is not just a practice of security; it is providing for the protection of the patient experience, clinical care, and brand trust within the organization. The IoMT space has become at least mutually exclusive from other traditional cyberspace domains for threat assessment, requiring additional context, diligence, and proactive defenses by security analysts. However, when the focus is on the appropriate domains, proper tools, and effective collaboration across the organization, hunting threats will represent an efficient way to address secure environments in modern healthcare.

Embracing a Proactive Security Philosophy

Threat hunting represents a proactive security paradigm. Threat hunting enables security analysts to act proactively, rather than waiting for alerts from automated detection. It allows security analysts to identify unknown activity, potential exploitation, indications of compromise, or behaviors that may indicate threat involvement, which might otherwise go undetected or take days/weeks to detect. Proactively detecting threats is crucial in the current state of security operations, as threat actors have become more effective in employing stealthy and adaptive techniques to undermine security principles.

Microsoft Sentinel is a great toolkit for this approach and exploration. Sentinel offers advanced capabilities for searching and examining, along with extensive telemetry and a workspace that encourages purposeful exploration. Conducting threat hunting on a relevant platform like Microsoft Sentinel increases the likelihood of identifying threats that may have been concealed in logs or expediting the resolution timeline of undetected attack or threat actor activities.

Why Alert-Only Security Doesn't Cut It

Automated alerts play a significant role in modern cybersecurity, but concerns about their inherent reactivity raise questions. Alerts work by matching known signatures already detected in the environments, detecting anomalies on the defined baselines, or raising flags when predetermined conditions are triggered. Since alerting is not automatic, responses happen after an analyst has assessed the alert. Regardless, an automated alert is still valuable, but it does have its limits.

Sophisticated attackers may be using an attacker credential, utilizing live off the land techniques, or exploiting a zero-day vulnerability. In those cases, alerts may never trigger, or they could trigger too late. As such, threat hunting is essential for exposing these elusive intrusions; threat hunting allows analysts to go deeper, look for different questions to ask, and search outside of the events and indicators currently being productively observed.

The Foundation: Sentinel Hunting Queries

At the core of the hunting capabilities in Sentinel are hunting queries. These queries are written in the Kusto Query Language (KQL), and they serve as valuable investigative tools to analyze log data.

Hunting queries examine specific behaviors, like identifying suspicious sign-ins, rare process executions, or unexpected network connections. And there is a vast library of hunting queries in Sentinel to help guide analysts. The templates are not the end; they are just the beginning, serving as templates for more sophisticated investigatory hunt queries based on what the analyst will uncover.

A hunting query isn't intended to validate an incident; instead, it identifies leads—a breadcrumb of evidence that needs additional inquiry/validation. The hunting is an iterative cycle that includes analytical reasoning and domain expertise.

Building a Valuable Hypothesis

A successful hunt should begin with designing and articulating a hypothesis. A hypothesis is a statement or assumption about possible attacker behavior in a specific environment. For instance, an analyst might suspect that a compromised user account is being used to move laterally through several systems. From that idea, the analyst can formulate a hypothesis: "If lateral movement occurs, we may see multiple logins from a single account across multiple systems in a short period." It can then be determined that the hunting effort is focused on either proving or disproving the hypothesis. Sentinel provides the collaborative workspace and capabilities to investigate this idea using queries, logs, and visual exploration.

Refining the Results: Identifying the Noise

When using a hunting query, the initial queries often produce a high volume of results, requiring the analyst to refine them to focus on the information that matters.

Sentinel can filter the results in various ways. Use the built-in filtering tools in Sentinel to filter the results from the query by time range, user account, IP address, or other dimensions. This allows the analyst to easily filter out the known-good activity and hone in on those events that are warranting some attention.

One way to narrow down the results is by comparing them across time. If the analyst can compare someone's activity today to the activity of the last week, it can help them identify new or unusual patterns that may indicate a new threat.

Hunting for Threat Campaigns

For the most part, threat hunting is usually driven by an understanding of ongoing campaigns. A campaign is a pattern of activity that is indicative of a particular threat actor or malware family.

Threat analysts can use this intelligence to hunt for signs that those patterned activities are being utilized within their environment. While not every campaign triggers alerts, Sentinel offers the opportunity in the hunting productivity workspace to query the environment against desired threat intelligence indicators and behavioral patterns. This method allows for a shift in thinking from "what has already been identified" to "what could be taking place here now without us knowing."

Mitigating Detection Gaps with MITRE ATT&CK

Organizations have detection gaps—areas where threats can exist and evade detection because of the lack of coverage.

Microsoft Sentinel helps analysts identify detection gaps by utilizing the MITRE ATT&CK framework, which provides information on standard attacker techniques. Microsoft Sentinel enables analysts to see the tactics covered by existing rules and the uncovered tactics, along with hunting queries that can be used to identify coverage gaps.

This strategy helps security teams mature their defense patterns by leveraging adversary tactics' conflict employment techniques, rather than relying on preexisting alert collections.

Hunting in Microsoft Sentinel: Prebuilt or Custom Paths

Threat hunts in Microsoft Sentinel can be initiated in one of two ways: using predefined discovery queries or launching an empty hunt using your logic.

Using predefined hunting queries provides structure and comfort. It can be ideal in a new environment when teams are getting started. Predefined queries can generate insights at a much quicker pace than building a custom hunt. Conversely, a custom hunt allows seasoned analysts to make queries from scratch based on a specific concern, a new tactic, or an unfolding incident.

Both scenarios are equally supported in the Microsoft Sentinel hunting workspace. Analysts make edits to their queries, clone queries, and reconfigure queries as new information becomes available.

Managing the Hunt Workspace

Microsoft Sentinel has a dedicated place for managing hunts. Each hunt session can be identified with a name, description, related queries, and notes. This workspace documents the hunt—it helps analysts get their thoughts organized, track what they find, and report out to others on the team.

The workspace environment encourages collaboration. Any team member can add their insights or re-examine the prior hunt. This allows analysts to see what was previously uncovered and how a particular query was analyzed.

From Hunt to Detection: Creating Analytics Rules

When a hunting query shows a repeatable pattern of malfeasance, the findings of that query become a candidate for detection.

Sentinel has the functionality to have an analyst convert a hunting query into a scheduled analytics rule. This analytical rule will execute on an automated schedule and will create alerts if suspicious behavior returns.

This ability allows analysts to move from manual investigation to automated detection. Once the behavior is understood and verified, it becomes a de facto part of the organization's defense in depth.

Real-Time Monitoring via Live Hunting

While hunts typically use historical data, Sentinel offers a novel feature to use hunting in a live sense. Instead of executing a hunting query at different time stamps in the past, an inquiry can be executed without time stamps. This allows for the same query to collect matching events from this point forward and trigger a flag for each event as they arise in real time.

Live hunting helps track a threat that is ongoing, active, or focused on an investigator's research question. The investigator will receive a real-time alert whenever results are returned, allowing immediate triage based on the urgency of the analysis. Being provided with a steady stream of data helps keep the investigator nimble to make decisions in critical situations.

Bookmarking Findings

As an analyst conducts the hunt and finds interesting findings, they can bookmark those findings. The analyst will bookmark the discovery, including the context of the discovery, the query that was executed, and the results obtained, or any notes/tags made. Bookmarks can be described in many ways (user, host, IP, etc.) and attached to phases of an investigation or incident. Bookmarks allow the analyst to compile their evidence around a hypothesis and save it for future reference in an identifiably labeled and easily retrievable fashion.

In the right hands, bookmarks can provide a veritable treasure trove of knowledge with considerable utility for follow-on investigations and historical reviews.

Incident Beacon

Bookmarks are just more than a personal record of activity—they can be moved upstream into incidents in Sentinel.

Analysts may want to utilize a bookmark with sufficient evidence of malicious activity to initiate a new incident or link to an event that is being investigated. This flow ensures that the findings from the hunters are recursively attached to the PRC (post-incident response) lifecycle using a single methodology, thereby preserving momentum and greater precision in resolving incidents to a conclusion.

The synthesis between hunting and incident response forces all the proactive work to have an operational context.

Visualize Your Connections

Microsoft Sentinel also features a built-in Entity Graph that visually organizes and represents the relationships between all the objects in a hunt: users, devices, applications, IP addresses, etc.

Entity graphs enable analysts to map connections and pivot off similar entities, thereby building a broader scope of adversarial engagements. Rather than seeing results in isolation, analysts can understand actions about others across an environment.

Entity graphs make it dramatically easier to identify evidence of lateral movement, privilege escalation, or synchronized attacks on multiple identities or endpoints. Simultaneous Hunting across Actor and Sentinel

Defensive operations benefit from a standard view, and Sentinel integrates directly with the portal used by Microsoft Defender.

This all-in-one functionality uniquely enables analysts to conduct simultaneous hunts over a larger set of data (e.g., telemetry on endpoints, identities, email, workloads in the cloud, etc.). Not only do analysts not have to switch from one tool to another to follow a thread, but they can now search, explore, analyze, and respond in one place.

Better integration enables deeper context and faster time to investigation and improves overall security posture.

Hunting Across Multiple Workspaces and Tenants

For large enterprises, managed service providers, or environments with many separate spaces or tenants, Sentinel allows analysts to hunt across multiple workspaces.

Analysts can configure access to multiple workspaces and write queries to look across tenants. Analysts can conduct global theme identification and follow the themes into unified investigations across business units, regions, or customers. It is a beneficial feature in complicated, distributed environments that require centralized threat intelligence and team-based threat hunting efforts.

Controlling Access and Permissions

Not everyone on the team needs the same access. Sentinel implements role-based access control (RBAC) to control who can run queries, see results, create rules, and promote incidents.

Providing the appropriate access allows you to impose some governance and limit the chance of misconduct. It also enables you to facilitate hunting roles in the Security Operations Center, allowing dedicated resources to hunt freely while maintaining some global control and capacity for oversight.

- Getting the roles right is vital for your security and productivity levels.
- Building hunting as a discipline and culture
- Hunting is not a single event but a discipline and culture.

Organizations that are successful at hunting develop the discipline of regular, released exploration—the formation of hypotheses, scheduled hunts, identifying findings, and positively challenging their models and methodologies. They create shared knowledge, turn repeated hunts into playbooks or reference guides, and share the attribution of hunting wins with the entire crew.

Cultivating a discipline and culture around hunting leads to creativity riding along with vigilance, plus a willingness and ability to adapt in an ever-changing threat landscape.

Understanding and Quantifying Hunting Effectiveness

With any hunting program running, teams must determine whether their hunting efforts are making an impact by defining or creating metrics. Examples of the metrics can include:

- The number of hunts over a given period
- Total Bookmarks created and promoted
- Total detection rules written from hunts
- Total coverage added to MITRE techniques
- Total response actions taken from the hunting results of suspicious activity
- Regular review of these metrics helps sharpen the hunting program, rationalize costs, and report value for the organization to leadership.

Threat hunting in Microsoft Sentinel is embraced as a paradigm shift from entirely reactive to proactive security. It enhances analysts' ability to explore, rationalize, and identify the unknown, whether that involves developing hypotheses, running complex queries, or translating findings into actionable steps. Retraining for hunting consists of a blend of art and science.

CHAPTER 4   THREAT DETECTION, INVESTIGATION, AND RESPONSE

Hunting with KQL

When integrated into the routine of a SOC, KQL not only improves detection but also deepens the security excellence culture of an organization. In a time where adversaries are evolving, defenders must grow faster, and threat hunting leads the way.

As the cybersecurity landscape continues to evolve, being able to hunt proactively for threats across your digital estate is vital. There will always be automated alerts or detections for events that you deem problematic. Still, once you move beyond these alerts and detections, you realize that there is a sea of raw event data, which contains the nuanced evidence of sophisticated adversarial activity and maliciousness throughout your organization. To look through this data and find hidden threats is why a powerful and flexible query language is not only important, but also essential for the modern security analyst.

In this section, we will take a closer look at the active threat hunting of threat actors within the security framework, a specialized query language that is used to dig deeply into security-specific event data. The query language gives you a less structured methodology (although structured) for working with the many avenues of immense information collected across endpoints, identities, email, and applications. The capability to master this language will change how you look at security events from merely watching them to actively hunting the information to create specific questions for your data and we will go through the basic components of this query language, the syntax, and the basic operators that allow you to filter, manipulate, and enrich data to find the needle of harmful activity in a sea of benign activity. Ready to explore new methods of controlling your security data and elevating your threat hunting game to a new dimension?

The Basics: A Read-Only, Data-Flow Language

On the surface, this advanced hunting query language is a read-only, data-flow language. When you create and execute queries on data, you are asking a question but not modifying the data itself. The integrity of your security data as "read-only" is essential. You can confidently investigate a query without the fear that you "accidentally" deleted a possible piece of evidence.

The concept of data flow is also essential. You can think of your query as a pipe from your perspective. Data coming from a source table enters through the pipe, and it is directed through a sophisticated flow of filtering conditional statements that you created.

At each operator, it takes a dataset as input, performs a task on the dataset (filtering, sorting, aggregating), and then directs the dataset to the next operator. This flow is your secret weapon, syntactically making a logical and meaningful query using simple language.

The syntax structure enhances the readability and ease of authoring queries. Just as with programming for data, queries began with a table of data and a series of functions that you developed and expressed with a pipe (|) function to denote each operator. The pipe provides clear visibility to the reader, enabling them to see where the data came from and track the transformations made on the data.

The Structure of a Query: Building Your First Hunt

To appreciate the beauty and power of the query language, we will look closely at a query syntax structure. All queries contain one or more statements, with one statement being the most popular—the tabular expression statement, wherein you take a table of input and create a table of output. Consider the following conceptual query:

```
DataTable
| where Timestamp > ago(7d)
| where ActionType == "FileCreated"
| summarize count() by FileName
```

Let's examine the aspects of this example:

- *DataTable*: This is the first step in our query. The lesson plan specifies the table of data we want to explore. The security model maintains a large schema of tables, each one containing a category of event data for a specific type of activity, for example, device actions, network events, or email activities. We will look further into the tables available later.

- *| (Pipe)*: This is the main connection point in our data-flow model. It indicates that the output of the previous statement will provide the input for the statement following it.

- *where Timestamp > ago(7d)*: This is our first filter operation. The where operator filters the DataTable to include only the records with a Timestamp that falls within the last seven days. Filtering records based on time is a very natural way to scope queries to the relevant timeframe and increase performance. The ago() function makes it simple to specify timeframes based on relative times.

- *where ActionType == "FileCreated"*: Here, we perform a second filter. We are now selecting from the data that passed through the first where clause, records where the ActionType is "FileCreated". This demonstrates how you can chain multiple operators together to filter your data down in incremental steps.

- *summarize count() by FileName*: This is an aggregation step. The summarize operator aggregates the filtered data by the FileName column, and then, for each file name, we use the count() function to count the number of records. The result is a new table with two columns: FileName and the number of times it had a creation event.

This simple example illustrates the core approach to building a query: you have a large dataset, for instance, a security-relevant dataset, to work with first, then filter down to the events you are focusing on, then aggregate the results to obtain helpful information.

Important Operators: Your Threat Hunting Toolbelt

The query language's potential allows you to use many operators. While this chapter cannot cover all the operators in depth, knowing a few essential operators will give you a firm ground to contribute to many hunting activities.

Filtering and Selecting

- *where*: As shown, the where operator is your primary mechanism for filtering data based on conditions you specify. You can create even more specific filters by using many comparing operators (i.e., ==, !=, >, <, >=, <=) and logical operators (and, or). When making character string comparisons, you can also use operators that look for case-insensitive comparisons, such as has, contains, starts with, and ends with, or similar operators that are case sensitive (i.e., has_cs).

- *project*: The project operator gives you the chance to select which columns you want to see in your output. This is useful for eliminating noise from your results while maintaining your investigational focus. The project operator also enables you to rename columns and create new columns based on simple calculations.

- *take and limit*: To view a sample of the data in a table quickly, use the take or limit operator followed by the number of rows you want to see. This is useful for opening a new table and examining the structure of the data contained in it without waiting for a long-running query to finish.

Aggregation and Summarization

- *summarize*: Perhaps one of the most powerful operators available is summarize. In essence, it lets you run statistical calculations against your data. If desired, you can group by one or more columns and apply aggregation functions like count(), dcount() (distinct count), sum(), avg(), min(), and max().

- *count*: A straightforward operator, count returns the number of rows in the input dataset.

Joining and Combining Data

- *join*: The join operator is a great way to combine rows from two different tables using a standard column. This can become very powerful by enriching your data. For example, you might join device event information to device information to associate an event with the operating system or machine group of the device. There are different types of joins, such as Inner, LeftOuter, and RightOuter, which dictate how records are matched between the two tables and, ultimately, which records will be in the result.

- *union*: The union operator combines the rows from two (or more) tables into one table. The tables will need to have the same number of columns and data types. This is a great way to get a specific indicator over multiple event types.

CHAPTER 4   THREAT DETECTION, INVESTIGATION, AND RESPONSE

Understanding the Schema: The Blueprint of Your Data

Understanding the sources of data available to you will inform your first quest. The query language is designed to operate on an existing, well-defined schema. A schema is made up of multiple tables, each with its columns. The tables provide a logical representation of security events and entities in your environment.

The schema describes the data available to you and how to access it. Some tables will be more relevant to your queries than others, but all the tables can provide clues when you look for specific tactics, techniques, and procedures in the attack life cycle.

Here are some examples of the types of tables that you will see

- *Device Events*: These tables provide a large amount of information related to what is happening on your endpoints. This includes anything from process creation events to network connections initiated from devices, registry changes, file creation and modification events, and logon events.

- *Email and Collaboration Events*: These tables relate to the flow of email, including, for example, information from email attachments, URLs that were included in an email, and directing information about what happens post-delivery. An important data source for hunting phishing and malware delivery campaigns.

- *Identity and Application Events*: Within these tables, you will find user authentication information, sign-in events from identity providers, and any events from cloud-based applications. Again, beneficial data for hunting compromised accounts or unusual user behavior.

- *Alert and Threat Intelligence Information*: The alert and threat intelligence information comes from the tables that include information about the alerts that get created by the security suite detection capabilities and threat intelligence information as indicators. The same information that triggers alerts can also help correlate with your findings during the hunt when referring to known threats.

Before you start to hunt, it's helpful to explore the schema. The UI of the advanced hunting tool will generally have a schema browser that will show you all the tables and columns of each table, including a description of what kind of data is contained within that column. Knowing the schema should significantly improve your ability to develop relevant and successful queries for what you are looking for.

If you want to defend your organization, it is worth the investment to learn how to use advanced hunting query language effectively. It unlocks the full potential of the vast security data you have access to, serving as the key to transitioning from a reactive alert investigation mindset to a more proactive threat hunting approach.

Learning is a continuous process, and developing mastery of an advanced hunting query language comes down to practice. Begin by formulating simple queries, examining the schema, tables, and operators, and then build upon the data relevant to hunting incidents. The more you use advanced hunting query language, the more fluent you will become with the key operator syntax, the more aware you will be of what could be a subtle signal of compromise, and the more effective you will be at being the gatekeeper of your organization.

Threat Hunting with the MITRE ATT&CK Framework

Quality threat hunting requires systematic searching for known adversarial behaviors, not random anomalies. This is precisely the benefit of the MITRE ATT&CK framework for the modern-day security analyst.

MITRE ATT&CK is a globally accessible curated knowledge base of adversary tactics and techniques, based on observation of real-world adversaries, which provides a common terminology for describing and analyzing adversary behavior in the field of cybersecurity. Consider it an encyclopedia of everything an attacker might do to achieve their objectives, from initial access to final impact.

Aligning our efforts with ATT&CK enables us to transition from a reactive posture (waiting for alerts to fire) to a more proactive one, where we think like an adversary. This involves forming hypotheses about how an adversary might act in our environments and utilizing our query skills to validate or disprove those hypotheses. This chapter will explore ways to use the intelligence and organization of the ATT&CK framework to perform more targeted, intelligent, and effective threat hunting, and specifically how ATT&CK is integrated within security platforms such as Microsoft Sentinel.

The Structure of ATT&CK: Tactics and Techniques

The ATT&CK framework is organized into a logical hierarchy, which represents the preferred life cycle of a cyberattack, and it is essential to understand the structure to leverage it properly.

Tactics (The "Why"): The tactic is the adversary's tactical goal—"The Why." The tactic represents the high-level goal the attacker is attempting to achieve. There are initial access, execution, persistence, privilege escalation, defense evasion, credential access, discovery, lateral movement, and exfiltration. In total, there are 14 tactics in the Enterprise ATT&CK matrix.

Techniques (The "How"): Within each tactic, there are several techniques. A method describes how an adversary achieves a tactical goal. For instance, while attaining the execution tactic, an adversary could use the Command and Scripting Interpreter technique. ATT&CK documents hundreds of these techniques as they have been observed in the wild.

Sub-techniques (The "Specific How"): Many techniques further divide into sub-techniques, which provide a more specific description of the behavior. For example, the Command and Scripting Interpreter technique (T1059) has several sub-techniques, such as PowerShell (T1059.001), Windows Command Shell (T1059.003), and Python (T1059.006). This level of detail is invaluable when developing accurate hunting queries.

By utilizing this Tactic-Technique-Sub-Technique hierarchy, we can parse a technically complex attack into several observable behaviors. This structured view is the ideal basis for systematic threat hunting.

From Framework to Hunt: A Hypothesis-Driven Approach

The primary concept behind ATT&CK-driven hunting is that when we are threat hunting, we have to start hunting for indicators of behavior (IOBs) rather than specific, known indicators of compromise (IOCs)—such as file hashes or IP addresses. An IOC is a static artifact that an adversary can easily change. A behavior, or technique, is such a fundamental part of their operation that it is less easy for them to change. The approach is based on a hypothesis-driven methodology:

Select a Technique: Select a specific ATT&CK technique or sub-technique upon which to focus. Your selection may be based on threat intelligence reports, an identified gap in your automated detections, or simply a desire to work through the ATT&CK matrix systematically.

Formulate a Hypothesis: Formulate a hypothesis that is clear and testable. For example, "An adversary may be utilizing PowerShell sub-techniques (T1059.001) to download and execute malicious code from the internet."

Determine Data Sources: Identify the specific data required to test your hypothesis. For PowerShell, you want process creation logs and any command-line arguments associated with those processes. If using something like Microsoft Sentinel, you would look for data in the DeviceProcessEvents table (which is populated by Microsoft Defender for Endpoint) or the SecurityEvents table (which comes from Windows Security Auditing, Event ID 4688).

Create a Hunting Query: With your understanding of the query language (e.g., KQL), create a query that can look at the given data sources to search for evidence of the behavior hypothesized.

Evaluating the Outcomes: Run the query, and consider the output. You are trying to differentiate between benign administrative activity and possibly malicious behavior. Getting this level of detail requires context and is not simple. For example, is that PowerShell command part of a known software deployment script, or is it an obfuscated one-liner that is connecting to a random unknown domain?

Response and Automation: When you discover a true positive, you can kickstart your incident response process. Just as importantly, you can create a new automated detection rule, leverage a successful hunt query into a proactive hunt, and turn the events into a lasting automated defense, allowing you to hunt for the next threat proactively.

Using ATT&CK with Microsoft Sentinel

Modern SIEM platforms like Microsoft Sentinel have built-in robust capabilities to operationalize the ATT&CK framework, unlike anything we have seen before.

Alerts and Incidents Mapping: Many of Sentinel's built-in analytics rules have been pre-mapped to ATT&CK tactics and techniques. When an alert is generated, it becomes a collection of activities implicated by the attackers and gives you greater context about the goals of the adversary across other imminent objectives. An incident accumulates alerts that may have been generated by aspects of multi-faceted or multi-stage attacks that move across ATT&CK tactics, providing an incident-level picture of the attack and the activity.

Hunting Queries: The "Hunting" page in Microsoft Sentinel has pre-built KQL queries built specifically for proactive threat hunting. Many of these queries apply to ATT&CK techniques that can be run on-demand or on a scheduled recurrence to search for suspicious activities that may not be high-fidelity enough to generate an alert but are certainly worth investigating.

Threat Intelligence Integration: Threat Intelligence platforms that funnel into Sentinel tag the potential indicators in their intelligence, mapping their Indicators of Compromise (IOCs) to ATT&CK TTPs (tactics, techniques, and procedures). This allows you to pivot from a threat actor to the specific methods and then consume them to hunt for that in your environment.

Coverage Analysis: Sentinel offers workbooks that visually display your engagements and detections across the ATT&CK matrix for your organization. This provides security managers with immediate visibility into ATT&CK techniques, including broad coverage of automated detection incidents and elements with no detection coverage, which act as "blind spot" detections. All this is a priority—the blind spots are where your next hunt will take place.

A Practical Example: Hunting for Scheduled Task Abuse

Let's walk through a hunting scenario using this methodology.

Technique Selection: We choose the technique Scheduled Task/Job (T1053), specifically the Scheduled Task (T1053.005) sub-technique. Adversaries frequently use the Windows Task Scheduler to establish persistence or execute malicious code at a later time.

Hypothesis: "An adversary has created a new scheduled task to execute a suspicious script or binary, potentially from an unusual location like C:\Users\Public\."

Data Sources: We need logs that record the creation of scheduled tasks. In Windows, this is Event ID 4698. In Sentinel, this data would likely be in the SecurityEvents table. We also might want to correlate this with process execution events from the DeviceProcessEvents table.

```
Hunting Query (KQL):
// Hunt for newly created scheduled tasks
SecurityEvent
| where EventID == 4698 // "A scheduled task was created"
| parse EventData with * 'TaskName' TaskName_raw * 'Command' Command_raw *
| project
    Timestamp,
    Computer,
    Account,
    TaskName = tostring(TaskName_raw),
    Command = tostring(Command_raw)
| where
    // Look for suspicious commands or paths
    Command has_any ("powershell", "cmd.exe", "wscript.exe", "cscript.exe")
    or Command has_any (@"C:\Users\Public", @"C:\Temp\", @"C:\Perflogs\")
```

Analysis: When we run this query, we're not just looking for any new scheduled task. We're looking for tasks that exhibit suspicious characteristics: tasks that run common scripting interpreters (which could be used to execute malicious code) or tasks that point to executables in world-writable directories where an attacker might place a payload. The results would need to be compared against known good tasks in the environment to identify true outliers.

The MITRE ATT&CK framework transforms threat hunting from an art into a science. It provides the structure, the common language, and the strategic guidance needed to hunt for adversaries in a systematic and repeatable way. Security analysts can stop chasing alerts and proactively dismantle attacks by combining the power of flexible query language with ATT&CK's comprehensive adversary knowledge base. A proactive cyber defense starts with hunting with ATT&CK, not just as a best practice.

CHAPTER 4 THREAT DETECTION, INVESTIGATION, AND RESPONSE

Integrating Threat Intelligence into Response Strategies

The Internet of Medical Things (IoMT) is one of the most significant innovations that have occurred in healthcare today. IoMT has transformed clinical workflows and patient care by facilitating real-time connections from medical devices to healthcare networks and patient data systems. At the same time, it also creates unique security challenges. The consequences of a compromised IoMT system can be more severe than in traditional IT environments, where your data may be at stake. When an IoMT system is compromised, there may be a risk to a human life.

In an environment that is so high? Stakes and security strategies require timely and relevant threat intelligence. Threat intelligence contains more than a list of malicious IPs or file hashes. It provides contextual insight into the tools, tactics, and procedures (TTPs) employed by threat actors. Along with that context of TTPs comes an understanding of what actors are trying to achieve and their methods to achieve it. In IoMT, where visibility is poor and attacks could exploit obscure issues or be dependent upon legacy devices running outdated software, it is also paramount to have context for understanding actions. Forearmed with context from threat intelligence, defenders can be alerted to early signs of compromise, assign priority to critical alerts, and take action at the right time.

Medical devices are fundamentally different than traditional computing endpoints in that they were not built to host modern security agents or keep secure logs. Making patches and updates can often require interrupting a clinical operation. Furthermore, many medical devices were designed without security in mind, operating on insecure protocols and vulnerable firmware. In essence, IoMT systems are valuable targets for threat actors. Threat intelligence helps to close this gap, allowing defenders to understand the threat indicators of attacks occurring elsewhere in the world and to strengthen their local defenses before a threat reaches their environment.

The threat landscape impacting healthcare is always evolving. Threat actors are constantly developing new strains of malware, adversarial infrastructure, and attack campaigns, too often targeting IoMT devices either as a primary or secondary assault. Threat intelligence enables organizations to detect unwanted changes in threat actor tactics, techniques, and procedures. Threats are identified not only based on new indicators of compromise but also from a strategic perspective—what groups are attacking, what vulnerabilities are being utilized, and what those impacts may be.

In this situation, defenders would shift from relying upon responsive and reactive threat detection to employing an intelligence-led security model that incorporates current knowledge of known active threats.

Within complex networks, such as hospitals or clinics, security operations centers receive thousands of alerts daily; rarely do more than a handful of alerts, and even fewer events, require significant resources (time) for validation and verification. None of those alerts has the same value, so the triaging of alerts is one of the most critical and challenging parts of an operator's day. Threat intelligence helps provide the context needed to differentiate important alerts from false positives. For instance, an outbound connection to an organization's designated IP address typically does not trigger alerts from the security operations center, given the numerous public-facing endpoints and applications. However, placing that same connection into context with recognized command-and-control infrastructure may prompt a more thorough investigation. Or to take another example, an unauthorized login on a diagnostic shipboard machine falls in the same category until the potential danger presented by the attempt can be placed into context with threat intelligence showing the unsuccessful login is pattern consistent with "brute force" tactics observed as being used by listed threat actors within a regional campaign.

Building Threat-Intelligent Security Architectures using Microsoft Sentinel

Microsoft Sentinel is an essential part of embedding threat intelligence into the architecture of an IoMT-aware security program. When contemplating defense, threat intelligence can assist organizations in leveraging a practically derived defense strategy that reflects how real, recurring attacks are manifesting in the respective threat landscape versus a potentially flawed theoretical risk methodology. Sentinel enables architects to apply both Microsoft's native threat intelligence and engineered third-party source intelligence to derive a comprehensive and real-time view of actor-driven activity ultimately.

Once an organization moves to the design phase, there are opportunities to extract existing assets (medical devices and clinical systems) that are mapped against commonly known threat actors and threat techniques. This can be a massive help for a risk assessment scheme, and if Sentinel can accept threat models using the MITRE ATT&CK framework, you can assign previously known behaviors of potential attackers into an IoMT environment with its specific PACS server or infusion pump and potentially different HL7 messages. You can play not only to comply but also with the known behaviors of actively engaged (and potentially profiting) threat groups.

To Engineer Sentinel to Activate Threat Intelligence

As an organization moves from the design phase of a Sentinel-based IoMT security project to engineering, the threat intelligence becomes operational at that stage. Inside your Sentinel deployment, your engineers configure ingestion methods for continuously ingesting newly identified threat indicators, whether housed within Microsoft's telemetry, trusted ISACs, or commercial intelligence providers. These indicators (IP addresses, domains, file hashes, process behavior, etc.) will now be ingested and retained in the Sentinel instance for both detection and retrospective detection capabilities.

Subsequently, your security engineers would programmatically insert those indicators into analytics rules, so not only should organizations be submitting threat data as generic alerts, but a far more sophisticated correlation will become evident by matching historic telemetry with previously known adversarial indicators and behaviors. For instance, a DNS request that might appear innocuous becomes concerning when viewed against a multitude of threat intelligence feeds and the corresponding associated data. With Sentinel, engineers can revise the rules as threat intelligence evolves, ensuring that their detection capabilities are up-to-date with current threats.

Engineering also includes configuring the hunting environment for Sentinel in a way that leverages threat intelligence. Security analysts write KQL (Kusto Query Language) queries to locate behavioral patterns associated with known threats. Sentinel enhances this process by providing out-of-the-box hunting queries based on up-to-date threat intelligence and allowing organizations to construct their threat-specific hunting activities. In IoMT scenarios, concerning capabilities and telemetry availability, this pre-emptive hunting process is beneficial.

Using Detect and Response Capabilities with Threat Intelligence

When deploying Sentinel into an active IoMT ecosystem, intelligence becomes an essential enabler of detection and response. Analysts and/or responders receive alerts that have been enriched with contextual data, i.e., known threat actors, campaign metadata, and recent attack history. The enriched data is essential for the analyst and/or responder to understand not only what happened, but also who did it and why.

Intelligence also plays an enormous part in alert prioritization during the deployment phase. In healthcare settings, where downtime can significantly impact patient care, understanding what alerts represent real threats goes a long way in helping the team efficiently prioritize how and when to respond to alerts. Sentinel assists this process by scoring and ranking alerts based on factors such as the presence of threat indicators and the confidentiality and integrity of the affected assets, along with the TTPs observed. This creates a more condensed and effective incident response process.

The inclusion of threat intelligence in Sentinel also shapes the utilization of automated responses. Playbooks, Sentinel's automation framework, can be used when indicators match known adversarial activity. For example, when an IoMT gateway device identifies an association with a known malicious domain, a playbook could isolate the network segment to which the IoMT gateway belongs, block that domain at the firewall, and notify the clinical staff. These automated responses are enabled with real-time intelligence, allowing for a rapid containment response with little human involvement.

Enabling Analysts to Leverage Intelligence in Investigations

Threat intelligence is a force multiplier for security analysts. Sentinel provides contextual information from threat feeds as it relates to every alert and incident, which enables analysts not only to see what occurred but also whether it's a part of a larger campaign or affiliated with individuals they know are adversarial. This enriched data is pulled directly into the Sentinel interface, which allows analysts an almost instant sense of what an alert may signify.

Investigations within Sentinel also have tools like the investigation graph that allow them to visualize the actions an attack has taken. When the investigation graph contains nodes that have ties to known threat intelligence indicators, an analyst can pivot quickly to their external data, identify lateral movement, and assess the attacker's objectives. When dealing with incidents impacting medical devices or clinical systems, it is critical to have this level of insight to contain an incident rapidly and accurately. Additionally, Sentinel allows analysts to model and run historical data, using known indicators of compromise for backward scanning. This post hoc analysis can uncover hidden, slow-moving, or long-aging threats that did not rise to the previous detection threshold. In the IoMT space, it is critical because threats can sometimes originate from devices that are either misconfigured or remain at a low observable level before clear signs of compromise emerge.

Automating Response Actions with Intelligence at the Core

Automation in Sentinel is not limited to alerting or notifications. Sentinel can identify threats and utilize threat intelligence to formulate sophisticated or conditional decision-making based on confidence in threat assessments, determination of the sophistication of the potential threat, and fidelity of the danger (high fidelity-low fidelity). When subject to a high-fidelity threat, Sentinel can initiate distinct plays that contain incidents across firewalls, endpoint protection platforms, and email. In healthcare, where timing is critical, speed and repeatability can offer an interruption or prevention to the remediation process. Ultimately, time is of the essence.

The playbooks can also be developed to dynamically ingest updated threat feeds, allowing Sentinel to keep up with adversary campaigns. If, for example, the healthcare ad hoc threat intel indicated an adverse threat actor leveraging a new ransomware campaign targeting hospital systems, Sentinel could initiate searching for relevant indicators in the environment and leverage remediation or response playbooks for the matches. This initiates the development of a living process designed to counter unknown, evolving threats, which are continually contextualized in terms of threat activities or events.

Integrating Continual Threat Hunting and Strategic Defense

Using threat intelligence in Sentinel will also aid in threat hunting. While perusing the risk assessment and its value, hunters can create a hypothesis based on known threats. Depending upon the threat, a hunter may focus on privileged lateral movement across subsegments that include devices or focus on identifying anomalous events in the critical care system by referencing the expected/known behaviors from their threat actors.

Every new piece of intelligence refines and focuses hunter actions. Sentinel provides an organization with a living threat picture. Through adaptive evolution, it recognizes changes in threat actors' behavior over time, matures detection logic, and understands how the role of the examining analyst with adversaries and adapted responses evolves.

Integrating threat intelligence into each layer of an organizational IoMT security strategy is not merely a technical activity or operational necessity; it is, in fact, a strategic incorporation. With Microsoft Sentinel's integrations, tools, and workflows, we can operationalize the model of intelligence across the security lifecycle: design, build/implementation, engineering, and investigation.

In healthcare, where timely disruptions threaten patient safety, operationalizing imperative concepts can provide valuable deliverables when they rely on timely independent issues, utilize relevant threat intelligence, and act with or recognize existing, expected capacities, which could prove invaluable. Adaptive security operations, informed by relevant threat intelligence sources, enable organizations to assess and mitigate potential security impacts. Sentinel provides organizations with the opportunity to initiate recognizing distinctions in their traditional, static security operational posture through theoretical and distinct procedures to create an adaptive and responsive security operation. Organizations can adapt their current processes and avoid being constrained by their existing security posture when encountering new, unknown unknowns or specific threats. For defenders in a healthcare context, an incentivized approach is a viable method to establish their role within rapidly evolving threat environments. It creates opportunities to capitalize on one-off capabilities within a ubiquitous response capability, creating a cohesive, adaptable, resilient, and robust defensive ecosystem.

Working with Threat Intelligence in Microsoft Sentinel

Threat intelligence is essential to detect, investigate, and respond to modern security operations. Microsoft Sentinel allows for the integration and management of threat intelligence to help security teams surpass adversaries. The experience working with threat intelligence is the same whether you are using the Defender portal or the Azure portal, and any organization can create, manage, and analyze threat information with ease.

A Transition to the Defender Portal

With Microsoft Sentinel growing and evolving, the Defender portal offers a unified experience for managing Sentinel and has become the standard experience for Sentinel users. Starting in July 2026, all Sentinel access will be fully supported through the Defender portal, and customers still utilizing the Azure portal will be redirected to the Defender portal. To assist, organizations should plan for the transition, including learning more about the capabilities inside the Defender interface.

Access the Threat Intelligence Interface

Getting started with threat intelligence using Sentinel means determining which portal to use. When accessing through the Defender portal, the path is straightforward: Threat intelligence ➤ Intel management. When using the Azure portal, the entry point is somewhat uneven, but the options available to the user after entering the interface remain the same.

Creating Threat Intelligence Objects with STIX

Sentinel provides the ability to create threat intelligence objects using Structured Threat Information Expression (STIX). STIX is an open, structured language for representing threat data. STIX provides an easier way to describe and understand threat data; it also allows for richer threat data and means better integration with other tools to enrich your intelligence. To initiate a new STIX object, navigate to the management console and select Add new ➤ TI object. When the procedure is complete, you will have to choose the type of object (indicator, threat actor, or attack pattern), and you will be presented with a form that will collect the necessary metadata. You must fill in the required fields, which will be marked; you will then be able to define sensitivity using the Traffic Light Protocol (TLP).

If your object has an existing relationship to another piece of threat intelligence, you can capture this relationship based on the relationship type and reference it. There is also the capability of creating objects in less cumbersome ways by using the copy functionality in Sentinel, which allows you to duplicate an object to create a similar object using the copied metadata to speed up the creation process.

Evolving and Managing Threat Intelligence

All threat data ingested or created requires curation based on appropriate timelines. However, Microsoft Sentinel provides security teams with numerous tools to engage and optimize their threat intelligence, such as ingestion rules for the suppression and curation of ingestion, builders for creating relationships to other objects, tagging, and advanced search.

Ingestion Rules Switch: To Suppress Source Data Ingestion

Ingestion rules provide an advantage by allowing security teams to suppress direct ingestion of the noisy, low-confidence indicators and enhance ingestion of those with a higher "truth." You can also extend the validated period of essential indicators, apply action tagging, or suppress indicator duplication.

To create an ingestion rule, navigate to the Ingestion rules section and define the conditions for object type source, confidence level, and action. For instance, you might have a rule that adds several days and designates a number from a trusted source as an "Extended" expiration for high-confidence indicators.

Rules will execute in a specific, defined order from lowest priority to highest, and each rule examines every incoming object. After you create your rules, you can start using them immediately.

Making Relationships Between Threat Intelligence Objects

Using the relationship builder, an analyst can create a logical relationship between two different STIX objects by linking them together, i.e., linking a threat actor to an attack pattern or indicator. Relationships provide context, additional investigative value, and additional data points.

To start, click Add new ➤ TI relationship, select the existing object, and establish the type of relationship. A threat actor will "Use" an attack pattern or may be "Attributed to" an entity that is known. You can create up to 20 _relationships at once, though more can be added through additional iterations.

Viewing Threat Intelligence

The Microsoft Sentinel management interface includes powerful tools to assist security teams in curating, organizing, and analyzing threat data. Filtering can be done against STIX object types, and logical conditions can be used in search. You can view detailed options for each indicator.

When leveraging search, you can use multiple conditions using logical operators AND & OR to refine your search.

Confirm that the interface only displays the most recent version of each object. For IP and domain indicators, Sentinel will enrich the data with GeoLocation and WhoIs information to assist investigations.

Tagging Threat Intelligence

Tags provide a fast and simple way to organize and classify threat intelligence objects. Tags can represent incidents or campaigns, but relationships are more appropriate for representing formal associations between entities.

You can tag multiple objects by selecting them in the interface and applying the desired tag. While tagging is free-form, using standard naming conventions/tags is a best practice to ensure consistency across your team.

For objects created within Sentinel, editing threat intelligence is simple. For objects that have been ingested, fields may be edited to include tags, expiration date, confidence score, and whether they are revoked. The latest version of any object will be visible in the interface, no matter the origin.

Querying Threat Intelligence Data

The management interface is a helpful way to work with data, but for more complex tasks, querying more often is needed. Microsoft Sentinel will store threat indicators in dedicated tables that allow for all the advanced search queries and integrations.

In the Defender portal, Advanced Hunting can be used under Investigation & response ➤ Hunting to explore those tables in KQL (Kusto Query Language).

Visualizing Threat Intelligence Using Workbooks

Most teams find that visualization makes the knowledge of threat intelligence more straightforward to understand. Microsoft Sentinel includes a workbook specifically for threat intelligence in the Threat Management ➤ Workbooks parameters. The Threat Intelligence workbook allows your team to view, analyze, and customize the threats you care about in an instant.

Once opened, you may opt in to edit the workbook by selecting Edit, then add any custom queries you wish. One way to create a chart showing the count of threat indicators by type is with:

```kusto
Copy
Edit
ThreatIntelligenceIndicator
| summarize count() by ThreatType
```

Please select a relevant visualization, such as a bar chart, and place it on your dashboard. Workbooks are highly customizable and can include many charts, queries, and filters combined to form a comprehensive dashboard tailored to your organization's requirements.

These workbooks are built around the Azure Monitor's Workbook infrastructure, which supports multiple ways to visualize data. By applying this capability, security teams can create interactive dashboards that highlight relevant threat intelligence for their environment.

To sum up, Microsoft Sentinel provides a strong and complex approach to threat intelligence. Where threat intelligence can include the structured construction of STIX objects, visualized in various fashions, and queried in powerful ways, Sentinel provides continuous and actionable threat intelligence in a streamlined and organized manner. Finally, organizations on the trajectory to fully utilize the Defender portal will heavily rely on these essentials for building a mature and responsive security operations program.

Using Copilot for Security Analysts in the Embedded Experience

Security operations have always relied on speed, clarity, and accuracy. Still, with the more convoluted nature of threats, as well as the escalation of security data volume, analysts will often find it tough to keep up with the scale of investigation and response workload. Microsoft Sentinel launched Security Copilot to help offset this frenetic pace. Security Copilot integrates artificial intelligence capabilities into the core of the MSD Sentinel solution, offering a new, meaningful way to interact with security data through natural language and intelligent assistance.

Security Copilot was designed to assist analysts every step of the way. When engaging with Copilot, analysts can use conversational language or technical language and get responses that provide detail and lift from the analyst workload. As a result, there is no requirement to have full knowledge of the query language or the specific tool. An analyst can ask, "What set off this alert?". Or whether this user has other incidents involved? Or if various indicators of compromise are essential? Security Copilot will typically respond with a summary of details or insightful supporting queries.

Security Copilot was built with Kusto Query Language (KQL) query generation and explanation, which, to many analysts, can be a significant hindrance to effective threat hunting or incident investigation. Security Copilot can generate and illustrate KQL queries on demand, providing detailed explanations for the logic behind the KQL syntax to users. Our goal is to help analysts become more familiar with the product, providing them with the information they need to be confident in their work, such as writing queries with ease and at a pace and rhythm that suits their assignments. It effectively unshackles the onboarding aspects that have been misplaced, making it easier to onboard new team members. Additionally, it provides endless advanced analysis and well-led analysis for those who have experienced the grind, fulfilling their obligations. In addition to the queries, Security Copilot provides in-depth incident analysis. It gives both incident decomposition, which identifies related alerts, affected entities, and potential root causes, as well as suggested next steps. This allows analysts to triage quickly and dedicate their time and efforts to the most pertinent areas. No longer are they lost in thousands of alerts, but they are presented with focused and relevant information so they may efficiently respond to incidents.

In the area of threat hunting, Security Copilot accelerates the journey from hypothesis to investigation. It allows analysts to ask questions such as "Have we seen this behavior from anywhere else in the environment?" or "Which endpoints have communicated with that suspicious domain recently?". They can leverage the AI assistant to support hunting activities because it builds the queries to execute, supports interpretation of the results, and does not require them to write complex logic by hand.

Operational tasks can also benefit from Copilot's guidance. Analysts can ask for help creating analytic rules or automation playbooks. For example, the analyst can ask the assistant to create a rule that detects a specified number of failed sign-in attempts, followed by escalation of privilege, or it could prepare a standardized playbook that automatically isolates the affected external devices. This standardizes responses and reduces the time it takes to operationalize new detection techniques.

Interacting with Copilot is easy and intuitive. Copilot is embedded in the Sentinel interface, allowing users to type prompts directly and receive responses in a dedicated conversation pane. The conversation that is taking place is contextual, meaning that

Copilot takes into context the current incident or data they are examining. Whether the analyst is sifting through logs, responding to alert triage, reviewing threat indicators, or performing other tasks, Copilot's responses provide reliable information related to the specific task.

For teams operating in life-threatening environments, such as during critical incidents, Copilot can reduce cognitive load. It is capable of managing mundane as well as highly technical details, which frees the analyst's time to focus on analysis, decision-making, and threat interpretation. It can also facilitate cross-role collaboration. For example, less experienced analysts can use Copilot to help understand complex scenarios, which are then presented in terms they can easily understand. Security leadership can also leverage AI summaries as ready-made reports to disseminate their findings to the broader security stakeholder community.

Security Copilot was built with privacy and enterprise compliance built in. It does not violate organizational data boundaries and guarantees that any information processed or analyzed is limited to what the organization approves. No highly sensitive data is sent or used beyond the purpose of security, which assures that customer confidentiality and compliance obligations are met.

In terms of day-to-day operations, Copilot generates the most benefit when dealing with large-scale alert reviews, multi-stage incident investigations, and exploratory threat hunts. It can assist teams in understanding the scope of incidents, connecting the dots for seemingly unrelated alerts, and quickly responding to time-sensitive alerts. From providing assistance on content development to query writing or summarizing the main insights based on findings, Security Copilot injects intelligence and clarity into every area a security analyst routinely operationalizes on behalf of their organization.

Security Copilot represents a significant shift in how defenders interact with Microsoft Sentinel. It provides basic building blocks that configure the complex interface between the human domain expertise and the extensive range of scale and complexity of security data. By using thousands of queries, regulators, defenders, and analysts can prioritize decisions, performance, and ultimately, action. Previous generations of defenders, accustomed to manual detection and slow responses, will now shape new norms for detecting threats.

As the cybersecurity threat landscape becomes increasingly personalized and agile in persistent environments, supporting tools that enhance the effectiveness of analysts is no longer optional. Security Copilot demonstrates this support and capability development that empowers security teams with intelligent and responsive capacity to support their needs in real time.

Internet of Medical Things (IoMT) View

The rapidly growing Internet of Medical Things (IoMT) has created a new paradigm of patient care, efficiency, and innovation; however, it has also created a large, complex attack surface. The IoMT security challenge shouldn't just be framed as an IT risk; it is a patient safety challenge. A sound security strategy will require a comprehensive view that considers every part of the lifecycle from conception and deployment to the daily work of security analysts. Integrating Microsoft Copilot for Security with Microsoft Sentinel creates a unique, end-to-end solution to the IoMT security challenge.

The IoMT Security Challenge: A Complex, Critical Space

While the IoMT technology environment creates security challenges, it also presents unique challenges that differ from those of traditional IT security. When thinking about IoMT security challenges, consider

- *Device Diversity*: An IoMT ecosystem can have a diverse range of devices, from modern, IP-enabled infusion pumps to legacy diagnostic equipment running an obsolete OS. In other words, standard security controls are nearly impossible to implement because your "devices" are too diverse.

- *Extensive Device Lifetimes*: Medical devices often have a considerably longer lifespan than typical IT assets. Thus, many medical devices run unsupported firmware and software, which creates existing and perpetual vulnerabilities.

- *Regulatory Compliance*: The healthcare environment is highly regulated, especially concerning protecting patient data (e.g., HIPAA). Non-compliance can result in significant fines and reputational harm.

- *Patient Safety*: A successful cyberattack on an IoMT device can result in life safety consequences, such as modifying the dosing of medications or impairing the delivery of an essential diagnostic procedure.

CHAPTER 4   THREAT DETECTION, INVESTIGATION, AND RESPONSE

- *Limited Security Features*: Many medical devices have not been purpose-built for security (e.g., not incorporating strong authentication, encryption, or basic patching). The Strategic Rationale: Why Copilot & Sentinel Empower the Right Decisions. The decision to use Copilot for Security and Microsoft Sentinel for IoMT security is a straightforward one, centered around an intelligent, unified, and scalable platform.

- *Unified Visibility*: As a cloud-native Security Information and Event Management (SIEM) and Security Orchestration, Automation and Response (SOAR) solution, Microsoft Sentinel provides a single pane of glass for the security data across the whole health organization, for both IT networks and cloud infrastructure, and importantly IoMT, as the integration with Microsoft Defenders for IoT ingestion from its connector does provide this critical visibility.

- *AI-Powered Threat Detection*: Because Sentinel has built-in machine learning and User and Entity Behavior Analytics (UEBA), which are crucial in detecting anomalous behavior in the large, complex, and noisy IoMT environment, including allowing early detection of sophisticated threats that would not have triggered a traditional signature-based detection process.

- *Automated Response*: Sentinel's SOAR functionality enables the automation of incident response playbooks, which is vital in such a fast-moving threat landscape, as the landscape in IoMT requires a rapid reaction to contain a threat effectively and does not cause harm to a patient in the process.

- *Natural Language Interface*: Copilot for Security will help democratize security analysis, allowing security personnel to interrogate complex security data in natural language. The implications for healthcare organizations without a team of dedicated cybersecurity experts with deep expertise in query language may also be the greatest advantage.

CHAPTER 4   THREAT DETECTION, INVESTIGATION, AND RESPONSE

From Design to Deployment: Designing and Deploying Secure IoMT Solutions

The work on the Copilot and Sentinel completes a more secure model for designing and deploying IoMT.

Secure by Design: Understanding the types of threats and vulnerabilities that Sentinel and Copilot were able to identify will help security architects push for medical devices that have higher security capabilities built into them. The information gathered from these tools could then be used to develop more secure security requirements for purchasing new devices.

- *Complete Data Ingestion*: During the deployment of IoMT systems, engineers can ensure that Microsoft Sentinel is ingesting all relevant data sources; logs from networks, firewalls, identity and access management solutions, and alerts and inventory data from Microsoft Defender for IoT are the most notable.

- *Custom Analytics and Playbooks*: Engineers can leverage Copilot functionality insights and create custom analytics rules within Sentinel that are specific to the IoMT environment of each organization. For example, engineers could create a rule to detect if a medical device establishes communication with an unauthorized external IP address. Additionally, automated response playbooks can identify a compromised device so that the device can be isolated from the environment.

The Security Analyst's Resource: Changing Operational Practices

The security analyst on the ground will indeed find both Copilot for Security and Microsoft Sentinel to be massive factors of change.

- *Acceleration of Incident Investigations*: When an alert for a possible IoMT security incident is triggered in Sentinel, the analyst can use Copilot to get a quick summary of that event in natural language. This summary includes details on the impacted device, the nature of the threat, and other user-related activity.

- *Natural Language to KQL*: Rather than spend time writing complex Kusto Query Language (KQL) queries to hunt for threats, the analyst can ask Copilot in plain English for information and obtain a KQL query provided and executed in Sentinel. For instance, the analyst can ask, "Show me all communication from infusion pumps to any IP address in North Korea in the past 24 hours." Copilot then converts the request, provides the KQL, and executes the results without delay.

- *Malicious Script Analysis*: If a suspicious script were suspected to be on a medical device or associated system, the analyst could ask Copilot to analyze the script and report what it is intended to do and its impact, if applicable. In a matter of seconds, a task that once required a very specialized malware analyst can be performed.

- *Guided Response and Remediation*: Copilot can provide the analyst with step-by-step guidance through incident response, helping to contain the threat, eradicate malware, and assist in the recovery of the system under attack. Guided response capabilities are beneficial for junior analysts who do not have experience dealing with IoMT security incidents.

- *Proactive Threat Hunting*: Copilot can help analysts perform proactive threat hunting by providing information about a threat actor's latest tactics, techniques, and procedures (TTPs). For example, an analyst can ask Copilot, "What are the common attack vectors for compromising MRI machines?" and receive a detailed response including actionable intelligence.

A Real-World Scenario: A Day in the Life of an IoMT Security Analyst
Here is the scenario:

- *Alert*: Microsoft Sentinel generates an alert stating that an infusion pump is making an unusual outbound connection to a known malicious IP address.

- *Triage with Copilot*: The security analyst instantly asks Copilot to summarize the incident. Copilot provides the analyst with a summary, which includes the device's location, the patient it is assigned to (assuming this is permissible and available), and the threat intelligence about the malicious IP address.

- *Investigation*: The analyst asks Copilot, "Has this device talked to any other suspicious IP addresses?" Copilot creates and runs all required KQL queries in Sentinel, returning the results. Additionally, it notes that the device had been communicating with another IP address belonging to a known ransomware group.

- *Containment*: The analyst, with Copilot's assistance, initiates an automated playbook in Sentinel to isolate the infusion pump from the network and eliminate any malicious communications from occurring.

- *Remediation*: The analyst works with the biomedical engineering team to take the device offline for forensic analysis and make it safe to be reimaged.

- *Reporting*: The analyst has Copilot generate an incident report for management and for compliance, with a lot less time than had it been done manually.

The integration of Microsoft Copilot for Security and Microsoft Sentinel represents a significant evolution in securing the Internet of Medical Things. It is a vibrant technical solution, and one with strategic purpose that meets the full lifecycle of securing IoMT. The integration provides a single pane of visibility, intelligent threat detection, and a natural language interface for security analysis, empowering healthcare organizations to professionally protect their patients, data, and reputation in an increasingly connected world. From the CISO who defines the security strategy to the engineer who deploys new devices to the analyst responding to threats, Copilot and Sentinel are enabling tools that provide essential intelligence to create a more secure and resilient healthcare ecosystem.

Summary

This chapter introduces the reader to the full range of security operations within Microsoft Sentinel, from how the analyst interacts on a day-to-day basis with its core features. It starts by orienting the security analyst to the Sentinel interface, data sources, and the depth of rich context that can be generated for monitoring and managing alerts. Then, it covers how to convert an organization's risk and threat models into defined detection and analytics rules, teaching the reader how to author, test, and iterate Kusto Query Language (KQL)–based rules that surface high-value security events without being overwhelmed by alerts.

Following the discussion on detection, the chapter moves to incident response management. Here, it explains how to orchestrate triage workflows, assign and track investigation tasks, and generate audit trails. The reader learns the best practices for incident investigations: creating timelines, pivoting across related alerts, and leveraging Sentinel's entity maps to visualize attackers' movements. The section will discuss automating some of the response components—when and how to utilize playbooks and Logic Apps to automatically contain threats, enhance incidents through external intelligence, and eliminate repetitive manual actions.

In a dedicated section, the text leverages the experience of disrupting an attack. Here, the focus is on leveraging Sentinel's orchestration components to disrupt steps in the adversary's kill chain, such as blocking malicious IP addresses, disabling an account, and triggering network segmentation. After this, the chapter builds further upon the capabilities of KQL for analysts, presenting approaches for writing efficient queries, creating reusable functions from existing queries, and visualizing delivered results to engage team pursuits as well as enhance queries based on prior results.

Moving towards the closing sections, the chapter shifts to being proactive by covering threat hunting. The reader learns how to formulate hypotheses, utilize IOC feeds, and leverage KQL to detect abuse that is executed more discreetly. As part of this section, the chapter illustrates several techniques for "hunting with KQL" by presenting sample patterns and constructing Kusto query constructs. The chapter wraps up with a description of how to utilize threat intelligence across the response lifecycle—curating indicators, using STIX objects to map relationships, and surfacing enrichment data—and as a prelude to introducing the embedded experience with Security Copilot, which gives the analyst an AI-augmented expertise that can assist in query generation, creating incident summaries, or suggesting next steps. In summation, this chapter arms analysts with a holistic, end-to-end playbook for detecting, investigating, and disrupting cyberattacks with Microsoft Sentinel.

Thank you for choosing to read this book. Wishing you success and confidence as you begin your journey in securing the Internet of Things (IoT).

Index

A

Access control lists (ACLs), 282
Access controls, 88
Account access, 303
Activity log, 269
Actuators, 5
Advanced persistent threats (APTs), 146
Advanced Security Information Model (ASIM), 78, 140, 281
    block diagram, 137, 138
    components, 137–143
    entity context, 145, 146
    Microsoft Sentinel, 138
    normalization, 135
    source, 134
    storage model, 139
    use cases, 136, 137
    value, 135, 136
Agility, 84
Alert correlation, 273–275
Alert fatigue, 259
Alert-only security, 307, 308
Alerts, 186, 322
Analytics logs plan, 129
Analytics rules, 209
    access and permissions, 211
    threat detection, 209
    types, 209–211
Anomaly rules, 210
Apache Log4j (Log4Shell), 216, 217
Archive Logs, 113

Artificial intelligence (AI), 3, 10, 23
Asset inventory, 189
Attack disruption mechanisms, 37
ATT&CK framework, 187–189
Automated investigation, 45
Automate schema mapping, 131
Automation, 67, 219, 235, 270, 284
    actions, 224, 225
    incident, 223
    management, 226
    response, 328, 329
    rules, 282
    tools, 285
    triggers, 224
    use cases and scenarios, 226
Automation rule, 31, 223
Auto Playbooks, 288
Auxiliary logs plan, 129
Azure activity, 26
Azure Data Explorer (ADX), 130, 131
Azure Lighthouse, 97–99, 104–106
Azure Logic Apps, 228
Azure Monitor Agent (AMA), 74, 115
Azure Storage, 26

B

Bandwidth, 96
Basic Logs, 113
Behavior analytics, 287
Blockchain, 10, 17
Bookmarking, 311

INDEX

Breaches
   security operations, 89
   Sentinel and Defender XDR, 89
   vulnerabilities, 88
Building blocks, 170, 171, 254, 255
Built-In queries, 213

C

Capability helps support continuous integration and deployment (CI/CD) pipelines, 227
Centralized architecture, 104
CloudAuditEvents, 68
Cloud-based analytics, 7
Cloud-based security, 22
Cloud integration, 53
Cloud management, 60–62
Cloud-Native Scale, 46
Cloud-native Security Information and Event Management (SIEM), 33
Cloud systems, 6
Command-and-control (C2) connections, 302
Communication modules, 5
Community contributions, 215
Compliance, 47
Computer Emergency Response Teams (CERTs), 174
Cross-Origin Resource Sharing (CORS), 199
Custom detection, 51
Custom logs, 116
Custom queries, 214, 215
Cyberattack, 286, 291
Cybersecurity, 1, 22, 46, 150, 163, 169, 234, 243, 244, 246, 247, 252, 272, 280, 282, 314, 335

   challenges, 10, 16, 17
   innovation and resilience, 16, 17
   Internet of Medical Things (IoMT) threats, 11–14
   multi-layered approach, 17, 18
   operation, 275
   resilience, 85
Cybersecurity Labelling Scheme for Medical Devices (CLS-MD), 15
Cyber Threat Intelligence (CTI), 175, 177
   Microsoft Sentinel, 124–127
   security operations, 122
   sources, 123
   types, 123, 124
Cyber threats, 11, 19, 38
Cybervictims, 18

D

Data collection optimization techniques
   automating, 113
   cloud and endpoint sources, 116
   custom and operational logs, 116
   data connectors, 117
   data source, 113
   evaluation, 113
   log data, 114, 115
   long-term retention, 113
   in Microsoft Sentinel, 114
   scenarios, 115
   Sentinel, 112
Data collection rules (DCRs), 113
Data connectors, 117, 179
   data source, 119
   defining, 117
   roles, 117
   Sentinel, 120, 121
   types, 118

use cases, 118
Data ingestion, 331
Data loss prevention (DLP), 80
Data normalization, 142–144, 281
    ASIM (Advanced Security Information Model), 135
    value, 135, 136
Data residency, 96
Data security, 71–73
Data-siloed entity, 3
Data sources, 164, 247, 248
Data visualization, 230, 231
Deep Packet Inspection (DPI), 83
Defender for Endpoint, 44
Defender plans options, 66
Defender portal, 32, 329
Defender XDR, 40, 44
    cloud integration, 53
    incident correlation and alerts, 52, 53
    incident generation, 53
    Microsoft Copilot, 53, 54
    Microsoft Sentinel, 48–51
    portal, 32
Denial-of-service (DDoS) attacks, 13
Deployment, 69–71, 194, 338
Designing, Log Analytics workspace
    multiple Azure Tenants, 104–106
    multiple workspaces, 96–98
    single workspace, 95, 96
Design phase, 110
Detection rule lifecycle, 260
deviceEvents, 68
Device Posture, 80
DevOps pipeline, 61
Digital assets, 66
Digital estate, 251
Digital twins, 10
Discovery phase, 109, 110

Disruption attack strategies, 287
    challenges, 289
    in Internet of Medical Things (IoMT), 288, 289
    Microsoft Sentinel, 290, 291
    security posture, 289
Distributed architecture, 104
Domains, 302–304

E

Ecosystem, 5
Electronic Health Record (EHR) systems, 21
End-to-end encryption, 6
Entities tab, 272
Entity graphs, 312
Extended Detection and Response (XDR), 1, 20, 32

F

Firmware, 13, 14

G

5G Connectivity, 10
Generative AI (Gen AI), 34, 53
General Data Protection Regulation (GDPR), 13
GitHub, 261

H

Healthcare ecosystem, 10, 11, 20
Healthcare security, 280
Health Insurance Portability and Accountability Act (HIPAA), 13, 85

INDEX

Hijacking, 13
Hunting, 162, 313
    built-In queries, 213
    community contributions, 215
    Kusto Query Language (KQL)
        ATT&CK framework, 320
        hypothesis-driven approach, 320, 321
        query structure, 315, 316
        read-only, data-flow language, 314
        Schema, 318–320
        threat actors, 314
        toolbelt, 316, 317
    management and modification, 214
    for scheduled task abuse, 322, 323
Hunting program, 313
Hunts, 30
    access and permissions, 313
    baseline establishment, 304
    bookmarking, 311
    clinical teams, 305
    to detection, 310
    education, 306
    Incident Beacon, 311, 312
    Microsoft Sentinel, 303, 304
    reactive security, 301
    threats, 300, 301
    visibility of devices, 305
    workspaces, 310
Hybrid architecture, 104
Hypothesis, 308, 309

I

IdentityInfo, 68
Implementation phase, 110
Incident automation, 223
Incident Beacon, 311, 312

Incident reports, 269
Incident response (IR), 286
Incidents, 30, 186, 212, 235, 260, 262
Incidents mapping, 322
Independent Software Vendors (ISVs), 104
Indication of compromise (IOC), 301
Indicators of Attack (IOAs), 123
Indicators of behavior (IOBs), 320
Indicators of compromise (IOCs), 123, 171, 173, 176, 178, 182, 235, 245, 259, 291, 304, 320, 322
InfoSecurity, 20
Insider threats, 14
Intelligence-sharing communities (ISACs), 176
Internet of Medical Things (IoMT), 79, 83, 132, 142, 154, 220, 280, 286, 300, 336
    advantages, 8, 9
    adversaries, 301
    analytics rules, 281
    automation rules, 282, 284
    Azure IoT Reference Architecture, 1
    challenges, 84
    components and architecture, 4–7
    connectivity, 2
    continuous monitoring and optimization, 284
    cyberattacks, 286–288
    cybersecurity challenges, 16, 17
    cybersecurity threats, 11–14
    definition, 2
    deployment, 338
    evolution, 3, 4
    future of, 10, 11
    global regulatory and legal pressures, 15
    healthcare security, 280

INDEX

health systems, 3
inspection, 83
Logic App Playbooks, 282
Microsoft Sentinel
    auditability, 21
    patient monitoring devices, 20
    SOAR capabilities, 21
    threat intelligence, 21
    vulnerability, 21
monitoring device, 2
normalization, 281
process-based approach, 281
real-World applications, 7, 8
regulations, 9
risk surface, 32
security challenge, 336, 337
technical controls, 79
threats, 11, 280
use cases, 7, 8
Internet of Things (IoT), 1, 3, 13, 19, 65, 286
    cloud platform, 1
    and Internet of Medical Things (IoMT), 32
    and IT ecosystems, 19
    Microsoft Defender, 63–66
    Microsoft Sentinel, 22–24
    and Operational Technology (OT), 64
    and privacy norms, 15
    risk surface, 32
    scalable strategy, 34
    security incidents, 277–279
Interoperability, 14
Inter-team collaboration, 261
Investigation Graph, 272, 279
IT Ecosystems, 238
IT Service Management (ITSM), 109

J
Jupyter notebooks, 30, 31

K
Kusto Query Language (KQL), 38, 45, 137, 140, 142, 153, 159, 200, 237, 243, 245, 256, 257, 264, 278, 292, 308, 339
    advantages, 293
    column control
        adding, 206
        removing, 206
        selection, 206
        working, 207
    custom queries, 214, 215
    for engineers, 248
    in incident investigation, 297
    in incident management, 296
        automation, 299
        context, 298
        logs, 298
        queries, 300
        refine and correlation data, 298
        save investigation queries, 299
        visualization, 299
    Microsoft Sentinel, 202, 293
    operators
        data, 204
        filtering, 204
        limiting, 204
        sorting, 205
        summarize, 205
    parsing, 208, 209
    queries in Sentinel, 295–297
    query language, 201
    query statements, 201

INDEX

Kusto Query Language (KQL) (*cont.*)
    query structure, 294
    security engineers, 165
    telemetry data, 200
    troubleshoot, 203
    valuable things, 202, 203
    variables, 208

L

Legacy software, 14
Life cycle management, 219, 220
Live hunting, 311
Log analytics, 89, 91, 95
Log analytics workspace, 73
Log data, 114, 115
Logic App Playbooks, 282, 283
Logic Apps, 186
Log management
    automate schema mapping, 131
    efficiency, 130
    lifecycle policies, 132–134
    in Microsoft Sentinel, 129, 132–134
    native integrations, 131
    organizations, 127
    primary security, 128
    secondary security data, 128
    Tiered log retention strategy, 130
Logs, 298

M

Machine learning (ML), 3, 211
Managed Security Service Providers (MSSPs), 174
Managed Service Providers (MSPs), 104
Man-in-the-middle (MitM), 13
Mean time to detection (MTTD), 66

Mean time to remediation (MTTR), 171
Mean time to resolution (MTTR), 255
Mean time to resolve (MTTR), 271
Medical device management, 1, 15
    bluetooth glucose monitors, 4
    cyber attackers, 8
    equipment, 7
    healthcare provider, 4
    integration, 2
    IoMT architecture, 5
    logs, 21
    telemetry data, 33
    vulnerabilities, 13
Medical Device Regulation (MDR), 15
Micro-segmentation, 80
Microsoft 365, 27
Microsoft Azure, 70
Microsoft Azure Portal, 24
Microsoft Copilot, 78
Microsoft Defender, 35
    access, 41
    for cloud, 41
    exposure management, 41
    key services, 39, 40
    navigating, 42, 43
    portal, 39, 44, 45
    security management, 36–39
    Sentinel, 40
    unified security hub, 39
Microsoft Defender Extended Detection and Response (EDR), 44, 45, 69
Microsoft Defender portal, 261
    AI-Assisted Security, 265
    alert correlation, 273–275
    alerts, 261
    alerts and source, 263
    attacks disruption, 264
    audit and reporting, 269

automated investigation, 264
correlation and intelligence, 263, 264
detection and response, 265
incident management, 264, 265
incident response workflow, 275-277
incidents, 262, 268
investigation, 268
investigative stage, 267
ownership, 267
renaming incidents, 269
security workflow, 266
Sentinel, 264
severity, 267
tags, 267
Microsoft Defender Threat Intelligence (MDTI), 178
Microsoft Defender XDR (Extended Detection and Response), 33, 35, 36, 40, 44, 80
for Cloud, 60-62
components, 90
data security and privacy, 71-73
Internet of Things (IoT), 63-66
investigation experience, 61-63
zero trust security, 86
Microsoft Entra Application, 182
Microsoft Entra ID, 26
Microsoft Exposure Management, 51
Microsoft Security Copilot, 38
Defender Portal, 53
description, 53
exposure management, 57-59
features of, 55-57
use cases, 54, 55
Microsoft Security Exposure Management, 37
Microsoft security rules, 210
Microsoft Security Services, 39, 40

Microsoft Sentinel, 86, 130, 140, 159, 172, 243
Action List, 124-127
advantage, 112
automated incident, 1
automation rules, 31
collection of data, 25, 26
data sources
Azure services, 74
costs/budgeting, 75
virtual machines, 74
data sources connection, 247, 248
detection and analytics, 91, 92
disruption attack strategies, 290, 291
hunting, 310
incidents, 30
Internet of Medical Things (IoMT), 20, 21
Internet of Things (IoT), 22-24
investigation capabilities, 27
Kusto Query Language (KQL), 293
log management, 132-134
medical data, 18
Microsoft Defender XDR (Extended Detection and Response), 48-51
migration, 107-113
approaches, 107, 108
multiple workspaces, 98-104
notebooks, 30, 31
OoB (Out of Box) security, 23-25
Playbooks, 31
security analysts, 246
Security Copilot, 150-156
security engineers, 163, 247
security information and event management (SIEM), 19
threat analysis, 30
threat detection, 27, 29, 30

INDEX

Microsoft Sentinel (*cont.*)
    User and Entity Behavior Analytics
        (UEBA), 148, 149
    Zero Trust, 78–81
Migration, 251
    approaches, 107, 108
    design, 110
    implementing, 110
    operationalization, 111
    phases
        discovery, 109, 110
Mitigation, 309
MITRE ATT&CK framework, 28, 46, 187–189, 309, 319
    asset inventory, 189
    detection capabilities, 190
    education, 191
    incident response rate, 190
    security control measures, 191
    threat modeling, 190
Models behavior, 146
Multicloud alerts, 63
Multi-factor authentication (MFA), 79, 83
Multiple Azure Tenants, 99, 104–106
Multiple workspaces, 96–98
Multitenancy structures, 97
Multitenant ecosystem, 227

N

Narrowband IoT (NB-IoT), 6
Native integrations, 131
Near-Real-Time (NRT), 210, 257
Network Access Control (NAC), 84, 282
Network Detection and Response (NDR), 305
Network segmentation, 80
Normalization, 26

O

Once-in-a-lifetime configuration, 81
Operationalization phase, 111
Operational logs, 116, 297
Operational technology (OT), 35
Order of Execution, 225, 226
Out-of-the-box (OoB) security, 23–25, 28, 60

P

780 PATCH Act (2023), 15
Patch management, 289
Patient-wearable sensors, 2
Performance optimization, 141
Personal health information (PHI), 13
Planning an Incident Response, 275–277
Playbooks, 31, 86, 110, 111, 121, 147, 165, 225, 228, 229, 235, 257, 282
    and automation, 285
Plugin-based functionality, 153
PowerShell script, 152
Precision medicine, 10
Prerequisites, 182
Privacy, 71–73
Protected health information (PHI), 79, 280
Protocol anomalies, 303

Q

Quantifiable value, 255, 256
Query languages, 294

R

Ransomware, 17, 18, 44, 287, 328
    attacks, 12, 284
    IoMT ecosystems, 12

playbook, 21
3rd-party network devices, 75
Reactive security, 301
Real-time alerts, 184
Real-time collaboration, 46, 47
Real-time monitoring, 311
Remediation, 45
Remote Patient Monitoring (RPM), 7
Renaming incidents, 269
Reporting, 230, 231
Resource library, 252
Retention, 132–134
Role-based access control (RBAC), 67, 97, 239, 312
Root cause analysis, 235
Rule execution, 224
Rule logic, 185

S

Scalable strategy, 34
Scaling operations, 238, 239
Scheduled rules, 210
Schema, 318–320
Security analysts, 338–340
    case management, 246
    digital transformation, 244
    Kusto Query Language (KQL), 245
    rules, 245
    Sentinel, 246
    substantial data, 244
    tuning and optimization, 246
    workbooks, 246
Security Copilot, 151, 252, 333
    core capabilities, 153–156
    defenders, 335
    integration, 153
    Internet of Medical Things (IoMT), 336
    Kusto Query Language (KQL), 334
    operational tasks, 334
    orchestration, 152
    privacy, 335
    standalone application, 152
    threat hunting, 334
Security coverage, 168
Security engineers
    building blocks, 170, 171
    communication, 162
    core capability, 161
    data sources, 164
    future-proofing, 172, 173
    hunting, 162
    Kusto Query Language (KQL), 165
    Microsoft Sentinel, 163
    operations, 167
    organizations, 160
    playbooks, 165
    security information and event management (SIEM), 167
    Security Operation Center (SOC), 166
    Sentinel, 167–170
    surveillance, 162
    Threat Intelligence (TI), 173
    threats, 164
Security exposure management, 33, 42, 50
Security incidents
    Alert correlation, 273–275
    analysts, 271
    interactive logging, 271
    Internet of Things (IoT) devices, 277–279
    investigation graph, 272
    investigation phase, 273
    investigative capabilities, 271
    investigators, 271
    tabs, 271

INDEX

Security information and event
    management (SIEM), 1, 19, 22, 32,
    35, 69, 76, 77, 83, 108, 162, 167,
    176, 251, 290, 293
  capabilities, 1
  end-to-end visibility, 33
  and Extended Detection and Response
    (XDR), 20
  Microsoft Defender, 47
  Microsoft Sentinel, 23
  and SOAR, 27
  vs. Microsoft Sentinel, 170, 253, 254
Security operations, 34, 35, 88, 250
  engineers, 167
  Zero Trust, 92–95
Security Operations Center (SOC), 37, 38,
    43–46, 54, 68, 91, 112, 139, 160,
    166, 213, 228, 249, 250, 253,
    255, 256
  centralized visibility, 234
  compliance, 236
  device diversity, 236, 237
  maturity, 236
  measurement, 239, 240
  Microsoft Sentinel, 234
  risk management, 236
  use cases, 237
Security orchestration, automation, and
    response (SOAR), 20, 22, 27, 32, 35,
    77, 108, 159, 161, 220–222, 245,
    249, 290
  capabilities, 21
Security workflow, 266
Sensors, 5, 8
Sentinel, 160, 309
  analytics rules, 257, 258
  automation rule, 264
  building blocks, 254, 255
  disruption attacks, 291
  disruption workflows, 292, 293
  future-proofing, 256
  Kusto Query Language (KQL), 295–297
  quantifiable value, 255, 256
  security engineers, 167–170
  Threat Intelligence (TI), 326
ServiceNow, 46, 282
Shared Access Signature (SAS), 198
Simulations, 68
Single workspace, 95, 96
Smart hospitals, 7
Smartwatches, 7
Spoofing, 303
Structured Threat Information eXpression
    (STIX) format, 123, 173, 176, 177,
    180–184, 330
Synchronization, 228
Syslog forwarders, 115

T

Tactics, techniques, and procedures
    (TTPs), 123, 176, 339
Tags, 267
Telehealth, 2
Telemedicine, 3, 7, 81
Telemetry, 121, 127, 278
Template Watchlists, 196
Threat detection, 29, 30, 234
  alert fatigue, 259
  analytics rules, 257, 258
  detection rule lifecycle, 260
  high-quality detections, 258, 259
  Incidents, 260
  Microsoft Sentinel, 256
  watchlists, 259
Threat hunting, 212, 302, 306, 334

domains, 302–304
in healthcare, 306
MITRE ATT&CK® framework, 319
security, 307
security practices, 215, 216
strategic defense, 328, 329
toolbelt, 316, 317
Threat Intelligence data connector, 178
Threat Intelligence Platforms (TIPs), 181
Threat Intelligence (TI), 1, 21, 28, 32, 37, 41, 43, 46, 53, 57, 58, 60, 68, 91, 161, 166, 167, 211, 235, 249, 259, 288, 304, 322
  alerts with metadata, 218, 219
  API
    application, 183
    Microsoft Entra Application, 182
    permissions, 183
  automating response, 328, 329
  content hub, 178
  data connector, 179
  detection and responds, 177, 178
  detection and response, 326, 327
  detection logic, 216
  incident creation, 218, 219
  ingestion, 183, 184
  integration options, 126, 127
  interface, 330
  into response strategies, 324–326
  investigations, 327
  management, 330
  Microsoft Sentinel, 173, 174, 329
  objects, 331
  querying, 332
  reviewing and publishing, 219
  rule creation, 185
  rule logic, 217
  security architectures, 325
  sources, 122
  stages, 121, 122
  Structured Threat Information Expression (STIX), 330
  tagging, 332
  use cases, 121
  value, 174–176
  viewing, 332
  workbooks, 332, 333
Threats, 276
  analysis, 30
  assets management, 43
  campaigns, 309
  detection, 248
  intelligence, 19
  Internet of Medical Things (IoMT), 280
  investigation and response, 42, 43
  modeling, 190
  security engineers, 164
  User and Entity Behavior Analytics (UEBA), 146
  zero trust security, 91, 92
Tiered log retention strategy, 130
Time to detect (TTD), 37
Time to respond (TTR), 37
Tools, tactics, and procedures (TTPs), 322, 324
Traffic filtering, 288
Traffic Light Protocol (TLP), 330
Transmitters, 6
Transport Layer Security (TLS), 84
Trusted Automated eXchange of Intelligence Information (TAXII)
  Azure portal, 180
  configuration details, 180
  management, 181
  threat detection, 180

U, V

Unification, 46
Unified data ingestion, 234
Unified security operations, 47, 66–69
User and Entity Behavior Analytics (UEBA), 78, 91, 144, 171, 234
  analytics, 145
  continuous improvement, 148–150
  data sources, 145
  insider threats, 147
  intelligent analytics, 148
  Microsoft Sentinel, 147
  resources—Sentinel, 144
  threat detection, 146

W, X, Y

Watchlists, 29, 166, 167, 245, 249, 259
  creation, 194
  deployment, 194
  high-value assets, 191
  limitations, 193, 194
  scenarios, 192
  security operations, 192
  uploading, 195–197
    to Azure Storage, 197, 198
    configure Cross-Origin Resource Sharing (CORS), 199
    Shared Access Signature (SAS), 198
    workspaces, 199, 200
Windows Event Forwarding, 115
Workbooks, 29, 166, 167, 230, 231, 249, 332, 333
  in Microsoft Sentinel, 232–235

Workflow collaboration, 46, 47, 277–279
Workspaces, 77, 312
  architecture, 98–104
  hunts, 310
  log volume, 89
  multiple, 96–98
  Multiple Azure Tenants, 104–106
  single, 95, 96
  Watchlists, 199, 200

Z

Zero Trust architecture, 16, 79–81
Zero Trust security model, 232, 239
  access controls, 88
  breaches, 88, 89
  challenges, 81, 82
  cloud and security Copilot, 90
  cybersecurity resilience, 85
  Extended Detection and Response (XDR) and Sentinel, 86
  foundational understanding, 77
  in healthcare, 81
  Microsoft Defender XDR, 86
  multidisciplinary approach, 82
  network segmentation, 83
  planning and prerequisites, 89
  principle, 87, 88
  risk assessments, 84
  role management, 92
  security operations, 92–95
  with Sentinel, 78–81
  threats, 91, 92
  vulnerabilities, 83, 84

GPSR Compliance

The European Union's (EU) General Product Safety Regulation (GPSR) is a set of rules that requires consumer products to be safe and our obligations to ensure this.

If you have any concerns about our products, you can contact us on

ProductSafety@springernature.com

In case Publisher is established outside the EU, the EU authorized representative is:

Springer Nature Customer Service Center GmbH
Europaplatz 3
69115 Heidelberg, Germany